Focus on What Matters

ALIGNING YOUR BUSINESS WITH YOUR PURPOSE

Learn how to implement the 7P Business Alignment Model—a purpose-driven, integrative, and holistic approach—to unlock more of your potential and create a greater sense of fulfillment.

Steven Kim

With contributing author Alfredo Romero

Book Cover Design Taryn Andersen and interior formatting by 100Covers.

ISBN

979-8-9985154-3-9 (Amazon)

Version 1.2 December 2025

Published by **Purpose Matters Press**

TABLE OF CONTENTS

DEDICATION

As fellow sons of immigrant parents, we dedicate this book to our families, honoring those who paved the way before us and those who will carry the legacy forward into new adventures.

> *To my father and mother, who sparked the entrepreneurial fire within me, and to my sons, Jaden and Kai, may you carry that flame boldly on your own purpose-driven journey.*
>
> *Steven Kim*

> *To my wife, Kristen, for her steadfast support through all my efforts, my parents who inspired and shaped my life's journey, and my sons, Lukas and Alec, who now carry that legacy into their own lives.*
>
> *Alfredo Romero*

DEDICATION TO THE READER

To our purpose-driven leaders—
May your work shape a better world and serve the greater good.

PREFACE—WHY THIS WORK MATTERS

If you've ever poured everything into your business, working long hours and making personal sacrifices to create something that matters then you can relate to my parents' story.

My parents immigrated to Los Angeles nearly sixty years ago on student visas to pursue the American dream and the hope for a better life. Their story is a testament to the idea that America is truly a land of opportunity. Like many immigrants, they worked tirelessly and made tremendous sacrifices to support their family and make the most of every opportunity.

At one point, my father slept in his car and showered at the local YMCA, to save money and send it back to help support his parents and six siblings in Korea, a country still recovering from the devastation of the Korean War.

After they met and married, my parents built a life together, operating several small businesses over four decades. These ranged from a hair goods business and a mini-market to plumbing, precision engineering and machining, and even an auto repair shop. It still amazes me and my two younger brothers that my father arrived in America with just a hundred dollars and no family here, and with my mother's support, built a life that eventually included a home with an ocean view in Palos Verdes by the time I was in middle school.

My mother stood beside him every step of the way, managing the household, raising three boys, and running the hair goods business while juggling her many roles as a mother, wife, and business owner.

As a second-generation Korean American born in Los Angeles and the eldest of three sons, I grew up working in the various family businesses my parents owned. That experience was common among many Korean Americans in my peer group, whose parents also ran small businesses. A typical week for my parents involved ten to twelve-hour workdays from Monday through Saturday, with Sundays reserved for church usually followed by lunch at a Korean Chinese restaurant and afternoons spent with extended family, often at my grandmother's apartment in Koreatown.

Growing up in that environment, witnessing both the highs and lows of entrepreneurship instilled in me a deep appreciation for small business owners. Over time, that appreciation evolved into a calling: creating tools and resources to help entrepreneurs succeed.

Despite their many achievements, I also witnessed the toll it took on their health and their ability to enjoy the very life they were working so hard to build. Near the end of his life, my father confided that he wished he had traveled more and spent more time with family instead of working so much. He regretted missing the precious moments that could never be lived again.

Perhaps that was all he knew what to do at the time. Like many of us, he did the best he could with the understanding he had. Yet when we look back, the regrets that surface from a life not fully aligned with what matters most become a stark reminder for us all. This realization deepened my conviction that aligning one's life and business with the key dimensions that truly matter must serve as the compass guiding my own work—and the work I now do with business owners who want to grow, and grow with purpose.

For the past fifteen years, I've had the privilege of working with hundreds of small and mid-sized business owners across industries ranging from manufacturing, construction and specialty trades, professional and technical services, advisory/consulting, logistics and distribution, wholesale, hospitality, and retail. Through these experiences, I've seen firsthand how our frameworks and methods can make a meaningful difference not only in the lives of business owners but also in the lives of employees who work for them.

Many of the owners by the time they start working with us have achieved a relatively high level of success. I've found what sets them apart isn't their accomplishments but their drive to keep learning, growing, and evolving. They're rarely content with the status quo and continuously striving to improve themselves, grow and keep building more of what matters.

With leaders like these in mind, my contributing author Alfredo and I wrote this book and created the 7P Business Alignment Model™ to offer a practical, purpose-driven roadmap—one designed to help you focus on what truly matters.

And yet, even for successful business owners, something often feels off. It's not for lack of effort or even ideas. You're taking action, solving problems, and moving things forward. But despite all the activity, it doesn't feel like things are clicking the way they should.

Success, in fact, can lead to burnout, overwhelm, or perhaps the sense that you're carrying too much of the weight of the business on your own. Sometimes that happens because you're not focusing on the right things in the right way. But more often, it's because the right things aren't working together to serve your purpose and the 7P Business Alignment Model™ helps you fix that.

If you've ever felt like your business keeps moving but not all parts working in the same direction or aligned with what matters, you're not alone. Most owners reach a point where progress starts to feel scattered where the effort is there, but alignment isn't. The 7P Business Alignment Model™ helps bring everything back into purpose-driven alignment. It gives you a clear, purpose-driven way to connect the seven core parts of your business—Purpose, Prioritization, People, Pipeline, Product, Process, and Profit—so they move together instead of pulling you in different directions and veering you off course.

When alignment happens, you are better able to focus on what truly matters and let go of what doesn't. By doing so, you can spend more of your time and energy becoming who you're meant to be, doing the work and achieving the results that matter most.

When your business is aligned with your purpose, you can bring out more of your potential and build a more fulfilling life for yourself, your team, and those you serve.

That's the journey I'm inviting you on and my hope is that this book helps you take it with greater clarity, confidence, and purpose.

INTRODUCTION—WHY ALIGNMENT MATTERS

Alignment

/əˈlīnmənt/

Noun: arrangement in a straight line or in correct or appropriate relative positions[1].

In business, alignment means the parts of your organization are positioned to move in the same direction toward what truly matters.

The Hidden Struggles of Business Owners

Most small business owners I meet aren't struggling because they don't work hard. Quite the opposite. They're often working too hard while juggling operations, putting out fires, and jumping from one urgent task to the next.

You may have thought, *"If I just work smarter, hire better, or find the right system, I'll finally get some relief."*

But what if the problem isn't your ability to juggle or any of the reasons you currently believe are holding your business back?

The deeper, often overlooked issue is misalignment—when the essential parts of your business aren't in the *'correct relative positions'* to what matters most. When effort is directed toward priorities that don't serve your deeper purpose, misalignment sets in, often leading to overwhelm, burnout, and chronic stress.

That's why **purpose-driven alignment** is so powerful. When your business aligns with your purpose and what matters most, you can grow with greater clarity, conviction, and fulfillment. You make better decisions, build stronger teams, and create meaningful results not just for your bottom line, but for your life.

We developed the **7P Business Alignment Model**™ as a practical, proven framework to focus attention where it matters and realign your business around your purpose. It's the antidote to misalignment applied across seven core dimensions: **Purpose, Prioritization, People, Pipeline, Product, Process, and Profit.**

When these areas are working in sync, your organization can operate with greater clarity, unity and shared direction, so growth becomes more meaningful and fulfilling.

A Rowboat Metaphor for Your Business

Running a business is a lot like rowing a boat. Each oar must be in the right relative position with one another and move together to generate forward momentum. Imagine each oar represents a different dimension of your business. No matter how strong your team is, if they're not rowing in sync, in the same direction, you end up wasting energy, drifting sideways, or worse, spinning in circles.

Defining Success and Getting in Sync

Before getting on the water, the crew must agree on the destination. Success isn't just about staying afloat—it could mean arriving safely, winning a race, or simply enjoying a nice day on the lake. If each rower has a different goal, the boat will struggle to move cohesively.

Similarly, a business without a clear mission, vision, and values may have employees who disagree on the proper course of action. For example, a product development team may prioritize quality and craftsmanship, while the marketing department pushes for rapid product launches to meet quarterly sales targets. If these teams don't align on what success looks like, conflict will arise, resulting from competing priorities.

Without a unified purpose, even the most skilled teams can find themselves rowing in circles, expending energy, but making little progress. This highlights the need for a shared vision and rhythm that keeps everyone moving in sync, maximizing the impact of every individual's effort.

Role of the Leader (Coxswain)

Once goals are set, a rowboat needs a leader, the coxswain. This person steers the boat, calls the race plan, motivates the rowers, and makes necessary adjustments.

In business, this leader is often the owner, founder, president, CEO, and/or senior leadership team. In smaller companies, the owner may take on multiple roles, much like a single two-oar boat where one person plans, rows, steers, and adapts. The leader ensures the boat moves in the right direction at the right speed, with every oar hitting the water at the right time. As businesses grow and mature, the business owners, like the coxswain, may not necessarily row themselves. Still, they know the ins and outs of each role and can step in to keep the team moving forward when needed.

The 7P Business Alignment Rowboat Metaphor

Just as a coxswain's role is crucial to a rowing team, a leader's ability to align the organization's efforts is vital for business success. Enter the 7P Business Alignment Model™ (BAM)—a framework that brings clarity and cohesion to your business, much like the synchronized rowing of a well-coordinated crew.

The model consists of seven key dimensions of your business: Purpose, Prioritization, People, Pipeline, Product, Process, and Profit. Six of these Ps are analogous to oars in a rowboat, with Purpose representing the destination and the reason you are rowing the boat in the first place. It is also the underlying source of strength and cohesion required to direct and power the rowboat's six oars effectively. Understanding how to coordinate these metaphorical "oars" in a unified manner will help you coach, steer, and motivate your organization to success.

However, just as a rowing team becomes inefficient when oars are out of sync, misalignment in any of these dimensions can lead to significant setbacks for your business. Whether it's a lack of clarity about your destination or inefficiencies in how you row together, misalignment produces frustration, wastes resources, and ultimately hinders progress:

- **Purpose:** Without a clear purpose, the crew won't agree on the direction, leading to confusion.

- **Prioritization:** Without clarity of priorities, the company may be pulled in too many directions, hindering its performance.
- **People:** Misaligned employees increase turnover and negatively impact the company culture.
- **Pipeline:** A misaligned pipeline can result in insufficient customers or ones who are not the right fit.
- **Product:** Misaligned products may fail to meet customer needs, not be profitable or make the most of company strengths.
- **Process:** Inefficiencies like oars dragging in the water lead to higher costs and reduced profitability.
- **Profit:** Declining profit can eventually sink the business

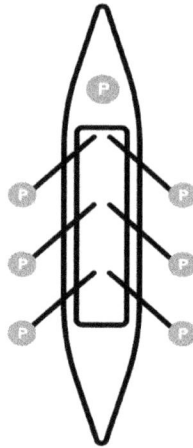

Staying in Sync Across the Business

Implementing the 7P Business Alignment Model™ helps create balanced execution, keeps the business boat afloat, and ensures it's moving in the right direction at a sustainable speed. Each member of a department may have their own goals in mind, sometimes "outperforming" their peers, but this is the equivalent of a single rower trying to make the boat go faster by themselves.

Each department may have its own goals, but focusing too much on one area can lead to imbalances. For example, if one side of the boat speeds up without the other side knowing, the boat veers off-course or in circles. A timely reminder from the leader ensures each rower is rowing in sync with the others, enabling them to keep the boat on course.

How to Use This Book

This book is designed to help you align your business with its purpose and stay on course by implementing the purpose-driven frameworks within the **7P Business Alignment Model**™ (BAM). Much like the McKinsey 7S Framework[2], which emphasizes organizational alignment across seven interconnected elements such as strategy, structure, systems, shared values, skills, style, and staff —the 7Ps provide a holistic and integrative way to view and guide your business. The book is organized into nine sections:

- **Sections 1–7**: Each section is dedicated to one of the 7Ps, offering in-depth insights, practical strategies, and actionable tools to help you align each P with your purpose.

- **Section 8**: Explores purpose-driven renewal and re-alignment with what matters most while also delving into leaving a meaningful legacy through succession planning or a successful exit.

- **Section 9**: Focuses on 7P Business Alignment Model™ implementation best practices, overcoming obstacles and challenges, and understanding the levels of support available to you.

Each section contains four chapters, for a total of 36 chapters. You can begin anywhere that aligns with your current priorities or pain points. That said, starting with Section 1: Purpose will provide greater clarity around your "end in mind" destination and help answer the foundational question: *Why are you rowing this boat in the first place?*

Section 1 – 1st "P" **Purpose**

Section 2 – 2nd "P" **Prioritization**

Section 3 – 3rd "P" **People**

Section 4 – 4th "P" **Pipeline (Sales/Marketing)**

Section 5 – 5th "P" **Product/Service**

Section 6 – 6th "P" **Process**

Section 7 – The 7th "P" **Profit**

Section 8 – **Renewal**

Section 9 – **Implementation**

We encourage you to read and review each chapter. In our experience, every client has different missing pieces in their unique puzzle—and we never know in advance which chapter will contain the critical insight that creates a breakthrough for you and your business. Each section of this book focuses on helping you and your team achieve purpose-driven alignment so you can move forward with greater clarity, momentum, and confidence.

Continuous Improvement and Learning

While this book brings together our accumulated learnings, best practices, tools, and methodologies, we continue to learn, refine, and apply the 7P Business Alignment Model™—both for our clients and within our own organization.

Staying true to our core values of continuous learning, improvement, and humble curiosity, we often use the phrase *"based on our current understanding"* to remind ourselves that the 7P BAM is an evolving, living framework. Today's version 1.0 represents the culmination and distillation of what we've learned to date, recognizing that no approach to success in the real world is ever the *"be-all, end-all"* solution.

Over the past decade, we've strengthened the frameworks within the 7P Business Alignment Model™ across diverse industries and client scenarios—helping business owners tackle real-world challenges and achieve meaningful improvements in how their businesses operate and grow.

In that same spirit of continuous improvement, this book was also created through the very principles it teaches. By applying the 7P Business Alignment Model™—particularly the *Product 'P' Purpose-Driven Innovation chapter*—I created this book as a living example of alignment in action. Each chapter was designed, refined, and tested as an expression of what it means to focus on what matters and align with purpose.

Customized Practical Application

You don't have to implement everything at once. Start with the chapters that speak directly to your current needs. We've found applying even one critical insight at the right time can make a meaningful difference in how your business runs or how you lead.

As clients adopt and implement the 7P Business Alignment Model™ (7P BAM), they develop a shared understanding and language for their organization's improvement efforts[3]—promoting a more collaborative and effective approach to tackling challenges.

The purpose-driven frameworks in this book are designed to help you better focus on what matters so you can become, do, and have more of what matters—and less of what doesn't.

From Insight to Action

Knowledge alone is not enough. The key lies in applying that knowledge with consistent, focused action. As Peter Drucker advised, "Don't tell me you had a good meeting; tell me what you're going to do on Monday that's different."[4]

In the spirit of Drucker's advice, this book isn't just about information—it's about facilitating transformation in how you lead, how your team works, and how your business grows. You'll see more clearly, act with greater purpose, and achieve the outcomes that matter most. Together, we'll cultivate what I call, "Your Company Way"[5] of solving problems, seizing opportunities, and aligning with your purpose so you can experience the relief and satisfaction of simplifying, executing, and accomplishing more of what truly matters.

Key Takeaways: Introduction to the 7P Business Alignment Model

1. **Alignment is Key to Business Success:** Like rowing a boat, every aspect of your organization must work together harmoniously toward a common goal. Misalignment in any dimension can hinder progress and waste resources.

2. **Purpose as the Guiding Star:** The "Purpose" dimension serves as the destination and guiding reason behind all actions. A

clear purpose ensures your team is aligned and motivated toward shared goals.

3. **The Leader's Role:** The leader acts as the coxswain, steering the organization, calling the race plan, and ensuring everyone is rowing in sync. Effective leadership is critical to maintaining alignment and navigating challenges.

4. **7P Framework for Purpose-Driven Alignment:** The 7P Business Alignment Model™ breaks down the complexities of running a business into seven dimensions:

    o **Purpose:** The destination and core reason for the business.

    o **Prioritization:** Deciding and communicating what matters most.

    o **People:** Aligning and developing your team.

    o **Pipeline:** Managing customer acquisition and retention.

    o **Product:** Ensuring offerings meet customer needs profitably.

    o **Process:** Streamlining operations for efficiency.

    o **Profit:** Achieving financial health and sustainability.

5. **Impact of Misalignment:** Misalignment in any of the 7Ps—whether unclear goals, conflicting priorities, or inefficiencies—can lead to frustration, wasted resources, and slow growth.

6. **Flexibility in Application:** The 7P BAM allows you to start with the dimension most relevant to your current challenges, enabling customized and practical application.

7. **Commitment to Continuous Learning:** The 7P BAM is an evolving framework based on real-world applications and continuous improvement.

8. **Action is Essential:** Insights and frameworks are only valuable if applied. As Peter Drucker emphasized, "Don't tell me you had a good meeting; tell me what you're going to do on Monday that's different."

PURPOSE—ALIGNING YOUR BUSINESS WITH WHAT MATTERS

"Life is never made unbearable by circumstances,
but only by lack of meaning and purpose." [1]
—Victor Frankl, *Man's Search for Meaning*

CHAPTER 1

WHAT MATTERS

"An unexamined life is not worth living"[2] *– Socrates*

The famous Greek philosopher Socrates argued that a life without introspection and self-reflection was not worth living. When faced with charges of corrupting the youth of Athens, Socrates stood firm in his beliefs and convictions about the importance of living an examined life. He saw it as his divine duty to seek truth and wisdom, even if it meant questioning and challenging societal norms and the status quo of his day.

His statement, "An unexamined life is not worth living," reflects his commitment to these ideals, even at the cost of his own life. Living an unexamined life implies neglecting to evaluate and consider one's beliefs and actions carefully. For example, failing to reflect critically on one's beliefs can lead to adopting "widely held but largely unexamined preconceptions."[3]

But what does it mean to examine (study carefully and in detail, often to make a judgment) one's life in a way that leads to a life worth living? And more importantly for us as leaders, how can this examination help us build better businesses, lead with purpose, and make decisions that bring us more of what truly matters?

The Value of Strategic Reflection:

In today's world of constant interruptions, pressures, and deadlines, business owners rarely have the luxury to pause. We live in an age of distraction and it's not just inconvenient. It's costly.

Distractions often pull our attention in competing directions, making it harder to slow down and reflect on what truly matters. What's needed is an intentional pause—one that allows us to slow down, so we're no longer held captive by the urgent but can instead focus on the important. Without making regular time and space for strategic reflection, we risk confusing activity with progress.

Reflection Isn't a Luxury. It's a Leadership Discipline.

Carving out time to think deeply about your business should not be viewed as a "wouldn't it be nice" or "I'll get to it when I have time" activity. In fact, it's one of the most vital responsibilities and disciplines of a purpose-driven leader. When you make time for strategic reflection, you rise above the noise and regain clarity to make better decisions. It's not stepping away from the business—it's stepping above it to see more clearly, choose more wisely, and lead more intentionally.

As Drucker advised, "Follow effective action with quiet reflection. From the reflection will come even more effective action."[4]

He also reminds us of the importance of distinguishing between efficiency vs effectiveness:

"Efficiency is doing things right; effectiveness is doing the right things."[5]

And even more firmly he warns us:

"There is nothing so useless as doing efficiently that which should not be done at all."[6]

In fact, when we fail to make time for reflection, we may end up becoming highly efficient at doing the wrong things.

The Power of an Alignment Reset™

A signature practice of the 7P Business Alignment Model™, the Alignment Reset™, facilitated by our Business Alignment Coaches helps owners and leadership teams zoom out from the day-to-day and evaluate whether their people, priorities, processes, and the rest of the 7Ps are still moving in sync with their long-term vision.

It also offers a practical way to apply Peter Drucker's principle of *systematic abandonment*. As Drucker wrote:

"The first step in a growth policy is not to decide where and how to grow. It is to decide what to abandon. In order to grow, a business must have a systematic policy to get rid of the outgrown, the obsolete, the unproductive... If we did not do this already, would we go into it now? If the answer is no, then the question must be, what do we do now?"[7]

Drucker challenges leaders to regularly examine whether existing products, services, or activities still align with their purpose and priorities. If something no longer delivers sufficient value or wouldn't be started today knowing what you know now, it deserves to be reconsidered, reshaped, or abandoned. For SMB owners, looking through the lens of systematic abandonment is especially important when evaluating legacy offerings, low-margin customers, or outdated processes.

Unlike traditional planning meetings or productivity check-ins, the Alignment Reset™ is about improving strategic clarity and making course corrections so you are more aligned with your purpose and with what matters most. It ensures you're not just doing things right, but *doing the right things*.

Systematic Abandonment in Practice: Key Questions

To apply this lens, here are three questions we often guide our clients through during an Alignment Reset™

1. If I weren't already doing this, would I choose to start it today?

   (e.g., product lines, customer relationships, services, processes)

2. Is this aligned with my current purpose, priorities, and goals—or is it a holdover from how we've always done things around here?

3. If I had the courage and clarity to let go of what no longer fits, what would I free up energy and resources to focus on instead?

These questions are simple, but they require honesty which can help you recognize where you may be holding onto something out of habit, fear, or inertia, rather than intentional purpose-driven alignment.

What You Gain from an Alignment Reset™

When practiced regularly, the Alignment Reset™ allows you and your team to:

- Reconnect daily activity with your larger purpose and strategic goals
- Spot early signs of misalignment across any of the 7Ps
- Make clear, focused decisions about what to adjust, refine, or remove

- Minimize distractions and re-center your efforts on what matters most

In our experience, some of the most profound breakthroughs don't come from adding more tools or strategies but from creating the space to reflect with intention so you can better focus on what matters and eliminate the things that don't.

Lead with Intention—Not Reaction

The Alignment Reset™ isn't just a tactic, but a mindset of intentional purpose-driven leadership. When built into your operating cadence, whether weekly, monthly, or quarterly, it helps you move from reacting to truly leading more effectively. As the saying goes, "one hour of clear thinking can save ten hours of misaligned doing."[8]

Through this structured time for reflection, key questions can emerge, insights can surface, and adjustments can be made, putting you and your business on a more purposeful and positive trajectory.

Reflection Questions:

- Are you currently setting aside regular time with your team—at least quarterly—for strategic reflection through **Alignment Resets™**?

- If not, how could you begin integrating this practice into your schedule?

- If you are already engaging in some practice of reflective thinking, are they helping you course-correct and stay aligned with your priorities? What changes could make them more impactful?

- How might regular reflective thinking benefit you and your business? What specific positive outcomes would you most like to see?

What Matters

In this chapter, we will introduce tools and guiding frameworks to help examine and reflect on one's life and business so one can better focus on what truly matters. However, to focus on what matters, it would be helpful to have greater clarity on what *actually matters* or what's *most important*. Then, we can work on ways to better focus on those things.

But *what matters*, and *what does that mean*?

To meaningfully answer this question of what matters requires context—what matters in terms of what? Answers can vary, depending on the many situational contexts and individual perspectives that one can draw from.

We acknowledge that the full scope of this important and profound question is beyond what any single chapter or book can fully address. However, if we take more time to reflect on our true priorities and learn to ask the right questions, we can better understand the underlying values and purposes that drive us. By doing so, we can work towards living a life that is more meaningful and worth living.

7P Business Alignment Model (BAM) Frameworks

To address the complexity of answering what matters, primarily in the context of your business, we've developed the 7P Business Alignment Model™. The frameworks within each of the 7Ps can help you break down the question of what matters in your business into more manageable parts. By doing so, we can better align those parts with your overall purpose and what matters most.

7P Business Alignment Model

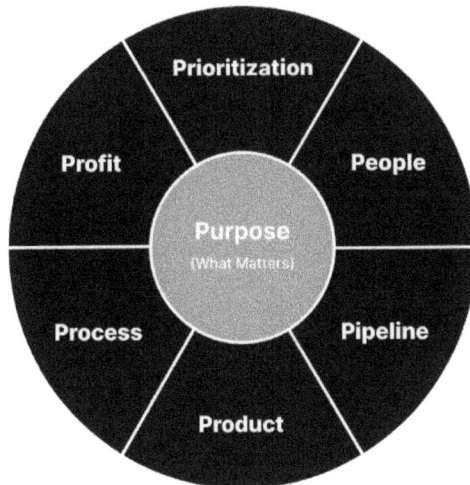

Prioritization

People

Profit

Purpose
(What Matters)

Process

Pipeline

Product

Each of the 7Ps contains *conceptual frameworks* that enable you to identify issues and problems in your business, think more clearly about them, and understand the causes of any misalignment as well as ways to correct them. The value of such frameworks is insightfully described by David Gray in an article for MIT Sloan Management Review:

> *"Any coherent thinking involves some form of conceptual framing. Conceptual frameworks are mental representations that order experience in ways that enable us to comprehend it. Take the ubiquitous income Profit and Loss (P&L) statement as an example: It's a simple yet powerful way to make sense of the myriad transactions that occur in business. Once we have framed financial exchanges as either revenues or expenses, we can begin asking and analyzing important questions about the business (such as why are we losing money?)*
>
> *By adding a further dimension of assets and liabilities—using a balance sheet framework—we can derive a huge range of ratios and relationships that provide further insight for managing and valuing the enterprise. These concepts—revenue, expense, asset, liability—are so familiar that we may not even recognize them as conceptual structures."[9]*

Throughout the book, we may start by defining terms followed by examples and client stories. We will also introduce conceptual frameworks—tools for organizing and clarifying ideas—to improve your thinking and decision-making process. From time to time, these frameworks may be presented in the form of tables, pyramids, and pies, providing visual references to help you see how different concepts align and fit together.

The 7P Problem-Solving Framework

Effective problem-solving starts with defining the problem properly and asking the right questions before attempting a solution. Albert Einstein is often credited with saying, "If I had an hour to solve a problem, I would spend the first fifty-five minutes finding out the right question to ask and then solve the problem in five minutes."[10]

Regardless of the exact ratio of time spent thinking of the right questions vs. trying to solve a problem, we tend to spend far less time and effort formulating the right questions than is optimal before attempting to solve the problems we face. To complicate matters further, how do we know if we're even asking the right questions in the first place? Learning to ask the right questions is a skill that develops with practice, benefits from diverse perspectives, and depends on breaking down complex problems into simpler, more manageable parts.

For example, broad questions like "How can I live a happy life?" or "How can I make my business more successful?" may be starting points for exploration, but are usually too difficult to tackle as a stand-alone question without further clarifying questions.

Our clients have found the 7P Business Alignment Model™ invaluable because it provides a structured approach and proven framework for deconstructing your business into more manageable components comprised of various dimensions—the 7Ps of your business. Doing so allows you to develop the right questions that can lead to the right solutions. Again, instead of viewing a complex problem like your business as a single entity with all of its moving parts, it's helpful to see it as a collection of smaller, interconnected parts that can be analyzed and addressed individually:

There's a saying, "A complex problem is a bunch of simple problems combined."[11]

Also, it's important to recognize that even the "smaller" or "simpler" solutions to individual challenges must be integrated and aligned with your overall purpose and desired end in mind while also considering the greater good of your business as a whole. Tackling isolated problems without this alignment can lead to short-term fixes that may create new issues elsewhere.

Developing the right solutions for these "simpler parts," as with any problem, requires, as we discussed previously, first and foremost, asking the right questions that frame the problem properly so it can lead us to the optimal solution. The questions we ask affect how we see the issue and even the options we consider.

That is why the 7P framework includes clarifying questions designed to help you think more clearly. By doing so, you can develop and execute a more effective plan of action to solve problems and challenges while making the most of the opportunities in your business. For example:

- **Purpose (P1):** Is everything we're doing aligned with our core mission and long-term vision?

- **Prioritization (P2):** Are we focusing on the most important tasks and opportunities?

- **People (P3):** Do we have the right team in place, and are they aligned with our values and goals?

- **Pipeline (P4):** Are our sales and marketing efforts focused on the right customers and delivering consistent results?

- **Product (P5):** Are we delivering value to customers in a way that differentiates us and serves real needs?

- **Process (P6):** Are our operations efficient, effective, and scalable?

- **Profit (P7):** Are we generating sustainable financial outcomes that support our purpose and reinvestment?

By asking clarifying questions for each of these components, the 7P framework helps ensure that you can make better decisions, and your solutions are aligned with your broader objectives and what matters most.

The Life Pie Alignment Framework™
A Holistic Approach to Fulfillment

While the 7P Business Alignment Model™ focuses on aligning your business with purpose, the Life Pie Alignment Framework broadens the lens. It helps you re-contextualize the Purpose 'P' by showing how business is just one slice of the larger whole of your life. By visualizing your life as a pie with interdependent slices, you can identify and evaluate your priorities to see where some adjustment or re-balancing may be needed.

Here's an example of one possible configuration for the slices of one's life pie:

- Health & Fitness

- Relationships (Family, Spouse/Partner, Children, Friends, Co-Workers)
- Business/Career
- Financial Health (Net Worth, Savings, Retirement Readiness)
- Personal Growth and Development
- Recreation/Hobbies
- Spiritual/Religion/Service

You can customize and describe your slices accordingly, though we recommend no more than seven. Although the 7P Business Alignment Model™ is primarily applied in the context of the business/profession slice of one's life pie, balancing the other key slices is also crucial for creating an overall sense of fulfillment and a life worth living.

We all know the stories of individuals who focused solely on their business or career at the expense of their health or relationships, resulting in debilitating illnesses or broken relationships and families. Toward the end of his life, my father regretted that he had devoted too much energy and attention to the business slice of his life pie and hadn't traveled and seen more of the world when he had the opportunity and the health to do so. During the last twenty years of his life, he had severe health challenges that left him mostly bedridden and prevented him from traveling and experiencing more of the world, a longing and wish he had from the time he was a young man.

My father's story is a cautionary tale reminding us of the importance of devoting enough attention to the various slices that make up one's life pie in a manner conducive to our overall well-being.

Knowing how to allocate the right proportion of energy and focus on the various slices of one's life pie is an ongoing challenge and hardly a straightforward thing to do. The proportion of energy devoted to various slices of one's life pie is dynamic and can change over time depending on your priorities and the phase of life you are currently in.

To deal with this energy allocation-balance challenge, we've designed the following Life Pie fulfillment ratings assessment as a self-reflection tool to determine where we might be out of balance and where slices of our life pie may be too small, or even non-existent for our own good.

The visual representation of the pie is especially useful when you want to illustrate and emphasize how each slice contributes to the whole.

Quantitatively, we can also track our time spent to determine the percentage that each slice occupies out of the total hours available, e.g., 24 hours a day or 168 hours a week. But when it comes to qualitative factors or importance, percentages can be misleading. Think about your vital organs like your heart, lungs, brain. You can't say one is "30% important" and another is "20%." Lose any one, since each is vital to the body's overall health and functioning, the whole system fails.

Assessing Your Life Pie

To gain deeper insight into your overall fulfillment, start by evaluating and rating each slice of your life pie. While your life pie slice descriptions may vary from those suggested below, we recommend limiting the number of slices to seven to make it more manageable. If necessary, you can create sub-slices within the main categories, but we suggest keeping those to a maximum of three. Below is one configuration featuring seven key categories that can comprise your life pie:

Life Pie

Life pie Categories:

1. Health & Fitness
2. Relationships (Family, Spouse/SO, Children, Friends, Co-Workers)
3. Business/Career
4. Money/Finances (Net Worth/Retirement Nest Egg/Savings)
5. Recreation/Hobbies
6. Personal Growth and Development
7. Spiritual/Service

Fulfillment Rating Instructions: Assessing Your Life Pie

Rate each slice of your **Life Pie** on a spectrum from **1 to 9**, where:

1-3 = Low Fulfillment (unsatisfying, draining, neglected)

4-6 = Mixed Fulfillment (adequate, tolerable, mixed)

7-9 = High Fulfillment (energizing, rewarding, deeply satisfying)

Life Fulfillment Assessment Guide

Important: Your ratings reflect your current phase of life—not forever. What feels "ideal" today may change as your priorities evolve.

1. **Current Rating (1-9):**

   Assign a number from 1 to 9 based on how fulfilling each category feels in your current phase of life.

2. **Why/What It Currently Looks Like Now:**
   - o Provide a brief explanation of why you assigned that rating.
   - o Describe your experiences, feelings, or current situations related to each category.

3. **Minimally Tolerable Rating (1-9):**

   Determine the minimally tolerable/acceptable rating for each category if currently below that level.

4. **Why/What Would Minimally Tolerable Look Like - by When?**

- o   Explain what a minimally tolerable rating would look like in your life.

- o   Set a timeline for when you aim to reach it if you are currently below it.

- o   The minimally tolerable or acceptable level may be the same as your current level. For example, a personal trainer who rates their current fitness level fulfillment at an eight may also assign a minimally tolerable level at an eight because their profession is tied to their fitness and may rate their ideal as a nine.

5. **Ideal Rating (1-9):**

Assign a number from 1 to 9 representing the vision or highest level of fulfillment you aspire to in each category by incorporating the "in this phase" parameter to make it more manageable.

6. **Why/What Would Ideal Look Like - by When?**

- o   Describe your ideal state for each category.

- o   Set a timeline for when you aim to achieve it.

7. **Steps to Move to the Next Higher Rating, Minimally Tolerable or Ideal:**

- o   Outline specific actions you can take to improve your fulfillment rating in each category.

- o   Focus on practical and achievable next steps.

Fulfillment Rating Summary:

Life pie Category	Current Rating (1-9)	What It Currently Looks Like Now	Minimally Tolerable Rating (1-9)	What Would Minimally Tolerable Look Like - by When?	Ideal Rating (1-9)	What Would Ideal Look Like - by When?	Steps to Move to the Next Higher Rating: Minimally Tolerable or Ideal
1. Health & Fitness							
2. Relationships (Family, Spouse/SO, Children)							

Life pie Category	Current Rating (1-9)	What It Currently Looks Like Now	Minimally Tolerable Rating (1-9)	What Would Minimally Tolerable Look Like - by When?	Ideal Rating (1-9)	What Would Ideal Look Like - by When?	Steps to Move to the Next Higher Rating: Minimally Tolerable or Ideal
3. Business/ Career							
4. Money/ Finances (Net Worth/ Retirement Nest Egg/ Savings)							
5. Personal Hobbies/ Recreation							
6. Personal Development/ Growth							
7. Spiritual/ Religion/ Service							

Life Pie Reflection Questions

After completing the table, take some time to reflect on your ratings and responses:

1. **Which slices of your life pie are perhaps "too thin"?**
   o   Look for ratings of 5 or below where attention and energy may be lacking.

2. **How might you begin to re-balance them?**
   o   Identify steps that would improve those ratings toward your baseline (minimally tolerable) or vision (ideal).

3. **How might improving one slice actually free up energy for others?**
   o   For example, would better health or stronger relationships improve your effectiveness in leading your business?

4. **What actions can you take to re-proportion your attention in ways that are more conducive to your overall well-being?**

o   Decide where to reallocate time, energy or resources so your life pie feels more balanced and fulfilling.

To illustrate how to fill out the worksheet, here's an example for the **Health & Fitness** category:

Life pie Category	Current Rating (1-9)	Why/What It Currently Looks Like Now	Minimally Tolerable Rating (1-9)	Why/What Would Minimally Tolerable Look Like - by When?	Ideal Rating (1-9)	Why/What Would Ideal Look Like - by When?	Steps to Move to the next higher rating: Minimally Tolerable or Ideal
1. Health & Fitness	4	Currently exercise 1x/ week; weight 198 lbs and body fat is ~25%; endurance is low—can only jog about 1 mile without stopping	6	Exercise 3x/ week, maintain weight ≤190 lbs and body fat ≤22% by end of Q3	8	Exercise 5x/ week, maintain weight ≤180 lbs and body fat ≤18% by year-end; run 5K under 30 min.	- Schedule workouts on the calendar. - Hire a personal trainer. - Join a fitness class. - Prepare workout gear in advance.

Tips for Using This Worksheet

- **Be honest with yourself:** Provide ratings that honestly reflect how you feel and include brief explanations to gain the most benefit from this exercise. Only share what you're comfortable sharing with your Business Alignment Coach.

- **Set Realistic Goals:** Ensure your minimally tolerable and ideal ratings are achievable within your timelines and try including the "in this phase" parameter to make it more manageable.

- **Take Action:** This worksheet's value lies in the steps you take to improve your fulfillment. Utilize an accountability partner, like our Business Alignment Coach (BAC), to support you in staying consistent and following through with your action plans.

- **Review Regularly:** Revisit this worksheet periodically to assess your progress and make necessary adjustments. The numerical ratings simply serve as reference points — a baseline to measure your improvement and growth.

By systematically evaluating each area of your life pie, you'll gain clarity on where to improve and take meaningful steps toward a more balanced and fulfilling life.

Maslow's Hierarchy of Needs

Another guiding framework to help determine what matters is Maslow's hierarchy of needs, or what I might refer to as the *what matters pyramid*. Abraham Maslow, a renowned psychologist, introduced the concept of a hierarchy of needs to explain human motivation. Maslow posits that certain essential—or *what matters*—priorities must be satisfied before individuals can pursue higher-order aspirations.

For example, physiological needs like water, food, and safety must be met before other needs like belonging, esteem, and self-actualization begin to matter. The pyramid operates under the premise that individuals must fulfill specific fundamental needs before advancing up the hierarchy toward more evolved ones.[12]

In other words, if you are suffocating from lack of air or dying of thirst, then "what matters" at that moment is air and water. Maslow split these needs into two groups: lower-order needs (physiological and safety), primarily met through physical external means, and higher-order needs (social, self-esteem, and self-actualization), which are satisfied internally.[13] When "times are good," and people's lower-order needs are met, one's attention on "what matters" can be directed and focused on fulfilling higher-order social, self-esteem, and self-actualization needs.

Maslow's hierarchy of needs

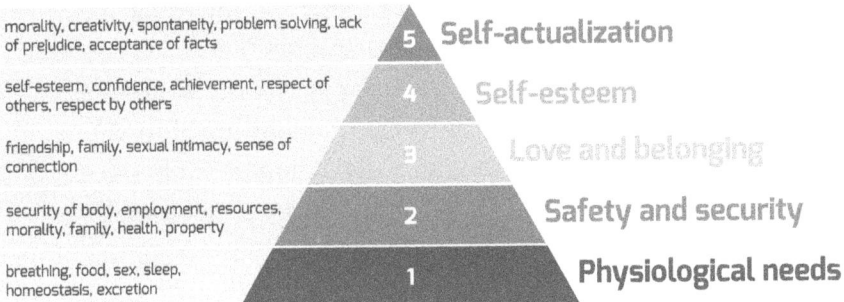

morality, creativity, spontaneity, problem solving, lack of prejudice, acceptance of facts	5	Self-actualization
self-esteem, confidence, achievement, respect of others, respect by others	4	Self-esteem
friendship, family, sexual intimacy, sense of connection	3	Love and belonging
security of body, employment, resources, morality, family, health, property	2	Safety and security
breathing, food, sex, sleep, homeostasis, excretion	1	Physiological needs

Yet while Maslow's hierarchy of needs generally holds true, history has shown us many instances of individuals and groups who have willingly sacrificed bodily comforts, livelihood, personal safety, even their own lives for a greater cause or purpose. These examples remind us that what matters is not always defined by survival but by meaning and purpose.

Practical Application: Maslow's Hierarchy applied in the Workplace

Maslow's hierarchy of needs can provide insights into understanding and meeting the needs of employees in the workplace. By addressing each level of the hierarchy, businesses can create an environment where employees feel valued, motivated, and engaged. Below are examples of how Maslow's theory can be practically applied in a business context:

1. **Physiological Needs:**

    Ensure employees earn a fair and livable wage to afford necessities like housing, food, and healthcare. Regular breaks and adequate mealtimes during work hours also help employees meet their fundamental needs.

2. **Safety Needs:**

    Provide job security through fair wages, consistent employment practices, and a physically safe and clean work environment. Offering benefits such as health insurance, retirement plans, and access to mental health resources reinforces a sense of stability and trust.

3. **Social Needs:**

    Relationships at work play a pivotal role in employee satisfaction and motivation. Organized activities like company outings, team-building exercises, or shared meals (such as monthly BBQs or team lunches) can foster a sense of community and belonging. Employees often stay in companies because of strong relationships with their managers and colleagues.

Conversely, employees may leave when these relationships are poor. The adage, *"Employees don't leave companies; they leave managers,"* highlights how critical relationships with managers and colleagues are to an employee's decision to stay or leave.

4. **Esteem Needs:**

   Recognize and reward employees for their achievements. Highlight stories and examples that showcase the behaviors and results the company values. Acknowledging accomplishments, whether through formal awards, informal praise, or opportunities for skill development, bolsters employees' confidence and self-worth.

5. **Self-Actualization Needs:**

   Try providing more challenging tasks that maximize your employees' strengths while providing a path toward advancement and career progression. Companies that employees see as ones that offer more opportunities for self-actualization in the form of professional development and training are more likely to have better employee retention and attract better employees. Supporting their employees' growth and development typically results in a more motivated, engaged, and loyal workforce.

Business Benefits of Supporting Self-Actualization

When businesses create a workplace that supports employees in meeting their fundamental needs and progressing toward self-actualization, the benefits go way beyond employee-individual fulfillment. This alignment between employee fulfillment and organizational goals not only enhances morale but also drives tangible outcomes like higher retention, improved engagement, and the ability to attract and retain top talent. By providing opportunities for self-actualization, companies can unlock more of the potential of their workforce and ensure that employees are not just surviving but thriving. This results in more employees who loyal and committed to the organization's long-term success.

1. **Enhanced Job Satisfaction:**
    o Employees who feel they are growing and reaching their full potential are generally more satisfied with their jobs. This satisfaction reduces turnover rates as employees are less likely to leave a company that supports their personal and professional growth.

2. **Increased Employee Engagement:**
    o When employees are engaged in meaningful work that allows them to express their talents, creativity, and skills, they are more likely to be committed to their roles and the company they work for.

3. **Attraction of Top Talent:**
    o Companies known for fostering environments where employees can achieve a greater degree of self-actualization become attractive to high achievers and top talent. Talented professionals seek out workplaces that offer opportunities for personal growth, challenging work, and the chance to make a significant impact.

4. **Positive Company Culture:**
    o Providing opportunities for self-actualization contributes to a positive company culture, which is crucial in retaining current employees and attracting new ones. Companies that encourage professional development and personal fulfillment often have stronger, more cohesive teams.

5. **Alignment with Purpose:**
    o Employees are more likely to stay with a company if they feel their work aligns with their values and goals. When a company provides opportunities for self-actualization, it helps employees align their work with their life's purpose, increasing their sense of loyalty and commitment.

Supporting Data and Research:

Several studies and surveys support the idea that opportunities for self-actualization and professional development are significant factors in employee retention and attraction.

For example:

- **Gallup's Employee Engagement Survey** consistently shows that opportunities for development and growth are top predictors of employee engagement.[14]

- **A Conference Board survey** found that 58% of workers would consider leaving their job if development opportunities were absent.[15]

- **An EdAssist survey** found that 53% of respondents reported that having access to professional development opportunities would encourage them to stay at their current job longer. Meanwhile, 60% of respondents said that a job with professional development opportunities would be more enticing than a job with regular pay raises.[16]

Providing opportunities for self-actualization benefits employees and gives companies a competitive edge in retaining and attracting top talent. By creating an environment where employees can grow, achieve, and fulfill more of their potential, companies can foster loyalty, improve job satisfaction, and build a stronger, more engaged workforce.

Reflection Questions for Promoting Self-Actualization in the Workplace

1. How does our organization currently support employees in aligning their work with their personal values, goals, and purpose?

2. What opportunities for learning, growth, and skill development do we offer to help employees improve and advance?

Following Your Bliss: Insights from Joseph Campbell

As a purpose-driven leader of a growth-minded organization, it's important to recognize that encouraging self-actualization within your organization impacts far beyond the workplace. Supporting employees on their journey toward self-actualization taps into a deeper, universal human need for fulfillment and purpose—a need that, when met, benefits the individual and the entire organization and positively impacts the greater societal good.

Joseph Campbell, a noted anthropologist, mythologist, and author of The Hero's Journey, infers that you can put yourself on a path to self-actualization when you 'follow your bliss.' In a PBS interview series with Bill Moyers titled *The Power of Myth*. Campbell encourages us to pursue an endeavor that brings the greatest sense of enduring fulfillment, combining both desire and purpose versus short-term, momentary, hedonistic pleasures.

He believed that if you followed your bliss, you would be assisted in ways that cannot be foreseen: "Follow your bliss, and the universe will open doors for you where there were only walls."[17] This idea resonates not just on an individual level but can also apply within the workplace, where fostering purpose and fulfillment in your employees can create environments where individuals and organizations thrive.

Discovering Ikigai: Your Reason for Being

While Campbell encourages us to 'follow our bliss,' the Japanese concept of *ikigai* takes the idea of aligning purpose and passion and builds on it further.[18]

It comes from the Japanese word "ikigai," which translates to "reason for being." The word is derived from "iki," meaning life, and "gai," meaning value or worth. Where Maslow's pyramid shows us the progression of how one prioritizes fundamental needs, *ikigai* helps us identify where our deepest fulfillment lies at the intersection of four essential dimensions:

1. **What You Love (Passion):** The activities, interests, or pursuits that bring you joy and energy. These are the things that you are most curious about and where time just flies by.

2. **What You Are Good At (Strengths):** The skills, talents, and natural abilities you excel at. These strengths set you apart and are often the foundation of the value you bring to your business and/or profession.

3. **What the World Needs (Mission):** The challenges, problems, or needs in the world that you can positively impact and give your work meaning beyond yourself. This is where your contribution connects with a greater good.

4. **What You Can Be Paid For (Profession):** The products, services, or expertise you can offer that create value in the marketplace and provide sustainable income. This ensures your *ikigai* is not only fulfilling but practical.

Your *ikigai,* often presented as a Venn diagram, lies at the intersection of these four dimensions. Essentially, *ikigai* is about finding that "sweet spot" where what you love, what the world needs, what you're good at, and what you can be paid for intersect to create a more meaningful and fulfilling life. It's the idea that life is most fulfilling when you can live in your *ikigai,* resulting in a greater sense of well-being and positive societal impact.

Applying the Ikigai Framework

To bring your *ikigai* into focus, consider the following steps:

1. **Identify Your Passions:** Reflect on the activities, interests, or hobbies that make you lose track of time. What are you most curious about and/or brings you the most joy and excitement?

2. **Recognize Your Talents:** Assess the skills and strengths that set you apart. What do others often seek your help or advice on?

3. **Understand the World's Needs:** Consider the problems or gaps in your community, industry, or the world. How can your talents and passions address these needs?

4. **Explore Financial Viability:** Consider how you can be compensated in a sustainable manner for your contributions. What value can you offer that others are willing to pay for?

Aligning Purpose with Action: The Path to Meaningful Growth

Taking time to examine what truly matters—free from daily distractions—creates the clarity and focus needed for meaningful growth. This reflection requires intentionality, accountability, and the discipline to realign actions with deeper priorities.

At Purpose Matters, this practice is essential to how we can fulfill our mission:

Empower growth-minded organizations to focus on what matters, align with their purpose, and achieve meaningful growth with greater fulfillment.

We bring this mission to life through the 7P Business Alignment Model™, a holistic and integrative framework designed to empower purpose-driven entrepreneurs and their teams to grow and evolve into ever-improving versions of themselves.

In addition, we believe when we create better alignment between the purpose of the business slice in the context of the overall purpose of one's life pie, we can create an enduring sense of fulfillment and meaningful growth for the business owner and the lives of the people they serve.

Expanding Beyond SMBs: Universal Principles of Purpose Alignment

Although these frameworks have been developed over more than a decade with owners of Small to Mid-Sized Businesses (SMBs), the underlying principles and questions apply far more broadly. They are, at their core, universal tools that empower you to better align with one's *purpose* and *what matters most*.

These same ideas can serve budding entrepreneurs testing their first venture, start-ups navigating rapid growth, university students clarifying their life direction, working professionals seeking career advancement and/or greater meaning, or non-profit directors striving to balance mission with sustainability.

In fact, if you replace the word business with life in *Aligning Your Business with Your Purpose*, it becomes *Aligning Your Life with Your Purpose*. This simple shift highlights a broader truth: these frameworks aren't just about business performance but also about living with meaning and purpose. Whether applied to work, relationships, education, or community leadership, the goal remains the same: aligning what matters most and how you show up every day.

Next Steps: Bringing Purpose to Life

Knowledge alone doesn't create change. Without effective frameworks, knowledge can stay dormant and never translate into action.

We live in an age of abundant information—books, podcasts, online courses, and now AI. Yet despite all this access, most people still struggle to apply what they know in meaningful ways.

That's because knowledge without a framework is like raw material without a blueprint. You can have all the tools and materials in the world, but without a plan to execute it, it's nearly impossible to build anything that endures.

To benefit from purpose-driven alignment, your purpose must move from vision to action. The chapters ahead show you how to do exactly that using the 7P Business Alignment Model™. In the Purpose chapter, you'll define your mission and vision—your true north—to guide decisions and keep you aligned and centered. As you move through each of the seven Ps, you'll learn how to put purpose into practice across every area of your business and life—helping you focus on what matters, unlock your potential, and build success that's both fulfilling and sustainable.

Frame and Framework: Aligning Who You Are with How You Lead

A frame (identity) shapes how you see yourself and the world around you. It's the lens through which you interpret experiences, form expectations, and define success. Your frame is tied to identity—it helps you answer, "Who am I, and who am I becoming?"

A framework (execution), on the other hand, provides the structure—the plan, blueprint, or playbook—that supports the behaviors reinforcing that identity. For example, if you see yourself as a healthy, fit person, you're more likely to follow the framework of regular exercise and balanced nutrition. As you consistently act on those habits, your identity strengthens, and that stronger identity reinforces those same behaviors.

The same principle applies in business and leadership. Seeing yourself as a purpose-driven leader creates the frame, while using a structured approach like the 7P Business Alignment Model™ provides the framework that sustains it.

Knowledge without a framework for applying it is useless. Most SMB owners already know far more than they can consistently execute. A framework helps you turn what you know into consistent action that builds better habits and produces meaningful results.

Without a framework to guide decisions and behaviors, what you know never becomes what you do. You see this in business all the time: a leader may read several books on business improvement or listen to countless podcasts yet still feel scattered on Monday morning. Without a framework, ideas don't translate into action or results. Once a clear structure is in place—like the 7P Business Alignment Model™— actions become more aligned and repeatable.

Over time, your actions and self-image begin to align, creating a positive feedback loop that builds confidence, focus, and fulfillment. Your frame and framework continually reinforce each other: the clearer your frame, the better your framework guides your actions; and the more consistently you follow your framework, the stronger and more aligned your frame becomes. Together, they create the conditions for meaningful growth and lasting change.

Key Takeaways for Chapter 1: What Matters

1. **The Importance of Reflection**: Drawing from Socrates' teaching that "an unexamined life is not worth living," this chapter emphasizes the essential role of introspection in identifying what truly matters in life and business. Reflection uncovers deeper values, beliefs, and priorities.

2. **Clarity Through Reflection**: Setting time aside for reflective thinking is essential—not optional. It helps leaders step back from daily noise, recalibrate, and realign actions with long-term goals and deeper priorities.

3. **Efficiency vs. Effectiveness**: As Peter Drucker noted, "Efficiency is doing things right; effectiveness is doing the right things." Reflection enables leaders to be more effectiveness vs efficient.

4. **The 7P Business Alignment Model**™: The 7P framework offers a holistic, practical way to navigate business complexity. By breaking challenges into the areas of Prioritization, People, Pipeline, Product, Process, Profit, and Purpose, it helps leaders align decisions, behaviors, and outcomes with overarching goals.

5. **Life Pie Alignment Framework**™: For personal alignment, the Life Pie provides a visual way to reflect on and balance key life areas—health, relationships, career, finances, and personal growth—ensuring no essential dimension is ignored.

6. **Maslow's Hierarchy of Needs**: Maslow's model shows that fulfilling foundational needs creates the conditions for pursuing higher-order growth. This principle applies both to personal development and to building engaged, high-performing teams.

7. **Encouraging Self-Actualization**: Supporting people in their growth toward self-actualization not only meets a fundamental human need but also strengthens engagement, retention, and organizational performance.

8. **The Concept of Ikigai**: Ikigai offers a practical framework for identifying one's "reason for being"—the intersection of what you love, what you're good at, what the world needs, and what you can be paid for. This helps cultivate deeper fulfillment and purpose.

9. **From Reflection to Action**: Reflection is valuable only when it leads to purposeful action. Leaders are encouraged to integrate regular reflection into their routines to align decisions and behaviors with values and purpose—turning clarity into meaningful growth.

10. **Expanding Beyond Business**: While the 7P BAM is written for SMB owners, its principles apply widely—to solopreneurs, professionals, students, and nonprofits. Aligning one's whole life with purpose, not just business, is what ultimately drives meaningful growth and fulfillment.

Reflection Questions for Chapter 1: What Matters

1. What's top of mind for me right now, and why does it matter?

2. Which of the 7Ps in my business feels most out of balance or most in need of improvement?

3. Looking at my Life Pie, which areas need more attention, and what small steps can I take to improve them?

4. How well does my current work or business align with my purpose and the impact I want to create?

5. After completing the Ikigai exercise, what did I learn about my strengths? How can I use those strengths in ways that bring fulfillment, create impact, and remain financially sustainable?

6. What are my top 1–2 takeaways from this chapter, and how will I apply them?

CHAPTER 2

CUSTOMER MATTERS

*"It is the customer who determines what a
business is. And what the customer buys and
considers value is never a product. It is always
utility, what a product or service does for him."[1]*
—Peter Drucker

What Matters to Your Customer: The Universal Principle Behind Every Purchase

I recall a Sunday afternoon visiting my father, sitting in his lazy chair, and asking him about the Rolex watch he often wore. He was a very frugal man who was loath to spend money on even relatively inexpensive consumer goods, like coffee, clothing, etc. I chided him about spending over $10,000 for such an expensive watch when he was such a "cheapskate" in many other areas of his life.

When I asked him why he had gotten such an expensive watch, he looked at it momentarily, and said "It makes me feel good." That's it. Nothing more needed to be said beyond those five words. I understood why: After working so hard for so many years, he could finally afford such an item and enjoyed the satisfaction, status, and feeling of importance that his Rolex watch imparted to him.

This anecdote highlights a universal truth underlying nearly every purchase decision: the pursuit of feeling "good." In business terms, that emotional payoff—the utility customers derive from how your product makes them feel—drives the real value you sell. Even when the goal is to avoid feeling "bad" or experiencing discomfort, the motivation is still directed toward a positive emotional state and away from a negative one.

No one buys a Rolex watch simply to tell the time. Customers purchase Rolex watches for the feelings of prestige, status, and self-importance that luxury-branded items often provide.[2] While some might argue that these good feelings are fleeting or superficial, such value judgments are beyond the scope of this book.

The essential takeaway is that nearly every business enterprise is ultimately tied to making the buyer feel some type of "good." From hospitality and retail to food services, manufacturing, and professional services, few businesses operate with the goal of making people feel "bad." However, simply understanding that your business is about creating positive feelings for customers isn't enough to answer the critical question, "What business are you in?"[3] As Drucker points out, if the customer determines the answer to this question, then it's crucial to dig deeper beyond the features of your products or services and identify the core benefit your business provides or the specific problem or pain point it solves for your customer.

Digging Deeper: What Business Are You Really In?

When we ask our clients, "*What business are you really in*?" their initial answers typically describe the surface-level activities of their business. For example, if you run an aluminum foundry, you make parts from aluminum casting; if you're an electrical contractor, you provide electrical contracting work; if you own a Subway franchise, you make and sell sandwiches; and if you own an architectural firm, you design plans. While these answers may be a good starting point, digging deeper into the underlying core customer benefits derived from your products and services, is critical to understanding what business you are really in.

Lessons from Marketing Myopia: Features vs. Benefits

In *Marketing Myopia*, Levitt famously illustrated how companies lose sight of their core benefits when they confuse features with customer value: "The railroads failed to ask this same question (what business are you 'really' in) and stopped growing. Why? Not because people no longer needed transportation. And not because other innovations (cars, airplanes) filled transportation needs. Rather, railroads stopped growing because railroads didn't move to fill those needs. Their executives incorrectly thought that they were in the railroad business, not the transportation business." [4]

As the titans of industry at the beginning of the 20th century, they viewed the world through the prism of the railroad business, which focused on laying down more tracks and building faster and bigger trains. They were attached to the features of trains and tracks versus the underlying core benefits of how they served customers—moving goods and people from point A to B safely and on time.

Their 'myopia', a vision condition in which close objects look clear but far objects look blurry, as pointed out by Levitt, prevented them from recognizing and capitalizing on the opportunities created by the emerging new technology arising from automobiles and planes. The growth of these new forms of transportation inevitably made railroads less dominant and subsequently became a smaller and smaller slice of the overall transportation market.

Levitt highlighted Hollywood and the movie business as another example of how other industries make the same mistake, putting themselves at risk of obsolescence. Hollywood defined its business incorrectly by thinking it was in the movie business when it was actually in the entertainment business. Levitt explains further how, with the advent of TV in the 1940s, many movie producers were blind to their own myopia regarding their industry. By being stuck or trapped in the existing paradigm of thinking they were in the "movie business," they rejected TV when they should have seen it as an opportunity to grow their "entertainment business" beyond just their movie business.[5]

Modern Example: Netflix vs. Blockbuster

A more recent and widely understood example of marketing myopia is the rise of Netflix and the fall of Blockbuster. Blockbuster saw itself as being in the video-rental business, focused on physical store locations, late fees, and DVD inventory management. It invested heavily in optimizing that model and resisted changing it. But customers didn't care about renting DVDs, they cared about convenient, affordable, and immediate access to entertainment.

Netflix, by contrast, understood it was in the on-demand entertainment business. It started with DVD-by-mail then pivoted into streaming, and later into content creation—always focused on delivering entertainment when and how people wanted it. Blockbuster's focus on the features of its old model blinded it to the benefits customers actually valued. Netflix stayed focused on the benefit of convenient, personalized entertainment and evolved its business model accordingly.

Just like the railroads and Hollywood studios before them, Blockbuster's mistake wasn't a lack of demand. It was a failure to recognize what business they were really in.

Whether you're a local contractor, cafe owner, or tech firm, the lesson is the same: customers don't buy your product—they buy the result it gives them. If your business model clings too tightly to how things have always been done, you risk missing the deeper opportunity to serve and grow in ways that matter to your customer.

As an SMB owner, the question isn't just what you sell in terms of features, but what outcome are your customers really buying. Additionally, you need to ask is your business model aligned to deliver it purposefully and profitably?

A modern-day example of a company that clearly understands what business they are in is Disney. Unlike early Hollywood studios, Disney has diversified beyond amusement parks and films into streaming services, TV networks like ABC and ESPN, merchandise, and resorts. By expanding into various entertainment avenues, Disney clearly understands its broader role in delivering entertainment rather than limiting itself to movies or amusement parks. This strategic approach allows Disney to grow and adapt, ensuring it remains a leader in the entertainment industry across multiple platforms.[6]

Refining the Scope of Your Business Benefits

However, framing your business in terms of its core benefits or utility, like "transportation or entertainment," is typically too wide of a lens to be practical for most businesses. We must refine and narrow the scope of what business we are in to guide decision making and develop a more actionable strategy relevant to your business core competencies.

For example, if you say you are in the education business, what type of education and for whom? Interestingly, the origin of the word "education" is from the Latin root *"educare,"* meaning "to lead out or bring forth."[7] Perhaps we can infer that through organized questions and the transference of knowledge, we can lead out, bring forth more of our potential, and achieve greater understanding. Peter Drucker exemplifies the power of asking the right questions, as illustrated by one of his former clients:

> "Drucker got us thinking through our problem and applying our own expertise and experience in a way we had never done before. This was amazingly effective and valuable, and we found valuable solutions to our issues that we had missed in the past. We discovered these ourselves because of his questions."[8]

The Business of Purpose Matters

Just like Netflix wasn't simply "in the DVD rental business" but understood and evolved into the *on-demand entertainment business*, Purpose Matters continues to grow into the *business of potential-development*—helping growth-minded SMB owners and their teams achieve greater clarity, alignment, and focus so they can grow more profitably, sustainably, and with greater fulfillment.

At its core, Purpose Matters is in the education business in the original sense of *educare*—drawing out the best in people and organizations through purposeful questioning, reflection, and actionable frameworks. Fractional executive support and alignment coaching are the means; the real product is a business that works with its purpose, not against it, producing both professional success and a sense of well-being for the owner and their team.

Who Is Our Customer?

When I meet with my clients and talk with their employees, I remind them that their paychecks and direct deposits don't come from a mythical money tree growing in the owner's backyard. It comes directly from the customers' bank accounts. They exchange their money for products and services rendered in ways that solve their problems and satisfy a want or need—*better than their next best available alternative*.

In the context of what matters in business, the customer and what they value matters. The customer is the individual or group that must be satisfied for the organization to achieve results.[9] They are the people who *value* and *want* the company's offering. In addition, identifying and understanding its primary and supporting customers is critical for the business owner's ability to prioritize *what matters most* by also prioritizing *who matters most*.

Who is our primary customer?

The primary customer is the individual or entity that directly benefits from the company's product or service.[10] The primary customer for a machine shop in the aerospace industry might be a large aerospace manufacturer requiring precision-machined parts for aircraft production.

For the machine shop, this customer defines their market and drives the shop's operational focus. Knowledge about the primary customer's needs—such as high precision, quick turnaround, and adherence to strict regulations—impacts everything from the type of machinery the shop invests in to the quality control measures it implements. It's critical to have one clear answer to this question. Focusing on too many customer segments can spread resources too thinly to be effective and inhibit the business's growth. While the aerospace manufacturer is the primary customer, they are not the only customer.

Beyond the Buyer: Other Key Stakeholders

While your primary customer is the one who pays for and receives your product or service, there are others—your team, investors, and vendors who also play a vital role in your business's success and whose needs must also be considered. [9] For example, skilled machinists who work in the machine shop are key stakeholders and might be motivated by the opportunity to work on innovative aerospace jobs. Suppliers may value long-term reliability and partnership and investors may be looking to grow the business for a successful exit.

These stakeholders aren't "customers" in the traditional sense, but their alignment to your purpose and satisfaction also matter. When you understand what they value, you can strengthen your overall ability to serve your primary customer more effectively.[11] We'll explore these relationships further in later chapters in the Product and Pipeline sections and provide frameworks to help you identify your primary customers and what they value while ensuring they align with your purpose, core competencies, and core values.

Key Takeaways for Chapter 2: Customer Matters

1. **The Customer Defines Your Business:**
   o As Peter Drucker emphasized, the customer determines what your business is by defining what they value. Success depends on your ability to understand and deliver on these values effectively.

2. **Focus on Core Benefits, Not Features:**
   o Customers buy based on the benefits they derive, not the technical features of your product or service. Identifying and emphasizing these core benefits helps align your offerings with their needs.

3. **Know Your Primary and Supporting Customers:**
   o Identify your primary customer (who directly uses your product or service) and your supporting customers (employees, suppliers, and investors). Both groups play critical roles in your success.

4. **Adapt to Meet Customer Needs:**
   o How customers' needs and preferences get met can change over time due to technological advancements, market trends, or regulatory shifts. Regularly reevaluate who your customers are and what they value to stay relevant and competitive.

5. **Avoid Marketing Myopia**
   o Focus on the broader value you deliver rather than narrowly defining your business by its current features or offerings. This perspective helps you innovate and avoid obsolescence, as illustrated by historical examples like the railroads and Hollywood.

6. **Customer-Centric Focus Drives Results**

   Understanding your customers' needs and solving their problems better than their alternatives creates value, fosters loyalty, and ensures long-term business success.

Reflection Questions Chapter 2: What Matters to the Customer

1. **What business are you *really* in, and how does your product or service deliver value beyond its features?**

   o How do you help your customers feel "good" or solve their pain points? Are you focusing on the core benefits or only the surface-level activities of your business?

2. **Who is your primary customer, and what do they value most about your product or service?**

   o Are you addressing their most pressing needs and delivering better solutions than their next best alternative?

3. **How do your supporting customers (e.g., employees, suppliers, investors) contribute to your success, and are you meeting their expectations?**

   o What steps could you take to strengthen relationships with these stakeholders?

4. **Are you proactively adapting to meet your customers' needs or changes in the market environment?**

   o What trends, technologies, or regulations might shift your customers' expectations, and how are you preparing to meet them?

5. **How does your team understand your primary customers and how do they prioritize them?**

   o   Are you spreading resources too thin by trying to serve too many segments, or are you focusing effectively on the customer who matters most to your growth?

6. **What stood out to you in this chapter or resonated most with you?**

7. **What are your top 1-2 takeaways from this chapter**, and what specific step can you take to put them into action and translate them into reality?

These reflective questions can help you stay more aligned with who your business is truly serving in terms of customer benefits while also staying adaptable to an ever-changing business landscape.

CHAPTER 3

CULTURE MATTERS

*"You can have a good strategy in place, but if you
don't have the culture and the enabling systems
that allow you to successfully implement that
strategy, the culture of the organization will defeat
the strategy."*[1]
— *Dick Clark, CEO, Merck*

Build a Culture that Reflects What Matters

This chapter provides practical strategies for defining and cultivating your company culture, enabling you to execute your strategic goals more effectively while aligned with your purpose.

Culture is how work really gets done when no one's watching. It's "how we do things around here"—the shared behaviors, attitudes, beliefs, and assumptions that shape how people work, decide, and interact every day. In practice, it's the behavioral norms and systems that either reinforce your strategy or undermine it.

The Chartered Management Institute describes the culture of an organization as "…its personality and character. Organizational culture is made up of shared values, beliefs, and assumptions about how people should behave and interact, how decisions should be made and how work activities should be carried out."[2]

Experts have long emphasized the vital role of culture in strategy execution. MIT professor Edgar Schein notes in Organizational Culture and Leadership, "Culture determines and limits strategy."[3] Similarly, the often-quoted saying attributed to Peter Drucker, "Culture eats strategy for breakfast,"[4] highlights that even the best strategies can fail without the right culture to sustain them.

Defining Company Culture

In our work with clients, we've found that cultural fit has become increasingly important when screening job applicants to find the "right-fit" employees. However, when asked to describe their culture, clients often struggle to articulate it, as culture can be ambiguous and difficult to define.

To address this challenge, we help clients define and articulate their culture as a reflection of how a company's core competencies and values are consistently practiced in daily decisions and behaviors. By developing real-world examples and stories that illustrate how these core values and competencies manifest in their workplace and customer interactions, we help owners and leadership teams identify, communicate, and reinforce their culture within the organization.

Defining Core Competencies

A company's core competencies are its unique strengths that set it apart and enable it to deliver distinct value to customers. As Warren Buffett wisely said, "Everybody's got a different circle of competence. The important thing is not how big the circle is. The important thing is staying inside the circle."[5] These "circles of competence" include specialized expertise, knowledge, operational efficiencies, and innovative processes that are difficult for competitors to replicate.

For instance, a precision engineering firm might specialize in producing high-tolerance components using cutting-edge technology and proprietary manufacturing techniques. This expertise and efficient workflows give the firm a competitive edge that is difficult for others to match. By staying within its circle of competence, a company can focus its efforts and resources on what it does best and deliver superior value to its customers while creating a solid foundation for sustainable success.

Core Competencies vs. Values

Football Team Example

- **Core Competency:** The Sea Kings High School football team's ability to **run the ball effectively is its core competency.** This strength comes from having a talented offensive line that can create running lanes and a skilled running back who can exploit those opportunities. These are technical capabilities, specific skills and assets that make the team effective in executing a running game strategy.

- **Core Values:** The team's values reflect the attitudes and behaviors that drive how the team operates and sustains this core competency. For instance, the Sea Kings value **discipline, physical toughness, and teamwork**. The offensive line embraces the mentality of outworking their opponents in the trenches, while the running back embodies grit and perseverance—qualities that embody what legendary NBA player, Kobe Bryant, referred to as the 'mamba mentality', a relentless focus, resilience, and never quitting on the play.

SMB (small and mid-sized business) Examples:

Digital Marketing Agency serving SMBs

- **Core Competency:** A digital marketing agency's ability to craft engaging marketing campaigns and utilize data-driven strategies effectively is its core competency. This strength comes from having skilled content creators who develop compelling stories and experienced analysts who turn customer data into actionable insights. These are technical capabilities—specific skills and tools that enable the agency to deliver impactful marketing results for their clients.

- **Core Values:** The agency's core values drive how these competencies are developed and sustained. For example, their creativity is cultivated in an environment where the values of collaboration and innovation are highly encouraged resulting in productive brainstorming sessions and fresh ideas. The value of data-driven decisions shapes their approach to client projects, where every campaign is built on measurable insights.

Managed Service Provider (MSP) providing outsourced IT services

- **Core Competency:** The ability to deliver proactive IT monitoring and rapid troubleshooting is a core competency. This technical strength stems from a highly skilled team that leverages advanced tools to prevent issues and resolve them quickly when they arise. These technical capabilities ensure clients experience seamless IT operations, minimizing downtime and disruptions.

- **Core Value:** The MSP's core value is **humanizing customer service** to make clients feel valued and supported. This goes beyond solving technical problems—it's about creating positive interactions at every touchpoint and cultivating a mindset of authentic and personable customer service.

Core Competencies Framework for Discovering Strengths

To help clarify your business's core competencies, reflect on the following questions. Writing them out on sticky notes or chart paper as part of a brainstorming session would be helpful. Additionally, connecting your answers to real-life examples—such as "just like the time when..." or "as evidenced by..." will make them more concrete and actionable.

1. **What Are Your Key Business Activities?**

    o What specific services or products do you provide that define your business?

2. **What Sets You Apart?**

    o What are the unique strengths or capabilities that differentiate your business from your customer's next best alternatives (competitors) and give you an edge? How do these strengths help you deliver distinct value to your customers?

    1. **Distinct value** refers to the unique benefits, solutions, or outcomes a company delivers to its customers that differentiate it from competitors. It is what makes your product or service useful and uniquely desirable, often addressing customer needs in a way that others cannot replicate. Distinct value combines tangible

attributes (e.g., price, quality, efficiency) with intangible qualities (e.g., brand reputation, customer experience, customer relationships, innovation).[6]

3. **What Are Your Core Strengths?**

   o In what areas does your business excel? (Consider skills, knowledge, and resources.)

   o What competencies or expertise have you developed more than others in your industry or ones they may not have?

4. **Do Employees Understand Your Company's Core Competencies and Use Them to Drive Success?**

   o How can we ensure employees utilize these core competencies to create more value for customers and the business?

5. **What Do Your Customers Value Most About Your Business?**

   o Based on customer feedback, what aspects of your business do they appreciate most?

   o What makes your customers choose you over your competitors? (Consider cost, quality, speed, or customer service.)

6. **What Resources Give You an Edge?**

   o Are there any physical, financial, or human resources you have that strengthen your competitive position compared to your customers' next best alternative?

7. **What Problems Do You Solve for Your Customers?**

   o What specific challenges or pain points do your products or services address for your target customers?

   o How does your business make life easier or better for your customers, and what measurable benefits do you deliver?

Building Success Through Core Competencies

Defining and focusing on core competencies helps employees understand what drives the company's success and clarifies where to concentrate their efforts. This clarity gives employees confidence, reduces wasted effort, and helps the company grow without burning out its people.

Purpose Matters Core Competencies

In working with our clients over the years, here are five core competencies and the resulting customer benefits that we've identified:

1. Strategic Focus and Purpose Alignment

Empower organizations to focus on what matters, prioritize effectively and align their business with their purpose by utilizing the **7P Business Alignment Model**™. By integrating the 7Ps: Purpose, Prioritization, People, Pipeline, Product, Process, and Profit, leaders gain clarity, make better decisions, and drive meaningful growth with greater fulfillment.

2. Team Development and Alignment

Professionalize their hiring and improve team alignment to attract and retain more of the right-fit employees who align with company purpose, values and goals. Using the Right-Fit Employee Profile, BDTC Framework, and structured evaluation tools, helps our clients reduce turnover, improve employee engagement, and build a more productive and committed workforce.

3. Strategic Marketing and Customer Alignment

Deliver strategic, data-driven marketing solutions to help organizations better identify, attract, and retain more of the high-value right-fit customers aligned with your core purpose, values, and competencies. By doing so, you can increase brand loyalty, profitability, and sustainable growth.

4. Problem Solving and Integrative Consultation™

We help leaders solve the real problem and not just the visible one while also looking through the lens of maximizing opportunities. Integrative Consultation™ helps clients uncover root causes, involve the right voices, and guide collaborative solutions across teams, priorities, and systems. We don't jump to answers—we help clarify the right questions, align thinking, and turn confusion into clear, coordinated action.

5. Process Optimization and Operational Alignment

We help SMBs streamline and document their core processes through mapping, playbooks, SOPs, and improving role clarity via frameworks like RASCI. This improves collaboration, efficiency, and accountability, ensuring daily operations align with strategy, purpose, and profitability.

Core Competencies Key Takeaways

1. **Understand Core Competencies as Unique Strengths:**

   Core competencies define what sets your business apart, encompassing expertise or combination of expertise, processes, or efficiencies that deliver exceptional customer value.

2. **Align Efforts with Core Competencies:**

   Focusing on your "circle of competence" ensures your resources are directed toward what your business does best, minimizing distractions while maximizing impact.

3. **Strengthen Culture to Reinforce Core Competencies:**

   Create a work environment that supports and encourages the strengths that set your business apart. A strong culture helps employees consistently apply your core competencies and ensures customers experience their full value.

Core Values: The Foundation of Company Behavior and Decision-Making

While core competencies represent the unique strengths that set your business apart and drive its success, core values are the guiding principles that influence an organization's behavior and decision-making.[7] These values reflect what the company stands for and considers important. Core values shape how your organization operates and interacts with stakeholders. They can also be described as how work gets done—the way things are done around here. Core values are often embedded in mission statements, codes of conduct, and policies, but their true impact is felt when the leadership team and employees genuinely embody them.

One way to evaluate how you are living your values, as described in an MIT Sloan Management Review article is to:

"list your values and allocate the number of hours per day (or week) you spend on choices that express these values, the quality of personal energy spent while engaging in these activities, and the amount of money you spend in their pursuit.

For instance, if personal growth is a value, what can you identify that you do each week to invest in it? Are you challenging yourself by learning a new skill? Are you setting aside time to learn this skill when you are fresh and energized? Are you spending money on a class or employing the right expert or coach to help you refine your new skill? Taking stock of how your stated values align to how you invest your time, energy, and money can help clarify how effectively you are living your values."[8]

Distinguishing between Stated vs. Actual Core Values

A critical distinction lies between stated values—what a company says it values—and actual core values, reflected by the behaviors and decisions made. This difference often becomes most apparent when priorities compete or when the company faces difficult choices. For example, a company that claims integrity as a core value might be tested when it faces the choice of adhering to ethical practices at the expense of profit or prioritizing profit at the expense of ethics. If the company consistently chooses more profit over ethical practices, it becomes evident that ethics is not genuinely one of its core values.

Actual core values consistently guide decisions and behaviors, even when significant costs or challenges are involved in upholding those values. In essence, a company's core values are demonstrated not by what it says but by what it does.

Values Under Pressure: Two SMB Tests

SMB Manufacturing Context (Using Quality as a Core Value)

Scenario:

A family-owned manufacturing company specializes in producing precision-engineered parts for medical devices. The company prominently states quality as one of its core values, emphasizing that its products meet the highest safety and performance standards, especially since its components are used in life-critical equipment.

The Test of Actual Values:

The company faces a situation where a key client requests a large order but imposes an aggressive deadline. Meeting the deadline would require skipping several quality control steps and possibly compromising the precision of the final product. Accepting the order could lead to significant short-term revenue while rejecting it could strain the relationship with the client.

- **Option 1:** The company refuses to skip the quality control steps, even if it means losing the contract. This decision demonstrates that quality is a core value, prioritized over financial gain.

- **Option 2:** The company chooses to cut corners to meet the deadline, risking the integrity of its products. This would reveal that quality is more of a stated value than an actual one.

Outcome:

If the company chooses Option 1, it shows its commitment to quality goes beyond marketing statements, reinforcing trust with existing customers who rely on its uncompromising standards. If it chooses Option 2, it risks reputational damage and potential liability should its compromised products fail in the field.

Key Takeaway:

Core values like *quality* are tested when a company must decide between maintaining its standards and pursuing short-term gains that may come at the expense of quality. For SMB manufacturers, consistently aligning actions with stated values builds long-term credibility with customers and employees, even if it involves short-term sacrifices.

SMB Context (Using Employee Well-Being as a Core Value)

Scenario:

A small manufacturing company claims *employee well-being* is a core value, proudly highlighting initiatives like flexible schedules, wellness programs, and a commitment to maintaining a safe work environment.

The Test of Actual Values:

The company lands a large order from a key client, requiring production to scale significantly to meet a tight deadline. The leadership faces a choice:

- **Option 1:** Push employees to work overtime for weeks without adequate rest, potentially leading to burnout and fatigue-related accidents. This would ensure meeting the client's deadline but may compromise employee well-being.

- **Option 2:** Hire additional temporary workers or negotiate an extended deadline with the client, even though this approach would reduce profit margins or risk losing the contract.

Outcome:

- If the company opts for **Option 1**, it could reveal that *employee well-being* is more of a stated value than an actual one, as it prioritizes financial gains over its stated commitment to employee well-being.

- If the company chooses **Option 2**, it could indicate through its actions that employee well-being is prioritized, reinforcing trust and loyalty among its workforce. We also understand that various employees may interpret these types of decisions differently. Some employees may welcome the overtime pay earned from the additional work.

Key Takeaway:

Core values like *employee well-being* are tested when a company must balance competing priorities. Actions that align with stated values foster a culture of trust and loyalty, leading to long-term employee retention and enhanced reputation in the industry. Conversely, actions that contradict stated values erode trust, potentially harming morale and productivity.

Defining and Demonstrating Core Values: Moving Beyond Abstract Values

SMB owners often struggle to define core values in a way that resonates and translates into actionable behaviors. Simply listing abstract values like "integrity" or "customer service" isn't enough; these values must be clearly defined and tied to tangible examples of how they influence daily operations.

For instance, a company valuing innovation might actively encourage employees to take calculated risks and experiment, while a company emphasizing customer satisfaction could focus on providing exceptional service and fostering strong client relationships. Owners and teams can bring these values to life by sharing stories and examples of value-driven decisions and behaviors. When defined and demonstrated effectively, core values serve as a guiding compass that shapes employee behavior, reinforces organizational culture, and ensures the company's actions are aligned with those core values.

Real-Life Scenarios and Storytelling

Using relatable examples in the context of their day-to-day operations can make core values more understandable and actionable for SMB owners and their employees. Consider a small business that values "Customer-Centric Excellence." This core value could come to life when a client faces a significant issue with a product or service. Instead of following a rigid policy, the team prioritizes the customer's needs by going above and beyond to resolve the issue, even if it means absorbing additional costs.

An example could be a local design-build firm receiving a call from a client who is unsatisfied with a completed landscaping project. Even if the issue stemmed from a client misunderstanding rather than a company error, the team might decide to revisit the project site and make adjustments without charging extra. For this particular company, this action would embody their version of "Customer-Centric Excellence" by putting the client's satisfaction above immediate profit.

These real-life examples make core values tangible, illustrating how values drive decision-making and actions, especially when prioritizing customer relationships over short-term financial gains. By sharing stories like these with their teams, SMB owners can reinforce the culture they want to build and show how core values influence decisions in meaningful ways.

Alignment of Core Values and Core Competencies

Another element of cultivating the right culture is ensuring alignment between core competencies and values. When what a company is good at (core competencies) aligns with what it stands for (core values), and both are practiced consistently, the result is a coherent culture that drives performance and employee engagement.

For instance, if a company values teamwork and collaboration, its core competencies might include effective communication, meetings, and project management skills. By aligning its core competencies with its core values, the company can create a cohesive culture that supports and is aligned with its strategic objectives and core purpose.[12]

Core Values vs Core Competencies: Client-Centric Example

To further clarify the distinction between core values and core competencies, let's explore the concept of 'client-centric,' which can describe both. As a core value, "client-centric" reflects the company's prioritization of the customer and the belief that the customer is at the center of everything the company does, as evidenced by how the company interacts with and serves the customer.

As a core competency, "client-centric" represents the company's specific set of skills or capabilities that the organization excels in, enabling it to deliver superior client-focused services or products. "Client-centric" as a core competency is focused on the *how* of the business's client interactions. It refers to the practical and operational capabilities of the business that enable it to deliver on its client-centric values.

In summary, "client-centric" as a core value refers to the organization's philosophy and commitment to client satisfaction, while "client-centric" as a core competency focuses more on the specific skills and capabilities that enable the organization to deliver on that core value effectively.[13] The following describes a few of the core values of our own organization:

Purpose Matters Core Values

Earned Trust Through Meaningful Results

Our aim is to deliver in a way that creates meaningful results while also making clients feel understood, empowered, and supported. Our goal is to earn not just customer satisfaction but the kind of trust that leads them to enthusiastically refer us to others and those they care about.

Growth Mindset with Humility

We embrace challenges and feedback with a humble posture of learning, knowing we don't have all the answers and never will. A Growth mindset isn't about arriving; it's about continuously improving.

We commit to continuous learning, reflection, and realignment with purpose so we can evolve into better versions of ourselves, serve others more fully, and make a more meaningful contribution over time.

Blunt Integrity, Delivered with Empathy

We don't sidestep hard conversations. We show up with candor, even when the truth is uncomfortable because that's what real partnership requires. But blunt doesn't mean cold. We lead with empathy, listen deeply, and speak directly from a place of respect, care, and belief in our clients' potential. We treat every client's business with the care, candor, and commitment we'd offer a close friend.

Purpose-Driven Alignment

We believe businesses thrive when they align with what matters most. We help our clients and ourselves build from a place of clarity, focus, and simplicity so they can execute what truly matters with purpose and confidence. This alignment isn't just about the strategic—it's also deeply personal, rooted in a clear sense of *why*. By doing so, we can then translate it into meaningful results.

Integrative Approach

We combine practical tools and proven methods across the 7Ps to help you solve real problems effectively. You don't get vague advice or one-size-fits-all templates. Instead, you get step-by-step guidance tailored to your business, with tools you can use right away to create meaningful results.

Holistic (Whole-Person) Alignment

The purpose of our Life Pie framework reminds us that we are whole people and not just roles or job titles. We take a holistic approach to each person and business we serve, recognizing that true alignment starts at the level of identity and well-being. Whether working with a client, team member, or partner, we lead with empathy, dignity, and the belief that meaningful work flows from a well-aligned life with what matters most.

Core Values Takeaways for SMB Owners

1. **Define and Communicate Values with Real-World Examples**: Illustrate values with stories that exemplify these values in your business.

2. **Distinguish Stated vs. Actual Values**: Identify values that are lived through consistent behaviors and decision-making, especially in challenging situations.

3. **Reflect on Values**: Evaluate how values are demonstrated in the business and adjust behaviors and decision making as necessary to ensure alignment with strategic goals and purpose.

Core Values Framework

1. **What Principles and Beliefs Are Central to Your Organization?**

   o What are the guiding principles or beliefs that shape your business decisions?

   o Which values do you consider non-negotiable regarding how your company operates?

o   How clearly defined are your company's core values? Are they specific and actionable, or do they feel abstract and open to interpretation?

o   What practical examples or behaviors can you use to illustrate each value in action?

2.   **How Do These Values Influence Your Day-to-Day Operations?**

o   How do these values impact the way you treat customers, employees, and partners?

3.   **Can You Identify Specific Examples Where These Values Have Guided Your Actions?**

o   Reflect on specific situations where your core values influenced a decision or action. How did it play out?

o   Are there moments where your values helped resolve a conflict or determine a course of action?

4.   **How Do You Communicate and Reinforce These Values to Your Employees?**

o   Do all employees understand our core values, and do they reflect the way things are done around here?

o   How are we ensuring that these values are consistently communicated and reinforced across the organization?

5.   **How Do Your Values Influence Customer Interactions and Relationships?**

o   How do your core values shape how you serve and interact with your customers?

Cultivating a Culture that Reflects Your Values and Competencies

Cultivating the right culture requires focused effort, commitment, and buy-in from your leadership team. Here are some practical steps for defining and cultivating a positive and aligned company culture:

- **Define Core Competencies and Core Values**: Define the core competencies and values critical to your company's success.

Engage employees at all levels in this process to ensure that the definitions are meaningful and relevant.

- **Communicate and Reinforce**: Communicate the core competencies and values to all employees and reinforce them through regular communication, training, and recognition programs. Ensure these elements are integrated into the company's mission statement and performance evaluations.

- **Lead by Example**: Effective leadership is crucial in shaping a company's culture. Leaders and, specifically, the owner(s) should model the behaviors and attitudes that reflect the company's core values and competencies. By demonstrating a commitment to these principles, leaders can set the tone for the rest of the organization.

- **Hire for Cultural Fit**: When hiring new employees, consider not only their technical skills and experience but also their alignment with the company's core values, competencies, and culture.

- **Foster a Positive Work Environment**: Create a work environment that supports and encourages the desired culture that reflects your core values and competencies. This can include everything from office layout and work policies to team-building activities, company-sponsored lunches, and employee recognition programs.

- **Measure and Adjust**: Regularly assess the company's culture by utilizing employee surveys, feedback sessions, and other tools to gather input and identify gaps and areas for improvement. Be open to making changes and continuously strive to strengthen the culture.

- **Celebrate Successes**: Recognize and celebrate employees who embody the company's core values and demonstrate its core competencies. Celebrate examples and stories of successes that reflect the desired culture.

The Benefits of a Strong Culture

The following benefits can be realized when culture is built on clear values, distinctive competencies, and consistently practiced:

Enhanced Employee Engagement: Employees who feel connected to the company's core values and competencies are more likely to be engaged and motivated. This leads to higher levels of productivity, creativity, and job satisfaction. Research has shown that organizations with high employee engagement outperform those with low engagement in terms of productivity and profitability.[10]

Attract Top Talent and Build a Stronger Brand: A positive and consistent culture can enhance a company's brand reputation and attract top talent. Companies with strong cultures are often considered desirable places to work and do business with, leading to increased opportunities and growth.[11]

The Gap Between Actual and Desired Culture

Every organization has two cultures—the one it has and the one it wants. The space between them is the culture gap: the difference between a company's current reality and the culture that truly aligns with its purpose. If left unaddressed, this gap can quietly erode engagement, trust, and long-term success.

For many SMB owners, this gap often results from a lack of clarity in defining and reinforcing the culture they want to build. In smaller organizations, where every employee has an outsized influence on culture, ensuring that daily behaviors reflect core values and business priorities becomes even more critical.

Leaders must take ownership of defining, modeling, and reinforcing culture while empowering employees to help sustain it. Culture thrives when both leaders and teams share responsibility for engagement, clarity of purpose, and execution. This shared commitment builds a thriving, purpose-aligned organization.[12]

Identity-Level Transformation and Bridging the Gap to a Purpose-Aligned Culture

Ultimately, the culture of your organization starts with you, the owner. You set the tone, not only through what you say but, more importantly, through who you are and how you consistently show up. Before you can expect your team to live out the company's core values and align with its purpose, you must align yourself with those values.

This is why identity-level alignment is critical. If you see yourself as an overworked technician who is "just trying to survive the day," your culture will inevitably reflect that mindset no matter how many mission statements you put on the wall. But if you see yourself as a purpose-driven leader, capable of building a thriving, values-based business, you begin to lead from a place of purpose focused alignment and strength.

In fact, one of the biggest obstacles we see with our clients is the gap between their current culture and the culture they aspire to create — one that aligns with their purpose, values, and long-term goals. The good news is that culture can be intentionally shaped and aligned when owners are willing to reflect on and adjust who they are becoming as leaders, not just what they expect from others.

Culture is built when leadership identity aligns with business purpose and when leaders model the behaviors they want to see in their teams. Culture-building isn't a leadership exercise alone but a shared responsibility lived out through their team's daily actions and interactions.

Yet owners and leaders hold the ultimate accountability for defining, sustaining, and reinforcing that culture. Everyone participates, but leadership provides the direction and consistency that keep it aligned.

For SMB owners—where each team member has a greater influence on culture than in larger companies—intentional culture design becomes even more essential. When owners take the time to define both their current and desired culture and align them with their core values and competencies, they build a stronger foundation for engagement, execution, and long-term success.

Identity-Level Transformation: The Starting Point for Cultural Change

"What you think, you become. What you feel, you attract. What you imagine, you create."[13]

—attributed to Buddha

So, how do you begin closing the gap between actual and desired culture? It starts by aligning yourself—at the identity level—with the kind of leader who can build that culture. Not with posters, team workshops, or new policies—but with how you see yourself as a leader and how you show up every day. This is not just about skills or external behavior change; it begins with shifting how you see yourself and how you lead from within.

If you want a culture of accountability, collaboration, or customer care, you must first embody those values. You can't expect your team to be accountable if you avoid tough conversations. And you can't create a culture of care if you lead with irritation, impatience, or emotional distance. Culture starts with you by how you show up, how you respond under pressure, and how you make others feel. This is why who you are becoming as a leader is the foundation for any cultural shift you want to create.

Identity Alignment Practices

1. Identity Journaling: Start by writing 2-3 minutes daily or weekly **from the perspective of the leader you are becoming**—one who aligns with your business purpose and the culture you want to build. Reflect on how you think, act, and make decisions as that person.[14]

- **Example Prompt**: *"What's one way I can lead this week so my actions reflect our core values?"*
- **Why it works**: Writing helps rewire your thinking, reinforce a new self-image, and align your actions with that identity.

2. Behavioral Alignment (Acting 'As If')

- "Act as if you have already become the person you want to be."[15]—Alfred Adler

Ask yourself throughout the day:

"What would my purpose-driven self do in this situation...What behaviors am I demonstrating that reflect and reinforce the core values and competencies of my company?"

Then **act on that answer**—whether that means how you handle a client issue, lead a meeting, or respond to a team challenge.

- **Why it works**: Actions shape identity. When you behave like the leader you want to become, you start thinking and believing like that person—closing the gap between intention and reality.[16]

3. Visualization of Future Self and Business

Spend 5–10 minutes daily **visualizing yourself leading a thriving, purpose-aligned organization**—making wise decisions, inspiring your team, and driving results in alignment with your values.

- **Why it works**: Visualization primes your brain to act consistently with that identity. It also builds confidence and mental rehearsal to succeed in key leadership moments.

By practicing identity alignment, SMB owners can cultivate an organization where employees feel empowered, valued, and deeply connected to the company's success and purpose.[17]

Key Takeaways: Chapter 3 Culture Matters

1. Culture Drives Strategy Execution

- A great strategy will fail without the right culture to support it. Culture shapes how people behave, make decisions, and work together, directly impacting your ability to achieve strategic goals.

- As Peter Drucker noted, *"Culture eats strategy for breakfast."* Defining and aligning your culture is essential for long-term success.

2. Culture = Shared Behaviors, Attitudes, and Beliefs

- Culture is more than words on a wall—it's "how things are done around here."

- It includes shared values, beliefs, and assumptions that guide how people behave, interact, and make decisions in daily work.
- Your culture is ultimately **defined by what is consistently practiced**, not just what is stated.

3. Clarify and Align Culture with Core Competencies and Values

- To build an effective culture, clarify your **core competencies** (what your business does best) and **core values** (what your business stands for).
- Together, these drive how your team operates and how customers experience your business.
- Real-world stories and examples of values and competencies in action help make your culture tangible and understandable.

4. Distinguish Core Competencies from Core Values (But Align Both)

- **Core competencies:** *what you do best* -the unique strengths (e.g., expertise, processes, or efficiencies) that deliver value to customers.
- **Core values** are guiding principles that shape *how you go about doing it,* the way you work, treat others, and make decisions.
- Aligning your **core competencies** with your **core values** creates a consistent culture that drives performance and employee engagement.

5. Lead by Example to Set the Tone for Culture

- Leaders shape culture by **modeling behaviors** aligned with the company's core values and competencies.
- What leaders do (especially in tough situations) sets the example for the entire team.
- When leaders live the culture, employees are more likely to follow suit.

6. Bridge the Gap Between Stated and Actual Values

- **Stated values** are what you say you believe; **actual values** are what you demonstrate through actions and decisions.

- Your real culture is reflected in choices made when values are tested—especially when money or pressure from competing priorities are involved.

- Align stated and actual values to build trust with employees, customers, and partners.

7. Hire and Develop for Cultural Fit

- Hiring for **cultural alignment** is as important as hiring for skills.

- Look for candidates who share your core values and can embody your company culture in how they work and interact.

- Ongoing training and performance reviews should reinforce your culture and values.

8. Define and Communicate Core Values Clearly

- Abstract values, such as "integrity" or "customer service," must be defined with real-life examples to guide behaviors.

- Ask: **What does this value look like in action?** Share stories that illustrate your values being lived out.

9. Culture and Core Competencies Strengthen Competitive Advantage

- Focusing on **what you do best** (core competencies) while living out **who you are** (core values) strengthens your market position and builds customer trust.

- Competitors may replicate products, but they can't easily copy a strong, values-driven culture.

10. Assess, Reinforce, and Continuously Improve Culture

- Culture is not "set and forget." Regularly **review, assess, and adjust** to keep it aligned with your mission and strategic goals.

- Use tools like employee feedback, team discussions, and culture surveys to evaluate alignment and make improvements.

11. Purpose Matters Example – Building Culture Through Competencies and Values

At **Purpose Matters**, we help clients define and cultivate their desired culture using these core competencies:

- **Strategic Focus & Business Alignment** – Helping clients align strategic focus and purpose to create their desired culture using frameworks like the 7P Business Alignment Model™.

- **Professionalized Hiring & Talent Alignment** – Improve hiring by attracting and then aligning their team to reflect the desired culture.

- **Strategic Data-Driven Marketing & Customer Alignment** – Ensuring customer value aligns with core values, core competencies and company culture.

12. Your leadership identity shapes your culture—whether you realize it or not.

- Culture change begins with how you see and carry yourself as a leader—not with posters or policies.

- If you want a culture of accountability, care, or innovation, you must first model those behaviors consistently.

- Your identity and daily actions set the standard for what's expected and accepted across your organization.

13. Culture Is a Shared Responsibility—But You Set the Tone

- While every employee helps shape culture, leaders are ultimately responsible for defining, guiding, and reinforcing it.

- In SMBs, where each person has more influence, leaders must be intentional about culture-building.

- A shared approach fosters engagement, purpose, and performance—but it starts with you.

Summary of Why Culture Matters for SMB Owners:

- **Culture is a competitive advantage.** It influences how work gets done, how employees engage, and how customers experience your business.

- **Culture alignment boosts growth and profitability.** When everyone is aligned around shared values and strengths, your business performs better.

- **Culture is shaped by daily actions.** Be intentional in defining, modeling, and reinforcing it—starting with leadership and spreading to the whole team.

Reflection Questions for Chapter 3: Culture Matters

1. Understanding and Defining Culture

- How would you describe your company's current culture? Does it align with your strategic goals and where you want to take the business?

- What are the "unspoken rules" or behaviors that define how work gets done and how people interact in your company?

- If an outsider observed your company for a day, what would they say about your culture? Would you agree with their assessment?

2. Identifying What's Helping or Holding You Back

- What parts of your culture are helping your business grow and align with your purpose?

- What parts of your culture may be holding your business back from achieving its goals?

3. Core Values and Competencies in Action

- What are some specific ways your team lives out (or doesn't live out) your company's core values and core competencies?

- How do your core competencies show up in daily operations, and how do they set you apart from competitors?

4. Leadership's Role in Shaping Culture

- As a leader, how are you modeling the culture you want to create? Where might you need to adjust?

- How do you address situations where employee behaviors—or your own—conflict with your company's values? Are your responses consistent and transparent?

5. Aligning and Embedding Culture

- How do you ensure that core values are reinforced in employee onboarding, training, and performance evaluations?
- What is one specific action you can take to better align your team's behaviors and decisions with your company's values and purpose?

6. Employee Engagement in Culture

- How do you empower employees to actively shape and contribute to the company culture?
- Are there specific employees or teams that embody your ideal culture? How can you recognize or share their example to inspire others?

7. Measuring and Adjusting Culture

- What tools or processes (e.g., surveys, feedback sessions) do you use to assess your culture? Are they effective?
- How do you identify and address gaps when you see behaviors that are out of alignment with your desired culture?

8. Hiring and Sustaining the Right Culture

- What steps do you take to ensure that new hires align with your core values during the hiring and onboarding process?
- What tangible actions (e.g., recognition, team-building activities) have you taken recently to reinforce and sustain the culture you want?

9. Aligning Identity and Desired Culture

- In what ways do my daily behaviors reflect the culture I expect from others?

- What value or behavior do I want to see more of in my team, and am I consistently modeling it myself?
- Which identity alignment practice (journaling, acting 'as if', or visualization) could I begin today to start shifting my leadership toward the purpose and culture I want to create this week?

10. What stood out to you in this chapter or resonated most with you?

- What story, insight, or idea felt especially relevant to your business or leadership right now?

11. What are your top 1–2 takeaways from this chapter?

- What is one specific step you can take to bring these takeaways to life and better align your culture with what matters and your purpose?

CHAPTER 4

PURPOSE MATTERS

Definition:

pur·pose /ˈpərpəs/

noun

1. The reason for which something is done, created, or for which something exists.[1]

Clarify Your Purpose

This chapter delves into the various dimensions of purpose and how to gain greater clarity about your core business purpose, encompassing your mission and vision. Purpose serves as the north star that informs and guides strategic decision making within a business. Without it, businesses risk drifting off course, misaligning resources, and ultimately falling short of their potential.

To explore the idea of purpose, we present the **Purpose Pyramid**, which provides a structured way to understand purpose on three levels: **General Purpose, Core Purpose,** and **Greater Purpose.**

Purpose Pyramid

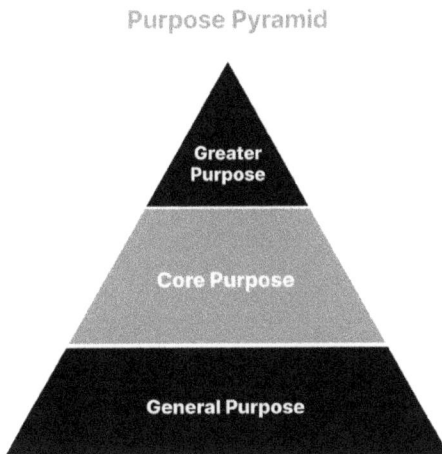

Purpose Pyramid: Understanding Purpose on Three Levels

1. General Purpose:

We've designated the "General Purpose" in the Purpose Pyramid as the universal or general reason why businesses exist. Peter Drucker powerfully encapsulates this reason with his statement: *"The purpose of business is to create and keep a customer."*[2] This principle emphasizes that every business exists to create and deliver value to its customers.

Throughout the book, a number of citations will draw from the prolific work of Peter Drucker, hailed by Business Week as "the man who invented management".[3] Drucker directly influenced a vast number of leaders from a wide range of organizations across all sectors of society, including General Electric, IBM, Intel, Procter & Gamble, Girl Scouts of the USA, The Salvation Army, Red Cross, United Farm Workers, and several presidential administrations. He was a writer, professor, management consultant, and self-described "social ecologist" who explored how humans organize themselves and interact much the way an ecologist would observe and analyze the biological world.[4]

2. Core Purpose:

At this level, your business's core purpose comprises your mission and vision, shaped by your culture, core competencies, and core values. Your mission defines your reason for existence and explains what your business does, who it serves, and how it creates value in the present. Your vision provides a future-oriented description or aspiration of how the world will look when your vision is realized.

3. Greater Purpose:

This level of purpose in the purpose pyramid addresses how a business contributes to society as a whole. Building on this concept, Peter Drucker tells us that *"Business enterprises ... are organs of society. They do not exist for their own sake, but to fulfill a specific social purpose and to satisfy a specific need of a society, a community, or individuals."*[5] The idea that businesses, like organs in a body, should serve a function that contributes to the overall health of society reflects a holistic approach—one that benefits everyone as more businesses embrace this mindset of contributing to the larger ecosystem to which they belong.

However, striving to create a better society by making positive contributions beyond the monetary goals of running a business is not always within one's control straightforward. For example, a knife manufacturer may contribute to the greater good by producing high-quality knives that enable people to dice vegetables to prepare meals for their families. In contrast, those same knives could also be misused as weapons to inflict harm, highlighting the inherent complexity and uncertainty of ensuring that the products of a business will be utilized for the greater societal good since the manufacturer cannot fully control or predict whether its products will be used constructively or destructively.

Businesses can also contribute to the greater societal good and make a positive impact starting from a more micro level simply by fostering a positive work environment and providing stable livelihoods for their employees. Doing so empowers individuals to support the well-being of their families as well as the community that they are a part of.

SMB owners can reflect on how their business decisions whether in hiring, production, marketing, or customer engagement align with their greater purpose by asking:

- Are we creating value beyond profit?
- Are we making decisions that align with our core values and benefit society as a whole?
- Are we fostering a culture where employees feel connected to a greater mission and proud of the impact they help create?

Purposeful Alignment with the 7P BAM

Gaining clarity on purpose across these three levels provides a guiding star for aligning the key elements of your business—the 7Ps. The 7P Business Alignment Model™ (BAM) ensures that the six operational elements—Prioritization, People, Pipeline, Product, Process, and Profit—work cohesively and in alignment with the overarching principle: Purpose. When your business activities align with your purpose pyramid, we believe this alignment can unlock more of your potential while creating a greater sense of fulfillment for you and those around you.

As Henry Stoever writes in *CEO Magazine*: "Alignment is key to harnessing the power of purpose effectively. Individuals are most engaged when their personal values align with the mission and goals of the organization. Companies that can articulate a clear purpose and demonstrate how each employee contributes to it foster a more motivated workforce."[6]

Purpose Misalignment Symptoms

However, misalignment between these 6 Ps with your purpose P can lead to unintended and unforeseen consequences. As George Labovitz stated in his book *The Power of Alignment*, "Misaligned companies, like cars out of alignment, can develop serious problems if not corrected quickly. They are hard to steer and don't respond well to changes in direction."[7] Misalignment and lack of clear purpose can manifest in various ways and have wide-ranging consequences. When your business and purpose are not aligned, you may experience one or more of the following symptoms:

Impact on Motivation and Burnout

If left untreated, a lack of clear purpose and misalignment can lead to decreased motivation and burnout, especially if your business activities do not align with your core values and purpose. The following might or might not apply to you, but the daily grind of running a business can start to feel more burdensome, making it harder to sustain the enthusiasm and commitment you once had.

You might feel stuck especially when you're exerting effort but making little or slow progress, and it feels like you're pressing both the accelerator and brakes at the same time. A sense of overwhelm and frustration can creep in, along with the nagging feeling that something isn't quite working or progressing as quickly as you'd like, without knowing exactly why. Over time, this can lead to a sense of stagnation, especially when your efforts aren't yielding the expected progress.

Lower Employee Engagement and Retention

Owners are not the only ones affected by misalignment. Employees can sense when a business lacks a purpose or is vague about its primary strategic objectives and goals. If the organization acts inconsistently with its stated core values, this perception can lower morale, reduce engagement, and lead to higher turnover rates, as employees may not feel their work is meaningful or aligned with their values.

Decision-Making Difficulties

Decision-making can be difficult without a clear strategic decision-making framework guided by your values and overall business purpose. You may feel like you are in a "holding pattern," an impasse filled with uncertainty about how to move forward.

Customer Perception

Misalignment also impacts how your customers experience your brand and company. Customers today increasingly seek to engage with brands they perceive as having a clear purpose and values aligned with their own. A groundbreaking global study ("Strength of Purpose" study of 8,000 global consumers and 75 companies) revealed a substantial business benefit to such purposeful brands, as consumers are four to six times more likely to buy from, trust, and champion companies with a meaningful purpose.[8]

This study shows that customers increasingly seek out and prefer doing business with companies that stand for something beyond their products or services. A business that clearly communicates and lives its purpose builds stronger brand identity and fosters deeper loyalty from its customers compared to competitors or their customers' next best alternative. Businesses that fail to articulate or live their purpose may struggle to differentiate themselves, reducing customer loyalty and trust.

Financial and Operational Challenges

Misalignment can also have negative financial implications. Businesses not aligned with their purpose may not optimally allocate resources based on their company's core values, core competencies, and the core customer benefits they provide. By not playing to their strengths, they may also miss out on "right-fit" opportunities for growth and struggle to differentiate themselves from their competition. Purpose misalignment can result in inefficient resource allocation, missed opportunities, and a failure to leverage core competencies. This reduces competitive advantage and may stifle growth.

Risk to One's Personal Fulfillment and Legacy

Lastly, misalignment with your purpose can affect your personal fulfillment and the legacy you hope to leave behind. Running a business that does not reflect your values or contribute to a meaningful purpose can lead to regrets and a feeling that the business (and the owner) did not live up to what the owner truly stands for or aspires to become and/or achieve. The emotional toll of running a business that feels misaligned with your values and aspirations can negatively impact your sense of fulfillment and peace of mind.

Addressing Misalignment

Addressing misalignment involves reassessing the business's direction, strategies, and practices to ensure they harmonize with the owner's core values and purpose. This reassessment may lead to making necessary adjustments and changes over time that can put you on a more optimal trajectory towards a more fulfilling and sustainable path for both owner and business.

When one focuses on and engages in core activities that align with their purpose, they typically experience a deeper sense of fulfillment, enthusiasm, and a feeling of "aliveness." They are more likely to wake up feeling energized and look forward to going to work. The next section will address how to overcome the misalignment challenge by identifying and clearly articulating a meaningful core purpose informed by one's core competencies, values, and culture.

Moving Toward Purpose Alignment and Transformation

Many of our clients find George Labovitz's "hard to steer" analogy strikingly relevant to their own businesses. When a company lacks alignment, navigating toward its goals whether it be revenue growth, profitable customers, more time, less frustration, or greater peace of mind becomes far more challenging. The **7P Business Alignment Model**™ **(BAM)** provides a structured approach to realign your business and team, making it easier to steer toward the outcomes you truly want.

However, even with the right frameworks in place, achieving different results requires more than just effort. It requires change. Our clients recognize that their current ways of thinking have brought them to where they are, but that same level of thinking is often insufficient to take them where they want to go. As often attributed to Albert Einstein (though the true origin is debated), "We cannot solve our problems with the same thinking we used when we created them."[9] This means reexamining perspectives, adjusting assumptions, and approaching challenges with a new mindset to discover better solutions.

By shifting the way we think, we naturally change how we make decisions, take action, and ultimately achieve results.

The Right Support Structure

However, meaningful changes are more likely to occur when one has the right support system. The good news? You don't have to do it alone. Transformation becomes significantly more achievable when guided by a structured approach. By implementing the purpose-driven alignment solutions within the 7P BAM, our Business Alignment Coach helps clients navigate this process, ensuring that meaningful changes occur not just in how they think, but in how they operate so they can ultimately achieve more of their potential and a greater sense of fulfillment.

Developing Your Core Purpose —Mission and Vision

The first phase in navigating this process of better alignment is charting the course and having a clear destination—the end in mind—informed by one's core purpose comprising the mission and vision.

In his book Creating the Organization of the Future, Dr. Bernie Jaworski presents the following description for developing one's mission: "A mission sets a common goal for all and enables everyone to align their roles to the mission. It provides guidance for decision-making as well as a framework for what to do and what not to do. When properly crafted, it enables the organization to stay focused and sets boundaries regarding which businesses to be in and which ones it should not be in."[10]

A well-crafted mission statement isn't just about words on paper; it should inspire action. When crafting a mission statement that truly inspires and motivates, Antoine de Saint-Exupéry, author of the beloved *The Little Prince*, offers a powerful metaphor:

"When you want to build a ship, do not begin by gathering wood, cutting boards, and distributing work, but awaken within the heart of man the desire for the vast and endless sea."[11]

This metaphor illustrates that genuine inspiration comes not from assigning tasks or directives but from a deep and shared desire to pursue something of significance that comes from one's heart.

Authentic Mission and Vision Statements

In the pursuit of significance, a mission statement should authentically reflect who you are, what you stand for, and what you aspire to be. We believe lofty-sounding statements that lack authenticity will fail to resonate and inspire. For example, here's a convoluted mission statement that we asked AI to generate as an example of what not to do when crafting one:

"We endeavor to proactively empower value-added synergies by leveraging innovative solutions across multifaceted operational touchpoints, driving scalable deliverables that transcend traditional benchmarks in customer-centric paradigms."[12]

Why This Doesn't Work:

1. **Overloaded with Jargon**: Words like "synergies," "value-added," and "touch points" sound fancy but lack concrete meaning.

2. **No Clear Purpose**: The statement doesn't explain *what the company actually does* or *who it serves*.

3. **Too Long and Complicated**: SMB owners and employees need clarity and focus—not statements that confuse or lose the reader.

4. **Disconnected from Reality**: There's no mention of customers, employees, or real-world outcomes that matter to stakeholders.

Developing a Mission Statement

We've found that crafting a good mission statement requires hard work, reflective thinking, and focused attention, free of distractions from day-to-day operations. We highly recommend including your leadership team to develop a shared understanding of your company's mission statement. To start with, we recommend setting some time, perhaps an hour to an hour and a half, and a quiet space dedicated to this exercise. The following framework provides an example of how to develop one for your company.

1. **Mission Statement:**

A mission statement defines an organization's fundamental purpose and answers the question, "Why does the organization exist?"

Characteristics of a good mission statement:

- Clear and understandable by all.
- Concise and memorable.
- Broad enough to allow for growth.

2. **Components of a Mission Statement:**

- Why does this company exist?
- What is the scope of the company's activities?
- What products or services are offered?
- Who are the customers served?
- What is the unique benefit to the customer?
- Statement of values and beliefs.

While the "Components of a Mission Statement" section outlines the core elements a strong mission often contains such as purpose, audience, unique benefits, and desired impact, real-world mission statements don't always include all these components in one sentence.

In Peter Drucker's book, *The Five Most Important Questions You Will Ever Ask About Your Organization*, he writes, "A mission cannot be impersonal; it has to have deep meaning, be something you believe in—something you know is right. A fundamental responsibility of leadership is to make sure that everybody knows the mission, understands it, and lives it." [13]

Mission Statement Examples:

Managed Service Provider (MSP) Mission Statement

1. Core Purpose and Reason for Existence:

"To simplify and optimize technology for small and medium-sized businesses, ensuring they have the IT infrastructure and support needed to operate efficiently and securely."

2. Identify Your Target Audience or Beneficiaries:

"We serve SMBs across industries that rely on seamless, secure, and scalable IT solutions to drive their daily operations, growth, and innovation."

3. Define What You Provide or Achieve:

"By delivering proactive IT management, cybersecurity, cloud solutions, and 24/7 support, we help businesses reduce downtime, enhance security, and streamline operations—allowing them to focus on their core business functions."

4. Highlight Key Values and Principles:

"With a commitment to reliability, innovation, and exceptional customer service, we act as a trusted technology partner, providing tailored solutions that align with each client's unique needs and goals."

5. Summarize the Impact or Result:

"Our goal is to empower SMBs to operate with confidence, free from IT concerns, so they can focus on scaling their business, increasing productivity, and achieving long-term success."

Final Mission Statement:

"Our mission is to simplify and optimize technology for small and medium-sized businesses by delivering proactive IT management, cybersecurity, cloud solutions, and 24/7 support. With a commitment to reliability, innovation, and customer-centric service, we empower SMBs to operate securely and efficiently, allowing them to scale and achieve their long-term business goals."

Mission Statement for Non-Profit Organization

Begin describing the organization's reason for existence. Use action-oriented language.

Example: "Our mission is to empower ..."

Identify Your Target Audience or Beneficiaries: Specify who the organization serves or benefits. This can include customers, clients, communities, or specific groups.

Example: " ... empower underprivileged youth ... "

Define What You Provide or Achieve: Regarding your core customer benefit—the customer's perceived problem or pain your business solves.

Example: " ... by providing access to quality education ... "

Highlight Key Values and Principles: Mention the core values, principles, or beliefs that guide your organization's actions and decision-making.

Example: "... with a commitment to equality, innovation and inclusivity."

Summarize the Impact or Result: State the impact or result your organization aspires to deliver.

Example: " ... so they can realize their full potential and lead fulfilling lives."

Edit and Refine: Combine the above elements into a concise and coherent statement. Keep it focused and free of jargon.

"Our mission is to empower underprivileged youth by providing access to quality education with a commitment to equality, innovation and inclusivity so they can realize their full potential and lead fulfilling lives."

Purpose Matters Mission:

Begin describing the organization's reason for existence. Use action-oriented language. Example: "Our mission is to *empower...*"

Identify Your Target Audience or Beneficiaries: Specify who the organization serves or benefits. **Example**: "... Growth-minded organizations ... "

Define What You Provide or Achieve: Regarding your core customer benefit—the customer's perceived problem or pain your business solves. **Example**: " ... help them focus on what truly matters and align their business with their purpose"

Highlight Key Values and Principles: Mention the core values, principles, or beliefs that guide your organization's actions and decision-making. Example: " ... Empowerment through strategic guidance and purpose-driven alignment utilizing the 7P BAM."

Summarize the Impact or Result: State the impact or result your organization aspires to deliver. Example: " ... unlock more of their potential, meaningful growth, and a greater sense of fulfillment."

Edit and Refine: Combine the above elements into a concise and coherent statement. Keep it focused and free of jargon.

Purpose Matters Mission: "Empower growth-minded organizations to focus on what matters, align with their purpose, and achieve meaningful growth with greater fulfillment."

Additional Examples of Other Mission Statements:

McDonald's: "Our mission is to make delicious feel-good moments easy for everyone."[14]

- **Why does this company exist?** To provide easy, enjoyable food experiences.
- **What customers are served?** Everyone.
- **What products or services are offered?** Fast food.
- **The unique benefit of the products or services to the customer:** Quick, tasty, feel-good moments and meals for all.

Coca-Cola Company: "To refresh the world in body, mind, and spirit. To inspire moments of optimism through our brand and our actions. To create value and make a difference everywhere we engage."[15]

- **Why does this company exist?** To refresh the world and inspire optimism.
- **What customers are served?** Global consumers of all ages and demographics.
- **What products or services are offered?** Beverages and brand-driven experiences.
- **The unique benefit of the products or services to the customer**: Provides physical refreshment, mental and emotional upliftment, and a sense of shared value and impact through engagement.

Tesla Mission Statement:

"To accelerate the world's transition to sustainable energy"[16]

- **Why does this company exist?** To speed up, accelerate the shift to sustainable energy.
- **What customers are served?** The world, everyone in the world on a global scale.
- **What products or services are offered?** Products or services that utilize sustainable forms of energy.
- **The unique benefit of the products or services to the customer**: Contributes to cleaner, sustainable energy use that benefits our planet.

Vision Statement Framework

While often overlapping with elements of a mission statement, a vision statement is more focused on describing the *future* state an organization strives to achieve. It answers the question: Where do we see ourselves in the long term, and/or what do we envision the world to look like or become as a result of the impact we've made?

Elements of Crafting a Vision Statement

Vision Statement: A good vision statement should be aspirational and inspiring. It describes the aspirational future the organization strives to create.

Values and principles: Incorporates guiding beliefs or principles that align with the organization's overall character.

1. **Start with a Forward-Looking Statement**

2. **Describe the Ideal State**

3. **Highlight Core Values and Principles**

4. **Set a Time Frame (optional)**

5. **Edit and Refine:** Combine the above elements into a concise and coherent statement. Keep it focused and free of jargon.

Vision Statement Framework and Examples:

Purpose Matters Vision Statement:

"A world where purpose-driven organizations align their potential with the greater good."

Analysis:

- **Ideal state:** *"A world where purpose-driven organizations align their potential with the greater good."* Envisions a world improved in the context of promoting the greater societal good.

- **Values and principles:** *"Purpose-driven, potential and for the greater good"* emphasizes a focus on purpose, realizing one's potential and societal benefit.

Amazon

Vision Statement:

"To be Earth's most customer-centric company, where customers can find and discover anything they might want to buy online, and endeavors to offer its customers the lowest possible prices."[17]

Analysis:

- **Ideal state:** *"A world where customers can find and discover anything they want to buy online at the lowest possible prices."* Reflects an all-encompassing, seamless marketplace.

- **Values and principles:** *"Customer-centricity"* and *affordability* emphasize customer-focused innovation and cost leadership.

Nike

Vision Statement:

"Bring inspiration and innovation to every athlete in the world."[18]
(*If you have a body, you are an athlete.*)

Analysis:

- **Ideal State:**

  Nike envisions a world where everyone is seen as an athlete and is inspired and empowered by its innovative products, promoting accessibility and inclusion for all.

- **Values and Principles:**

1. **Inspiration:** Motivating individuals to push their limits and achieve their goals.

2. **Innovation:** Delivering cutting-edge products through creativity and advanced technology.

3. **Inclusion:** Embracing the belief that every person has athletic potential.

5. IKEA

Vision Statement:
"To create a better everyday life for the many people."[19]

Analysis:

- **Ideal State:**

  IKEA envisions a world where everyone has access to practical and affordable home solutions that improve their daily lives.

- **Values and Principles:**

1. **Affordability:** High-quality products at prices accessible to everyone.

2. **Simplicity:** Functional and easy-to-use designs for everyday living.

3. **Inclusion:** Serving a broad audience with solutions for diverse needs.

6. Tesla

Vision Statement:

"To create the most compelling car company of the 21st century by driving the world's transition to electric vehicles."[20]

- **Ideal State:**

Tesla aims to be the leading car company of the 21st century, recognized for driving the global shift to electric vehicles and sustainable energy solutions.

- **Values and Principles:**

1. **Innovation:** Constantly creating cutting-edge technology and setting new industry standards.

2. **Sustainability:** Committed to reducing fossil fuel dependence and promoting greater sustainability.

3. **Customer Focus:** Designing exciting, high-performance products that captivate customers.

4. **Leadership:** Taking the lead in transforming the automotive industry toward a sustainable future.

5. **Ambition:** Striving to be the best and inspire global change in transportation.

Refining Your Mission and Vision Statements:

- Revisit and revise periodically to ensure they align with the organization's goals and values.

- Evaluate and check in to see that they continue to serve as a source of inspiration and guidance for employees, stakeholders, and partners.

Key Takeaways Chapter 4: Purpose Matters

1. **Purpose is Your North Star**: A clear purpose guides your business decisions and actions, ensuring alignment with your mission and vision.

2. **Purpose Connects to Action**: It bridges your long-term goals with day-to-day tasks, keeping your team focused on what matters most.

3. **Purpose Inspires Engagement**: When your team and customers connect with your purpose, they feel more motivated and aligned with your goals.

4. **Purpose Sets You Apart**: Businesses driven by purpose stand out in the marketplace and attract loyal customers and employees.

5. **Purpose Evolves Over Time**: As your business grows, revisiting and refining your purpose ensures it remains relevant and impactful.

6. **Purpose Builds Resilience**: During tough times, a strong purpose provides clarity and motivation to keep moving forward.

7. **Alignment Brings Fulfillment**: A business aligned with its purpose leads to greater satisfaction for owners, employees, and customers alike.

Reflection Questions Chapter 4: Purpose Matters

1. Are your day-to-day actions aligned with your purpose? If not, what feels out of sync? (Gets right to the heart of whether purpose is lived out or just words on a wall.)

2. Is your mission clear and easy to explain? How could you make it simpler or stronger? (Clarity of mission is foundational for alignment and communication.)

3. Do you keep your purpose in mind when making big business decisions, (e.g., personnel, infrastructure investments, product/service development, facilities and property)?

4. What's one step you can take to keep your purpose front and center?

5. Can you think of a recent decision that supported—or went against—your purpose? What did you learn from it?

6. What excites and motivates you most about your business's purpose?

7. What stood out to you in this chapter or resonated most with you?

8. What are your top 1-2 takeaways from this chapter? What's one specific action you can take to bring them to life in your business or leadership?

PRIORITIZATION— ALIGNING YOUR PRIORITIES WITH YOUR PURPOSE

CHAPTER 5

CHART THE COURSE:OKRs

*"To begin with the end in mind means to start
with a clear understanding of your destination."[1]*
— Stephen R. Covey, The 7 Habits of
Highly Effective People

Harnessing the Power of OKRs

Once you've clarified your purpose, the next challenge is focusing your energy on what truly matters so your daily actions move you closer to it. That's where charting the course with OKRs comes into play.

The Objectives and Key Results (OKRs) framework has been used by some of the world's most successful companies—Amazon, Tesla, Google, Microsoft, and Facebook—to set measurable goals, align them with their missions, and track progress.[2]

In *Objectives and Key Results: Driving Focus, Alignment, and Engagement with OKRs*, Niven and Lamorte define OKRs as "A critical thinking framework and ongoing discipline that seeks to ensure employees work together, focusing their efforts to make measurable contributions that drive the company forward."[3]

For SMB owners, this framework offers a structured approach to charting a course that enables you to achieve your strategic objectives and desired outcomes.

Critical Thinking Defined: What, then, is *critical thinking*? Google offered several definitions for critical thinking; however, the AI-generated one synthesized the best definitions we came across:

"Critical thinking is a disciplined process of analyzing, evaluating, and interpreting information to form a judgment or make a decision. It involves questioning assumptions, exploring different perspectives, and using logic and reason to reach a conclusion. Critical thinking is applicable and important in all areas of life, including education, business, and everyday interactions."[4]

When we think critically, we can also ask the right questions to assist with making informed judgments and better decisions, increasing the likelihood of finding the right answers. As Peter Drucker wisely noted, "The most serious mistakes are not being made as a result of the wrong answers. The truly dangerous thing is asking the wrong questions."[5]

The Role of Frameworks: A "framework" in the context of consulting and learning provides structured questions that facilitate and guide our critical thinking. A framework helps to outline the key components of a process or concept. For example, the OKRs framework breaks strategic goals into Objectives (what you want to achieve) and Key Results (how you measure progress).

Understanding OKRs: The Core Questions

OKRs (objectives and key results) help answer two critical questions:

1. Where do I want to go?
2. How will I know I'm getting there or pacing myself to get there?

As outlined by Andrew S. Grove in *High Output Management*, the standard OKR formula is: "I will (Objective) as measured by (Key Results)."[6]

Defining Objectives within OKRs

An objective is a qualitative and aspirational goal that an individual, team, or company wants to achieve. It should be meaningful and aligned with the company's mission and vision, providing inspiration and direction.[7]

What makes a good objective in the context of OKRs?

A good objective should be:

1. **Inspirational**: Motivate and inspire the team, offering a clear vision of the organization's goal.
2. **Clear and Concise**: Easily understandable, avoiding vague or overly complex language.

3. **Strategic**: Align with the company's broader goals and strategic direction.

4. **Actionable**: Guide the team's efforts toward specific actions or outcomes.

Additional elements of a strong objective include being vision-driven, inspiring, and directional; aligning with company goals; focusing on what matters most; showing a clear destination; and creating meaningful impact.

Examples of Objectives:

- Delight our customers with an exceptional service experience.

- Expand our presence in the local market to become the go-to brand for small businesses.

- Build a high-performing team through skill development and improved collaboration.

- Transform our operations to improve efficiency and reduce costs without sacrificing quality.

Key Results (KRs) are specific, measurable outcomes used to track the progress toward achieving an Objective within the OKR (Objectives and Key Results) framework. Each Key Result is designed to provide clear criteria for determining whether the Objective has been met and quantify what success looks like for the Objective.

Key Results are SMART

- **Specific**: Key Results are clear and precise, leaving no ambiguity about what needs to be achieved.

- **Measurable**: Key Results include metrics or milestones that can be tracked, such as percentages, numbers, or deadlines.

- **Achievable**: While challenging, Key Results should be attainable with the resources and time available.

- **Relevant**: They should directly contribute to achieving the associated Objective.

- **Time-bound**: Key Results are tied to specific deadlines or time frames, ensuring a clear endpoint for accomplishment.[8]

Key Results Examples:

If the Objective is to "Improve customer satisfaction," the Key Results might include:

1. Increase the customer satisfaction score from 80% to 90% by the end of Q3.

2. Reduce the average customer support response time from twenty-four to twelve hours by the end of Q2.

3. Achieve a Net Promoter Score (NPS) of 9 by the end of the year from 30% of our customers compared to 20% previously.

Key Results define the specific outcomes that must be achieved to meet an Objective. They provide a clear, quantifiable way to assess progress and success within the OKR framework.

A Few Things to Remember About OKRs

-   OKRs should be ambitious, achievable, well-defined, and part of a continuous improvement effort.

-   OKRs are not to-do lists; they should connect specific performance periods (monthly, quarterly, etc.) to broader business goals and strategies.

The History of OKRs

OKRs (Objectives and Key Results) are rooted in Management by Objectives (MBO), a concept developed by Peter Drucker in the 1950s to align organizational goals with employee performance. Andy Grove, then CEO of Intel, expanded on this idea by creating the OKRs framework, which provided a way to set clear objectives and define measurable key results (KRs) to track progress. John Doerr, who worked under Grove's tutelage at Intel, was deeply influenced by this approach and later introduced OKRs to Google in 1999.

During a meeting around a ping-pong table that doubled as its boardroom table, Doerr presented to Google founders Larry Page and Sergey Brin how OKRs could help the start-up better focus and execute. Google adopted OKRs, which played a crucial role in its exponential growth. Doerr presented the following OKRs to Google's founders and their leadership team during this meeting.[9]

Objective: Build a planning model for their company, as measured by three key results:

Key Results:

- KR1: I would finish my presentation on time.

- KR2: We'd create a sample set of quarterly Google OKRs.

- KR3: I'd gain management agreement for a three-month OKR trial.[10]

Google then established its company strategy with this strategic goal-setting framework; the rest is history. Since then, the simplicity and effectiveness of OKRs in setting the company's strategic direction have been embraced by numerous leading companies, including Amazon, LinkedIn, Microsoft, Netflix, and Uber.

Here's an example of how Doerr applied the OKR framework to a personal-family goal. Doerr was asked about his personal OKR in an interview on *Recode Decode*.

He answered, "You know, my daughters have both left home, but I had read, and I believe that having family dinners together was a good thing. So, I set an OKR, shared it with my team to be home for dinner by six p.m. twenty nights a month, and be present, turning off the phone system. I put a switch on the router. We shut down the internet to the whole house. It's not only the quantity but the quality." [11]

This personal goal would be written out like this:

Objective: Have more quality family time, as evidenced by ...

Key Results:

- KR1: Get home for dinner by six p.m., twenty nights a month.

- KR2: Be present by turning off the internet router to eliminate distractions.

Translating Mission and Vision into OKRs

Translating mission and vision into OKRs involves breaking down high-level objectives into specific, actionable, measurable goals aligning with the company's core purpose.

Step 1: Clarify Your Mission and Vision

Mission Statement: Describes the organization's reason for being and answers the question, why do we exist and for whom?"

Vision Statement: Describes what your organization aspires to become and the future you hope to create. It answers the question What kind of future are we working toward—and how will the world be better because of us?

Step 2: Translate Mission into Strategic Objectives Strategic objectives should align with the mission and vision, setting the organization's long-term direction.

Step 3: Break Down Strategic Objectives into OKRs

Objective: Typically, a qualitative statement describing what you want to achieve. It should align with your mission and vision and provide direction without attaching numerical values.

Key Results: Quantitative measures or milestones that track the progress towards achieving the objective. These should be SMART (Specific, Measurable, Achievable, Relevant, and Time-bound).

OKR Example: Purpose Matters

Mission: To empower growth-minded organizations to focus on what matters and align their business with their purpose to create meaningful growth and greater fulfillment.

Objective: Empower growth-minded organizations to improve their performance through purpose-aligned solutions.

> o **Key Result 1 (KR1)**: Secure three 7P Alignment clients by the end of the quarter who align with our purpose and values.

o **Key Result 2 (KR2)**: Increase the percentage of current clients who give Purpose Matters an NPS score of 9 or higher from 30% to 50 % by the end of the fiscal year.

o **Key Result 3 (KR3)**: Increase overall employee productivity across client organizations by 10% by the end of the fiscal year, measured through improvement in employee output and lower labor costs from 27% to 25% of total sales.

This example illustrates how to craft an objective that maintains a more inspiring, strategic focus connected with the company mission rather than simply stating financial objectives like "grow revenues" or "increase market share." The key results ensure that the objective is actionable and measurable, striking a balance between inspiration and practicality.

However, you may find articulating your objectives in a more straightforward manner like increase market share or grow revenues also helpful depending on your preferences.

Step 4: Differentiate Between Quantitative and Qualitative

Quantitative Objectives: Statements focused on numerical and objective measures. For example, "increase sales revenue" as measured by a 20% year-over-year increase in quarterly revenue by the end of Q4.

Qualitative Objectives: Aspirational and descriptive goals. For example, "Create a more inclusive and engaging workplace where employees feel valued and motivated," as measured by increased employee participation in quarterly company events and the implementation of a mentorship program matching 50% of employees with mentors by the end of the year.

By following this structured approach, organizations can ensure their OKRs align with their mission and vision, providing a clearer path to achieving their strategic goals.

OKR Example: Dental Services Client

Mission: As an independent, community-based, employee-owned company, we protect and empower our plan members, helping them promote and maintain their oral health and wellness through education and preventive programs while assuring high-quality dental care at a reasonable cost.

Motto: A great reason to smile ... going the extra mile.

Vision: To become known as the leading advocate for prepaid dental plan members.

Objectives and Key Results:

Objective 1: Remain in Good Standing with Regulators

Key Results:

- Zero violations and fines from regulators by end of the fiscal year.
- Successful completion of milestones 1 through 8 ahead of schedule by July 31st, 2025.
- No required corrective actions following the completion of the current CAP (Corrective Action Plan).
- Receive and maintain approval for all rates and form filings by end of current quarter.

Objective 2: Grow Revenues

Key Results:

- Increase individual member retention from 65% to 75% by end of current fiscal year.
- Increase current group member retention from 96% to 99% by end of current fiscal year.
- Restore revenues to at least the prior year's level by end of the current fiscal year.

Objective 3: Maintain Financial Sustainability

Key Results:

- Improve current operating profit levels to 10% operating profit by the end of fiscal year.

Objective 4: Develop a Healthy Pipeline

Key Results:

- Target large, prominent, respected, and recognized "brand name" groups, with 30 unique Risk Management Consultants generating at least 20 RFPs by the end of fiscal year.

- Secure 2 enrolled groups (cases) from each currently active broker (50), totaling 100 new enrolled groups by the end of fiscal year.

- Develop 50 new broker relationships, producing on average 3 RFPs and 1 new enrolled group each, totaling 50 new enrolled groups by March 31st, 2025.

- Establish a baseline Net Promoter Score (NPS) for each category by the end of the quarter:
  - Achieve a Broker NPS of 9-plus with at least 30% of our Brokers.
  - Achieve a Risk Management Consultant NPS of 9-plus with at least 30% of the RMCs.
  - Achieve a group purchaser NPS of 9-plus with at least 30% of purchasers.

Objective 5: Improve Member Dental Health and Wellness

Key Results:

- Establish a baseline for the percentage of completed treatment plans for current plan members by the end of the quarter.

- Increase the percentage of completed treatment plans year-over-year by at least 10% by the end of the fiscal year.

- Conduct an NPS plan member loyalty survey to establish a baseline NPS by the end of the quarter.

- Achieve a plan member NPS of 9 for a minimum of 30% of plan participants over the next 90 days.

OKR Example: Overhead Crane Maintenance and Service Firm

Mission Statement: We keep our clients' operations safe and running at peak efficiency by providing expert overhead crane maintenance and service—delivered with uncompromising safety, reliability, and customer care.

Vision Statement: To be the most trusted name in overhead crane service, known for industry-leading safety, rapid response, and long-term client partnerships.

Objectives and Key Results:

Objective 1: Enhance Customer Satisfaction

Key Results:

- Achieve a 90% or higher customer satisfaction score in quarterly surveys by the end of the year.

- Reduce service response time to under 24 hours for 95% of service calls by the end of Q3.

- Implement a follow-up system to check customer satisfaction within 48 hours of service completion by the end of the current Quarter

Objective 2: Increase Market Share

Key Results:

- Increase the number of new clients by 15% over the next quarter.

- Implement a referral program that results in 30 new client referrals by the end of the fiscal year.

- Launch a targeted marketing campaign that reaches 500 qualified prospects by the end of the current fiscal year.

Objective 3: Enhance Staff Training and Development

Key Results:

- Conduct monthly training sessions for all technicians on the latest maintenance technologies and safety practices by the end of the current quarter.

- Achieve a 100% completion rate of continuing education courses for all staff members by the end of Q3.

- Develop and implement a mentorship program for new technicians by the end of Q4.

Objective 4: Optimize Operational Efficiency

Key Results:

- Reduce maintenance scheduling errors by 50% over the next quarter.

- Implement a computerized maintenance management system (CMMS) to streamline service order processing by the end of the current fiscal year.

- Decrease supply costs by 10% through better inventory management and supplier negotiations by the end of the current fiscal year.

Objective 5: Improve Safety Standards

Key Results:

- Achieve zero incidents of workplace injuries within the next quarter.

- Conduct safety audits for 100% of service sites monthly.

- Implement a new safety training program and ensure all employees complete it within the next three months.

OKRs: Measuring What Matters

A study by the U.S. Census Bureau's Center for Economic Studies found that companies with structured management practices, such as performance monitoring and target setting, achieved better financial results.[12] This finding underscores the importance of the role of goal-setting frameworks like OKRs (Objectives and Key Results) in driving organizational success.

Peter Drucker's often quoted although not verified saying "You can't manage what you don't measure,"[13] highlights the critical need to identify and track key metrics. However, knowing what to measure and which metrics matter is not always straightforward.

William Bruce Cameron insightfully observes in Informal Sociology, "Not everything that can be counted counts, and not everything that counts can be counted."[14] This observation illustrates the challenge of measuring intangible factors like trust, enthusiasm, and sincerity, which, while difficult to quantify, are integral to successful business outcomes. And other measurable things may or may not matter to the extent that we believe they matter.

This is why going through the process of creating a well-thought-out, clearly defined, and articulated mission and vision is so important. It provides the strategic context needed to determine what truly matters, enabling you to better measure what matters most. Doing so helps you create a more effective and relevant set of OKRs—Objectives and Key Results—that align with your organization's mission and vision.

Key Takeaways Chapter 5 Chart the Course: OKRs

1. **OKRs Provide Clarity:** Objectives and Key Results provide a structured way to align strategic goals with measurable outcomes.

2. **Focus on What Matters Most:** Objectives ensures teams remain focused on priorities aligned with purpose.

3. **Set SMART Key Results:** Specific, Measurable, Achievable, Relevant, and Time-bound. Key Results track progress and drive meaningful change.

4. **Inspire Team Engagement:** OKRs serve as a tool to motivate and align teams, making goals clear, attainable, and impactful.

5. **Adapt for Continuous Improvement:** Regularly review and adjust OKRs to stay responsive to changing conditions, new opportunities and business challenges.

Reflection Questions: Chapter 5 Chart the Course: OKRs

1. Do your Objectives and Key Results align with your mission and vision?

2. Are your OKRs focused on the most critical priorities for your business right now?

3. Are your Key Results SMART: specific, measurable, achievable and relevant with set deadlines?

4. Are your objectives inspiring and motivating for your team?

5. How often do you review and adjust your OKRs to reflect new opportunities or challenges?

6. What stood out to you in this chapter or resonated most with you?

7. What are your top 1-2 takeaways from this chapter? What's one specific action you can take to bring them to life in your business or leadership?

CHAPTER 6

STAY THE COURSE: OKR BEST PRACTICES

"The Apollo mission was off course 90% of the time, but they still reached the moon by continually making small adjustments."[1]
— Anonymous

As we transition from *Charting the Course* with OKRs to *Staying the Course*, it's important to recognize that developing Objectives and Key Results (OKRs) is the first step toward aligning your priorities with your purpose. The real challenge lies in maintaining focus, consistent effort, and constantly making course corrections as needed.

In *OKRs Field Book*, Ben Lamorte emphasizes best practices for ongoing implementation, such as simplicity and focus, regular reviews, alignment across teams, and adaptability.[2] This chapter will delve into some of the best practices for implementation and ensuring that your OKR planning and execution efforts become an integral part of your operations.

Objectives and Key Results

- Initially, develop up to three Objectives at the organizational level. This limitation ensures that the company focuses on the most critical initiatives without overextending resources or spreading them too thin to be effective.

- Include broader strategic goals like increasing sales, improving operational efficiency, innovation, or customer satisfaction

- When crafting Objectives, it's also helpful to provide context by answering the question "Why now?" to clarify how the Objective addresses urgent challenges or opportunities, offering inspirational direction for the organization.

- OKR Scope: Focus exclusively on developing OKRs at the broader company-wide level initially. This simplifies alignment, ensuring all teams and departments work towards common company-wide goals. Later, OKRs can be set at departmental or individual levels, aligning with the broader organizational OKRs.[3]

Key Results

- Define two to four Key Results per Objective to ensure a reasonable number for each Objective supported by clear, measurable outcomes.

- Key results should be specific, measurable, attainable, relevant, and time-bound (SMART). For example, if the Objective is "Expand market presence," a Key Result could be "Open one new regional office within four months."

Understanding the Difference Between Key Performance Indicators (KPIs) and Key Results (KRs)

Key Performance Indicators (KPIs)

- **Definition**: KPIs are metrics that measure ongoing performance in specific areas to provide a snapshot of business health.

- **Examples**: Monthly/Annual revenue, gross profit margins, labor cost percentage, profitability percentage, customer counts and satisfaction scores, website traffic, etc.

Key Results

- **Definition**: Key Results are specific outcomes tied to an Objective, indicating what needs to be achieved. They are time-bound and can change with each OKR cycle.

- **Examples:** "Increase customer satisfaction score from 75% to 85% by the end of the four-month period."

Integration of KPIs and Key Results

KPIs inform the setting of Key Results. For instance, if a KPI shows a dip in customer satisfaction scores, a Key Result can target improving this metric within a specific timeframe. While KPIs track ongoing performance, Key Results focus on achieving specific x to y outcomes over time.

Setting and Evaluating Different Levels of Key Result Outcomes

When setting Key Results, it's helpful to define three distinct levels of achievement. This provides clarity for what's minimally acceptable, realistically achievable, and aspirationally possible—allowing your team to measure progress while maintaining motivation and focus.

Minimally Tolerable Outcomes

These are baseline goals that are necessary to keep the business operational. They define the minimum performance level required to avoid failure and ensure that critical targets are met.

Realistically Achievable Outcomes

Achievable outcomes are practical and attainable goals with reasonable performance targets given current resources and capabilities. These target goals are based on achieving steady, sustainable progress.

Ambitiously Achievable Outcomes

Setting highly ambitious goals can encourage exceptional performance. They aim for significant stretch goals and breakthroughs.

Examples: Three Levels of Key Results

Objective: Grow revenues by acquiring and retaining the right fit customers to ensure sustainable business growth.

Minimally Tolerable Outcomes (MTO)

- **Key Result 1:** Secure contracts with at least four new right-fit customers by the end of Q3 to maintain current revenue levels and cover basic operational costs.

- **Key Result 2:** Achieve a customer retention rate of at least 75% among existing right-fit customers by the end of the fiscal year, ensuring stable revenue.

- **Key Result 3:** Generate $75,000 in new revenue from right-fit customers by the end of Q4, meeting the minimum required growth to sustain operations.

Realistically Achievable Outcomes (RAO)

- **Key Result 1:** Secure contracts with six new right-fit customers by the end of Q3, representing a 20% increase in the right-fit customer base.

- **Key Result 2:** Improve customer retention rate to 80% among existing right-fit customers by the end of the fiscal year, reducing churn and supporting moderate revenue growth.

- **Key Result 3:** Generate $100,000 in new revenue from right-fit customers by the end of Q4, reflecting steady and sustainable growth.

Ambitiously Achievable Outcomes (ASO)

- **Key Result 1:** Secure contracts with ten new right-fit customers by the end of Q3, significantly expanding the customer base and driving revenue growth.

- **Key Result 2:** Achieve a customer retention rate of 85% among existing right-fit customers by the end of the fiscal year, positioning the company as a leader in customer satisfaction and loyalty.

- **Key Result 3:** Generate $150,000 in new revenue from right-fit customers by the end of Q4, pushing the company towards strong and ambitious growth targets.

OKR Four-Month Review Cycle

Studies have shown that conducting comprehensive OKR reviews every four months can be as effective as the traditional quarterly cycle. This period allows for substantial progress without conflicting with quarterly reviews and the sales team's pressure to close quarters strongly. It balances long-term focus and flexibility. Ben Lamorte recommends in his OKR Field Book starting with a four-month review cycle to distinguish OKRs from quarterly focused goals and milestones.[4]

Key Benefits of a 4-month Review Cycle

- **Enhanced Focus:** By separating OKR reviews from quarterly financial reviews, teams can focus on strategic objectives without the pressure of immediate financial targets.

- **Adequate Time for Progress**: A four-month period provides ample time for meaningful progress toward key results, allowing for a thorough evaluation of achievements and challenges.

- **Reduced Overlap with Other Reviews**: This schedule helps avoid overlap with other critical reviews, such as financial quarter-ends, reducing stress and workload.

- **Flexibility and Adaptation**: The slightly extended timeframe offers flexibility to adapt to changes in the market or business environment, ensuring that OKRs remain relevant and achievable.

- **Clearer Distinction from Routine Goals**: It helps differentiate between strategic OKRs and routine operational goals, reinforcing the focus on long-term success and innovation.

OKR Regular Check-Ins:

Schedule check-ins every week or two weeks to start.

Regular check-ins provide a structure to establish a feedback loop that allows teams to receive feedback and adjust their key results as needed. These consistent reviews ensure that progress is measured, challenges are identified early, and priorities remain aligned with strategic objectives. They also help maintain engagement by giving teams a sense of ownership and clarity about their role in achieving company-wide OKRs. Purpose:

Annual Review

- **Recommendation**: Conduct an annual review to reflect on the year's performance, celebrate successes, and plan for the following year.

- **Purpose**: Assess the overall effectiveness of the OKR process and align future goals with the company's strategic vision.

Role of an OKR Champion

If you can, appoint an OKR champion alongside the business owner. This person manages the OKR process and documentation and ensures consistency. The OKR champion coordinates the creation, communication, and alignment of various groups with the organizational

OKRs. They also help organize review meetings and track progress. This role helps maintain focus on strategic priorities, fosters accountability, and embeds the OKR process into the company culture and daily operations. When your team is aligned with the company OKRs, they can work together in a collaborative and unified manner, ensuring that all "6P oars" are rowing in sync to reach your destination 7th P- Purpose.

Key Results should be SMART:

- **Specific**: Clearly define the expected outcome.
  - o Example: "Launch the new product line by October 31st."
- **Measurable**: Include metrics to gauge success.
  - o Example: "Achieve a 25% increase in sales revenue."
- **Attainable**: Set realistic yet challenging targets.
  - o Example: "Reduce production costs by 10%."
- **Relevant**: Align with the overall objective and company goals.
  - o Example: "Expand customer base by acquiring 50 new clients."
- **Time-Bound**: Specify a clear deadline.
  - o Example: "Complete the new CRM system implementation by December 31st."

Minimum Time Commitment

Commit to a minimum of eight to twelve months for learning and implementing OKRs, with most clients committing to twelve to sixteen months to complete at least three or four OKR cycles consisting of 3-4 months.

Shared Folder for OKRs

Use a shared folder (e.g., Google Drive or One Drive) to store a draft of the OKRs in Word or Excel. This allows for real-time updates and facilitates easy access during bi-weekly updates and cycle reviews.

Common OKR Implementation Challenges

When working with clients, we've found these to be the most common, and they can hinder the effectiveness of this goal-setting framework and prevent organizations from achieving their strategic objectives. Here are some of the most common pitfalls:

1. Lack of Buy-In from Leadership

Problem: If leadership and teams are not fully committed to the OKR process, it can lead to half-hearted implementation and poor results. If the owner and their key leaders don't fully embrace and champion the OKR framework, it's unlikely that the rest of the organization will. Without strong support from the top, OKRs can quickly become a one-time check the box exercise rather than a meaningful strategic tool that's used regularly. Without a commitment from leadership, OKRs may lack the necessary visibility and importance within the organization, leading to poor adoption and execution.

Solution:

o **Educate and Align Leadership:** Begin by educating the leadership team on the benefits of the OKR framework. Clearly articulate how OKRs can drive focus, alignment, and measurable progress toward the company's strategic goals. Use case studies and examples from successful companies to illustrate the impact of well-implemented OKRs.

o **Involve Leadership in OKR Creation:** Engage leaders in the process of setting OKRs, ensuring their objectives align with the organization's overall mission and vision. When leaders are actively involved in creating

OKRs, they are more likely to take ownership and champion the process.

o **Demonstrate Commitment Through Action:** Leadership should demonstrate their commitment by regularly communicating the importance of OKRs, reviewing progress in meetings, and linking OKRs to performance evaluations and rewards. This visibility reinforces the significance of the framework and encourages the rest of the organization to follow suit.

2. Setting Too Many Objectives

Problem: Overloading the organization with too many Objectives can dilute focus and make it challenging to prioritize efforts.

Solution: Limit the number of Objectives to a manageable number (typically up to three) to ensure focus and clarity.

3. Vague or Unmeasurable Key Results

Problem: Key Results that are not specific or measurable make it difficult to track progress and success.

Solution: Ensure Key Results are specific, measurable, attainable, relevant, and time-bound (SMART).

4. Setting Key Results that are too ambitious or too easy

Problem: Key Results that are too challenging can demotivate teams if they seem unattainable, while Key Results that are too easy may not push teams to excel.

Solution: Strike a balance by setting ambitious yet achievable Objectives that stretch the team's capabilities without being discouraging.

5. Lack of Alignment with Company Mission and Vision

Problem: OKRs that do not align with the broader company mission and vision can lead to misaligned efforts and wasted resources.

Solution: Ensure that all OKRs are linked to the company's overall strategic goals, providing a clear line of sight from individual contributions to the company's mission.

6. Infrequent Reviews and Adjustments

Problem: Not regularly reviewing (set it and forget it) and adjusting OKRs can result in outdated or irrelevant goals that do not reflect current priorities or market conditions.

Solution: Schedule regular check-ins (e.g., bi-weekly or monthly) and formal reviews (quarterly or every four months) to evaluate progress and make necessary adjustments.

7. Confusing OKRs with To-Do Lists

Problem: Treating OKRs as a list of tasks rather than a framework for achieving strategic goals can limit their impact and effectiveness.

Solution: Focus on outcomes rather than tasks. OKRs should define what needs to be achieved and the metrics to measure success, not a checklist of activities.

8. Not Celebrating Successes and/or Learning from Failures

Problem: Failing to acknowledge achievements or analyze failures can demotivate teams and reduce the effectiveness of OKRs.

Solution: Celebrate wins and view failures as learning and feedback opportunities to improve. This approach helps maintain morale and fosters a culture of continuous improvement.

If not properly addressed, these pitfalls can undermine the effectiveness of OKRs. Awareness of these common issues enables organizations to implement strategies to avoid them, ensuring that OKRs are a powerful tool for driving alignment, focus, and success.[5]

Integrating Critical Thinking into Your Business: The 7P Business Alignment Model

Each of the seven Ps in our 7P Business Alignment Model™ contains "critical thinking frameworks," such as the OKR strategic goal-setting framework designed to help you ask better questions, capitalize on opportunities, and overcome business challenges. These frameworks ultimately empower you to achieve the most important results while unlocking more of your potential.

However, for these frameworks to have a meaningful impact, they also require a commitment to OPI—ongoing performance improvements. This means the "ongoing discipline"[6] referred to by Niven and Lamorte requires consistent allocation of time and resources to make incremental progress over time, leading to significant improvements in your overall business performance and peace of mind.

Key Takeaways Chapter 6: Stay the Course: OKR Best Practices

By following these best practices in the spirit of learning and continuous improvement, organizations can stay the course, effectively align their teams, track progress, and achieve their strategic goals, ultimately driving long-term success and growth.

1. **Stay Focused on Strategic Priorities:** OKRs help prioritize what matters most, ensuring the organization stays focused on critical goals while avoiding unnecessary distractions or resource waste.

2. **Differentiate KPIs and Key Results:** While KPIs measure ongoing performance, Key Results are specific, time-bound outcomes that gauge progress toward strategic objectives.

3. **Encourage Goal-Setting Balance:** Incorporating minimally tolerable, realistically achievable, and aspirational stretch outcomes ensures motivation without overextending your team.

4. **Commit to Regular Review Cycles:** Implementing structured review processes, such as a four-month OKR review cycle and bi-weekly check-ins, ensures continuous progress and agility.

5. **Leverage Leadership and Accountability:** Assigning an OKR champion fosters alignment, accountability, and cultural integration, supporting successful implementation.

6. **Cultivate a Learning Culture:** Celebrating successes and embracing failures as learning opportunities can enhance morale and promote a culture of continuous improvement.

Reflection Questions Chapter 6: Stay the Course: OKR Best Practices

1. Are your OKRs (Objectives and Key Results) clearly tied to your company's mission and long-term vision? How do they help move you closer to your big-picture goals?

2. Are your Objectives focused on the most urgent challenges or best opportunities in your business right now? How well do they reflect your current top priorities?

3. Do your Key Results strike the right balance between realistic, "must-hit" goals and stretch goals that push your team to grow? How do they motivate your team to take action?

4. How often do you review and adjust your OKRs? Are your check-ins helping you catch problems early and stay on track?

5. Is your team actively engaged in the OKR process? How well is your OKR champion helping to build teamwork, accountability, and alignment across different roles and departments?

6. What lessons have you learned from past wins or mistakes? How have you used those lessons to improve and adjust your OKRs moving forward?

7. What stood out to you in this chapter or resonated most with you?

8. What are your top 1-2 takeaways from this chapter? What's one specific step you can take to put them into action in your business or leadership?

CHAPTER 7

FOCUSING ON WHAT MATTERS

"The key is not to prioritize what's on your schedule, but to schedule your priorities."— Stephen Covey

Stephen Covey's timeless advice reminds us to focus first on what truly matters before filling our schedules. But in today's world, the challenge goes beyond managing time—it's managing attention.

"We can't control everything that demands our attention, but we can choose what deserves it."— Steven Kim

Definitions: Focus and Distraction

Focus: /ˈfōkəs/ Noun

1. The center of interest or activity.[2]
    Example: "This generation has made the environment a focus of attention."

Distraction: /dəˈstrakSH(ə)n/ Noun

1. A thing that prevents someone from giving full attention to something else.[3]

    Example: "The company found passenger travel a distraction from the main business of moving freight."

Why Focus Matters

If you're like most business owners, you probably feel stretched thin and pulled in too many directions. Your days are filled with activities including putting out fires, managing employees, responding to clients, and handling operational, financial, and customer issues. But even with all that effort, the progress and results often fall short of what you expect. A big reason is that our focus gets spread across too many areas, leaving us often feeling overwhelmed and scattered.

Instead of concentrating on the few vital things that would really move the needle, we end up giving more and more energy to the less important ones. Over time, this imbalance drains us and becomes a recipe for burnout and frustration.

This chapter is about helping you reverse that pattern so you can better focus on what matters most. It's about cultivating a **purpose-driven focus** that aligns your team, channels your energy, and produces results that actually matter.

Warren Buffett once shared a story about a dinner party where guests were asked to name the one word that most accounted for their success. Both he and Bill Gates wrote down the same word: **FOCUS**.[4]

Why Focus Is Hard—And Why It Matters Now More Than Ever

Living in a world with ever-increasing distractions competing for our attention makes it more difficult to say no and focus on what matters. Until the mid-1980s, there were only a handful of TV channels, but today, cable subscribers can choose from over 200 channels, not counting streaming services like Netflix, Amazon Prime, and Hulu.

With so many things vying for our limited attention, including our overflowing inboxes, we need better tools to filter out and say no to the things that matter least and yes to the things that matter most. Steve Jobs' perspective on focus emphasizes the power of saying no, especially to the things that matter least.

"People think focus means saying yes to the thing you've got to focus on. But that's not what it means at all. It means saying no to the hundred other good ideas that there are. You have to pick carefully."[5]

Consequently, we need to be more intentional about effectively utilizing our time and attention by first minimizing and then eliminating the distractions that pull us away from what truly matters.

When we learn to focus on the few vital things, this can empower us and make it less likely that the less important things will derail us. In working with our clients, we've found that burnout and feeling overwhelmed often arise when our attention and focus are spread too thin over too many things for a prolonged period.

As we attempt to juggle more and more balls, our ability to keep them all in the air at some point reaches its limit, and the balls inevitably come crashing down. When this condition persists, it can turn into chronic stress and fatigue, and we run the risk of mentally and physically breaking down. If you're feeling that pressure, you're not alone. You're not failing. You're living in a world that makes focus harder than ever, which is why you have to protect it—on purpose.

The Magnifying Glass: A Metaphor for Focus

When I was a kid, I was fascinated by how a magnifying glass could harness the sun's energy to start a fire. But it only worked if you held the lens steady in one spot. Move it around too much, and the heat never concentrates enough to spark a fire.

The same is true in business. You may have the sunlight, the energy, resources and capabilities, but if you keep moving the lens, scattering your team's energy across too many projects, nothing catches fire.

That's where the 7P Business Alignment Model™ comes in. It acts as your magnifying glass, while your Business Alignment Coach ensures that you have a steady hand holding it in place. By working together, you can learn to focus your energy across the seven essential dimensions of your business—Purpose, Prioritization, People, Pipeline, Product, Process, and Profit in a manner that enables you to ignite the results that truly matter.

Coaching for Consistency

Of course, even with the right tools, holding the focus steady isn't easy. That's why our Business Alignment Coaches are invaluable—not to necessarily push you harder, but to help you focus better.

They walk with you to build the habits of focused alignment that create real traction not only from short bursts of intensity but from steady, consistent effort over time.

The Focus Alignment Framework:

From Scattered Energy to Strategic Focus

The magnifying glass metaphor reminds us that clarity and effectiveness don't necessarily come from constant motion but from focused intention. You can work as hard as you want, but if you're not focused enough on the right things in the right way, your effort won't produce the desired outcomes.

To help owners move from scattered to focused, we developed the Focus Alignment Framework™ (FAF). It's more than a productivity tool but one that also helps us improve our strategic clarity and focus.

The FAF helps you:

- Understand and establish a baseline of where your time is actually going,

- Identify which tasks truly align with your strategic objectives, and

- Build the discipline to focus on what matters most, day after day.

Unlike generic time management hacks that may focus on getting more done, the FAF helps you get more of the right things done consistently and sustainably.

The FAF is both a reflection tool and a prioritization system. It helps you and your team translate high-level strategic goals into aligned daily and weekly actions. Whether you're reviewing how you spend your time, planning your week, or evaluating what to delegate, the FAF guides you to focus where it counts.

The framework is built on four pillars:

1. Alignment

The first step in the FAF is to establish clear, strategic priorities embodied in your OKRs (Objectives and Key Results) that are fully aligned with the company's broader mission and vision. If you've already defined your first P (Purpose) consisting of your mission and vision, and developed your strategic OKRs, you can now begin aligning your day-to-day tasks and duties around these objectives. This alignment ensures that every action you take connects directly to your company's larger purpose and strategic objectives.

2. Prioritization (Daily, Weekly, Monthly)

Once your strategic priorities are clarified and incorporated into OKRs (Objectives and Key Results), the next step is to reserve daily time for focused thinking and intentional prioritization. We call this habit *"prioritizing prioritization"*—setting aside time each day or week to deliberately assess and organize your tasks and commitments before jumping into action.

This intentional time block ensures that the most important tasks, meetings, and duties are not only identified but also scheduled and assigned to the right person whether that's you or someone on your team. Without this prioritization habit, it's easy to get caught up in reacting to whatever is loudest or most urgent in the moment, rather than staying focused on what actually moves the needle for your business.

A critical element of effective prioritization is learning to distinguish between tasks that are urgent, important, or both so that you don't confuse "busy" work with high-impact work. One tool to help make these distinctions is the Eisenhower Matrix, also known as the Urgent-Important Matrix.

The **Eisenhower Matrix** divides tasks into four quadrants:

1. **Important and Urgent**: DO IT NOW- These are urgent customer issues, deadlines, and problems that require immediate attention. They must be handled now, but ideally, through better planning and prevention, fewer tasks should land in this quadrant over time.

2. **Important but Not Urgent**: SCHEDULE IT- These are strategic, high-value activities—like planning, relationship building, leadership development, and building capacity for long-term business growth. These tasks are often neglected because they don't demand immediate action, but focusing here is what can grow and sustain your business.

3. **Urgent but Not Important**: DELEGATE -These are tasks that feel pressing but don't significantly contribute to your goals, like unnecessary meetings, interruptions, or minor issues. These are often candidates for **delegation** or elimination.

4. **Not Urgent and Not Important**: DELETE - These are distractions—time-wasting activities that provide little to no value. These should be **eliminated** or minimized as much as possible.

	URGENT	NOT URGENT
IMPORTANT	DO ✓	📅 SCHEDULE
NOT IMPORTANT	DELEGATE 👥	🗑 ELIMINATE

Zero-Based Time Budgeting (ZBTB)

Another framework that helps us better focus on what matters is the concept of Zero-Based Time Budgeting (ZBTB). Think of it as a thought experiment: you start with a blank slate, as if you had no existing obligations, and decide how to use every hour based on what will create the biggest impact.

Instead of automatically carrying over last week's commitments and meetings, ZBTB pushes you to re-evaluate all activities based on their alignment with your current strategic objectives and purpose.

It builds on the principle of systematic abandonment referred to in the Discover What Matters chapter but applies it to a daily or weekly time frame.

ZBTB helps you let go of tasks that no longer move the needle and intentionally design your time around what matters most, rather than defaulting to existing patterns that no longer serve you.

3. Measurement

To focus on what matters, you first need to know where your time and attention are actually going. You can't improve what you don't measure. Without tracking, it's difficult to tell whether your time is moving you toward your goals or getting taken up by distractions and busy work.

That's why we recommend using a simple time-tracking tool like Toggl. We'll walk through how to use these tools in the next chapter. By looking at the data, you can see where your time and energy go and make better decisions about how to spend them. Combined with Zero-Based Time Budgeting, this gives you the ability to reset, redirect, and stay aligned with what matters most.

4. Reflection: Pause to Learn and Realign

The final pillar of the Focus Alignment Framework (FAF) is reflection—the habit of stepping back regularly to see how well your time, decisions, and actions align with your purpose and priorities.

Reflection isn't about guilt for not doing enough or beating yourself up for falling short. It's about learning, adjusting, and improving—bit by bit, day by day.

Reflection allows you to:

- Learn from what worked and why
- Learn from what didn't
- Refocus your efforts to align with what matters most

Here are a few questions to guide your reflection:

- Did I spend my time on what mattered most—or just what felt most urgent?
- Which tasks, meetings, or efforts moved us closer to our OKRs and purpose?
- Where did things take longer than expected—and what can I learn from that?
- What energized me or my team? What drained us—and why?
- What would I do differently if I had this week to do over again?

When practiced consistently, you can begin to develop the *habit of reflective thinking* that is so critical to driving a culture of continuous improvement and purposeful progress for you, your team, and your business.

Focus Alignment Framework (FAF): Excel Worksheet

The **Focus Alignment Framework (FAF)** is presented as an Excel-based critical thinking tool designed to establish a clear baseline of the tasks consuming your attention on a daily, weekly, and monthly basis. Beyond simply listing current tasks, the FAF encourages reflecting on the tasks you *should* be doing to better utilize your strengths and address the needs of the business. By taking inventory of how you spend your time, you can evaluate whether your efforts align with what what matters and identify opportunities to focus your strengths and resources on activities that drive the company forward.

Applying the FAF

When applying FAF, your Business Alignment Coach will often interview key employees about their typical workweek to build a general narrative, later translated into task statements for the FAF worksheet.

For the purposes of the FAF, we avoid the granularity of listing task steps. For example, if twenty items are listed in the FAF, either there are too many tasks and duties to begin with, or we've listed task steps. We aim for a practical level of distinction that finds the sweet spot between one that is too broad and general and one that is too granular and specific.

For example, if the answer to "What did you do all week?" is "office work," that may be too general to be useful. On the other hand, the answer "I turned on my computer, answered an email, and filed a paper" may be too detailed and granular for this exercise. A more appropriate task statement in the context of an Admin Assistant could be: Manage incoming correspondence and route messages to the right person.

In doing this exercise with our clients, we've found that many employees have difficulty articulating and documenting what they do in the form of a well-written task statement. Fortunately, our Business Alignment Coaches can help you and your team with this process.

Building Toward Standard Operating Procedures (SOPs) and Position Guides

Another advantage of FAF is that documenting tasks enables you to build and refine Standard Operating Procedures (SOPs) and position guides or job descriptions for each role. Well-written guides speed up onboarding, clarify role expectations, and align new hires with your company's purpose and goals from day one. Over time, FAF not only helps you focus on what matters today but also builds the systems that sustain focus, alignment, and high performance as you grow.

Tree Diagram for Position Guide Tasks and Duties

The Tree Diagram helps visualize the relationship between position tasks, duties, and objectives:

- **Tree Trunk:** The position title.
- **Major Branches:** Core tasks and duties (up to 5-7).
- **Leaves:** Task steps that detail the actions required to complete the tasks.
- **Fruits:** Outcomes/benefits for the customer or company.

Defining Tasks and Duties: Basic Steps

1. **Write Task Statements:**

   Start each task with a verb, indicate how it is performed, and state the objective. For example, "Loads pallets using a forklift."

2. **Perform Task Analysis:**

   Describe the task frequency, difficulty, importance, and priority.

3. **List Task Steps:**

   Provide step-by-step instructions for each task.

4. **Combine Tasks into Duties:**

   Group-related tasks to form duties.

Example Task Statements vs Task Steps

Task:

   "Orders manufacturing parts when the system flags a part as being low in stock."

Task Steps for a Buyer:

   Look up usage for the item for the previous twelve months.

   Calculate the average monthly use.

   Add the planned growth rate for the product line.

   Check parts catalogs for best buy rates.

   Place purchase order.

Example Duties

Duty: Manage and optimize inventory levels

Tasks:

- Monitor stock levels.
- Reorder supplies when low.
- Verify inventory records.
- Conduct regular stock audits.

Detailed Example of Tasks, Task Steps, and Duties

Duty: Prepare and submit financial reports in a timely and accurate manner so that informed business decisions can be made:

Tasks:

- Prepare and submit monthly financial reports.
- Conduct quarterly financial reviews.
- Maintain financial records and documentation.
- Assist in the annual budgeting process.

Task Steps:

1. Gather financial data from various departments.
2. Verify the accuracy of the data.
3. Compile the data into a standard report format.
4. Analyze the data to identify trends.
5. Submit the report to the finance manager.

Using the FAF Task and Duty Evaluation Criteria:

The FAF Matrix helps you evaluate tasks based on a 1-10 least to most important rating scale across several dimensions, including importance/value to the company, personal enjoyment, importance and urgency, importance to train, level of skill/knowledge required, and difficulty of delegation. By systematically rating tasks, you can better prioritize and ensure your efforts align with your strategic goals.

However, we've found that if you rate everything or assign too many things as a 10 - the highest level of importance, you'll have difficulty distinguishing what's most important and prioritizing effectively.

As Patrick Lencioni reminds us "If everything is important, then nothing is."[6]

Focus Alignment Framework Excel Worksheet and Instructions:

Based on your current understanding of your business, make a list of all the tasks and duties that you perform (preferably in the order of importance). List additional tasks that you feel you should be performing but are not currently and mark them with an asterisk (*). Estimate the time in hours per week on average you typically spend on each. If applicable, fill in the primary time block for the task or duty. You can further categorize task and duties in terms of: CC Creating Customers KC- Keeping Customers, P-D-T People, Data Things, D-W-M (Daily, Weekly, Monthly) describing the typical frequency spent on that particular task						
Name of person that has **Primary, Back-up,Tiertiary** (back up for the back up) responsibility for a particular task or duty			**Date:**		**Yrs of Service:**	
Value: **How Valuable/Important** is this task or duty to the business -what's the consequence of not doing it (Least 1- to Most -10)			**Employee Name:**		**Hrly Rate:**	
Love-Loathe: Degree of personal value you get from doing it: Loathe it -1 to Love it-10 (Loathe it tasks are ones that drain your energy vs Love it -energizes you)	**Dept:**		**Job Title:**		**Reports to:**	
Degree of **Importance and Urgency**: (1-least 10-most) To what extent could I let this go **Level of Experience, Judgement Skill:** required in terms of relative hourly/salary pay rate: (Lowest hourly/salary-1 to Highest hourly/salary-10)	**Importance to Train** 1-lowest would be a task or duty that a qualified person could easily be hired to do to 10-Highest criritcal tasks that would be difficult to hire and train for					
Difficulty of Delegating (Easiest 1- Most Difficult-10): How easily can I delegate this task to someone else on my behalf	**Rank Order of Importance** 1-Least to 10-Most Important in terms of the contribution-impact to the overall performance outcome-evaluation for the Position- How big of a "slice" is this task-duty to the overall position's "performance pie" with 10 being the largest					

PDT	**Task-Duty Description**	Name of Primary	Name of Backup	Name of Tiertiery	D -W- M	Primary Time Block if applicable	**Avg Time Spent per week- Hrs**	**Ideal time spent per week-Hrs**	**Importance Value: Least to Most (1-10)**	**Loathe it-1 to Love it-10**	**Important and Urgent-Least to Most (1-10)**	**Level of Skill, Experience Judgement (1-10)**	**Degree of Delegatibility**	**Importance to train**	**Rank order of Importance (1-10)**	**Delegate? If Yes:H-Hire-or T-Train To Whom? By When?**
						TOT	**0**	**0**								

The above is an image of our FAF excel worksheet that our clients use to input the following data. Based on your current understanding of your business, list all the tasks and duties you perform, preferably in the order of importance. Include additional tasks you believe you *should be* performing but are not currently, and mark these with an asterisk (*). Estimate the average time in hours per week that you typically spend on each task or duty. If applicable, indicate the primary time block for each task (e.g., daily, weekly, monthly). If helpful, you can further categorize tasks and duties using the following codes:

- **CC** - Creating Customers
- **KC** - Keeping Customers
- **P-D-T** - People, Data, Things related task or duty

Enter the Name or Initials of the Person Responsible for the Task/ Duty

- o **Primary:**

- o **Backup:**

- o **Tertiary (Backup for the Backup):**

Primary Time Block if applicable: Is there a set time that this task takes place

- o Relative Frequency of task: Is this task typically performed on a daily, weekly, or monthly basis: D-W-M

Task Evaluation Criteria:

Value to Company (Column A):

- o How valuable/important is this task or duty to the business? What's the consequence of not doing it?

- o **Rate from 1 (Least) to 10 (Most):**

  - 10-9: Its contribution is critical to the company's overall objectives.

  - 8-7: It contributes in a significant way towards the company's overall objectives.

  - 6-5: It contributes at times towards the company's overall objectives.

  - 4-3: It has no impact, positive or negative.

  - 2-1: Negative impact - wasteful activity.

Love it and loathe it (B):

- o How much personal value/enjoyment do you get from doing this task? Do you loathe it (drains you of energy) or love it (energizes you)?

- o **Rate from 1 (Loathe it) to 10 (Love it):**

  - 10-9: Definitely keep - Love it. It energizes me and is one of the best parts of my job.

  - 8-7: Probably keep - I enjoy this activity for the most part.

- 6-5: Not sure - This task has good and bad points.
- 4-3: Most likely drop - I find this activity somewhat tiresome.
- 2-1: Definitely drop - I dislike doing it, and it drains me (loathe it).

Importance and Urgency (C):

o If you only had two hours before you had to leave for your vacation, which category would this activity fall into?

o **Rate from 1 (Least) to 10 (Most):**

- 10-9: Most important and super urgent - Essential. This takes top priority and must be done immediately or by the end of the day.
- 8-7: Important and urgent - I need to get this done within the next day or two.
- 6-5: Important - Somewhat urgent. I need to get this done this week.
- 4-3: Discretionary - I'll get to it when time allows.
- 2-1: Optional - Unimportant and not urgent. I can cut this immediately.

Level of Experience and Skill, Judgment (D):

o How do we calibrate the relative level of skill, experience, or judgment required 1-least to 10 Most. If helpful, try calibrating based on the relative market hourly pay or where it falls in the salary ranges within your company as it pertains to this task or duty.

o **Rate from 1 (Lowest hourly/salary pay rate) to 10 (Highest hourly/salary pay rate):**

- 10-9: Highest hourly pay rate (90-100% - top 10%).

- 8-7: Top tier (70-90%) hourly pay rate in the company.

- 6-5: Average hourly pay rate in the company (30-60%).

- 4-3: Below the company average (bottom 20%).

- 2-1: Bottom tier hourly pay rate (bottom 10%).

Difficulty of Delegating (E):

o How easily can you delegate this task to someone else on your behalf?

o **Rate from 1 (Easiest) to 10 (Most Difficult):**

- 10-9: Only I (or someone senior to me) can handle this task/duty. A high degree of judgment and/or experience is required, and a poor decision would be costly.

- 8-7: This task is best done by me or one of my peers and requires a fair amount of judgment and experience, where a poor decision would be somewhat costly.

- 6-5: If structured properly, this task could be handled satisfactorily by someone junior to me.

- 4-3: This task could easily be handled by a (junior) employee or outsourced to a third party.

- 2-1: This task could be dropped altogether.

Importance to Train (F):

o How important is it to train someone internally for this particular task or duty?

o **Rate from 1 (Lowest) to 10 (Highest):**

- 8-10: Highest importance to train someone internally - Essential tasks that would be difficult to outsource and/or make up the core competency of the company.

- 5-7: Somewhat important to train someone internally.

- 1-4: Low importance to train someone internally - A task that could be outsourced by a qualified person or company (e.g., IT, CPA, Payroll, Janitorial).

Rank Order of Importance (G):

o How important is this task or duty in terms of its contribution/impact to the overall performance outcome and evaluation for the position?

o **Rate from 1 (Least Important) to 10 (Most Important):**

o (This rating reflects how big of a "slice" this task or duty is in the position's "performance pie," with 10 being the largest.)

Delegate? (H):

o If yes, to whom and by when?

o Hire or cross-train internally?

Employee Information:

- Employee Name:
- Hourly Rate:
- Department:
- Job Title:
- Reports to:
- Years of Service:

By implementing the Focus Alignment Framework, business owners and their teams can break down objectives and key results, connecting them directly to the tasks and duties that drive those outcomes. This structured approach aligns daily and weekly actions with broader organizational goals, resulting in meaningful improvements in overall productivity.

Maximizing Time and Impact with the Focus Alignment Framework™ (FAF)

- **Prioritize What Matters Most:** The FAF Matrix Ratings sheet ranks tasks by value to the company, urgency, enjoyment, and ease of delegation—so you focus on the highest-impact work.

- **See Where Time Really Goes:** Estimate time spent on each task, then compare with actual tracked time (covered in the next chapter) to spot inefficiencies and reclaim hours.

- **Delegate with Confidence:** Identify tasks others can handle, freeing you to focus on strategy, growth, and work only you can do.

- **Plan with Purpose:** Use FAF alongside the Eisenhower Box and Zero-Based Time Budget (ZBTB) for a structured daily, weekly, and monthly plan that aligns with your business goals.

- **Align Effort with Goals:** Systematically evaluate tasks to ensure your team's time is directed toward what matters most, reducing busy work and increasing meaningful progress.

Final Thought: Aligning Time, Tasks, and Purpose

Ultimately, time is your most valuable and limited resource. By utilizing tools like the Focus Alignment Framework™, ZBTB and the Eisenhower Box, you can improve how your time is spent and ensure that every hour is better aligned with your purpose and goals. This approach helps you break free from the trap of endless busy work and focus on the few critical actions that truly move the needle—for your business, your team, and your own sense of fulfillment.

Key Takeaways 7: Focusing on What Matters

1. **Focus drives growth.** Business owners and their teams are often overwhelmed because they're trying to do too much. By focusing on what matters most, you free up time, energy, and resources for what truly drives success.

2. **The Focus Alignment Framework (FAF)** helps break down big-picture goals (OKRs) into clear, manageable tasks and duties that align with the company's purpose, mission, and vision.

3. **Prioritizing high-impact tasks** allows owners and teams to focus on the work that adds the most value—not just what feels urgent. FAF helps identify which tasks should be done by the owner, which can be delegated, and which should be dropped.

4. **Time management and focus are connected.** By tracking where your time goes and reviewing how tasks align with strategic goals, you can cut out low-value work and invest more time where it counts.

5. **Delegation is key.** You can't do it all. FAF helps identify tasks that should be handed off and supports this with structured position guides, job descriptions, and SOPs to ensure things get done right.

6. **Reflection and course correction** are essential. Regularly reviewing how time and effort are spent helps businesses stay aligned, adjust quickly, and prevent overwhelm and burnout.

Reflection Questions Chapter 7: Focusing on What Matters

1. Prioritization

- What are your three most important daily tasks?
- How well do they align with your strategic goals or OKRs?
- Are there tasks you're currently doing that you could delegate or eliminate to make room for more valuable activities?

2. Managing Distractions

- What are some things that pull your attention away from important work each week?
- What can you do to reduce or eliminate them?

3. Alignment with Purpose and Vision

- Are your daily, weekly, and monthly activities aligned with your mission, vision, and long-term goals?
- If not, what changes would bring better alignment?

4. Delegation and Training

- What tasks could you delegate or train others to handle?
- What processes or documentation (like SOPs or task guides) would help ensure these tasks are done well?

5. Reflection and Improvement

- Looking back on your day or week, did you focus on what mattered most—or just what felt urgent?
- What's one thing you could do differently next week to improve your focus?

6. What stood out to you in this chapter or resonated most with you?

7. What are your top 1-2 takeaways from this chapter?

8. What's one action you can take to put them into practice in your business or leadership?

CHAPTER 8

ALIGNING YOUR TIME WITH WHAT MATTERS

"Effective executives, in my observation, do not start with their tasks. They start with their time. And they do not start out with planning. They start by finding out where their time goes."[1]
—Peter F. Drucker, The Effective Executive

Few things show what really matters to us more than how we spend our time.

Yet days and weeks slip by, leaving you with the unsettling question: "Where did all the hours go?" Understanding how you actually spend your time and establishing a baseline of where those hours are going across key categories is the first step toward making meaningful improvements in both personal and organizational performance.

No matter who we are, we all have the same 24 hours each day to work from. Depending on how much sleep you get (ideally 7-8 hours), you have at the start of each day sixteen fresh hours to achieve a productive day doing more of what matters. This seems like a huge chunk of time to work with, and even the most experienced leaders often end the day wondering: *What did I really accomplish?*

The real challenge is learning to become more intentional and focused on doing more of what matters—hour by hour, day by day. While this book primarily addresses the business professional slice of your Life Pie, what matters doesn't just refer to work-related responsibilities. We've found that improving focus as a daily practice is far more effective than trying to change habits by the week or month. When asked how to improve oneself, a wise sage replied, *"Little by little, day by day,"* reminding us of the power and sustainability of a daily approach.

Sharpening Focus with Time Tracking

Measuring where your time goes isn't about micromanagement—it's about gaining clarity. Without this visibility, you risk holding on to tasks you should be delegating, saying yes to low-value work, or letting important priorities slip through the cracks. Time tracking tools like **Toggl** make it simple to log and analyze your hours, giving you data to see where your time truly goes. By doing so you can then adjust, refocus and invest more of your energy in what truly matters. You can try out a free version of Toggl at www.toggl.com.

Using the Toggl time-tracking app together with the **Focus Alignment Framework (FAF)** can significantly improve your ability to focus on your most important tasks and duties. Once you complete the FAF, you can then enter your key tasks into Toggl labeled as "projects" so that you have an accessible drop-down menu of tasks to pick from as you track those activities throughout the day and week.

Once you start accumulating this time-spent data over several weeks, you will be able to discern patterns and gain greater awareness of how your most precious resource—**time**—is currently getting utilized. This, in turn, enables you to make more informed decisions about delegation, scheduling, and where to invest your attention.

As Peter Drucker wisely noted, "Time is the scarcest resource, and unless it is managed, nothing else can be managed."[2]

Peter Drucker's 3-Step Time Management Approach[3] (Adapted from The Effective Executive)

1. **Record It**

   You can't manage what you don't track. Use tools like Toggl to create visibility into where your time is actually going.

2. **Ask Hard Questions**

   What would happen if this task wasn't done at all?

   Could someone else do this as well—or better—than I can?

   Am I unintentionally creating time waste for others?

3. **Consolidate It**

Protect uninterrupted blocks of time for high-value work.

Set aside **2-3 hour sessions** for *deep work*—distraction-free focus devoted to complex, cognitively demanding tasks such as strategic thinking, evaluation, or creative problem-solving.

Reserve separate **60–90 minute blocks** for *high-impact work*—critical actions that directly move your top priorities forward, such as key client meetings, hiring decisions, or revenue-driving initiatives that directly advance your top priorities.

Typically, shorter, less than 30 minute scattered time frames rarely allow for enough depth or meaningful progress. The goal isn't to fill every hour but to *align your time with what matters most.*

Carving out What Matters Time™

Developing the habit of setting aside discretionary time—open, self-directed blocks devoted to deep, high-impact work we call What Matters Time™—can transform both your productivity and peace of mind.

At first, reserving unscheduled time might feel counterintuitive to the idea of maximizing productivity. Yet these intentional time blocks are not a luxury—they're an investment. What Matters Time™ gives you the mental space to think strategically, solve problems creatively, and realign your actions with what truly matters.

Early mornings, when your mind is clear and interruptions are minimal, often provide the best window to reflect on what matters most, what matters now, and why.

Here are some key ways to use What Matters Time™—and why it matters.

Category	What Matters Time™ (WMT) Value
1. Strategic Planning and Innovation	Discretionary time gives SMB owners the mental space needed for strategic thinking. It allows them to step back from daily operations and focus on long-term goals, innovation, and business development.

Category	What Matters Time™ (WMT) Value
2. Problem-Solving and Decision-Making	Having blocks of WMT (What Matters Time) scheduled daily and/or weekly improves the ability to address unexpected challenges thoughtfully. This flexibility can lead to better decision-making and more effective problem resolution.
3. Employee and Customer Engagement	Owners can use WMT to engage more deeply with employees and customers, enhancing relationships, improving morale, and boosting customer satisfaction through proactive interaction and feedback.
4. Personal Development	Continuous learning and personal development benefit SMB owners directly. WMT can be used for reading, attending seminars, or learning new skills that improve both personal and business outcomes.
5. Work-Life Balance	WMT helps address personal needs, reduce stress, and maintain a healthier work-life balance, which is essential for sustained productivity and well-being.
6. Adaptability and Resilience	WMT empowers owners to better adapt to change, enabling them to pivot effectively when managing crises, adjusting to market shifts, or seizing new opportunities.
7. Creative Thinking	Creativity flourishes with mental space free from scheduled tasks. WMT can foster innovative ideas and creative solutions to drive the business forward.
8. Reflection and Review	WMT provides the opportunity for regular reflection on what's working and what's not, facilitating continuous improvement by evaluating business performance and making process adjustments.
9. Networking and Relationship Building	Professional relationships are key to business growth. WMT can be used to network, attend industry events, or meet potential partners, leading to new opportunities and collaborations.

In summary, leaving open spaces in your daily/weekly schedule with blocks of discretionary What Matters Time (WMT) are not just idle periods; they are strategic assets for SMB owners that enable them to work "on" their business and personal lives vs being consumed "in" the day-to-day of their business. Learning how to allocate the right amount of WMT is both an art and science. It depends of course, on the owner's or employee's individual circumstances and can change over time.

Our Business Alignment Coaches (BACs) can be a great sounding board to identify the ideal time blocks to start with. Perhaps starting with an hour or two per week might be manageable to begin with and then adjust as you go. The key is to become more intentional about creating the mental space so you can ultimately make a bigger impact on your business performance and even your own well-being.

Measuring and Putting What Matters into Action

To put What Matters Time into action and ensure you're actually spending time on what drives the most value, it helps to pair reflection with real data. That's where time tracking tools like Toggl come in. By tracking how time is actually spent across your most important tasks, you gain the clarity needed to align intention with reality. It's not about micromanaging every minute—it's about making sure your time reflects what matters most. The following step-by-step guide outlines how to use Toggl alongside the Focus Alignment Framework to make more informed decisions about where to invest your time and energy.

Utilizing Toggl Time Tracking App:

Step 1: Identify Key Tasks

- **Key Tasks:** From the Focus Alignment Framework, identify 5-7 key tasks most critical to your business objectives. These should be the tasks with high scores in "Value to Company" and ideally "Personal Enjoyment".

Step 2: Create Projects in Toggl

- **Set Up Projects:** In Toggl, create projects corresponding to these key tasks. For example, if one of your primary duties is "Client Acquisition," you can create a project named "Prospect Discovery Meetings" as one of the key tasks you perform to acquire clients.

- **Task Assignment:** If you're working in a team, assign these tasks-projects to relevant team members who are responsible for them.

- **Color Code Projects:** We recommend color-coding different tasks - projects in Toggl for easier visibility and organization. Assign and standardize specific colors to each task-project to quickly identify it in reports and on the Toggl dashboard.

Step 3: Track Time

- **Track Each Task:** As you or your team members work on these key tasks, you have the ability to start and stop the timer in

Toggl or just enter the time manually to track how much time is spent on each task.

- o **Duration of Tracking:** We recommend tracking at least 2-4 weeks of completed data to gather enough information to spot trends and make reasonable inferences about your time usage.

- **Use Tags:** For advanced users of Toggl, you can increase granularity using tags within Toggl to track time spent on specific client projects or jobs.

Step 4: Monitor and Analyze

- **Generate Reports:** At regular intervals (e.g., weekly or monthly), generate reports in Toggl to see how much time was spent on each key task. Analyze the time allocation to see how it aligns with your established priorities in the Focus Alignment Framework.

- **Compare with Goals:** Compare the actual time spent on key tasks against your Focus Alignment Framework's time estimates and expectations. This comparison can help identify specific tasks that are more time-consuming than anticipated or if they're being neglected.

Step 5: Make Adjustments

- **Refine Task Management:** Use the insights from Toggl reports to refine your task management strategy. If a key task is taking too much of the available time for the week, consider whether some parts can be delegated or if the process can be streamlined.

- **Update the FAF Focus Alignment Framework:** If you notice patterns, such as consistently underestimating or overestimating the time required for certain tasks, update the FAF to reflect these realities.

Step 6: Continuous Improvement

- **Regular Reviews:** Incorporate time-tracking data into your regular reviews of the Focus Alignment Framework. Use this data to continuously improve how tasks are prioritized and managed.

- **Adjust Toggl Projects:** As priorities shift or new tasks emerge, update the projects in Toggl to ensure that time tracking remains aligned with your current business objectives.

Toggl Implementation Challenges and Best Practices:

One of the biggest challenges our clients face when using Toggl is simply remembering to use it during their workday so they can accurately track their time. As a result, we've found that setting up focus accountability/alignment partners—pairing each employee with another employee to take turns reminding each other every couple of hours or so throughout the day via text/phone—is extremely helpful, especially during the first two to four weeks. Until the time tracking becomes part of the daily routine, everyone can benefit from periodic reminders.

The following lists the most common implementation challenges and best practices to overcome them.

1. **Forgetting to enter Time Data:**

    o **Practical Tracking:** Instead of tracking time minute by minute, we've found that it's more practical to estimate time spent on each task/project by updating your Toggl time tracker every couple of hours. This method is especially useful if you are frequently switching between tasks. The goal is to get rough estimates to establish overall time usage patterns on a daily and weekly basis. Aim to account for 80 percent of your normal workweek schedule. For example, if you work a forty-hour week, aim to track approximately thirty-two hours in Toggl.

    o **Best Practice:** SMBs often juggle multiple tasks, making it easy to forget about time tracking. Use Toggl's built-in reminders or browser extensions that prompt you to start the timer when accessing work-related apps or websites.

2. **Inconsistent Use Across Team Members**

o **Best Practice**: In SMBs, team members may have varied levels of familiarity and engagement with tools like Toggl. Conducting initial and ongoing training sessions can help emphasize the importance of consistent time tracking. Establish clear expectations that getting a minimum of time tracking data of 2-4 weeks, accounting for a minimum of 80% of their total hours worked is essential. Regularly review Toggl time reports weekly with the team to ensure everyone is on board and keeping up with tracking.

3. **Over complicating the Setup of Task Projects**

o **Best Practice**: SMBs benefit from keeping things as simple and straightforward as possible. Start with a minimal number of major tasks up to 5-7 that you'd like to track your time on. These are then set up as "projects" in Toggl, expanding only when necessary. This approach reduces complexity and makes the tool more user-friendly.

4. **Procrastination and Resistance to Tracking Time**

o **Best Practice**: Resistance to time tracking is common in SMBs, where employees may feel it adds unnecessary pressure. Communicate the benefits clearly. Time tracking can help manage workloads, improve productivity, and identify inefficiencies. To make it more engaging, consider gamifying the process with friendly competition or incentives for consistent use. Encouraging the use of Toggl's mobile app or desktop widget for quick and easy time entries can also reduce friction.

5. **Difficulty in Categorizing Tasks**

o **Best Practice**: Provide clear guidelines and examples of how to categorize common tasks. If you and your team have gone through the Focus Alignment Framework, you should have standardized naming conventions for each role's key tasks. Limiting the number of tasks to a manageable level also helps avoid confusion. Regularly review time entries to ensure they are correctly cate-gorized and assigned the correct task-project label in Toggl and provide feedback to improve accuracy.

6. **Overcoming the Initial Learning Curve**

   o **Best Practice**: Introducing new tools like Toggl can be daunting for SMBs with limited time for train-ing. Utilize online Toggl training videos and/or your Business Alignment Coach via Zoom meetings to get everyone up to speed quickly. Designating a Toggl "champion" within the team who can assist others as they get familiar with the tool can be highly beneficial.

7. **Analyzing and Acting on the Data**

   o **Best Practice**: If analyzed effectively, SMBs can derive significant value from time-tracking data. Set clear goals for what you want to achieve with the data—whether it's improving client billing accuracy or iden-tifying workflow bottlenecks. Schedule regular review sessions to discuss insights from Toggl data and explore how we can improve with actionable steps. Utilizing Toggl's visual reporting features can make data more accessible and easier to act upon, ensuring it aligns with your business objectives.

8. **Privacy Concerns**

   o **Best Practice**: In SMBs, where teams are often close-knit, privacy concerns around time tracking can arise. Clearly communicate how time-tracking data will be used, emphasizing its role in improving produc-tivity rather than micromanagement. Ensure that all time-tracking data is stored securely, with access limit-ed to authorized personnel only.

9. **Adapting to Changes in Routine**

   o **Best Practice**: SMBs may experience changes in rou-tine based on new projects, priorities, or client needs. Encourage your team to adjust their Toggl setup as needed to reflect these changes. Regularly incorporate Toggl usage into project planning and status update meetings, ensuring that time tracking evolves alongside your business. Schedule periodic check-ins where employees can suggest improvements to the time-tracking process.

This approach ensures that your SMB can overcome common challenges associated with time tracking, leading to more efficient operations and better overall business performance.

Benefits of Using Time Tracking App

- **Data-Driven Decision-Making:** It's been said that you can only improve what you measure and Toggl provides real-time data on how time is spent, allowing you to make informed decisions about task prioritization and resource allocation.

- **Improved Productivity:** By tracking time on key tasks, you can identify inefficiencies and adjust to improve productivity.

- **Enhanced Focus:** With Toggl generated time data, you can see if your time is spent on tasks that align with your strategic priorities and reduce time wasted on low-value activities.

- **Better Delegation:** Time-tracking data can highlight tasks that are taking too much time, helping you identify opportunities for delegation.

Time is our most precious and limited resource—unlike money or material goods, it cannot be rented, hired, bought, or extended. Each of us has the same twenty-four hours in a day, and how we utilize that time is crucial not just for achieving more but for unlocking our true potential and finding deeper fulfillment.

By integrating the Toggl time-tracking app with the Focus Alignment Framework (FAF), you and your organization can be empowered to carve out more What Matters Time so you can focus on what's truly important. This combination helps you track where your time goes, enabling you to make meaningful, continuous improvements in how you manage your life and business.

Peter Drucker's timeless principles of recording, managing, and consolidating time, when combined with the FAF and Toggl's time tracking, allow you to make informed, data-driven decisions that can elevate your productivity. By doing so, you can improve your ability to take back control of your time from distractions and spend more time on the things that matter most.

Although we just presented Toggl in the context of your business, it can also be used to track how time is spent in other areas of your life pie, including personal and family. As you regularly check in and repeat this process (our clients have found that going through this exercise about every six to twelve months has been invaluable to improving their overall productivity and focus), you'll determine if there are slices of your life pie that need attention or out of balance with the rest. By doing so you can take a more holistic approach to creating a greater sense of fulfillment in every aspect of your life, including your business.

Key Takeaways Chapter 8 Aligning Your Time with What Matters

1. **Time is your most limited and valuable resource.** Unlike money or people, you can't buy or hire more time which means how you manage your time is directly tied to your ability to grow your business and live a fulfilling life.

2. **If you're not tracking your time, you're flying blind.** Most business owners think they know where their time goes, but few can say with certainty. Time tracking creates the clarity you need to see where your hours are actually going and what's hindering or helping your business progress.

3. **Using a time tracking tool like Toggl, combined with the Focus Alignment Framework (FAF),** helps you get an honest picture of how well your time is aligned with what matters most. By labeling your most important tasks as projects in Toggl, you can start measuring if you're actually spending time on what moves the needle.

4. **Peter Drucker's timeless advice: Record, Manage, Consolidate** gives you a roadmap for mastering time

management. First, record your time to understand it. Second, manage your time by eliminating or delegating tasks that don't make the best use of your time. Third, consolidate your time by blocking out focused chunks of time for your highest-value work.

5. **What Matters Time (WMT) is a strategic asset.** Building regular discretionary blocks of time into your schedule allows you to step back, think strategically, and focus on high-value activities like innovation, key relationships, and problem-solving instead of getting stuck in day-to-day firefighting.

6. **Building a time tracking habit takes intentional effort.** Overcoming initial resistance and setting up simple, easy-to-use tracking categories makes all the difference. Team accountability, reminders, and gradually tracking more of your time (tracking 80% of your work week) help make it stick.

7. **Regularly reviewing time data leads to continuous improvement.** Looking at how you're spending your time and comparing it to your estimates in your Focus Alignment Framework helps you adjust, delegate, and re-focus so you're always aligning your time with what truly matters to you and your business.

8. **Time tracking isn't just for business — it can transform your whole life.** Using tools like Toggl to also track family time, personal development, or health activities can help you see where adjustments need to be made resulting in living more intentionally and feeling more fulfilled.

Reflection Questions – Chapter 8: Aligning Your Time with What Matters

1. Where is my time really going?

- What are the top 5-7 tasks or activities I spend the most time on each week?
- Which of these tasks are truly moving my business forward and which aren't?

2. Am I working on what matters most?

- How much of my time is spent on high-impact, "what matters" activities (e.g., strategic planning, client relationships, growth), people/team development)?
- What important tasks or goals am I not giving enough time to?

3. How can I create more What Matters Time (WMT) in my schedule?

- What's one small step I can take this week to block out time for my most important priorities?
- If I had an extra 2 hours this week to focus on what matters, what would I do with that time?

4. What should I stop doing or delegate?

- What tasks do I handle that someone else on my team could do just as well or better?
- What's one task I'm willing to delegate or outsource this month to free up my time?

5. How will I keep improving how I use my time?

- When will I review my time-tracking data (weekly, monthly) to identify adjustments?
- What's one change I can make in the next 30 days to better align my time with what matters?

6. What stood out to me as I reflected on these questions?

- What surprised me the most about how I'm currently spending my time?
- What is one insight I gained that I want to act on right away?

Optional Bonus Question (Personal & Professional Integration):

- If I tracked my personal time (e.g., family, health, service, learning), what patterns might I see?
- What adjustments would I want to make to live a more balanced and fulfilled life?

PEOPLE—ALIGNING YOUR TEAM WITH PURPOSE

CHAPTER 9

DEVELOP THE RIGHT-FIT PROFILE

"Hire character. Train skill." [1]
— *Peter Schutz, former CEO of Porsche*

Hiring for Character, Training for Skills: Aligning Employees with Your Purpose

Peter Schutz's quote highlights hiring employees with the right character and then training them to develop their skills. Conversely, if you hire employees with the right skills but the wrong character, changing their character is very difficult. Ideally, we want to hire employees with the right skills and character. In addition, we want to hire and retain employees aligned with our company's culture, values, and purpose.

If you've worked through the preceding Purpose section, which we recommend our clients start with, you will have a clearer understanding of what culture and values mean for your particular organization. With this clarity, you can better align new hires and current employees with your purpose. Again, skills can be learned and developed, but character and cultural fit typically cannot. Hiring employees based on their character and alignment with your culture and values is a critical component of what makes an employee the right-fit for your company.

Making Right-fit Distinctions

Yet how do we define the right-fit in terms of the particular skills or competencies and character or traits needed for a particular role? We all know that "I need a good employee" is inadequate and too vague to be useful for recruiters or anyone when it comes to sourcing and finding the right-fit employees for your company. Although the business owner usually knows what they want and can identify what the right-fit looks like, they may have difficulty articulating it. Beyond just a list of tasks and duties, owners might not have well-documented position guides regarding the character traits, skills, and competencies, enabling recruiters and others looking on their behalf to act effectively.

More importantly, our clients have found it invaluable when we can help them think through these traits and competencies in the context of their **Desired Performance Outcomes (DPOs)** of a particular position. In other words, what is the problem or pain we are trying to solve when hiring for this role? What key benefits are you looking to achieve for each new hire that will lessen your frustration and ultimately enhance your peace of mind? To begin the process of addressing this challenge, this chapter introduces two practical frameworks:

1. **Baseline Differentiating Traits/Competencies (BDTC) Framework**

2. **People-Data-Things (PDT) Framework**

These tools will help you make better distinctions about what the right-fit consists of, both the skills (competencies) and character (traits) for each role in your company, while also considering your company's culture and values.

Right-fit Employee Profile Benefits

- Clarify and communicate the essential traits and competencies required to achieve the Desired Performance Outcomes (DPOs) for that position.

- Provide stories and examples specific to your company of how these traits and competencies show up on the job so your employees understand what it means to perform well.

- Help establish minimum performance standards and facilitate more productive performance evaluation conversations with employees.

- Improve hiring processes by screening for the right-fit candidates based on baseline and differentiating competencies and traits.

By utilizing these frameworks, you'll establish better criteria for making informed hiring decisions and conducting effective performance evaluations for employees. By doing so, you can positively impact your team's ability to align with your company's purpose and contribute to its success.

Baseline vs. Differentiating and Traits vs. Competencies

Baseline Traits/Competencies are the essential attributes a person must have to perform the job adequately. If these are missing or underdeveloped, the individual cannot meet the role's basic expectations. However, it's important not to include the basics given for a particular role, such as the ability to read and write English or use a computer, when hiring an office administrative assistant. A trait/competency like "attendance" would be considered a given for higher-level management positions. For an entry-level admin or receptionist role, "develops others" or "team leadership" would most likely not be considered a baseline trait/competency for that level role but may be a baseline competency when hiring for a manager.

Differentiating Traits/Competencies, on the other hand, are what distinguish top performers from average ones. These go beyond baseline requirements and reflect the attributes demonstrated by your best employees. When selecting differentiating traits/competencies, focus on qualities you've observed in your top performers that contribute to exceptional performance. Differentiating traits are ones that stand out and are consistently demonstrated over time. You could also identify a differentiating trait as one of the baseline traits that top performers demonstrate at a significantly higher level, distinguishing them from average employees.

Competencies vs Traits: Competencies refer to skills and capabilities, while traits describe a person's characteristics and predispositions—how they are wired. For example, outgoing or friendliness may describe a person's traits, whereas the ability to delegate would align with someone's competency. We understand that it may be difficult to decide if something is more of a trait or competency. However, to simplify the use of the framework, we've been using trait and competencies interchangeably and not making the further distinction of creating a separate list for baseline differentiating traits and one for baseline differentiating competencies.

FOCUS ON WHAT MATTERS

BDTC Sports Example:

- For a baseball pitcher, the **baseline** competency might be the ability to throw a ball accurately at 95 MPH. However, for a first baseman, that particular baseline competency for a pitcher would not apply even though they are both baseball players. A baseline competency for the first baseman may be a set of defensive skills. Givens would refer to the fact that they both can run, catch, field and throw.

- A **differentiating** trait for either could be grace under pressure, demonstrated by clutch performance during the playoffs.

SMB Related Examples:

- For a customer service representative, a **baseline** competency might be the ability to respond to customer inquiries accurately and efficiently within a set timeframe. However, for a sales associate, that particular baseline competency for a customer service role would not apply, even though both roles involve interacting with customers. Givens would refer to the fact that both roles require strong communication skills and a customer-centric attitude.

- A **differentiating** trait could be emotional intelligence, demonstrated by the ability to diffuse tense situations and turn dissatisfied customers into happy satisfied ones.

- For a graphic designer, a **baseline** competency might be proficiency in design software like Adobe Creative Suite. However, for a web developer who works more on the server side that particular baseline competency for a graphic designer may not apply, even though both roles contribute to creating a visually appealing website. Givens would refer to the fact that both roles require creativity and attention to detail.

- A **differentiating** trait could be innovative thinking, demonstrated by the ability to develop original concepts that align with the brand's identity and stand out in a competitive market.

Instructions for Developing a Position's Baseline and Differentiating Traits/ Competencies

Initial Baseline Traits/Competencies Selection

1. **Review the definitions** of the listed traits and competencies (see the grouped list at the end of this chapter).

2. **Select up to 10** baseline traits/competencies that seem most important and relevant for the position. Remember that baseline traits/competencies are ones that, if any are missing, would most likely disqualify a person for the position.

Note: Keep in mind that competencies are typically skill-based, while traits describe a person's natural characteristics or predisposition. Don't get stuck on whether something is a trait or competency. We understand that sometimes the lines can blur when distinguishing and deciding if something is a trait or competency. The goal is to identify what combination of traits/competencies matters most for the role.

Narrowing Down to the Top Traits/Competencies

- Refine your initial list of 10 to the top 5-7 traits/competencies most relevant to the position.

- Exclude "givens". For example, "attendance" would be a given for a managerial role.

Note: Avoid Redundancy

Choose traits and competencies that complement rather than overlap. For example, if "trust builder" is selected, avoid choosing "influencer" unless both are distinctly relevant.

Context Matters: Adapting Traits to the Role

It's essential to tailor baseline and differentiating traits to the specific demands of each position.

- For transactional roles (e.g., fast-food worker), traits like "influence" may not be relevant.

- For strategic roles (e.g., business development executive), competencies like "influence" and "relationship building" are likely critical.

Higher-order competencies often encompass simpler traits. For example, "influence" might include "communication" as a foundational skill, but it is broader in scope.

Developing a Position's Differentiating Traits/Competencies

After you've selected the baseline traits/competencies, review the entire list again and select up to 2-4 differentiating traits/competencies (mark them with an asterisk *) that, in your experience, distinguish your top performers from those who are just adequate. In some cases, you may pick one of the baseline traits/competencies already selected as one of your differentiating ones by virtue of the fact that exceptional performers separate themselves from the average performers through their ability to demonstrate that same baseline trait/competency to a much higher degree.

Traits/Competencies in Action: Stories and Examples

Using examples to illustrate traits and competencies makes expectations clearer and more actionable.

Example: Service Orientation

- **Nordstrom Employee:** Stays late to ensure a customer has a tailored suit delivered to their hotel by 8 a.m. for a meeting.
- **Walmart Employee:** Helps a customer find an item in-store and loads it into their car.

These stories help employees visualize success within the context of their roles and your company culture. Different companies have different service standards; both are right for their contexts, but that doesn't necessarily mean that one way is right or better since Nordstrom and Walmart have very different service models and customer service expectations.

Example: Communication - Call Center Representative

- **Baseline:** Communicates product info clearly. After a billing inquiry, the customer fully understands their bill and next steps—no confusion.
- **Differentiating:** In addition to clarity, shows empathy and offers a proactive solution that the customer feels good about.

This level of care and relationship-building separates excellent from average performers.

Using stories and examples helps everyone understand what success looks like in action. Highlight and celebrate these as they occur. Over time, this encourages a culture where the "right-fit" behaviors are celebrated and aligned with your purpose.

Flexibility of the Framework

This Baseline–Differentiating Traits/Competency framework isn't meant to be the only factor in defining performance criteria for a role. You may find additional traits or competencies worth including based on your company's culture or the unique demands of a position.

Our clients have found this set to be comprehensive enough to be useful without overwhelming them with too many choices. It's best understood as necessary but not sufficient—these traits and competencies are essential for strong performance, but on their own, they don't guarantee success. Role-specific skills, cultural fit, and situational factors may still be required.

And remember, if you asked five managers from five different companies to create a list of seven baseline and differentiating traits/competencies for the same role, you'd likely get five different lists—each shaped by that company's culture and how the manager views the position.

Comparing BDTCs: Manager and Direct Report

A valuable exercise involves having managers and direct reports independently identify baseline and differentiating traits for a position, then compare their lists and why they chose them.

This process fosters:

1. **Clarity:** Align on the Ideal Employee Profile (IEP) and role expectations.

2. **Empowerment:** Help employees understand what matters most in their performance.

3. **Better Alignment**: Create shared performance metrics tied to the Desired Performance Outcomes DPO's aligned with organizational goals.

By going through the BDTC framework managers and their direct reports can have a productive dialogue to determine what the Right-fit Employee Profile looks like for a given role in terms of the essential traits and competencies required. Additionally, they can gain insights into how their perspectives compare to one another. As part of this exercise, it may also be helpful for managers to consider, if you were to replace this role with a new hire and start from scratch, what traits and competencies would you want from your ideal candidate based on the current needs of the business and desired performance outcomes for this position?

BDTC Framework Summary

The BDTC framework enables you to define success more clearly for each position in your organization, promoting better alignment between your employees and the needs of your business. By celebrating and reinforcing key traits and competencies through stories and examples, you can create a workplace culture that aligns with your purpose and generate a greater sense of fulfillment for everyone involved.

Definition of Traits/Competencies (Grouped by Category: See Appendix for complete list)

Management/Sales Traits/Competencies

- **Accountability:** Enjoys taking responsibility for accomplishments, progress and challenges on the job.

- **Commitment:** Demonstrates and communicates a genuine devotion to and enthusiasm for the brand, product, company, and customer.

- **Decision Making:** Weighs the cost and benefits before making choices and takes responsibility for the risks involved.

- **Delegation:** Can effectively assign work to others and coordinate their workflow with appropriate follow-up and encouragement.

- **Develops Others:** Places others in situations that will utilize and make their strengths most productive, providing timely constructive feedback.

- **Emotional Intelligence:** Understands how emotions factor into motivation, decision-making, and trust, discerning and appropriately responding to emotional dynamics at play in co-workers and customers.

- **Influence:** Uses credibility, expertise, trustworthiness, and empathetic understanding to affect how others think, feel, and act.

- **Motivator:** Is good at motivating and moving individuals and/ or groups of people to take action.

- **Negotiation:** Good at and enjoys reaching mutually beneficial agreements and mediating favorable terms.

- **Professional Presence:** Represents oneself in a confident, respectable, and business-oriented manner.

- **Resilience:** Ability to stay motivated in the face of challenges and to "bounce back" after unsuccessful attempts.

- **Strategic Thinking:** Ability to develop effective plans aligned with company goals and objectives given its personnel, resources, and capabilities.

- **Stress Tolerance:** Can perform calmly and effectively in high-stress and ambiguous situations.

- **Team Leadership:** Can successfully motivate, manage, and support a strong and cohesive team.

- **Trust Builder:** Communicates in ways that inspire trust and confidence: demonstrates a high degree of competency, purity of motive (cares about others), and authenticity/relatability.

- **Verbal Charm:** Ability to "win over" through confident and personable tonality, establishing rapport and influence through voice.

Advanced Traits/Competencies

- **Adaptive Communication:** This trait goes beyond general communication skills and involves the ability to adjust one's communication style to effectively connect with a diverse range of individuals and situations.

- **Strategic Resource Management:** For roles involving resource allocation—like budget, staff, or materials—the ability to strategically manage resources for optimal efficiency and effectiveness.

- **Customer/Client Centric:** Focusing not just on service orientation but on deeply understanding customer needs, behaviors, and trends to drive better service and product innovation.

- **Culture Fit:** Understanding and aligning with the company's values, ethics, and work environment. This might be a differentiating trait, as it can significantly impact an employee's ability to thrive within a specific organizational context.

Problem Solving & Process Traits/Competencies

- **Analytical Thinking:** Ability to address complex issues by breaking them into manageable components or logical steps, analyzing information, and drawing sound conclusions based on evidence-based reasoning.

- **Creativity:** Can create innovative, unexpected solutions by drawing inspiration from a variety of sources, including one's own intuitive insight.

- **Innovation:** Designs new, unexpected, and ingenious solutions to meet potential customers' desires and appeal to their needs.

- **Optimization:** Passion for making something, a product, process, or decision as functional and practical as possible.

- **Problem Formulation:** Ability to clearly define and structure complex problems before attempting to solve them. This task involves breaking down more significant issues into manageable components.

- **Problem Sensitivity:** Can foresee when something is wrong or likely to go wrong.

- **Troubleshooting:** Ability to navigate and enjoy analyzing the details of a problem, solving it with the best chance of success while adapting the approach as needed.

Relational Competencies/Traits

- **Collaboration:** Works effectively with coworkers and customers, integrating their capabilities and perspectives.

- **Concern for Others:** Is sensitive to others' needs and feelings and takes steps to be helpful on the job.

- **Emotional Intelligence:** Understands how emotions factor into motivation, decision-making, and trust, discerning and appropriately responding to emotional dynamics in coworkers and customers.

- **Friendliness:** Is warm and welcoming toward other employees, customers, and management; genuinely likes other people.

- **Rapport:** Ability to establish a close and harmonious relationship by understanding one another's feelings or ideas and communicating well.

- **Service Orientation:** Passion for helping others and seeking ways to meet their needs.

Technical Competencies (examples)

- **Computer Literacy:** Ability to use computers and related technology efficiently.

- **Word Proficiency:** Proficiency in using Microsoft Word for various tasks.

- **Excel Proficiency:** Using Microsoft Excel for data analysis and reporting.

- **Digital Literacy:** Understanding and capability to use digital tools and platforms.

- **Mathematical Aptitude:** Ability to understand and work with mathematical concepts.

- **CAD:** Proficiency in using Computer-Aided Design software.

- **Mechanical Aptitude:** Understanding of mechanical systems and processes.

- **QuickBooks:** Proficiency in using QuickBooks for financial management.

- **Microsoft Dynamics** - Proficiency in more advanced accounting systems

The People-Data-Things (PDT) Framework: Aligning Employee Strengths

The People-Data-Things (PDT) Framework (See Appendix) is another practical tool for SMB owners to ensure that employees are in roles that align with their natural strengths, skills, and inclinations. This framework categorizes tasks into three primary domains: interaction with people, engagement with data, and handling of things (physical objects or machinery). By aligning employees' tasks with their inherent strengths in these areas, businesses can optimize productivity, job satisfaction, and overall performance.

People: Interaction and communication tasks under the "People" category involve direct interaction with others, whether through communication, negotiation, collaboration, or customer service. Employees who excel in these tasks typically possess strong interpersonal skills, emotional intelligence, and a natural inclination toward working with others.

Examples of People-Related Tasks:

- Customer service and support roles where empathy and communication are key.

- Sales positions requiring persuasive communication and relationship-building.

- Leadership and management roles involve guiding teams, resolving conflicts, and motivating employees.

- Human resources tasks such as recruiting, training, and employee relations.

People Alignment Tip: Employees with a natural affinity for understanding and interacting with people should be assigned tasks that leverage these strengths. For example, placing an employee with strong interpersonal skills in a role that requires frequent customer interaction can lead to higher satisfaction for both the employee and the customer.

Data: Analysis and Interpretation "Data" tasks involve handling, analyzing, and interpreting information. Employees in this category work with numbers, statistics, reports, and other forms of data to make informed decisions, identify trends, and generate insights. Strengths in this area include analytical thinking, attention to detail, and proficiency with data tools and methodologies.

Examples of Data-Related Tasks:

- Financial analysis and accounting roles where precision and accuracy are crucial.

- Data entry and management tasks that require careful handling of information.

- Market research and data analysis positions that involve identifying trends and patterns.

- IT and technical support roles that require problem-solving based on data interpretation.

Data Alignment Tip: Employees with strong analytical skills and a preference for working with information should be assigned data-related tasks. For instance, someone who is detail-oriented and enjoys working with spreadsheets and databases would excel in roles involving data management or financial analysis.

Things: Handling and operations tasks in the "Things" category involve working directly with physical objects, machinery, tools, or equipment. Employees who thrive in this domain typically have strong spatial awareness, physical dexterity, and technical skills. These tasks often require hands-on work, precision, and mechanical aptitude.

Examples of Things-Related Tasks:

- Assembly line work where physical precision and manual dexterity are required.

- Operating machinery such as forklifts, production equipment, or vehicles.

- Maintenance and repair tasks that involve fixing or assembling mechanical parts.

- Warehouse roles that include stocking, organizing, and moving goods.

Things Alignment Tip: Employees who are skilled in handling tools, machinery, or physical materials should be placed in roles that require these abilities. For example, an individual with a knack for mechanical work and problem-solving would be well-suited to a maintenance or equipment operation role.

Ensuring Proper Alignment for SMB owners, understanding their employees' strengths and natural inclinations through the PDT Framework is essential for optimizing individual and organizational performance. Misalignment—such as placing a highly analytical person who doesn't enjoy working with people in a role that requires constant interaction with people—can lead to frustration, decreased productivity, and job dissatisfaction.

- **Assessment:** Regularly assess employees' strengths, preferences, and performance in their current roles.

- **Role Adjustment:** Be open to adjusting roles and responsibilities to better align with employees' strengths (People, Data and Things).

- **Training and Development:** Invest in training to help employees develop skills in areas that align with their strengths and also offer opportunities to grow in those areas.

Roles Requiring a Combination of PDT Strengths

While some roles primarily fall into one category of the People-Data-Things (PDT) Framework, many jobs require a blend of these categories. For instance, management consultants or managers often involve a combination of "People" and "Data" skills. In these positions, individuals must interact with and lead people while analyzing data to inform decisions, track progress, and drive strategic outcomes.

For example, a manager might be responsible for guiding a team (people) toward achieving business goals, while also interpreting sales reports and performance metrics (data) to ensure that the team is on the right path. A management consultant may need to interview clients and stakeholders (people) to understand business challenges and then assess company data (data) to provide actionable solutions.

Similarly, some roles may involve "Things" and "Data" combinations, such as IT or manufacturing roles that require technical precision, hands-on work with equipment, and analysis of operational data.

PDT Framework Instructions:

In the appendix, review each word and its definition as you did with the BDTC Framework. Select up to 3-5 tasks and duties in each category designated under People-Data-Things. Try to rank each of them based on their respective categories if it is helpful to do so.

PDT Framework Summary

The key to effective role alignment is ensuring that the employee's natural strengths and preferences match the demands of their role. Identifying individual strengths in the PDT Framework helps place the right employees in the right roles, leading to better performance, and job satisfaction.

By utilizing the PDT Framework, SMB owners can create a more effective, engaged, and motivated workforce, ensuring that each employee is in a role where they can excel and contribute most effectively to the organization's success. Attracting and developing the "right-fit" employees for each position in your business is essential to unlocking your organization's potential, saving money by reducing turnover and training costs, and creating a greater sense of fulfillment for both you and your employees.

Key Takeaways for Chapter 9: Develop the Right-fit Profile

1. **Hire for Character, Train for Skills**

   Aligning new hires with your company's culture, values, and purpose is critical. Skills can be taught, but character and culture fit are essential for long-term success.

2. **Clarify the Right-Fit Employee Profile:**

   Utilize the **Baseline Differentiating Traits and Competencies (BDTC)** and **People-Data-Things (PDT)** frameworks to help define the essential character traits, competencies, to develop role clarity needed to perform well and align with company purpose.

3. **Distinguish Between Baseline and Differentiating Traits/ Competencies**

   Baseline traits/competencies are non-negotiable for performing a role adequately, while **differentiating traits/competencies** are exhibited by your top performers and set them apart.

4. **Traits vs. Competencies**

   Traits describe a person's natural character and disposition (e.g., attention to detail), while competencies are skills and capabilities (e.g., delegation). Both are essential in building a right-fit employee profile, and should be considered together.

5. **Use Real-World Examples to Clarify Expectations**

   Stories and examples of how traits and competencies show up on the job help employees understand what success looks like in action and reinforce company values and culture.

6. **Adapt Criteria to Fit Each Role and Context**

   Tailor baseline and differentiating traits to the specific needs of each position. What's essential for a manager may not apply to an entry-level role, and vice versa.

7. **Leverage the People-Data-Things (PDT) Framework to Align Strengths**

   Align employee strengths with role demands by understanding whether a position primarily requires **people interaction**, **data analysis**, or **handling things (equipment/tools)**—or a combination. This helps improve fit, performance, and job satisfaction.

8. **Align Hiring and Role Expectations with Company Culture and Purpose** Defining what "right-fit" looks like in the context of your culture and purpose ensures that new hires contribute to long-term success and employee engagement

Defining what "right-fit" looks like in the context of your culture and purpose ensures that new hires contribute to long-term success and employee engagement.

Clarify Expectations for Performance and Evaluation

A well-defined right-fit profile enables clearer job expectations, better performance reviews, and more productive development conversations.

9. **Use Frameworks to Improve Hiring, Training, and Employee Development**

   Applying BDTC and PDT frameworks allows you to align hiring and training practices with what matters most, reducing costly turnover and improving employee retention and satisfaction.

Reflection Questions Chapter 9 Develop the Right-Fit Profile:

1. Defining the Right-Fit for Your Business

- What character traits and values are non-negotiable for anyone working in your company?

- How clearly have you defined the traits and competencies required for each role?

2. Baseline and Differentiating Traits/Competencies

- What **baseline traits and competencies** must every person in a specific role possess to perform adequately?

- What **differentiating traits or competencies** set apart your top performers from average employees in that role?

- How could clearly defining these traits/competencies improve your hiring and employee development processes?

3. Aligning with Culture and Purpose

- How well are your current employees aligned with your company's culture, values, and purpose?

- What impact does hiring for culture fit have on team cohesion and performance?

4. Practical Examples and Stories

- Can you identify examples of current employees who embody the right-fit traits/competencies? What specific behaviors make them successful in their roles?

- How could sharing these examples help clarify expectations for other employees?

5. Aligning Roles with Strengths (People-Data-Things Framework)

- For each key role in your company, does the work align with what employees naturally enjoy and are good at (People, Data, Things)?

- Are there current employees in roles that don't align with their strengths? How could you adjust roles or responsibilities to improve their performance and job satisfaction?

6. Hiring and Performance Standards

- Do you have a documented right-fit employee profile or position guide for key roles? If not, what's the first step you can take to create one?

- How would having a right-fit employee profile improve your hiring decisions and reduce turnover?

7. Leadership and Development Conversations

- How could a clearly defined set of baseline and differentiating traits/competencies help you have more productive conversations with employees about performance and development?

- What challenges do you face when evaluating whether an employee is the right fit, and how could these frameworks help address those challenges?

8. Continuous Improvement and Refinement

- When was the last time you reviewed the traits and competencies required for key roles?

- How can you ensure these profiles are updated regularly to reflect your company's evolving needs and purpose?

9. What stood out to you in this chapter or resonated most with you?

- What insight, story, or idea felt especially relevant to your business and hiring process right now?

- What's one thing you feel motivated to act on because of this chapter?

10. What are your top 1-2 takeaways from this chapter?

- What specific step can you take to put these insights into action in your business to improve hiring, training, or role alignment?

By reflecting on these questions and applying the frameworks discussed, organizations can develop a more effective and purpose-driven approach to right-fit employee selection and development.

CHAPTER 10

HIRE RIGHT-FIT EMPLOYEES

"People are not your most important asset.
The right people are."[1]
–Jim Collins author of Good to Great

Obstacles to Hiring Right-Fit Employees

Small to Mid-Sized Business (SMB) Owners and their existing staff often lack the expertise of a professional recruiter. They also find themselves spread thin and juggling too many responsibilities to focus on adequately sourcing and screening for the best candidates. This lack of focus can result in a less-than-ideal candidate pool, reducing the likelihood of making the best hiring decision.

In addition, instead of following the adage of hiring slowly and firing quickly, they often do the opposite—hiring quickly and firing slowly. This knee-jerk reaction of hiring quickly is often driven by the urgency to fill vacant positions when someone leaves or is let go. On the other hand, we've found that employers are often slow to fire and wait too long to let employees go, even when performance issues become evident.

Bridging the Gap in Talent Acquisition

In our experience, we've found that business owners often underestimate both the time and skill required to source enough suitable candidates to choose from adequately. In addition, they don't realize how much they lose out on the best candidates available, often hired by their competitors who put in the most effort to find them.[2]

In response to this challenge, our clients partner with us so we can professionalize their talent acquisition process and bridge the gap between current efforts and what needs to be done to improve the probability of success when it comes to hiring the right fit employees for their business. They appreciate the advantage they can gain from professional resources that can put in the necessary time and effort beyond what they can do with their limited staff and in-house resources.

Leveraging Job Platforms for Effective Recruiting

Part of what makes it especially challenging for SMB owners is that using job platforms like Indeed and Zip Recruiter requires constant monitoring and optimization to ensure keywords in job titles and descriptions align with what qualified candidates are searching for. You and your staff compete against seasoned recruiters who are more adept at using these platforms and are quicker at engaging the best-qualified candidates.

Since good talent usually gets hired fast, the sourcing and screening process requires diligent follow-through and timely responses to potential candidates. When it falls on the shoulders of the owner, or someone on their staff who handles HR and recruiting responsibilities, screening resumes and communicating with candidates promptly may often fall through the cracks amid juggling other day-to-day tasks.

It also matters how you effectively communicate your employment value proposition, especially when it comes to high-in-demand candidates who are also being recruited by your competition. SMBs may not have a well-articulated and defined employment value proposition that can make a compelling case for how their company is better than the candidate's next best alternative.

When we work with our clients, we take on the role of a "talent matchmaker" and take the time to better understand their company culture and employment value proposition. By doing so, we can then help them develop and articulate it to attract more of the right fit candidates. Also, if they hire only a handful of employees each year, they will not have the experience and expertise of professional recruiters, who typically hire hundreds annually. Professional recruiters also benefit from the latest talent acquisition systems and technologies that enable them to edge out their competition and hire more timely and cost-effectively.

Case Study: Optimizing Hiring for the "Right Fit" Employee

Frank's Hiring Challenge

One of our clients, "Frank", the owner of a Southern California-based landscape design-build firm with around 30 employees, called us frantically. "Sally", their "Controller" for the last three years, had just given her two-week notice. "We need to find her replacement and get a job posted on Indeed ASAP for another Controller!" Frank cried out.

Assessing the Situation

I told Frank, "Let's schedule a Zoom call this week to figure out how to best find her replacement." During our call, I explained the need for tactical and strategic approaches to solve this hiring problem. I also reframed the "problem" as an opportunity to optimize the next hire based on the current and critical needs of the business. The tactical approach would focus on ensuring the urgent day-to-day tasks and duties—the "blocking and tackling" aspects of the prior Controller's job—are covered. These are critical tasks that, if left undone, could negatively impact the company. In these situations, we've found that a designated backup or often the owner will temporarily fill the gap until a replacement is found.

First, we needed to figure out what Sally was currently doing for the company, so I scheduled a meeting with Sally to get a detailed account of her daily, weekly, and monthly tasks and the approximate time spent on each. We also reviewed Sally's job description as a starting point. Then, we compared it with her day-to-day activities, listing her tasks and duties in our Focus Alignment Framework Excel spreadsheet (see Chapter 7 FAF).

Strategic Hiring Questions and Optimization

Beyond understanding the tactical aspects of her job, it was also essential to ask Sally more strategic questions that considered how we might optimize the next hire based on the company's goals and objectives at that time. Additionally, we evaluated whether there was someone within the company who could be promoted or cross-trained in her role. By better understanding Sally's role and how it fit the company's needs, we identified key areas for improvement. This analysis enabled us to find a candidate who would fit the role as it was configured at the time and could also bring needed strengths to the team to address areas of improvement. Combining tactical and strategic considerations when hiring helped us position the new hire not only as a replacement but also as an improved addition to the team.

Aligning Titles with Function and Compensation

As we analyzed Sally's day-to-day tasks and duties, it became clear that her role was more akin to that of an administrative bookkeeper or AP/AR clerk than a traditional Controller. When I asked about her title: she explained it evolved as she took on more responsibilities and managed all office tasks, "running the office and handling all the admin side of everything." Based on her perception of her role and increasing responsibilities, she gave herself the elevated title of "controller." The owner had acquiesced, reasoning that as long as the work was done, the title didn't really matter to him. Over three years, her title morphed from AP Admin Coordinator to "Controller," even though her day-to-day tasks and duties didn't align with that title or role.

Understanding the Pay Ecosystem

I informed Frank that based on Sally's tasks and duties, the title of Controller was inappropriate, especially in a company with only 30 employees. Also, her current pay rate of $32 per hour is not in line with the pay ranges of Controllers. Controllers typically have over ten years of experience in accounting and advanced degrees and work in larger organizations with 150+ employees. The average pay for a Controller can range between $120K and $180K annually.

Given the pay ranges of Frank's current employees, a $120K+ salary would be higher than all his highest-paid employees, some who have been with the company for over 20 years. Bringing in someone at that pay level could create a skewed pay structure in their existing pay ecosystem and likely create resentment amongst existing employees. They could feel undervalued if a new person gets hired for a non-core role at a much higher pay rate.

It's a good practice for employers to ensure that employees properly align job titles with actual duties and appropriate compensation related to those titles to maintain organizational fairness and pay equity. Misalignment in titles and compensation, for example, posting for a Controller but paying at the level of an existing Accounts Payable (AP) clerk's salary, would preclude you from attracting qualified controller candidates at that pay level. Conversely, if you put the pay ranges too high for an Accounts Payable Clerk, you may find it challenging to find qualified candidates who fit that role since they are more likely looking for pay ranges in line with AP Clerk. With higher pay ranges than a typical AP Clerk would earn, you may also get overqualified candidates applying for that position.

By appropriately and accurately defining the tasks, duties, and desired outcomes for each role, along with the appropriate compensation for those roles, businesses can improve their probability of success in attracting the right candidates to apply for their jobs.

Navigating Pay Inflation: Ensuring Fair and Competitive Compensation

Taking the time to understand the existing "pay ecosystem" and taking a payroll census consisting of each employee's name, start date, job title, reporting relationships, and compensation: hourly pay rate or annual salary is essential to knowing what pay ranges can or should be offered when hiring for the company. In recent years, with increased inflation, pay has gone up. In some instances, this has created situations where the increased market pay rates may be higher than what your existing personnel is making.[3]

When the overall "pay tide" rises, it lifts all boats, and if you are not willing to rise with the tide of inflation by adjusting your pay rates accordingly, you may find yourself "underwater." This means that your current employees are getting paid below market rates, which will hinder you when attracting qualified personnel or, worse, risk losing your current employees to another employer. We define market rates as the average pay rate for a role based on experience, knowledge, and competencies while also considering demographic considerations like location, firm size, industry, etc.

As a result, our clients may need to increase the pay for their existing employees to keep up with rising pay levels and mitigate the risk of losing them to their competitors, who might offer more pay and better benefits. In addition, they do not want to risk alienating their current employees, especially if employees find out their pay is less than the new hires for the same role. Even though SMB owners would rather employees not talk about their pay with fellow employees, it's always better, in my view, to operate under the assumption that pay will be discussed or found out eventually. By creating a culture of transparency and fairness, there's less likelihood of any issues resulting from disgruntled workers feeling they've been treated unfairly.

Optimizing Job Titles

Our talent acquisition team consulted to determine the appropriate job titles while considering the traits, skills, and experience required needed for performing the required tasks and duties based on the company's needs and budget. In addition, they needed to consider the keywords in job posting titles to maximize visibility with candidates most qualified and suitable for the position when posting the job on a platform like Indeed. Sometimes, it's helpful to adjust keywords in job posting titles in order to improve responses from viable candidates.

Addressing Immediate Needs and Traits for the Role

Based on the critical and urgent needs of the business pertaining to that role, we determined that we needed someone with accounting-bookkeeping skills, preferably experienced in using Quick Books online accounting software, as it is widely used by small to mid-sized businesses. We were looking for someone with particular traits most conducive to the role while also fitting in with the team culture. One particular trait we were looking for in the candidate is the ability to handle and embrace chaotic challenges, including dealing with vendors demanding payments, arranging and negotiating with the IRS back payroll tax payments, and dealing with cash flow issues.

Developing the Right Fit Employee Profile

Based on the salary budget of $26-$29 per hour for this role, we determined that the ideal candidate should be in the early stages of their career but not freshly graduated from college. We needed someone with a few years of experience who was looking to take the next step in their career development. This role would involve day-to-day accounting activities such as entering payments and expenses and assigning them to the correct chart of accounts. It could also grow into a management-leadership role, potentially overseeing a department, including a part-time accounting admin or AP clerk.

We sought someone comfortable in a small business environment, capable of wearing multiple hats, and taking the initiative to think and problem-solve beyond just the doing the bare minimums of the job. The ideal candidate needed a high degree of learning agility and a relish for sorting things out and fixing issues. They also had to have a strong desire to take an active role in developing and implementing the right systems and processes to improve operational performance.

In an SMB team environment, you don't have the luxury of employees with the mindset of "it's not my job" who prefer to stay in narrow lanes, operating as well-defined specialized cogs in a large corporate machine. Typically, employees who are scrappy, resilient, and willing to juggle multiple responsibilities in a relatively unstructured and often chaotic environment are more likely to thrive in a small business or start-up organization.

The upside for these employees is that because their roles are not so narrowly defined, they have greater learning opportunities and a broader scope of responsibilities than would be typical in larger companies. They can also work more independently while dealing with fewer bureaucratic hurdles since they often work directly with the owner or senior leadership team.

Optimizing Job Posting Keywords

After we understand "what problem we are trying to solve" with each hire, we need to develop the appropriate job title that includes the keywords candidates with the necessary traits, competencies, and relevant experience are most likely searching for. It's a balancing act between not using a title that is too generic and not being overly specific to your organization. For example, using a title like "customer ninja master" might be too specific to the company, while "customer service representative" might be too broad.

This process requires researching, testing, and iterating job title keywords on major job platforms such as Indeed, Zip Recruiter, and LinkedIn. The goal is to find the most effective ones based on the company's needs. We must strike a balance between a job title that is too generic or broad and one that is too specific without the keywords that qualified candidates typically search for.

Internal Job Titles vs. Job Posting Titles

Additionally, the internal job title might not be appropriate or optimal for job posting purposes depending on how aligned the job duties, responsibilities, required skills, pay, and experience are with the title commensurate to those duties. For example, a small business with 40 employees might call the person who does their bookkeeping and accounting AP/AR with an annual salary of $60K a "Controller." However, a typical Controller earns at least double that amount and is usually found in larger organizations. Using the title "Controller" would be inappropriate based on average market pay since the job posting is your company's marketing piece designed to attract qualified candidates who search using specific keywords.

After discussing this with Sally and Frank, the owner, we determined that, based on company needs and budgetary considerations, the hourly pay range offered would be more in line with a job posting for an Accounting Admin position. We eventually hired someone who met our requirements and has since become a valuable addition to the team and a positive contributor.

Framework for Talent Optimization

Identifying Pain Points and Desired Performance Outcomes

We need to consult and figure out how we can best optimize the next hire based on the critical needs of the business. A good consultant presents a framework of questions to help the client get to the heart of the problem and gain insights. We need to ask:

- What problem or "pain" are we trying to solve by hiring for this role?

- What is the desired performance outcome regarding the 5-7 key slices of the performance pie.

- What are the relative weightings and importance of each "slice" as a percentage of the whole 100% "pie"?

Screening for Right Fit Traits and Competencies

Developing criteria for what Right Fit looks like allows us to get a better feel for the relative importance the hiring manager or owner assigns to each "performance slice." Then, as recruiters, we can screen for these traits and competencies based on how the manager or owner views the role. If each slice is approximately equal, then there is no point in "splitting hairs." Usually, it's impractical for most clients to figure out if one slice is 28% or 31%. We must ascertain if one slice is significantly more critical than the rest. For example, if customer service skills are weighted as 50% versus Excel skills at 10%, it is essential to make that distinction. Once we develop a set of 5-7 competencies or traits, we can craft a set of interview questions to then screen for those competencies or traits.

Interviewing for Right Fit Hires

We've found that critical incident-type questions work best and usually start with prompts like

"Tell me about a time when or can you describe a situation in which..." These questions give us better insights into the candidate's proficiency in those desired traits/competencies. Critical incident questions focus on past behavior, often the best predictor of future performance.[4] These questions also allow interviewers to gain a more detailed and realistic understanding of how a candidate handles real-world situations.

For example, if punctuality is a trait, you might ask if they think of themselves as punctual and how they've demonstrated that in their work history. It's recommended that you ask each candidate the same set of questions in the same order and rate the answers given on a scale of 1-10 that reflects how much you perceive each trait is demonstrated. (see appendix) Once the questions are answered, you and others involved in the interview can add up the scores. The actual totals for each candidate serve as a way to calibrate and compare against other candidates so you can determine the one(s) who will go on to the next stage. We've found it helpful to simply answer the question of, based on what you've heard, seen, and felt, how confident you are to take the candidate to the next step in the process, which could also be making an offer.

Even after the person is hired, you can't know how they will work out until after 30-60 days in many instances. It's helpful to be modest concerning what we think we can know about a particular candidate until we've gathered more work-related data points beyond a 45-minute Zoom or in-person interview at your office. By not trying to answer if this person is right for the job or if we should hire them in the earlier stages of the vetting and screening process, you make the vetting process more manageable, less taxing, and less prone to biases and errors.

One of our favorite responses to our clients when they tell us about the positive progress a new hire is making is encapsulated in these four words: "So far, so good." Even after a year or at any time in the future, it still applies —perhaps with the addition of asking, "How can we support you in making it even better?" You can also include job-specific tests and job samples whenever feasible. By following a structured interviewing process, employers can ensure greater consistency in their methods and minimize personal bias.[5]

Screening Questions Summary:

- Develop a set of 5-7 key competencies or traits required for the role.

    o Craft interview questions that test for these traits, using critical incident questions starting with "Tell me about a time when..." Example: If punctuality is important, ask candidates how they've demonstrated punctuality in their work history.

- Ask each candidate the same questions in the same order to maintain consistency.

- Have each interviewer rate each answer on a scale of 1-10 based on how well the candidate demonstrates each trait.

- Total the scores for each candidate to calibrate and compare them between the interviewers. It's fine to include one's intuition and gut feel to complement the scores.

- Use the scores to determine which candidates advance to the next stage or receive a job offer.

- Include job-specific tests and work samples when feasible to further assess candidates' abilities.

- Follow a structured interviewing process to ensure consistency and minimize personal bias throughout the hiring process.

Clarifying Essential Tasks and Duties

We can help clients understand the relative importance of each competency or trait by considering the negative impact or consequences if the trait is missing. Our BDTC Baseline Differentiating Traits and Competencies used to develop the Right Fit Employee Profile in the prior chapter can also help us clarify the most important 5-7 competencies or traits pertinent to the role. By doing so, these traits and competencies can also inform the overall performance pie we are using to evaluate success for the role. Then, we can also develop appropriate interview screening questions based on these traits and competencies across all candidates.

Identifying these traits and competencies doesn't mean they are the be-all and end-all in describing what is needed for the role. They fall under the rubric of "necessary but not sufficient." However, we've found that it's a manageable framework and a starting point for many owners to clarify their thinking on the essential traits, competencies and desired performance outcome for each role they are hiring for. This understanding often evolves based on how they configure and optimize the role to meet the changing needs of their business.

Crafting a Compelling Job Posting

After identifying the key traits, competencies, and essential tasks and duties in the broader context of the problem we are solving in hiring for this position, we need to craft a compelling Job Posting. **The job posting is not the same as a job description.** We've seen instances where it appears that an existing company job description was copied and pasted into an Indeed or Zip Recruiter job posting ad. Typically this is way too much information to serve as an effective job posting. Although the job description can serve as a useful starting point, the job posting is akin to a marketing piece selling prospective candidates on your employment value proposition consisting of what makes working at your company unique and better (including benefits, compensation, opportunities for growth, values and work environment), compared to their next best alternative.

We've found that the shorter and more succinct the job posting in terms of what's in it for the job seeker and the key traits and competencies required, the more effective the job posting, resulting in more of the "right fit" applicants applying to your job posting.

By consulting with our clients to understand their culture and employer value proposition, we can craft a compelling job posting around that in ways that are also authentic to who they are. By doing so, we can put the employer's best foot forward and attract as many qualified right fit candidates to apply, thus increasing the number of qualified candidates they can choose from and improving the probability of making a better hiring decision.

The job posting should also address the question of what it is about working for your company and this job opportunity that makes it better and different from their next best alternative. If their skill set and experience are in high demand, you are competing with other employers and often larger companies with a more established organizational infrastructure, employee resources and benefits, e.g. health insurance, 401k, PTO, etc., than what typically can be offered by an SMB enterprise. You are also competing with their current employer if they are employed and the option of staying where they are vs. making a change. To make a job change, employees typically must see a significant upside and positive difference compared to where they are currently.

Making Informed Decisions

Ultimately, all decisions whether in business or life, must be made based on the best and most relevant information available at the time. That means weighing trade-offs, considering likely outcomes, and making the best call for your situation—not chasing the perfect answer. Once a decision is made, we must live with the results, recognizing that there's no way to go back in time and test countless "what if" scenarios to determine the definitive "right" choice.

For example, one could argue for hiring an experienced Controller at $150K–$200K per year, a salary equal to what the owner might be earning. The assumption would be that a higher investment yields greater returns—the classic "you get what you pay for" mindset. While this may be a valid argument, it's equally important to weigh whether such a decision aligns with the company's current needs and financial realities.

The key lies in constant reflection and adaptability. By reviewing the outcomes of our decisions, we can better identify what worked, what didn't, and why. From there, we can learn, improve, and make course corrections when things differ from our expectations. Decision-making isn't just about getting it right the first time; it's a process of continuously striving for better outcomes through thoughtful evaluation and adjustments while aligning with what matters most.

Key Takeaways Chapter 10 Hire Right-Fit Employees

The challenges of hiring the right fit employees for SMBs include overwhelmed staff, underestimated time to hire the right fit employees, and the lack of specialized expertise in optimizing and effectively managing job platforms. Purpose Matters can address some of these challenges by performing the initial stages of the talent sourcing and acquisition process while professionalizing your hiring so you can increase the probability of attracting and hiring the best candidates for your business.

We also focus on optimizing the next right-fit hire based on current organizational needs rather than merely filling a position. A right-fit hire is qualified, fits your culture, and will stay long-term. In other words, as Lou Adler states in his book Hire with Your Head, "Hire for the anniversary dates, not just the start date." [6] By having more "right fit" employees, our clients can build a stronger, more capable team with greater peace of mind.

We ensure that job titles, descriptions, and required competencies and traits align with the actual needs of the business. This method improves the likelihood of finding the right fit and ensures long-term success and satisfaction for both the employer and the employee.

Effectively optimizing the hiring process involves understanding the critical needs of the business and crafting job postings that attract suitable candidates. By clarifying the problem or "pain," the hire is meant to solve and the desired outcomes we are hiring for, we can then determine and screen for the required competencies and traits most conducive to delivering these outcomes.

By guiding our clients through a series of clarifying questions within the frameworks of our 7P Business Alignment Model™, such as the BDTC (Baseline-Differentiating Traits/Competencies), PDT (People-Data-Things), and FAF (Focus Alignment Framework), we can help them develop the right fit employee profile. Doing so empowers our clients to make better, more informed hiring decisions resulting in better business outcomes and retaining more of the right-fit hires who align with the company's culture and purpose.

1. **Right Fit Employees Are Key to Success:**

    o   It's not about hiring just anyone; it's about finding candidates who align with your company's culture, purpose, and needs. Hiring the right fit employees reduces turnover, increases engagement, and contributes to long-term success.

2. **Professionalizing the Hiring Process Improves Outcomes:**

    o   SMBs often lack the expertise and time required to optimize hiring. Using tools, frameworks, and professional support ensures better candidate sourcing, screening, and decision-making.

3. **Strategic Hiring Focuses on Outcomes, Not Just Filling Roles:**

    o   A right fit hire should address specific pain points and deliver measurable outcomes. Understanding the problem the hire is solving and aligning the role with current business needs leads to smarter decisions.

4. **Crafting a Compelling Job Posting is Crucial:**

   o A job posting should be concise, engaging, and sell your employment value proposition. It's not just about listing duties; it's about attracting the right candidates by highlighting what makes your company better than their alternatives.

5. **Align Job Titles and Compensation Appropriately:**

   o Misaligned job titles or compensation can lead to mismatched expectations, poor candidate pools, and dissatisfaction. Ensure titles and pay accurately reflect the role's responsibilities and market benchmarks.

6. **Use Structured and Consistent Interviewing:**

   o Developing clear competencies and crafting consistent interview questions ensures fairness, reduces bias, and increases the likelihood of identifying the best candidates.

7. **Optimize for Retention, Not Just Recruitment:**

   o Hiring should focus on long-term success, aiming to find candidates who will thrive and grow with your organization over time. The goal is to "hire for the anniversary date, not just the start date."

Reflection Questions Chapter 10 Hire Right-Fit Employees

1. **What problem or "pain" is this role meant to solve, and what outcomes are you hiring for?**

   o Have you clearly defined the key traits and competencies needed to address this pain point and achieve these outcomes?

2. **How effectively does your current hiring process attract and identify the right-fit candidates?**

   o Are your job titles, postings, and compensation aligned with the actual requirements of the role and prospective employee's expectations based on the job posting?

3. **What is your employment value proposition, and how does it differentiate your company from competitors?**

   o Are you clearly communicating why candidates should choose your organization over their next best alternative?

4. **How consistent and structured is your interview process?**

   o Do you use the same questions and rating systems across candidates to minimize bias and ensure fair evaluation of key competencies?

5. **How well are you optimizing your hiring for long-term retention and alignment with your company's culture and purpose?**

   o Are you hiring with the goal of creating enduring relationships that contribute to team cohesion and organizational success?

6. **What stood out to you in this chapter or resonated most with you?**

7. **What are your top 1-2 takeaways from this chapter?** What's one specific action you can take to put them into practice in your business or leadership

CHAPTER 11

BUILD THE RIGHT-FIT TEAM

"Train people well enough so they can leave, treat them well enough so they don't want to,"[1]
– Richard Branson

Structuring Your Organization for Success

Developing a team that aligns with your business purpose is essential for long-term success and unlocking your organization's full potential. If you've worked through the frameworks in the purpose section, you should have a clearer sense of your company's core purpose, which is encapsulated by your mission and vision. This clarity serves as the foundation for identifying and attracting right-fit employees, those who not only have the skills required but also share your values and believe in where your business is headed.

In this chapter, we'll explore ways to structure your organization to support the growth of a right-fit team:

- Designing clear roles and responsibilities
- Creating functional alignment across departments
- Ensuring every team member contributes in a way that drives results and reflects your purpose.

We'll also introduce a practical framework and template for creating Position Guides—a simple but powerful tool for documenting expectations and responsibilities. These guides help managers and team members to assess performance, coach for growth, and ensure alignment across the team. When structure, clarity, and purpose come together, you don't just hire employees—you build a team where the right people are in the right roles to help take your business to the next level.

Organizational Growth Challenges for SMBs

For small and mid-sized businesses (SMBs), where individuals often wear multiple hats, having clearly defined roles and responsibilities is especially challenging. Unlike larger organizations where employees can specialize in more narrowly defined roles, many SMBs start with the founder(s) and a few other key personnel handling most everything else. As the business grows, additional personnel are needed to support this growth. However, as the organization expands, so does the complexity and potential for miscommunication between the owner and their employees.

As various departments develop within the business, they also risk becoming siloed and not adequately communicating with one another.[2] It becomes increasingly difficult to ensure everyone is rowing the boat in a coordinated manner as they strive towards the company's goals and objectives.

Among the employees, there may not even be a shared and unified understanding of the company's primary goals and objectives. Tasks and duties may overlap between employees, and you may have too many cooks in the kitchen, resulting in miscommunication, lack of accountability, and inefficiency. Without clear accountability as to who owns the task and is responsible, important tasks may get overlooked or not be attended to in a timely manner.

Importance of Cross-Training to Reduce Risk of Disruption

In addition to knowing who does what, it's essential to ensure that important tasks and critical functions are not overly reliant on a single individual. Cross-training multiple employees provides adequate backups - and even backups for the backups - in case someone gets sick, goes on vacation, or leaves unexpectedly.

This reduces the likelihood that the owner feels held hostage by a key employee and prevents employees from developing a sense of entitlement due to a perception of being "irreplaceable". More importantly, it benefits employees by giving them greater peace of mind when they can take time off without worrying about unfinished work or constantly checking emails. Having well-documented processes and cross-trained team members also ensures that negative issues stemming from an employee's performance or attitude don't leave the business vulnerable.

In an SMB with 50 or fewer employees, positions often default to having the owner or key managers act as backups - or at the very least, as the backup for the backups. To ensure a business has adequate backups beyond the owner, it's essential to proactively cross-train employees for each critical position whenever possible. By doing so you reduce the risk of disruptions and having to scramble to hire if the primary person responsible is no longer available. Particularly in SMBs, where a single person often handles multiple roles and responsibilities, owners don't have the luxury of larger organizations with specialized roles assigned to just a single employee.

Reflection Questions:

- Are adequate backups in place for each critical position?
- If not, what steps can you take to cross-train employees and document standard operating procedures (SOPs) for the role's tasks so someone could fill in if necessary?

Avoiding Personality-Driven Organizational Structures

Another challenge SMBs face as they grow is allowing long-time employees to shape their roles around their personal strengths and preferences rather than adapting to the company's evolving needs. When positions are defined by individuals rather than business requirements, it can lead to inefficiencies and sub-par performance that does not align with company objectives.

Roles should instead be designed based on the core functional needs of the business. By doing this, the business is better positioned to continue operating efficiently when hiring to replace key employees who may retire, become unavailable or leave.

Implementing a Functional Structure

A functional organizational structure solves the problem of personality-driven roles by aligning job functions with business needs rather than individual strengths. Each role is defined by its tasks and responsibilities, not by the person currently in that role. In addition, to reduce confusion and competing priorities, each functional box or role should also have only one boss or one other functional box that they report to.

Our clients have found it very helpful when we can work with them to design their organizational chart with the right functional boxes that are documented in the form of position guides (see appendix for sample position guide template). These position guides are not just a list of tasks performed but also include the position's baseline and differentiating traits and competencies most conducive to producing the desired performance outcomes. (see Chapter 9, developing the Right-Fit Employee Profile BDTC Framework)

For example, on a baseball team, the various positions—e.g., pitcher, catcher, first baseman—are like functional boxes, each requiring specific traits and competencies that are most conducive to success in that role. Similarly, you need to design your organizational chart with the right functional boxes by understanding the "game" your business is playing based on your industry segment, the type and size of your business, and the customer benefits you are delivering.

In smaller companies, it's not uncommon for the same person—especially the owner(s)—to cover multiple positions: "playing third base and shortstop." As you continue to grow, this, of course, becomes unsustainable. When you start to play in the "big leagues," you can't compete at a higher level and/or capacity unless you have all your positions adequately covered. By doing so you can position your team to perform well and win. Imagine how severely disadvantaged a professional baseball team would be if it were missing even a single position, such as a left fielder.

Benefits of a Functional Structure for Building the Right-Fit Team

1. **Clarity:** Employees understand their roles and how they contribute to the company's goals.

2. **Improved Communication:** A functional structure reduces silos and fosters better collaboration across departments.

3. **Efficiency:** Clearly defined responsibilities improve productivity and reduce redundancy.

4. **Employee Development:** Having clearly defined functional roles to refer to can uncover skill gaps, enabling targeted training and succession planning.

5. **Sustainability:** Having well-defined documented roles helps cross-train and prepare for succession planning so the business can adapt to changes when key personnel leave and minimize disruption.

Delegation and Authority

Effective delegation is a crucial component of a functional organization. By delegating tasks and responsibilities, managers free themselves to focus on higher-level strategic decisions. However, delegation is not about giving up control; it's about empowering employees to take ownership of their tasks while ensuring they have the authority to make necessary decisions.

For delegation to succeed:

- Employees need clarity about their responsibilities, scope of their authority, and how their performance will be evaluated.

- Managers must avoid micromanaging, as this stifles creativity and damages employee morale.

- Leaders should focus on managing for results while providing support and guidance that empowers and retains their best employees.

Succession Planning and Employee Development

A functional structure supports succession planning by also identifying gaps in skills and knowledge. This enables you to create targeted development plans, ensuring the business remains sustainable during employee transitions. By focusing on roles rather than individuals, SMBs can cross-train multiple employees to fill critical positions, reducing dependency on one or a few key personnel. Succession planning also provides employees with clear advancement opportunities, improving retention and job satisfaction.

Building Team Strengths through Proper Alignment

Peter Drucker's insights provide a valuable framework for understanding how to build a successful team and structure. Drucker advises us that *"The task of leadership is to create an alignment of strengths so strong that it makes the system's weaknesses irrelevant."*[3]

Key Points from Drucker's Quote:

1. **Focus on Strengths**: Rather than trying to fix weaknesses, good leaders should concentrate on maximizing the potential of each individual's strengths.

2. **Alignment is Key**: The true power of a team comes from coordinating individual strengths, so they work cohesively towards a common goal.

3. **Irrelevance of Weaknesses**: When strengths are effectively aligned, weaknesses become less important and are mitigated by the collective strengths of the team.

By focusing on aligning strengths with business needs, SMB owners can build teams that perform at a high level despite any individual shortcomings. A functional organizational structure ensures that roles are defined by business needs, not personalities and that each employee knows exactly what is expected of them. By focusing on leveraging strengths and aligning them with the needs of the business, you can empower your team to unlock their full potential and contribute to the long-term success of your company.

Leveraging Employee Feedback for Functional Alignment

As you already know, the strength of any organization comes from its people. To effectively utilize your employee's strengths, it is essential to have open lines of communication with them and get their feedback on what factors help versus hinder them in fulfilling what is expected of them. SMB owners can benefit from a better understanding of employee experiences, job satisfaction, and how well the company's structure supports both personal and organizational goals.

An effective team is placing people in the right roles and creating an environment where individuals feel valued, supported, and aligned with overall organizational goals. By gathering employee feedback, we can also address gaps and better understand employee sentiments and perspectives. The Confidential Employee Survey found in the appendix provides a valuable tool for employers to get a better sense of employee sentiments. When administered properly, it gives employees a chance to express what's working, what could be improved, and address any critical gaps that need attention.

When we work with our clients, we conduct these interviews with key employees and ensure the confidentiality of individual responses while providing the employer with an aggregate summary of feedback and any relevant patterns and recurring themes uncovered. When employees trust that their responses are confidential, they are more likely to provide candid feedback, enabling them to address concerns and implement meaningful changes.

Sometimes, the results of the survey simply confirm what the owners already know. Other times, they may provide unexpected but needed insights into the organization's health and where improvements are needed. The purpose of conducting such a survey and obtaining feedback from employees is to develop action steps resulting in a more engaged, productive, and aligned workforce.

(See Appendix: Sample Confidential Employee Survey)

Confidential Survey Key Takeaways:

- **Identify Strengths and Areas for Improvement**: Understand what is working well and pinpoint areas that require attention.

- **Enhance Employee Engagement**: Demonstrate that you value employee input, which can boost morale and commitment.

- **Align Roles with Company Goals**: Ensure that employees feel their roles contribute meaningfully to the organization's mission, fostering a sense of purpose.

- **Develop Actionable Strategies**: Use the feedback to inform decisions that improve processes, policies, and workplace culture.

Implementing confidential employee surveys not only provides valuable insights but also builds trust within your organization. Employees who feel heard and valued are more likely to be engaged and aligned with the company's vision. However, failing to act on the survey's findings can be very damaging to morale. Employers must make good faith efforts to implement recommended improvements to avoid eroding trust and engagement.

The Critical Importance of People Decisions

In summary, as Peter Drucker wisely points out, *"Executives spend more time on managing people and making people decisions than on anything else—and they should. No other decisions are so long lasting in their consequences or so difficult to unmake..*[4] *Peter Drucker*

Key Takeaways for Chapter 11: Build the Right- Fit Team

1. **A Well-Structured Team Drives Business Success**

   A strong team aligned with the company's purpose, values, and goals is essential for long-term success. Clear organizational structures, defined roles, and functional alignment help ensure employees contribute effectively.

2. **SMBs Face Unique Growth Challenges**

   In smaller businesses, employees often wear multiple hats. As the company grows, overlapping responsibilities, lack of accountability, and miscommunication can hinder efficiency. Creating a structured organization reduces these challenges.

3. **Cross-Training Mitigates Business Disruptions**

   Relying too heavily on one person for critical tasks increases risk. Cross-training employees ensures business continuity, provides backup for key functions, and prevents single points of failure in the organization.

4. **Avoid Personality-Driven Structures**

   Roles should be defined by business needs rather than tailored around individual strengths or preferences. Structuring roles based on function rather than people ensures sustainability and scalability as the company grows.

5. **A Functional Structure Enhances Efficiency and Clarity**

   A functional organizational structure improves communication, clarifies responsibilities, and aligns employees with company objectives. Employees understand their roles, reducing confusion and enhancing performance.

6. **Delegation and Authority Empower Employees**

   Effective delegation allows managers to focus on strategic priorities while empowering employees to take ownership of tasks that are better handled by them. However, successful delegation requires clarity on responsibilities and authority.

7. **Succession Planning Strengthens Business Resilience**

   Identifying skill gaps and preparing employees for future leadership roles ensures business sustainability. Succession planning fosters growth opportunities for employees and reduces disruption when key personnel leave.

8. **Leveraging Strengths Maximize Team Performance**

   Aligning individual strengths with business needs, rather than focusing on weaknesses, improves productivity and morale. As Peter Drucker stated, "The task of leadership is to create an alignment of strengths so strong that it makes the system's weaknesses irrelevant."

9. **Employee Feedback Enhances Organizational Alignment**

   Confidential employee surveys provide insights into what's working and what needs improvement. Addressing feedback strengthens engagement, improves job satisfaction, and ensures employees feel heard and valued.

10. **Hiring and Structuring the Right-Fit Team Sets the Business Up for Scalable Growth**

By defining roles, setting expectations, and building a well-organized team, SMB owners can position their businesses for sustainable expansion and long-term success.

Reflection Questions for Chapter 11: Build the Right-Fit Team

1. **Organizational Clarity and Structure:**
   - o Does everyone on your team have a clear understanding of their roles and responsibilities?
   - o Are there areas of role overlap or confusion that need to be addressed?

2. **Cross-Training and Business Continuity:**
   - o Have you identified critical tasks that depend too heavily on one person?
   - o What steps can you take to cross-train employees and document key processes?

3. **Functional Structure vs. Personality-Driven Roles:**
   - o Are your positions defined based on business needs, or have they evolved around individual employees?
   - o If a key employee left tomorrow, would their role be easy to fill based on a documented job description?

4. **Delegation and Employee Empowerment:**
   - o Do your employees feel empowered to make decisions within their roles?
   - o Where are you holding on to tasks that could be effectively delegated?

5. **Succession Planning and Team Development:**
   - o Have you identified employees who have the potential to take on more responsibility?
   - o What skills gaps exist within your team, and how can you proactively develop employees to fill those gaps?

6. **Maximizing Strengths and Team Alignment:**

- o Are employees working in roles that align with their strengths?
- o How can you better match employee skills with business needs to maximize performance?

7. **Employee Feedback and Engagement:**
   - o How often do you gather employee feedback on their experience within the organization?
   - o How do you ensure that feedback leads to meaningful changes rather than going ignored?

8. **Ensuring a Scalable Team Structure:**
   - o Is your current team structure sustainable as your business grows?
   - o What adjustments need to be made to scale your team effectively?

9. **What stood out or resonated with you the most in this chapter?**
   - o Was there a concept, framework, or example that felt particularly relevant to your business?

10. **What's one thing you will implement based on what you've learned?**
    - o What specific action will you take in the next week or month to improve your team's structure, delegation, or alignment?

CHAPTER 12

LET GO OF MISFIT EMPLOYEES

*"Failure isn't hiring the wrong
employees—it's keeping them."*
— *Steven Kim, Founder and Principal,
Purpose Matters*

Weeding out Misfit Employees

We've reframed firing or letting go employees as "weeding out" misfit employees as a more constructive mindset when making decisions that can change an employee's status in your company. Firing or rather weeding out misfit employees is one of the toughest and most critical tasks for any business owner.

We all know that misfit employees, those whose skills, attitudes, or values don't align with the needs of their role or the organization, can negatively impact team morale, productivity, and business performance.

Yet, the challenge for many business owners and their managers arises not from identifying these misfits but rather from their inability to act decisively and promptly to address the issues the misfit employees are causing. Delaying action typically worsens the situation over time.

Why Misfit Employees Persist

One of the primary reasons business owners struggle to address misfit employees is the lack of clear performance expectations and standards. When performance standards are not explicitly defined—whether for the first 60, 90, or 365 days—it becomes challenging to course-correct, leading to poor performance lingering far longer than it should.

However, when we work with clients to clarify their standards and help them think through challenging employee situations, they often realize they should have let the misfit employee go months, perhaps even years ago, especially when considering the overall good of their business. Fortunately, when they take the required actions, the relief from finally taking measures for the well-being of all parties concerned is greater than the regret that they should have done it sooner. Another significant factor is the mental strain involved in making tough personnel decisions. Firing an employee remains among the most difficult and emotionally taxing tasks for any manager or business owner.

As Peter Drucker wisely counsels us:

"There are no more important decisions within an organization than people decisions: staffing a job, placing people into jobs and assignments, promoting people, letting them go, and so on. No matter how carefully organizations hire people, they won't perform if put into jobs that are the wrong ones for them. No matter how brilliant and clever top management decisions are regarding a company's business, its strategy, its products or services, they will not produce results if the company's people decisions do not work out."[1]

In addition, conducting effective personnel evaluations can be a cognitively demanding process that requires thoughtful consideration and effort. Too often, managers focus on surface-level frustrations—such as *"Why is this employee so lazy, so difficult, or such a pain to work with?"* rather than addressing the deeper issues that could guide effective solutions. Clear, intentional thinking and asking the right questions about roles, expectations, and alignment are essential to overcoming these challenges and creating a more productive team.

As Henry Ford famously said, *"Thinking is hard work. That may be the reason so few engage in it."*[2] Similarly, Peter Drucker pointed out, *"The most serious mistakes are not being made as a result of wrong answers. The truly dangerous thing is asking the wrong questions."* [3]

Key Questions to Ask

To effectively weed out misfit employees and also make better use of your current employees, you need to start with the right questions:

1. **What matters?** What are the desired performance outcomes (DPOs) for this role?

2. **How do we define success?** What key metrics and measures will determine if those outcomes are achieved?

3. **What are the priorities?** Which performance areas or metrics carry the most weight?

4. **How do we evaluate?** What framework will we use to assess and compare performance fairly and objectively?

Establishing Minimally Acceptable Standards

In our experience working with clients, one of the ways that owners and managers can clarify performance standards is to establish a range of values from a baseline of what is minimally acceptable/tolerable to acceptable, good, and ideal excellent. Additionally, employers need a plan, such as a performance improvement plan, to address employees whose performance falls below minimally acceptable standards. Employers need a clearly defined threshold—a "line in the sand," so to speak—to determine when corrective actions are necessary and if the required improvement is not achieved when it is time to let misfit employees go.

The 7P BAM Employee Evaluation Frameworks

Learning to ask the right questions is key to making confident, informed decisions about employee performance. The evaluation tools within the 7P Business Alignment Model™ (BAM) are designed to help you do just that by giving you a structured way to assess, clarify, and take action on personnel matters when needed.

This chapter introduces two powerful frameworks that help business owners and managers move beyond vague impressions and empower you to take more decisive actions, whether that means making better use of your team's strengths or letting go of employees who no longer fit.

The Frameworks:

1. **Performance Evaluation Framework (PEF)** Aligns employee performance with defined objectives and behaviors. (see Appendix for completed PEF sample)

2. **A-B-C Player Evaluation Framework** – Helps you categorize team members based on contribution, alignment, and growth potential.

By applying these tools, you'll be able to:

- Define and communicate clear performance standards
- Set measurable, role-specific expectations
- Identify opportunities for development, reassignment, or exit
- Build a more aligned, high-performing team over time

These frameworks aren't just about evaluation—they're about making clearer decisions with less second-guessing. They help you see who's contributing, who's coasting, and who may be holding the team back. With that clarity, you can invest more intentionally in your right-fit employees and address misalignment before it turns into frustration, disengagement, or wasted efforts.

The following gives you a partial view of the Performance Evaluation Framework (PEF). The full version is in the Appendix. Each PEF can be customized for each of your company's key roles.

Key Components of the PEF:

1. **Overall Desired Performance Outcome (DPO):**

   A clear summary of each role's expected results and contributions aligned with organizational goals.

2. **Performance Rating Scale:**

   A 1-10 rating system for evaluating employee performance. This scale provides a standardized method to assess employees objectively and consistently.

3. **Performance Criteria:**

   Key performance areas—or "slices" of the performance pie—specific to each role. These slices can be weighted based on their importance and the percentage of time spent on each slice, ensuring evaluations are tailored to the unique responsibilities DPO's of each position.

4. **Goal Setting with OKRs:**

    Use Objectives and Key Results (OKRs) to set measurable and impactful goals. Each role should have clearly defined objectives, with 1-3 key results tied to each objective. This approach ensures alignment with organizational priorities and provides measurable benchmarks for performance.

5. **Baseline and Differentiating Traits and Competencies Ratings:**

    Evaluate employees on both **baseline competencies** (essential traits required for the role) and **differentiating competencies** (traits that distinguish top performers). Incorporate the People, Data, Things framework (PDT Ratings) as needed to further assess an employee's strengths and alignment with role expectations.

6. **Performance Improvement Plan and Employee Development:** For employees whose performance falls below acceptable standards, the PEF provides a space in comments below each performance slice to describe a Performance Improvement Plan (PIP). This structured plan outlines clear expectations, timelines, and actionable steps for improvement. Additionally, the PEF supports employee development by identifying opportunities for growth and offering tailored coaching and training programs.

7. **Overall Assessment:**

    The PEF can also be utilized to consolidate performance ratings, traits and competencies evaluations, and OKRs into a comprehensive overall assessment. This provides a holistic view of an employee's performance and contributions, serving as a basis for decisions regarding promotions, role adjustments, compensation, or transitions out of the role.

Why the PEF Works

The PEF clarifies expectations and facilitates objective evaluations, helping to identify areas where misfit employees fall short and where right-fit employees can improve further. The framework promotes transparency and fairness in evaluations by setting measurable standards with weighted performance criteria.

Incorporating OKRs, traits and competencies ratings, and structured improvement plans provides managers with actionable insights and tools to address under performance and encourage employee development. At the end of the evaluation, the overall rating assessment gives employers a better understanding of each employee's total contributions.

Here's an example for a **Desired Performance Outcome DPO** for one of our Talent Acquisition Specialists:

Employee Name-Title/Dept	Bart Adams	Talent Acquisition Partner/Recruiting
Position Summary in terms of Desired Performance Outcome (DPO)	PRODUCT/SERVICE: Help our clients hire more of the "right fit, A- player" employees by attracting and sourcing a higher quality pool of candidates for our clients to interview and choose from. Deliver this service faster and more cost-effectively than they can on their own, resulting in better hiring decisions and better hires over time. Help owners create a winning team of positive contributors to enable them to achieve their most important goals and profitably grow their company.	

Performance Rating Scale

This tool provides a framework for both the manager and direct report to evaluate performance along with a means to document feedback about employee performance during the review process. Performance for various criteria and metrics can be rated from 1 to 10 using the following performance level descriptions. It also provides recommendations for development and performance improvement for each rating along with additional space for comments:

Example: An employee who consistently exceeds sales targets, improves processes, and mentors peers might receive a rating of 9, highlighting their exceptional contributions and leadership within the team.

RATING	PERFORMANCE	Description / Action Required
9-10	Excellent	Track record of performing at a high level over time, resulting in a significantly positive impact—should mentor and serve as a model worth emulating. (10 rating given after consistent performance over time that redefines your standards of excellence)
7-8	Good to Very Good	Performs well, meets, and at times exceeds the expectations of an employee in this position, making a valuable contribution, is capable of more responsibility, needs little or no supervision, and should have new opportunities.
5-6	Needs Improvement	Performance less than that of a fully proficient employee in this position; needs improvement along with guidance and support (acceptable if still in training)
3-4	Poor	Performance is inconsistent and results in insufficient contribution: Immediate and substantial improvement necessary or face dismissal.
1-2	Very Poor	Under-performing over an extended period and having a negative impact on the organization—should have been "weeded" out a long time ago (Management should be held accountable)

Performance Evaluation Framework

The Performance Evaluation Framework helps us document and define the 5-7 key slices that comprise the DPO -Desired Performance Outcome pie for a specific position or role. These slices represent the major areas of responsibility and contribution to the role.

For each slice:

- Approximate the time spent on that area as a percentage.
- Assign a weight/importance as a percentage, ensuring the total adds up to 100%.

Each slice can be seen as the major **"tree branches"** of the role, while the **OKRs (Objectives and Key Results)** can be visualized as the **"fruits" of the branches**, representing the tangible outcomes of the role's efforts.

OKRs (Objectives and Key Results)

OKRs provide a **goal-setting framework** to help employees and managers focus on what matters most.

O – Objectives:

Objectives represent the **overall outcomes** you aim to achieve. To maintain focus and clarity, each role should have no more than 2-4 objectives.

KR – Key Results:

Key Results describe the **specific, measurable outcomes** needed to achieve each objective. Each objective should ideally have 1-3 key results.

Key Results can take two forms:

1. **Quantitative Goals:** Measurable outcomes expressed as a range or target (e.g., X to Y).
2. **Milestone Goals:** Tasks or projects to be completed that may not have specific numeric KPIs but can still be assessed for completion.

Key Terms

- **KPIs (Key Performance Indicators):**

  Relevant metrics that help measure the success of a Key Result (e.g., profit margin percentage, customer retention rate).

- **Milestone Goals:**

  Goals that may not have direct numeric measures but are assessed based on whether they are completed e.g., implement a new marketing email campaign.

OKR Examples

1. **Financial Objective:** Increase Sales

   o **Key Result 1:** Increase annual sales by 18% from last year's level.

   o *KPI: Sales*

2. **Financial Objective:** Improve profitability.

   o **Key Result 1:** Increase gross margin percentage from 27% to 30%.

   o *KPI: Gross Profit %.*

3. **Health Objective:** Get in shape fast.

   o **Key Result 1:** Reduce body fat percentage from 25% to 21%.

   o *KPI: Body Fat %.*

   o **Key Result 2:** Improve flexibility

   o *Milestone Goal: Attend a weekly yoga class.*

Personalizing the Framework

Comments Section:

Utilize the comments section to document:

   o Observations about performance gaps.

   o Recommendations for improvement.

   o Highlight progress toward achieving objectives and key results.

PEF Traits and Competencies

The PEF can also evaluate employees based on how well they exhibit and perform both **baseline** and **differentiating** traits/competencies:

- o **Baseline Competencies:** Essential traits required for effective job performance.

- o **Differentiating Competencies:** Advanced skills and behaviors that distinguish top performers.

Each competency is assessed through observable behaviors and specific examples, ensuring objective evaluation and targeted development.

PEF Employee Development (Self and Manager Assessment 1-10 Ratings)

The Performance Evaluation Framework (PEF) encourages a two-way dialogue between employees and managers: This framework equips managers and employees to go beyond just evaluating performance—it provides space for constructive feedback and professional growth.

- o **Self-Assessment Ratings:** Employees reflect on their strengths, areas for improvement, training needs, and career aspirations.

- o **Manager Assessment Ratings:** Managers provide insights into the employee's performance, suggest development opportunities, and discuss potential career progression.

This collaborative approach fosters greater self-awareness, engagement, and personalized career growth and development.

PEF Overall Performance Rating

The framework consolidates assessments from all sections to provide a holistic performance score, considering both results (**what**) and behaviors (**how**). This comprehensive rating informs decisions regarding promotions, compensation, and development initiatives.

Example: An employee demonstrating strong results and exemplary competencies across all areas might receive an overall rating of **8**, indicating very good performance with potential for further advancement.

Acknowledgment and Continuous Improvement

The evaluation process concludes with an acknowledgment section, where both manager and employee sign off, confirming mutual understanding and agreement regarding both evaluation of current and expected performance outcomes.

Benefits of the Framework

- **Clarity and Transparency:** Defined criteria and expectations ensure that employees understand how their performance is measured and what is required for success.

- **Alignment with Organizational Goals:** The framework ensures that individual goals are in sync with broader company objectives.

- **Improved Communication:** Regular, structured feedback can create opportunities for open dialogue between managers and employees, leading to improved relationships and workplace morale.

- **Targeted Development:** Identifying specific strengths and weaknesses allows for personalized development plans, aiding in employee growth and retention.

- **Objective Evaluation:** Utilizing standardized metrics and observable behaviors reduces bias and promotes fairness in performance assessments. The framework allows the individual and their manager to provide ratings for each component and compare answers.

- **Documenting performance evaluations:** Helps SMBs mitigate HR risks by creating a clear, objective record of employee performance, expectations, and actions to address deficiencies.

- This documentation provides evidence to support decisions related to promotions, compensation, or terminations, reducing the risk of wrongful termination claims or disputes. It also demonstrates compliance with legal and regulatory requirements, fostering transparency and fairness in HR practices.

PEF Implementation Best Practices

- **Standardize Criteria:** Use clear, consistent criteria across all evaluations. By focusing on measurable outcomes, specific examples of behavior, and their corresponding results, you minimize bias and establish a uniform standard for evaluating performance.

- **Engage Employees Early and Often:** To foster ownership and engagement, involve employees in setting their objectives and understanding the evaluation criteria.

- **Provide Ongoing Feedback:** Regular check-ins and updates ensure continuous performance discussions rather than confined to annual reviews.

- **Train Managers Effectively:** Equip managers with the necessary skills and tools to conduct evaluations thoughtfully and constructively.

- **Leverage Data:** Use collected performance data to inform broader organizational strategies and identify trends or areas needing attention.

- **Perform an organizational audit:** Using your organizational chart, rate each employee based on their overall PEF rating and A-B-C assessment introduced in the next section.

The A-B-C Performance Employee Evaluation Framework

In addition to the Performance Evaluation Framework (PEF), the A-B-C Player Evaluation Framework offers a practical and straightforward method for assessing your team. This "quick and dirty" approach provides a more generalized employee performance evaluation. By combining both frameworks, owners and managers can make better-informed personnel decisions, effectively identify under performers, and remove misfit employees sooner rather than later. This ensures your team is composed of contributors who drive performance, not hinder it.

Customizing the A-B-C Framework

The following A-B-C player criteria provide examples of what can be used but you can certainly customize to fit your company's unique culture and standards. Use past and current employees as reference points to define what "A," "B," and "C" players look like in your organization. Visualizing an employee who exemplifies the "A" player rating in each role helps calibrate your ratings for "B" and "C" players.

It's also important to recognize that, in most organizations, approximately 10-15% of employees are A players, another 10-15% are C players, and the majority—about 70-80%—are B players.

The Impact of Letting Go of C Players

Many business owners procrastinate over letting go of or "weeding out" a C player. But when performance standards are clearly defined, it becomes much easier to take action—action that may have been necessary months or even years earlier. Removing misfits often boosts morale within the organization because it reinforces a sense of accountability and fairness.

The remaining employees will notice that leadership enforces standards for the benefit of the team and the company. Conversely, allowing under performers to stay not only damages morale but also causes employees to lose respect for management, as they see that poor performance is tolerated.

With a clear standard of expected performance, including what is minimally acceptable, you can confidently act in the organization's best interest.

The A-B-C Player Characteristics

A Players ☺

High performers who exceed expectations, drive growth, and elevate team dynamics.

Characteristics:

- **Dependability:** Consistently deliver exceptional results with minimal supervision while meeting or exceeding deadlines.

- **Role Model:** Set the standard for others through their performance, attitude, and work ethic; can actively mentor others and attract other high performers to the organization.

- **Adaptability:** Excel in adjusting to new challenges, roles, or tasks without requiring extensive guidance.

- **Problem-solving:** Identify and address challenges proactively, offering creative and effective solutions with minimal support.

- **Team Collaboration:** Actively lead and inspire others, fostering a culture of trust, positivity, and shared success.

- **Initiative:** Consistently generate and implement forward-thinking ideas, driving continuous improvement and innovation across the organization.

How to Manage A Players:

- **Retain and Reward:** Expand their roles, ensure they are paid well, offer performance-based bonuses, and provide opportunities for growth to retain them.

- **Challenge and Develop:** Engage them with new responsibilities and challenges to maintain motivation and career growth.

B Players 😊

Reliable contributors who meet expectations and demonstrate potential for growth.

Characteristics:

- **Dependability:** Deliver consistent results with occasional guidance or supervision needed; dependable team members who maintain steady performance.

- **Competent Model:** Perform well within their scope but lack the exceptional qualities to serve as the role model for others.

- **Adaptability:** Show a willingness to grow but require additional support when faced with new or unexpected challenges.

- **Problem-Solving:** Make an effort to resolve issues but may require assistance to reach optimal solutions or avoid delays.

- **Team Collaboration:** Work effectively with others but tend to follow rather than lead; contribute to team success without being central drivers.
- **Initiative:** Occasionally propose ideas or solutions, showing glimpses of creativity and a willingness to improve.

How to Manage B Players:

- **Support and Coach:** Invest in mentoring, training, and targeted feedback to help them reach their potential and possibly develop into an A player.
- **Retain and Develop:** Value them as reliable team members, even if they do not evolve into A players, as they provide organizational stability and consistency.

C Players ☹

Under performers who struggle to meet expectations may hinder team success.

Characteristics:

- **Dependability:** Frequently fail to meet deadlines or deliver quality work without extensive supervision.
- **Mismatched Role:** Often placed in roles unsuited to their skills or interests, leading to repeated under performance.
- **Adaptability:** Struggle to adapt to new challenges or responsibilities, even with detailed instructions.
- **Problem-Solving:** Avoid taking ownership of issues, often escalating problems or leaving tasks incomplete.
- **Team Collaboration:** Poor communication, a lack of contribution, or negative attitudes can create friction within teams.
- **Initiative:** Rarely show initiative or bring new ideas, operating reactively rather than proactively.

How to Manage C Players:

- **Performance Improvement Plan (PIP):** Communicate performance expectations and provide a timeline for improvement through a performance improvement plan

- **Transition Out:** If no progress is made, swiftly transition them out of the organization or if possible reassessing them to another role that makes better use of their strengths, provided there are not attitude or culture misalignment. Prolonging their stay can undermine team morale and productivity.

Holistic Evaluation for the Entire Organization:

We've found that conducting performance evaluations for the entire organization at the same time each year (during a less busy period of the year) allows you to better assess and evaluate each employee's contribution slice and overall impact relative to the whole performance pie of your organization.

By doing so, you have the context of the entire organization to compare against each employee's contribution, which also informs their pay and total compensation. By taking this holistic approach, you are more likely to produce a fairer evaluation for each employee and, subsequently, the respective compensation based on their contribution as part of the whole. Alternatively, if this is not possible, conducting performance evaluations on the employee anniversary date can also work and is far better than not conducting them at all.

Smile or Frown Test:

One simple yet powerful question we often ask our clients to consider is: *"When you think about [employee's name], on balance, does he/she make you smile or frown? And why?"*

While the Smile or Frown Test provides a quick, overall intuitive assessment of an employee's impact, it works best when combined with objective performance metrics from the PEF and ABC framework to ensure decisions are both fair and actionable.

Key Takeaways: Evaluate to Elevate a High Performing Team

As you implement these frameworks, remember that the goal isn't just to evaluate—it's to elevate your team's performance. Use it to identify strengths, address areas for improvement, and set the stage for continuous growth. Breaking down roles into clear, measurable performance criteria and fostering open dialogue ensures everyone knows where they stand, where they need to grow, and any gaps that need to be addressed.

Remember, the goal is to have team members who are "rowing in sync" with others to contribute to the team's cohesion and effectiveness. By focusing on both what your employees achieve and how they achieve it, you'll build a culture of accountability, development, and excellence. By aligning individual roles and objectives with the organization's overall objectives, every team member can play a vital role in collectively rowing the boat, so it moves harmoniously toward its ultimate goal.

Key Takeaways: Chapter 12 Let Go of Misfit Employees

1. **Reframe Firing as Weeding Out Misfit Employees**:

   Misfit employees—those whose skills, attitudes, or values don't align with their roles or the organization—negatively impact team morale and business performance. Addressing these misfits promptly improves organizational health and team morale.

2. **Why Misfits Persist**:

   Misfits often remain due to unclear performance standards, emotional difficulty on the part of the owner when making personnel decisions, and a lack of structured evaluations. Delayed action typically only worsen their impact.

3. **Clear Performance Expectations are Crucial**:

   Establish minimally acceptable standards and use structured tools like performance improvement plans (PIPs) to guide decisions. Clarity reduces ambiguity and fosters decisive action.

4. **Key Frameworks for Evaluation**:

   o **Performance Evaluation Framework (PEF)**: Defines roles, performance expectations, and measurable goals. Includes metrics like OKRs (Objectives and Key Results), performance rating scales, and competency assessments.

o **A-B-C Player Framework**: Classifies employees into A (top performers), B (reliable contributors), and C (under performers), and provides management recommendations for each category.

5. **Prioritize Holistic Evaluations**:

Conduct organization-wide evaluations at the same time to assess individual contributions relative to the whole company while also better aligning performance with compensation.

6. **Proactive Employee Management**:

Invest in A players through challenges and rewards, develop B players through mentoring, and promptly address or transition out C players. Clear communication and perceived fair evaluations are essential for team success.

7. **Decision Support Tools**:

Tools like the Smile or Frown Test, combined with objective frameworks like the PEF offer both intuitive and data-driven approaches for evaluating employees.

Reflection Questions Chapter 12: Let Go of Misfit Employees

1. **Performance Standards**:

Are performance expectations for each role clearly defined and communicated? How can they be improved to minimize ambiguity and support employee success?

2. **Evaluation Frameworks**:

Are you utilizing structured evaluation tools like the PEF or A-B-C Player Framework? What additional steps can you take to ensure evaluations are objective and actionable?

3. **Acting Decisively**:

Are there any misfit employees whose impact you've delayed addressing? What actions can you take now to align your team with organizational goals?

4. **Holistic Assessments**:

Do your evaluation processes account for the overall contribution of each employee to the organization? How can you ensure fairness in performance reviews and compensation decisions?

Employee Development:

How are you investing in your A players to keep them engaged and motivated? What coaching or mentoring opportunities can you provide to help B players reach their potential?

5. **Alignment with Values:**

   Does your current approach to employee evaluation and management align with your company's mission and values? What adjustments can you make to reinforce alignment?

6. **Continuous Improvement:**

   How can you create a culture of regular, constructive feedback to support ongoing employee growth and team success?

7. **What stood out or resonated with you the most in this chapter**

8. **What's one thing you will implement based on what you've learned?**

PIPELINE—SERVING THE RIGHT CUSTOMERS ON PURPOSE

CHAPTER 13

IDENTIFY THE RIGHT FIT CUSTOMER

"You never really understand a person until you consider their point of view"[1]
—Harper Lee

Defining Your Customers

What is the definition of a customer? Is it everyone who visits your website or enters your store? Do you count them as customers only when they purchase your product or service? Figuring out who your customer is might be trickier than it sounds. Many businesses define their customers as the people or organizations that bring in revenue for a product or service. Some businesses target their marketing to key influencers, not end users per se, but those who impact final buying decisions.

For example, a pharmaceutical company may target prescribing doctors instead of patients, and a golf course equipment company may promote its product to golf course designers rather than golf course owners. Other businesses, like non-profit organizations, may provide their products or services for free to their end-user customers but must consider their donors and benefactors as customers as well. Suddenly, the question "Who is your customer?" becomes more complicated.

The Importance of Identifying the Right Customer

Defining who your customers are and ensuring that your business is positioned correctly to serve them can be one of the most essential parts of making your business successful. Choosing a suitable customer base can include not just choosing who you want to do business with but also who you should not serve. Spending too much effort on the wrong customer can waste time and resources. This is why creating a Right Fit Customer Profile (RFCP) for your business is crucial. The RFCP will help you understand in depth the people and organizations you can serve best and where you can make the highest impact with your product offering.

A Right Fit Customer Profile is a great tool to help you understand and reach your best customers and ensure your customer base is properly aligned with your purpose. Think about the typical luxury car driver. Imagine what they look like. What brands do they buy? Where do they live? How much do they earn? What are their hobbies? Now imagine trying to sell an economy car or a work truck to someone who normally buys a luxury car. No marketing campaign could effectively reach this customer. It would be irresponsible to even try. An economy vehicle would not typically meet the needs or satisfy the pain points of someone who is used to the features of a luxury car.

Even if you were to make a few sales, you would probably have high product returns or customer service issues and lower customer retention rates. In short, this campaign would be a waste of time and resources. Identifying and targeting the "right customer" and ensuring that your product and messaging resonate with their needs is crucial to making your marketing effective and profitable.

We're not saying you shouldn't sell to a broad range of customers. However, we suggest that understanding who your ideal customer is and ensuring they align with your purpose can make your marketing campaigns more effective.

A deeper bond with your brand can also improve customer retention rates and streamline your sales process. Emotional branding is crucial for creating strong connections with customers, encouraging them to feel a deeper bond with your brand.[2] By identifying your right-fit customers and marketing to meet their needs, you can achieve better sales outcomes, keep your customers happy, and make the most of your marketing budget.

Creating Your RFCP (Right Fit Customer Profile)

To create an effective RFCP, start by looking at your current customers. Who are your top buyers? Go through your existing database and look at which individuals and companies have been with you the longest and/or which ones have given you stellar reviews. Regardless of how they initially became your customer, these customers are the most loyal and more likely to believe in and support your mission and vision.

Now, carefully review this list of top customers to find out what they have in common. For example, are they larger or smaller companies? Public or private? Are they located in specific areas? Pay attention to what they share in demographics and psychographics because this will help you better understand the types of customers your business attracts and serves well. Use the following framework to help you develop your company's RFCP.

Right Fit Customer Profile Framework

- **Profile Name:** [Baby Boomer, Luxury Buyer, SMB Owner, etc.]
- **Demographics:**
    o   Age: [25-34, 35-44, 45-54, 55-64, 65+]

    o   Gender: [Male, Female,]

    o   Income: [$75,000-$99,999, $100,000-$124,999, $125,000-$149,999, $150,000-$199,999, $200,000+]

    o   Education: [High School Graduate, Some College, Bachelor's Degree, Master's Degree, Doctorate]

    o   Occupation: [Entry-Level, Mid-Level Professional, Senior-Level Executive, Business Owner, Retired]

- **Psychographics:**
    o   Interests: [Hobbies, activities, and areas of interest such as sports, reading, travel]

    o   Values: [Core beliefs such as sustainability, community involvement, innovation]

    o   Lifestyle: [Living habits and daily routines such as health-conscious, tech-savvy, frequent traveler]

- o Buying Behavior: [Shopping patterns like online shopper, bargain hunter, brand loyalist]
- **Primary Needs and Pain Points (what keeps them up at night):**
  - o [Identify the key challenges and problems that this customer faces which your product/service can help solve.]
- **Preferred Solutions:**
  - o [Describe what solutions this customer is looking for. This can include specific features, benefits, or types of services/products they prioritize to address their needs and pain points.]
- **Communication Preferences:** [Email, Phone, In-person meetings, social media, Video calls, Text messaging]

TABLE 1: Purpose Matters Right-Fit Customer Profile (RFCP)

Category	Details
Company Size	15-80 employees (with potential for 10-100)
Annual Revenue	$2M-$25M
Industries	Manufacturing, Construction, Professional and Technical Services, Contract trades, Transportation, Logistics, Wholesale/Distribution, Skilled Trades, Specialized Business Services
Geography	Greater Los Angeles Region, Orange County, San Bernardino & Riverside Counties.
Age	40+
Gender	Predominantly Male, but open to female business owners and executives
Annual Income	$200k-$1M+
Education	BA/BS, MBA, or equivalent business experience

Values & Beliefs

Category	Details
Core Values	G.O.E.S. – Growth-Oriented, Open to Learning, Economically Viable, Strategic Thinkers
Business Philosophy	Purpose-driven leadership with a focus on long-term success over short-term gains

Employee & Culture Focus	Believes in building strong teams, prioritizing culture, and investing in their employees
Approach to Growth	Values expert guidance and operational clarity to drive sustainable business growth

Interests & Hobbies

Category	Details
Reading	Business, leadership, and personal development books
Networking	Attending industry-specific conferences, mastermind groups, and networking events
Strategic Forums	Engaging in strategic business forums like Vistage, YPO, and EO
Professional Growth	Actively seeking best practices for better business and talent management, operations, marketing and process improvement.

Lifestyle

Category	Details
Work-Life Balance	Balancing work and personal fulfillment but often feeling overwhelmed with daily operations.
Business Focus	Open to innovative business frameworks that allow them to focus on higher-level strategy and free up more time
Priorities	Prioritize efficiency, profitability, and work-life balance

Job Titles

Title
Principal
Owner
President
CEO
Managing Partner
Founder
COO (in growth-stage companies)

Background

Category	Details
Entrepreneurial Mindset	Has built their business through hard work and persistence
Experience	Firsthand experience with business challenges like hiring, retention, customer acquisition, and scaling
Creativity & Problem-Solving	Highly creative problem solver who looks for ways to innovate and stay ahead of the competition

Risk & Strategy	Willing to take calculated risks but values structured guidance to refine operations and reduce inefficiencies

Customers' Goals

Category	Details
Business Strategy	Align business strategy, employees, and processes with a clear purpose to drive profitability
Labor Optimization	Lower labor costs while improving employee engagement and productivity
Self-Sustaining Model	Create a business model that doesn't require their constant hands-on involvement
Customer Focus	Optimize customer acquisition and retention strategies to attract right-fit clients
Operational Efficiency	Reduce inefficiencies and scale with clarity

Pain Points (The pain-gap matters enough that they are looking for solutions)

Category Examples	Details
Workforce Challenges	Employee turnover and hiring challenges
Labor Costs	Rising labor costs and inefficiencies in workforce productivity
Work-Life Balance	Feeling overwhelmed and constantly stressed resulting in burn-out
Operational Bottlenecks	Unclear priorities and processes creating inefficiencies and higher costs
Customer Alignment	Struggling to attract and retain enough of the right-fit customers to drive sustainable and long term growth.

Where to Reach Them

Category	Details
Trusted Advisors	CPA firms, fractional CFOs, business coaches, insurance brokers, legal advisors
Business Networks	Vistage, YPO, EO, industry-specific roundtables
Industry Events	Construction, IT, Professional Services, Skilled Trades Conferences & Trade Associations
Marketing Channels	Selective LinkedIn & Email Marketing—High-value insights (not generic social media outreach)
Referrals	Highly value trusted recommendations from peers

Suggested Keywords
Business alignment consulting
Reduce employee turnover

Hiring & retention best practices
Increase profitability through better people alignment
Small business leadership
Right-fit employee hiring
Operational efficiency & process improvement

Suggested Messaging

"Are you spending too much time putting out fires instead of focusing on real growth?"
"What if you could attract and retain employees who truly align with your vision?"
"Scaling a business doesn't have to mean more stress. Learn how to align your team for sustainable success."
"Struggling with high turnover? The cost of keeping the wrong employees is higher than hiring the right ones."
"Is your business working in harmony, or are misaligned priorities slowing your growth?"
"Your purpose should drive your profit—let's make sure your business is aligned for both."

Identify Key Traits: Alignment of Core Values and Core Competencies with your Right Fit Customer Profile

Trait 1: Alignment with Core Values

- **Description:** Customers who share and resonate with our company's core values.
- **Indicators:** Positive feedback on our company's mission, values, and long-term partnership interests.

Trait 2: Alignment with Core Competencies

- **Description:** Customers who benefit from and value our company's core competencies.
- **Indicators:** Positive feedback on our company's mission, core values and competencies.

Trait 3: Profitability

- **Description:** Customers who contribute positively to our bottom line.
- **Indicators:** High lifetime value (LTV), healthy, sustainable profit margins.

Trait 4: Growth Potential

- **Description:** Customers who show potential for future growth and expansion.

- **Indicators:** Increasing order sizes, expansion into new markets, or product lines.

Trait 5: Low Maintenance

- **Description:** Customers who require minimal support and resources.

- **Indicators:** Few support tickets, low return rates, positive and constructive feedback.

Trait 6: Advocacy

- **Description:** Customers who are likely to promote our products/services.

- **Indicators:** High Net Promoter Score (NPS), and customer referrals.

Checking Your RFCP Against Your Core Purpose

Once you've completed your Right Fit Customer Profile (RFCP), take the time to compare it with your company's core purpose, which consists of one's mission, vision, core values, and core competencies. Ask yourself:

- Are they well-aligned?

- What specific reasons might explain why these customers are attracted to your business?

Customers often remain loyal for intangible reasons not easily measurable or explicitly defined. In industries with abundant choices, loyalty often stems from shared values, or the positive emotions customers experience when interacting with your brand.[2] Understanding these factors can help you craft the right messaging to attract new customers and deepen connections with existing ones who share similar values.

Identifying Potential Misalignments

If you sense a disconnect between your RFCP and your core values or competencies, this may indicate missing information or misperceptions. Consider:

- Are there aspects of your business that customers value but you haven't formally acknowledged? For example, stellar customer service agents may embody your mission in ways that aren't reflected in your official statements or documents.

- Do customers see your company differently than you do? Their perspectives might highlight overlooked strengths or inconsistencies in how your brand is perceived versus how it's presented.

You can often address these misalignments by engaging your customers:

- Discuss why they chose your business

- What do they value most about your products, services, or interactions.

- What might their answers reveal in terms of insights you've taken for granted or were unaware of.

The Importance of Alignment

Ensuring alignment between your RFCP and your company's purpose is critical for creating effective marketing strategies and building long-term relationships. Without this alignment, you risk developing strategies or messages that fail to resonate with your ideal customers.

By regularly assessing how your RFCP aligns with your mission and values, you can ensure that every aspect of your business— from product offerings to customer communication—is in sync with what matters most to your audience. This alignment fosters stronger customer loyalty, attracts like-minded individuals and organizations, and positions your business for sustainable growth.

Finding More Customers Using the RFCP

Once you are comfortable that your RFCP aligns with your business's purpose, you're ready to attract more of these right-fit customers. In the next chapter, we'll discuss how to do this. Remember, finding and understanding your right fit customer isn't just about making more sales. It's about building a community of people who believe in what you do and are happy to support you.

Key Takeaways Chapter 13: Identify the Right Fit Customer

1. **Clearly Define Your Customer**

   Understanding who your customers are is foundational to aligning your pipeline with your purpose. Your customers may include direct buyers, influencers, or beneficiaries, depending on your business model. A clear and nuanced definition ensures your resources are focused on those who truly drive value for your organization.

2. **The Importance of a Right Fit Customer Profile (RFCP)**

   Creating a Right-Fit Customer Profile helps you identify the customers who most closely align with your core values and competencies and who benefit most from your offerings. By focusing on these customers, you improve the effectiveness of your marketing, sales, and customer retention efforts while avoiding the waste associated with targeting misaligned prospects.

3. **Avoiding Misalignment**

   A misalignment between your RFCP and your mission, core values and core competencies can lead to wasted resources, ineffective strategies, and dissatisfied customers. Regularly validate your understanding of your RFCP against your core values, competencies, and purpose to ensure consistency and coherence.

4. **Identifying Key Traits of Ideal Customers**

   An effective RFCP also includes key traits such as profitability, growth potential, low maintenance, and advocacy. Customers with these traits not only contribute positively to your bottom line but also support long-term business growth.

5. **Building a Community Around Shared Values**

   Finding your ideal customers goes beyond just increasing sales; it's about building a community of loyal advocates who believe in your purpose and are aligned with your core values and competencies. These customer advocates not only drive revenue but also serve as brand ambassadors who are essential to your community-building efforts and growth.

Reflection Questions: Chapter 13: Identify the Right Fit Customer

1. **Who are your most loyal and profitable customers, and what common traits do they share?**

   o Reflect on your top customers and analyze their demographics, psychographics, and behaviors to understand what makes them the "right fit" for your business.

2. **How well does your current customer base align with your company's mission, core values, and core competencies?**

   o Consider whether your existing customers resonate with and support your business' purpose and long-term goals.

3. **Are there customers that do not align with your RFCP?**

   o Identify customers who may drain resources, fail to benefit from your offerings, or conflict with your values and focus.

4. **What specific pain points or needs do your right-fit customers have that your products or services solve effectively?**

   o Reflect on how your offerings address your ideal customers' challenges and whether your solutions create value that aligns with their expectations.

FOCUS ON WHAT MATTERS

5. **How can you refine your messaging and marketing strategies to attract more customers who align with your RFCP?**

   o Think about how to tailor your marketing and communication efforts to resonate with your right-fit customers, focusing on their values, needs, and preferred communication channels.

6. **What stood out or resonated with you the most in this chapter?**

   o Was there a concept, framework, or example that felt particularly relevant to your business?

7. **What's one thing you will implement based on what you've learned?**

CHAPTER 14

ATTRACT RIGHT FIT CUSTOMERS

"The more advocates you have the
fewer ads you have to buy"[1]
—*Dharmesh Shah Co-Founder of Hub Spot*

Using the Right Fit Customer Profile (RFCP) for Effective Segmentation

Attracting the right-fit customer starts with knowing who you're truly meant to serve. While most businesses segment customers by broad traits—like industry, age, or location—this chapter invites you to go deeper: to clarify not just who your customer is, but what they value, why they buy, and how you can serve them better than anyone else.

Customer segmentation is the process of dividing your audience into smaller, more focused groups based on shared characteristics like needs, behaviors, or values. When done strategically, segmentation doesn't just sharpen your marketing—it amplifies your impact by helping you speak more directly to those you're built to serve.

In the last chapter, we provided a framework to help you develop your Right-Fit Customer Profile (RFCP). In this chapter, we'll explore how strategic segmentation can help you refine that profile so you can craft your messaging with what matters most to your ideal customers.

The Strategic Segmentation Advantage

Strategic customer segmentation can give your business a competitive edge by helping you identify and define a customer category or subset that others may be overlooking or under serving. If these customers are aligned with your core purpose, competencies and values, you can then position yourself to better serve their needs and stand out in that niche. The key is to find the "sweet spot"—a segment specific enough that can resonate with your offerings in a manner that is different and better than your competition yet still provides a large enough pool of potential right-fit customers for your business to be financially sustainable.

Most businesses might target broad categories: "active women", "tech enthusiasts", or "small business owners" vs a more narrowly defined yet strategically segmented customer target.

For example:

- **Generic Target Customer:** "Active Women"
- **Segmented Target Customer:** "Active women who prioritize eco-friendly, sustainable clothing".

With this sharper focus, your messaging can become more relevant and personal to your segmented target customer.

For example:

- **Generic Tagline**: *"Get Active in Fashion with [Brand Name]."*
- **Segment-Specific Tagline**: *"With [Brand Name], You Can Get Both You and Mother Earth in Shape."*

By speaking directly to customer values, your brand becomes more attractive to the customers who truly fit with your offerings while differentiating you from competitors.

Understanding Customer Needs Through Segmentation

Strategic customer segmentation allows you to use your RFCP to ensure your marketing and outreach speak directly to your target audience's unique needs. If your message isn't resonating, the issue may not be your product or service but how you're communicating its value.

As Harvard Business School professor Theodore Levitt observed, *"People don't want to buy a quarter-inch drill. They want a quarter-inch hole!"*[2] Customers buy outcomes, not products. Even when multiple customer segments buy the same product, their motivations for doing so can vary widely.

Example: Consider a simple drill bit

- A **contractor** may purchase a drill bit for its durability to complete multiple projects.

- A **DIY homeowner** may buy the same bit to mount a single shelf for displaying a family photo.

Understanding these motivations helps you tailor your communication to each segment's values which makes your offering more relevant to their needs and outcomes.

Detailed Example: A single drill bit appeals to various customer segments—contractors, DIY homeowners, hobbyists, and trade schools. While they all want to drill holes, the primary reasons they value a particular drill bit differ:

Feature	DIY Homeowner	Contractor	Hobbyist	Trade School
Durability		✓		
Value (Price)	✓			✓
Versatility	✓			✓
Wear-Mark Indicator		✓	✓	✓
Longevity		✓		✓
Sturdiness		✓		
Accuracy		✓	✓	
Sharp Edges		✓	✓	
Warranty	✓			

Selling to these different customers doesn't require changing the product—just the message. For example:

- A **contractor** values durability and a wear-mark indicator. Highlighting these features ensures your product feels tailored to their needs.

- A **homeowner** values versatility and affordability. Messaging focused on these benefits will resonate with them.

Tailoring Messages for Maximum Impact

By segmenting customers and crafting targeted messages, you align your product's benefits with each group's needs, enhancing the relevance of your offerings.

  o   Who is your audience? (Identify the segment)

o What problems are you solving? (Pinpoint their pain points)

o How does your product help? (Highlight specific benefits they value)

o Why should they choose you? (Differentiate your offering)

If any segment grows large and viable enough, you can use these insights to develop product extensions tailored specifically to them. For instance, if contractors consistently request drill bits with enhanced durability, introducing a "Pro Series" line could meet their needs without alienating other customers.

Ensuring Alignment Between Product and Customer Needs

Revisit your RFCP regularly to ensure alignment between your products, messaging, and customer needs. List each segment's pain points and desired outcomes and evaluate whether your communication highlights these.

To assess financial viability, consider metrics like segment size, purchasing power, and growth potential. A segment that is too small or has a low spending capacity may not justify the resources required to acquire them cost effectively.

Developing your Right Fit Customer Profile and strategic segmentation ensures you focus on what matters most to your right-fit customers, enabling sustainable growth.

Purpose Driven Customer Journey Mapping

Once you've identified your key segments, ensure their experience with your company is effective and appropriate to their buying -purchasing patterns.

Understand the different stages a customer goes through before making a purchase and their experience with your company and ensure they are aligned with your purpose.

- **Questions:**

  o How do customers discover your business?

o What steps do they take before making a purchase?

o What are the key touch points in their journey?

o What is the typical sales cycle (time to complete the buying process) What are the pain points or obstacles they face at each stage?

o Is each step of the customer buying journey aligned with your purpose?

Key Takeaways Chapter 14: Attract the Right Fit Customers

Effective segmentation is more than just targeting; it's about identifying and understanding the unique needs of your right-fit customers. Once you know what your customers value, you can craft tailored messages highlighting your product's relevance to each segment.

This approach enhances your marketing efforts, positions your business for sustainable growth, and builds a community of loyal advocates who align with your purpose and values. By revisiting your Right Fit Customer Profile (RFCP), refining your messaging, and ensuring alignment with customer needs, you can create a business that resonates deeply with those you serve and achieve lasting success.

1. **Strategic Segmentation Sharpens Your Focus.**

   Strategic segmentation sharpens your focus. Broad categories dilute your message. The more clearly you define your right-fit customer, the more effectively you can connect with them.

2. **The Right-Fit Customer Profile (RFCP) Drives Relevance.**

   When you understand what your ideal customer values, where to reach them, and how to speak their language, your marketing becomes more focused, cost-effective, and impactful.

3. **Tailored Messaging Builds Trust and Resonance.**

   It's not just about what your product does—it's about what your customer needs. Speak directly to each segment's motivations and desired outcomes.

4. **Align Customer Needs with Your Business Purpose.**

Your strongest customers are those who align with your values and purpose. When your messaging reflects that alignment, you attract more loyal advocates—not just more buyers.

5. **Balance Focus with Scalability.**

   Define and choose segments that are narrow enough to resonate, but broad enough to sustain profitable growth. Avoid spreading yourself too thin—or going too niche. Targeting overlooked or underserved customer segments that are still large enough to be financially viable affords your business opportunities to dominate niches and differentiate from competitors.

6. **Revisit and Refine Your RFCP Regularly.**

   Customer needs shift. Markets evolve. Your segmentation strategy and messaging should adapt to changing conditions so your outreach remains relevant.

7. **Purpose-Driven Customer Journeys Matter.** Every step from discovery to decision and delivery should reflect your core purpose, values and competencies. When the customer journey is aligned with your purpose, you deepen customer trust and can create a more fulfilling experience.

Reflection Questions Chapter 14: Attract the Right-Fit Customers

1. **Is your customer segment specific yet large enough to be financially viable?**

   o Is your segment focused enough to resonate yet broad enough to support sustainable growth?

2. **Does your messaging address what your segmented customers value?**

   o Are you emphasizing the benefits each segment values most, or is your messaging too generalized?

3. **Are there under served segments you could uniquely serve?**

   o Are there overlooked needs or market gaps your business could address better than competitors?

4. **How often do you revisit and refine your segmentation strategy?**

   o Are you adapting to market changes or customer behavior shifts?

5. **What stood out or resonated with you the most in this chapter?**

   o Was there a concept, framework, or example that felt particularly relevant to your business?

6. **What's one thing you will implement based on what you've learned?**

CHAPTER 15

RETAIN AND GROW LOYAL CUSTOMERS

*"Get closer than ever to your customer. So close,
in fact, that you tell them what they need well
before they realize it themselves."[1] –Steve Jobs*

Why a Loyal Customer Base Matters for SMBs

You no doubt have heard the phrase "If you build it, they will come,"[2] from the movie *Field of Dreams*. This often-quoted line, when used by marketing professionals suggests that having a great product alone will attract customers. Another similar line is attributed to Ralph Waldo Emerson, "Build a better mousetrap and the world will beat a path to your door."[3]

However, while a having a good product is essential, experience shows us that alone rarely guarantees business success. To thrive, you also need a loyal base of customers who not only value what you offer but also return again and again. This chapter explores how to create and maintain that loyal base, which is key to maximizing customer lifetime value (CLV), optimizing your marketing efforts, and driving sustainable growth.

Understanding and Leveraging Customer Lifetime Value (CLV)

Customer Lifetime Value (CLV) is a vital metric for understanding the long-term impact of each customer on your business. CLV measures the total revenue you can expect from a customer throughout their relationship with your company.[4] For SMBs, knowing CLV helps in making strategic decisions about investments in customer acquisition, improving retention, and its impact on business growth.

Example: Calculating CLV for a Coffee Shop

Imagine you own a small coffee shop. You have a group of "regulars" that visit your shop either on the way to work or because they live in the neighborhood. Here's how you can calculate and understand the CLV of your regular customers.

1. **Average Purchase Value**: The average customer visits 3 times a week, spending $5 per visit.

   o   *Weekly Spend*: $5 x 3 = $15

2. **Annual Spend**: $15 per week x 52 weeks = $780 per year.

3. **Customer Life span**: The average customer relationship lasts 5 years

4. **CLV**: $780 x 5 = $3,900

This shows how even a modest daily purchase adds up significantly over time. Loyal customers don't just provide consistent revenue—they represent long-term value that's far greater than a single transaction.

Example: Calculating CLV for an IT Support Provider

Now consider a small IT support business serving local SMBs. You provide managed services under monthly contracts.

1. **Average Monthly Contract Value**: $2,430

2. **Annual Spend**: $2,430 x 12 = $29,160

3. **Customer Life span**: 2 years

4. **CLV**: $29,160 x 2 = $58,320

This shows how each loyal customer can generate tens of thousands of dollars in long term value. Losing just one client early means losing not only monthly income but also the long-term value of a multi-year relationship.

That's why retention is critical—whether your business relies on small, frequent purchases or larger, recurring contracts, CLV underscores the same truth: loyal customers are the foundation of sustainable growth. They deliver higher revenue, cost less to maintain, and often become advocates who promote your business to others like them.

Why CLV Matters

1. **Strategic Marketing Investments**: With a better understanding of your average CLV, you can make better decisions on marketing spend and total customer acquisition costs as a % of CLV and total revenues.

2. **Enhanced Customer Retention**: You can implement and optimize retention strategies informed by CLV—optimizing loyalty programs that also increases repeat business.

3. **Sustainable Growth**: Retaining and increasing high-CLV customers provides a more reliable revenue stream, allowing you to build a stable foundation for long-term success.

Increasing customer life-time value, while important, is not the only reason to focus your business on serving your ideal customers. Aligning your business with your ideal customer also means that you will have happier customers and higher satisfaction scores. This can be reflected in several different ways, all of which only serve to make your business better and more profitable.

Measuring Churn Rate: An Early Warning System

Another way to measure the loyalty of your customer base is to monitor your churn rate. **Churn Rate** is the rate at which customers stop doing business with your company within a given period. High churn indicates potential issues in customer satisfaction or value alignment.

Example: If you started the year with 200 customers and lost 40 by year's end, your churn rate is 20% (40 ÷ 200).

Keeping churn low means focusing on retention strategies that keep customers satisfied and engaged. Other organizations measure **Retention Rate**, which is the inverse of churn rate. In other words, a churn rate of 20% is equivalent to a customer retention rate of 80% (1 −0.2). These rates vary by industry as shown on the chart:[5]

Customer Retention By Industry

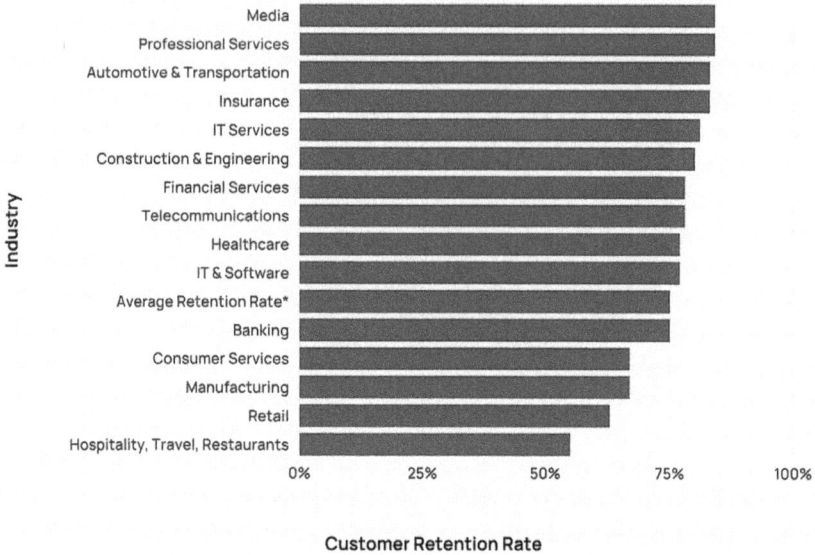

Customer Retention Rate

Benefits of Serving the Right-Fit Customers

Having the right fit customers leads to increased profitability, stream-lined marketing efforts, and higher customer satisfaction, resulting in:

1. **Reduced Returns and Fewer Refunds**: Customers who see value in your products or services are less likely to return items or request refunds, reducing customer service burdens and costs.

2. **More Effective Marketing**: With a clear understanding of your ideal customer, you can create precise marketing messages and promotions that resonate, attracting those who are most likely to become loyal, repeat customers.

3. **Higher Referrals**: Satisfied customers who align with your business are more likely to recommend your business to others, becoming advocates and generating word-of-mouth growth.

Gathering Customer Feedback and Benchmarking Against Competitors

A crucial aspect of retention is gathering ongoing feedback from your customers. This helps you assess:

- **Customer Satisfaction**: Are you meeting or exceeding their expectations?

- **Comparative Performance**: How do your products or services measure up to your customers' other options?

- **Value Alignment**: Are your core values resonating with your customers' values? Customers often remain loyal to businesses that reflect their principles.

Encourage customers to share feedback through surveys, reviews, and direct communication. Use this information to identify areas of improvement, allowing you to stay aligned with customer needs and maintain loyalty.

Aligning Your Marketing and Messaging with Customer Needs

Tailoring your marketing messages to align with the needs and values of your ideal customer is essential. To do this effectively:

1. **Understand Your Customers' Pain Points**: Revisit your Right Fit Customer Profile (RFCP) and identify common challenges or needs. Address these points directly in your marketing.

2. **Know Where to Reach Them**: Are there specific platforms, communities, or publications where your customers gather? Focus on these areas to maximize reach and relevance.

3. **Highlight Relevant Features**: Customize messaging to emphasize the product features that your target segments value most, ensuring you capture attention and resonate with your audience.

Practical Tips for Retaining Right fit Customers

1. **Implement Loyalty Programs**: Reward repeat customers with discounts, exclusive offers, or perks to show appreciation and encourage ongoing engagement.

2. **Use Personalized Marketing**: Leverage customer data to send tailored messages that address specific needs, enhancing customer satisfaction.

3. **Actively Engage with Feedback**: Respond to feedback promptly, making changes as necessary to improve the customer experience and show you value their input.

Key Takeaways Chapter 15: Retain and Grow Loyal Customers

1. **Customer Loyalty Drives Growth:**

   Loyal customers lower marketing costs, increase lifetime value (CLV), and spread your business through referrals and advocacy.

2. **Understand and Leverage Customer Lifetime Value (CLV):**

   CLV highlights the long-term revenue potential of each customer, enabling you to make better and more strategic investments in customer acquisition, retention and loyalty programs.

3. **Monitor Churn and Retention Rates:**

   Churn rate offers insight into customer satisfaction and value alignment. Regularly tracking retention and churn helps identify potential issues and areas for improvement.

4. **Serve Right-Fit Customers for Higher Profitability:**

   Focusing on customers who align with your business values and offerings reduces returns, increases referrals, and ensures efficient marketing strategies.

5. **Feedback is Key to Retention:**

Gathering and acting on customer feedback helps assess satisfaction, benchmark against competitors, and address pain points effectively, building stronger relationships.

6. **Tailor Marketing Messages to Customer Needs:**

   Align your marketing efforts with your customers' values, pain points, and preferred communication channels to create personalized and impactful campaigns.

7. **Implement Practical Retention Strategies:**

   Loyalty programs, personalized marketing, and proactive engagement with feedback foster ongoing customer satisfaction and long-term loyalty.

8. **Retention lowers overall CAC Customer Acquisition Costs:**

   Retaining existing customers is more cost-effective than acquiring new ones, emphasizing the importance of maintaining strong relationships with your right-fit customers.

Reflection Questions Chapter 15: Retain and Grow Loyal Customers

These questions encourage SMB owners to consider customer engagement over time and at each stage of the customer buying journey and life cycle to improve customer retention and loyalty.

1. **What is your CLV and Customer Retention Rate for your various customer segments? How does it compare to your industry average?**

   o   Do you have the data to calculate these? You should measure these values regularly (annually) to ensure that your strategies are effective.

2. **How well do you understand the life cycle of your typical customer?**

   o   Consider your customers' journey from their first interaction with your brand to their continued engagement. Are there specific points in the life cycle where engagement tends to drop off? What strategies can you implement to keep customers engaged at each stage?

3. **Is your customer segment well-defined and actionable?**

   o Is it narrow enough to target effectively yet broad enough to sustain growth?

4. **What strategies do you have in place to improve this retention rate?**

   o Examine how your customers interact with you and whether they are incentivized to continue doing business with you.

5. **What stood out or resonated with you the most in this chapter?**

   o Was there a concept, framework, or example that felt particularly relevant to your business?

6. **What's one thing you will implement based on what you've learned?**

   o What specific action will you take in the next week or month to improve your customer loyalty and retention?

CHAPTER 16

LET GO OF MISFIT CUSTOMERS

"Sometimes the best thing you can do for your business is to let your unprofitable customers go to your competition and let them worry about them."
— *Alfredo Romero*

Volume vs. Value in Customer Acquisition

In today's fiercely competitive business landscape, volume is often equated with success. Businesses are constantly striving for more likes, comments, and reviews. So, it comes as no surprise that many organizations believe that the more customers a company has, the better its prospects. However, sometimes, having fewer total but more right-fit customers can be a strategic move that benefits your business. In this chapter, we will delve into the reasons why "firing" or weeding out your misfit customers can ultimately lead to long-term success.

The Problem with Misfit Customers

Misfit customers can cause a lot of problems and hurt your bottom line. They unnecessarily drain time, money, and energy away from your other customers. They can also make your team unhappy and disrupt your business. It is critical to focus your limited resources on the right-fit customers who are better aligned with your business to help it grow and succeed. Doing this will improve your profitability, increase the efficiency of your marketing efforts, and, ultimately, improve your peace of mind.

Customer Utility and Business Profitability

As discussed previously, Peter Drucker reminds us, "The purpose of business is to create and keep a customer."[1] This seems straightforward enough; no one sets up a lemonade stand on a hot summer day simply to spend time outdoors. From the smallest start-up to the largest Fortune 500 company, every business is striving to provide a good or service to someone that will pay for it.

However, being a successful business doesn't stop at simply providing something for customers to buy. A successful business must also focus on bringing in more revenue than it spends on costs, earning a profit, and meeting its objectives. This means that business must generate a profit that enables the business to sustainably grow over the long term. In other words, both you and your customers should receive a net positive benefit.

But individuals are always looking for the best deal. The goal of a customer is to maximize their own utility by exchanging currency for available goods or services, ideally spending as little time or money as possible for the greatest amount of benefit. The time spent of course, can vary from person to person: some shoppers are happy to hop online, pick a product, click buy, and move on. Others spend hours researching, comparing features, and price shopping before they decide to buy.

Customer satisfaction is often tied to how well a product or service meets or exceeds their expectations. It is also closely linked to buyer's remorse, the regret a customer feels when their purchasing decision does not deliver the expected outcomes. The more a customer cares about their purchase, the more they will typically expect. All this results in the fact that customers focus on whether they are getting their money's worth rather than whether their interaction with your business is profitable for you. Their primary concern is that the product or service delivers the expected value, ensuring they feel satisfied with their purchase.

Ensuring Sustainable Profitability

While it is important to care about your customers' needs, you must also ensure that serving those needs is sustainably profitable. Sustainable profitability is the ability of a business to consistently make a profit over the long term while ensuring it can continue to thrive and grow, adapt to market changes, and meet stakeholder expectations without compromising future performance.

So, adding to our Peter Drucker quote, "The purpose of a successful business is to create and keep customers", we would qualify that with "to keep those customers that are economically profitable while ensuring a sustainable business." One way to achieve this is by identifying and weeding out customers who are not the right fit for your organization.

Identifying Misfit Customers That Erode Your Profits

While you may think that all your customers are profitable, a closer look at the associated costs of delivering your product or service, including opportunity and indirect costs, might reveal that some customers are not sustainably profitable. We cover this topic of opportunity costs and economic profit vs. profit in more detail in Chapter 25. By analyzing beyond just the direct costs (COGS) of your products or services and looking at the impact of indirect costs incurred by misfit customers, you can better identify which customers are not profitable and worth serving.

Identifying sustainably profitable customers is not always straightforward. You may have a handful of customers that immediately come to mind as costing more than they are worth, but many others may surprise you. Thus, it's crucial to determine which customers are the right fit. As we discussed in Chapter 13, a right-fit customer is one that aligns with your organization's values, competencies, and mission. By completing the Right Fit Customer Profile (RFCP), you gain a clearer understanding of what these customers look like and how they align with your company.

Methods for Identifying and Focusing on Right-Fit Customers

Determining which of your customers are sustainably profitable and compared to those that are not can be done in a variety of ways, each with their distinct advantages. Below are some methods we have used with our clients to help them focus their efforts on the right-fit customers while weeding out the misfit ones.

1. **Sales and Gross Margin Mix Analysis**: This technique evaluates your existing customers and their revenue relative to the company's total revenue. It also examines the relative gross profit contribution each customer contributes to the whole.

2. **Indirect Cost Analysis**: By taking into account indirect or "hidden" costs of serving customers, you can also identify and weed out customers that may negatively impact profitability so you can better focus on the right fit customers who contributes more positively to your bottom line.

3. **Comparative Value Pricing Analysis**: Understanding what your customers value and matching that with what they perceive they are getting from your company relative to their next best alternative helps ensure alignment and improves customer satisfaction leading to repeat sales and higher customer value.

Sales Mix Analysis

In a strategic marketing session with one of our clients, we performed a quantitative data-driven analysis and a qualitative assessment using sales mix analysis. This helped us prioritize and optimally reallocate their resources towards their most valuable customers.

First Step: Quantitative Analysis

We started by creating a detailed analysis of our client's customers, ranking them by yearly sales in descending order. Overall, the client had sales of $3.4M and a list of nearly 950 active customers. However, when we reviewed the report, we saw that 80% of total sales ($2.7M) were from only 22% of the customers. Drilling down further, we noticed that the top 40 customers—only 4% of total customers—generated $1.6M, or nearly half of total revenue.

See Table 1 below:

Table 1: Sales Mix Analysis Customers Ranked by Sales

Customer Rank	Percentage of Customers	Sales	Percentage of Sales
1 – 40	4%	$1,600,000	47%
41-210	18%	$1,100,000	32%
211-950	72%	$700,000	21%
Total	**100%**	**$3,400,000**	**100%**

While the client had calculated their average sales per customer at around $3,600, our analysis showed that the top 40 customers averaged around $40,000 each. This means the top 40 customers had an average sale value of more than ten times higher than the average customer. We were able to show to the client that a small fraction of their customer base contributed most of their revenue. This underscores the importance of adequately allocating resources and focusing their efforts on maintaining and building a solid relationship with these high-value accounts.

Strategic Recommendations to Client

1. **Focus on High-Value Customers**: Allocate resources more in line with the each customer's overall value and impact to the company. Focus on and strengthen relationships with the top 40 customers who contribute nearly half of the revenue.

2. **Optimize Marketing Efforts**: Identify other customers similar to the top 40 high-value customers and redirect marketing and customer service efforts towards attracting new customers in this group.

3. **Phase Out Misfit Customers**: Reduce resource allocation and/ or focus on customers towards the bottom of the list. While this may result in losing some of them, it will have negligible impact on overall profit, yet enable them to redirect resources more optimally.

4. **Regular Reviews**: Implement regular reviews of customer profitability and alignment to ensure the business continues to focus on the right customers.

Indirect Cost Analysis

Indirect costs are expenses related to serving your customer base that are not often found in your Profit & Loss statement as direct (COGS) costs of goods. These can include customer service, warranty claims, worker's comp, salespeople's time, and even the owner's time, which often doesn't get accounted for. Not calculating these as direct customer costs can result in underestimating the true costs of serving each customer. By assigning a cost per customer to each indirect cost, you can calculate how these costs impact customer profitability.

Steps to Analyze Indirect Costs:

1. **Identify Indirect Costs**: List out all indirect costs that your business incurs, such as customer service hours, warranty claims, and sales visits.

2. **Assign Costs to Customers**: Determine a cost value for each type of indirect cost. For example, product returns are usually 66% of the original item's price,[2] and an hour of customer service time might cost $50.

3. **Run Customer Reports**: Generate reports to see which customers are incurring these indirect costs most frequently. Look for patterns of over-utilization, such as frequent customer service calls or repeated product returns.

4. **Analyze Profitability**: Compare the revenue generated by these customers against the indirect costs they incur. This will help you identify which customers are truly profitable and which are not.

Example:

Let's consider two customers, A and B, and analyze their impact on indirect costs. Your organization has three salespeople and 120 customers. You have decided to split the accounts evenly so that each salesperson handles 40 accounts each. This means that each salesperson spends about 30 hours on each account annually. At $50/hour, the cost of "sales" for each account is about $1,500 annually:

Table 2a: Indirect Cost Analysis Salesperson Allocation

Number of Customers	Salespeople	Accounts per Salesperson	Allocated hours per account	Each Sales person hrs/ year	Each Sales Person cost @ $50/hr per year
120	3	40	30	1,200	$1,500

If every customer were exactly the same size, this would not be a problem. However, you find that Customer A brings in about $15,000 annually while Customer B is ten times larger. Each of these customers' Gross Profit comes to about 50% as shown below:

Table 2b: Indirect Cost Analysis Direct Cost Profitability

Metrics	Customer A	Customer B
Sales	$15,000	$150,000
Direct Costs	$7,500	$75,000
Gross Profit	$7,500	$75,000
Gross Profit %	50%	50%

However, if you also include the cost of sales, you have to add an additional $1,500 to the cost of serving each customer. This paints an entirely different picture:

Table 2c: Indirect Cost Analysis Direct and Indirect Cost Profitability

Metrics	Customer A	Customer B
Sales	$15,000	$150,000
Direct Costs	$7,500	$75,000
Additional Sales Cost	$1,500	$1,500
New Gross Profit	$6,000	$73,500
New Gross Profit %	40%	49%

Customer A is still profitable but by a lot less. Spending extra salesperson resources on Customer B makes more sense because it yields a higher Gross Profit than Customer A. If costs increase to the point where Customer A is no longer profitable, consider scaling back on visits or other services. If this results in Customer A no longer doing business with you, it may allow you to focus on finding other customers who are better aligned with ensuring a lucrative and sustainable business. This approach ensures that your sales efforts are directed towards the most profitable customers, maximizing ROI and enhancing overall business performance.

Comparative Value Pricing Analysis

Another valuable tool for assessing alignment with your right-fit customers and helping identify misfit customers is the Comparative Value Pricing Analysis — evaluating what customers value most with how well they perceive your company delivers on those values, compared to their next best alternative, and the relative pricing differential between both options.

This gives you visibility into:

- Which customers are the best fit for your business
- Where your strengths differentiate you compared to others
- Where gaps exist
- Where misfit customers may emerge (whose priorities you do not match or align well with)

Using Weighted Decision Criteria to Understand Customer Priorities

The key to this analysis is understanding that not all customer values carry equal weight in the buying decision.

Rather than simply asking customers if a factor is "important," we've found that it can be helpful to ask them how much each factor drives their purchase decisions.

For example:

"When deciding which company to buy from, how much does each of the following factors influence your decision? Please distribute 100% across these factors based on how important each one is to your choice."

This ensures the weights reflect real purchase drivers — not vague preferences.

Conducting the Survey

After determining your Right-Fit Customer Profile (RFCP), identify 4-6 key decision criteria most relevant to your customers. In addition, it's useful to ask if there is a significant decision criteria that is missing from the list.

Example criteria might include:

- Value for Money (Price)
- Customer Service (Responsiveness, Support)
- Timely Delivery
- Reliability
- Availability of Product

Step 1: Depending on the number of customers, ask 12-20 current customers to assign % importance to each factor (total = 100%).

Step 2: Ask customers to rate how well your company performs on each factor (scale of 1–10).

Rating scale definition:

1 = Very Poor — fails to meet expectations

5 = Average — meets basic expectations

10 = Excellent — consistently exceeds expectations

Step 3: Ask customers to rate how well their Next Best Alternative performs on each factor (same 1–10 scale).

Defining the "Next Best Alternative"

When asking about the "Next Best Alternative," clarify that this should be:

"The company or solution (or no solution) you would most likely choose if you didn't buy from us — based on your real-world experience and options — not a theoretical ideal or abstract market leader."

Examples:

- A competitor they've used before
- A competitor they are considering
- The most common substitute in the market or geography

This ensures the comparison stays grounded and actionable.

Step 4: Ask customers any additional feedback (Customer Feedback Column) and key factors that accounted for their ratings for both client and next best alternative.

Conducting the Survey

We surveyed customers, asking them to rate these values in terms of weighted importance and how they perceived these were being provided by the client and their nearest (NBAR) competitor. Table 3 shows the results of one such survey.

Table 3: Comparative Value Pricing Survey Results

Decision Criteria (Value)	Importance to Customer	Client Company Rating (1-10)	Client Result	Next Best Alternative Rating (NBAR)	NBAR Result	Diff.	Customer Feedback
A	B	C	D: B x C	E	F: B x E	G: D - F	H
Value for Money	30%	9.0	2.7	8.0	2.4	0.3	"Good value but could be more competitive."
Customer Service	40%	9.0	3.6	6.5	2.6	1.0	"Exceptional service, very responsive."
Timeliness of Delivery	10%	8.0	0.8	8.0	0.8	0.0	"Deliveries are always on time."
Reliability	15%	7.0	1.05	7.0	1.05	0.0	"Product reliability needs improvement."
Availability of Product	5%	7.0	0.35	7.0	0.35	0.0	"Always in stock when needed."
Totals	100%	-	8.5	-	7.2	-	-

Comparative Value Pricing Insights

In the example table above:

The overall weighted score for the client company was calculated to be 8.5.

The next best alternative scored 7.2. This suggests the client delivers ~18% more perceived value.

Therefore, pricing up to 18% higher than the next best alternative could be justified — while retaining alignment with customers who truly value that differentiation.

Why This Analysis Helps Weed Out Misfit Customers

By clarifying which values drive purchase decisions, you'll quickly see where your strengths align with your right-fit customers' priorities and where customers are buying for reasons your business is not built to compete on. If some customers assign 50%+ to lowest price, but your model is not built on competing with the lowest prices but on delivering premium service, then those are likely misfit customers.

You can adjust messaging and pricing to naturally filter them out.

Similarly, if your company scores much higher on service and reliability than competitors, use that to attract customers who prioritize those values — and confidently set pricing to reflect the added value.

Summary

Comparative Value Pricing Analysis helps you focus on right-fit market segments, confidently price for the value you provide, and naturally filter out misfit customers whose values and expectations don't align with your purpose or strengths.

Clients can better understand their relative strengths and weaknesses and identify areas of improvement based on customer feedback. When you have greater clarity on your strengths compared to competitors, you can then target customers and compete in markets where those strengths matter to the customer to the degree that gives you a decisive advantage. Also when your core competencies and values align with the customer's value criteria, you can then develop more effective and custom-tailored marketing and messaging to appeal to those right-fit customers while weeding out the misfit ones.

The Comparative Value Pricing framework gives SMB owners a simple, powerful way to:

- Better understand what drives their customers' decisions
- See how they stack up against real competitors
- Strengthen alignment with right-fit customers
- Use pricing and positioning to naturally weed out misfit customers
- Drive sustainable, purpose-aligned growth

Reflection Question

- Based on customer feedback, which decision criteria most drive your best and less than ideal customers' buying choices, and where do your strengths align or misalign with those priorities?

Key Takeaways Chapter 16: Let Go of Misfit Customers

In a world where customer acquisition is often seen as the primary focus, considering the option of firing some customers may seem counterintuitive. However, it's essential to understand that not every customer is worth keeping. Misfit customers drain profits, frustrate your team, and distract from your best opportunities. By identifying who truly aligns with your values and contributes to sustainable profitability, you free up energy and resources to serve the right customers — the ones who help your business thrive.

1. **Not All Customers Are Worth Keeping** – Misfit customers drain profits, frustrate your team, and take energy away from right-fit customers who matter most.

2. **Quality Over Quantity** – More customers don't always mean more profits. Prioritizing high-value, right-fit customers who align with your company's values and mission will lead to greater long-term success.

3. **The Hidden Costs of Misfit Customers** – Many businesses fail to account for the indirect costs of serving misfit customers, such as excessive customer service time, frequent product returns, or unnecessary customization requests. Identifying and reducing these costs is key to improving profitability.

4. **Right-Fit Customers Drive Growth** – Customers who share your business values, appreciate your offerings, and require fewer resources to serve are more profitable, contribute to a positive work environment, and strengthen your brand.

5. **Focusing on Sustainable Profitability** – Beyond revenue, true profitability comes from customers who bring long-term value without disproportionately increasing costs. Regularly evaluating the financial impact of your customer base ensures that you're focusing on those who help your business thrive.

6. **Methods to Identify Misfit Customers**

   o **Sales Mix Analysis** – Identify the small percentage of customers generating the majority of your revenue and gross profit in order to reallocate resources to them.

   o **Indirect Cost Analysis** – Examine hidden costs (e.g., customer service, product returns) to determine true customer profitability.

   o **Comparative Value Pricing Analysis** – Evaluate whether your pricing reflects the additional value you provide compared to your competitors.

7. **Strategically Letting Go** – Firing misfit customers allows you to focus energy and resources on customers who are a better fit for your business, improving overall efficiency and profitability.

8. **Empowering Your Team Through Customer Alignment** – When your business serves right-fit customers, employees experience less frustration, feel more valued, and can provide better service. Involving your team in identifying misfit customers creates alignment across your organization.

9. **Continuous Customer Review is Essential** – Customer needs and business priorities evolve. Regularly evaluating your

customer base ensures alignment with your strategic goals and profitability targets.

10. **Long-Term Success Comes from Focus** – Letting go of misfit customers may feel counterintuitive, but it allows you to build a stronger, more sustainable, and more customer-centric business that attracts and retains high-value customers.

Reflection Questions Chapter 16: Let Go of Misfit Customers

Reflection Questions: Chapter 16 - Weeding Out Misfit Customers

1. **What stood out to you most in this chapter?**
   o Did any of the insights challenge your current perspective on customer acquisition and retention?
   o How does this concept of letting go of misfit customers apply to your business's current customer base?

2. **What's one action you will implement based on what you've learned?**
   o How will you evaluate customer profitability, reallocate resources, or make adjustments to your sales and marketing strategy?
   o What specific step will you take in the next 30 days to improve your focus on right-fit customers?

3. **Who are your misfit customers?**
   o Are there customers who consume excessive time, resources, or attention compared to the value they bring?
   o What characteristics or behaviors define these misfit customers?

4. **How are you currently identifying and prioritizing your most valuable customers?**

   o   Have you analyzed customer profitability beyond revenue?

   o   Do you have systems in place to track customer-related costs such as service time, returns, or support requests?

5. **How does your current customer base align with your business values and mission?**

   o   Are you attracting customers who share your company's purpose and appreciate the unique value you provide?

   o   What steps can you take to refine your customer acquisition strategy to focus on better-fit customers?

6. **How would letting go of misfit customers improve your business?**

   o   What positive impacts could this have on your profitability, team morale, and operational efficiency?

   o   What concerns or fears do you have about "firing" customers, and how can you address them?

7. **How do you plan to balance customer service with sustainable profitability?**

   o   Are there specific policies or processes you need to adjust to ensure you are serving customers effectively without compromising long-term profitability?

   o   How can you set clearer expectations with customers to avoid overextending your resources?

By reflecting on these questions and taking deliberate action, you can ensure that your customer base supports—not hinders—your business's long-term success.

PRODUCT—ALIGNING YOUR PRODUCT/SERVICE WITH YOUR PURPOSE

CHAPTER 17

ALIGN YOUR PRODUCT/SERVICE

*"When you align your products and services
with your purpose, you unlock the potential
for meaningful growth and deeper fulfillment."*
— Steven Kim, Founder of Purpose Matters

Aligning Your Products with Your Company's Core Purpose

Aligning your products and services with your organization's core purpose ensures that what you offer not only meets market needs but also reflects your company's **purpose, values, and strengths**.

The benefits your products create for customers are the most tangible expression of that purpose. Your core purpose—shaped by your mission, vision, competencies, values, and culture—serves as a framework for decision-making and strategy. When your products and services stay in sync with that purpose, you foster deeper customer loyalty, drive meaningful growth, and stand apart from competitors.

Purpose: The Why Behind Your Business

As we covered in Chapter 4, your core purpose is the fundamental reason your business exists beyond making a profit. It is the "why" that drives you and your team every day. A clear purpose inspires, guides, and keeps your organization aligned with what matters most.

For example, your purpose might be:

- "To improve people's lives through accessible technology."
- "To provide healthy, sustainable food options to our community."

Identifying Core Competencies

Once your purpose is clear, the next step is understanding your core competencies—the unique strengths that enable you to fulfill that purpose and deliver value. These are what you do exceptionally well and what customers can't easily get elsewhere.

Core competencies could include:

- Technological expertise
- Exceptional customer service
- Efficient operations/supply chain management
- Innovative design capabilities

Ask yourself:

- What specific skills, resources, or processes set us apart from competitors or your customer's next best alternative?
- What do customers consistently say they value most about our business?
- Which of these strengths would be difficult for others to copy?

The harder a capability is to replicate, the stronger your long-term advantage.

Identify the unique attributes of your business: Specialized knowledge, proprietary technology, a well-trained team, or an efficient process that competitors lack.

For example:

- o Do you have a patented process or exclusive partnership that gives you an edge?
- o Are your products crafted with a quality standard that your customers value and competitors struggle to match?

What have customers mentioned to you about why they selected your business?

Listening to your customers is crucial. Their feedback can reveal the real reasons they value your offerings.

- o Are they impressed by your exceptional customer service, reliability, or innovative solutions?

- o Do they prefer your brand for its responsiveness, dependability, or ease of doing business?

- o Is there a common theme among the positive online reviews or testimonials from your customers?

Which of these attributes would be difficult for competitors or their next best alternative to duplicate?

Consider how easy it would be for a competitor to replicate your strengths. The more challenging it is for others to match your capabilities, the stronger your competitive position.

- o Do your strengths rely on significant capital investment, specialized expertise, or exclusive relationships that competitors cannot easily replicate?

- o Are these strengths embedded in your culture or standardized in your processes and systems, so they consistently deliver value and are hard to imitate?

Why This Matters:

When you clearly define and leverage the attributes that differentiate your business, you are better able to create a value proposition that resonates deeply with customers. Unique, hard-to-replicate capabilities not only set you apart in the market but also can build trust and loyalty among your customer base.

By understanding and continuously strengthening these unique qualities, you can position your business as the preferred choice in your industry. This strategic clarity ensures you're not just competing on price or features but offering something truly distinctive that customers can't find elsewhere.

Do Your Strengths Create Real and Lasting Value for Customers?

To evaluate whether your strengths truly matter, focus on their impact on your customers' needs and wants. Real value means your offerings directly solve problems or deliver clear benefits customers can feel. Lasting value means these benefits hold up over time, building reliability, trust, and loyalty.

What aspects of your business offerings directly address your customers' most pressing needs?

Start by identifying the specific challenges or unmet needs your customers face. For example:

o   Does your product simplify a complex process or solve a recurring issue for your customers?

o   Is your service filling a gap in the market that others have overlooked?

How do your strengths solve customer pain points or enhance their overall experience?

o   Do your offerings save time, money (reduce costs), or provide exceptional quality?

o   Are you removing barriers, like poor accessibility or confusing processes?

o   Do you deliver a seamless and enjoyable experience that keeps customers returning?

By connecting your strengths to your customers' needs and eager wants, you not only ensure relevance but also solidify your role as a trusted partner in their success.

Which of your core competencies are sustainable and can contribute to long-term growth?

Sustainability means your strengths are not fleeting or easily exhausted. Instead, they should remain relevant and valuable as your business scales:

- **Longevity:** Are your core competencies built on foundational strengths like proprietary technology, deeply rooted expertise, or strong customer relationships that endure over time?

- **Scalability:** Can your competencies grow alongside your business? For instance, an efficient supply chain or innovative production method could help you scale effectively as demand increases.

- **Resilience:** Do these strengths continue to provide consistent value, even as market conditions evolve?

Core Competencies Example for a Design Firm:

Let's consider a design firm. The firm's owner identifies their company's unique ability to deeply understand client needs and deliver customized creative solutions on tight deadlines.

This capability helped them attract high-value clients, strengthen customer loyalty, and generate repeat business while reinforcing the firm's reputation for excellence.

Clients often said, "We wouldn't work with anyone else—they just don't get us the way you do."

The firm defined its core competencies as:

The design firm defines its core competencies as:

- Ability to gain deep client knowledge
- Creative and customized solutions
- Quick turnaround.

Practical Tools for Identifying Competencies

While many core competencies are readily apparent, many organizations use some of the following tools to help them identify what other qualities make them stand out:

1. **Internal Analysis (SWOT):** A SWOT analysis is an exercise where you identify your company's **S**trengths, **W**eaknesses, **O**pportunities, and **T**hreats. Core competencies can be found in strengths and opportunities.

2. **Customer Feedback Surveys (NPS Score):** Listen to your customers. What do they value most about your products or services? Their insights can highlight your core competencies.

3. **Benchmarking:** Compare your financial performance with competitors to see where you excel or may have a competitive advantage.

Leveraging Core Competencies

Once you've identified your core competencies, the next step is to use them strategically. Focus on strengthening and applying these capabilities in ways that create greater value for your customers. As Peter Drucker famously said, "Making strengths productive is the unique purpose of any organization." [1]

For example:

- If **innovative design** is a core competency, focus on creating cutting-edge products that set trends.

- If **exceptional customer service** sets you apart, ensure every product or service enhances the customer experience.

From Competencies to Core Values

While core competencies focus on what your company *does* exceptionally well, core values reflect *why* and *how* you do it. Your core values are the fundamental beliefs, a compass that guides decision-making, shapes company culture, and informs interactions with customers, employees, and partners. Review your mission and vision statements to see any recurring themes that inform your core values.

Examples of Values may include things like: Integrity, Customer Focus, Innovation, Teamwork, Accountability, Quality, Respect, Continuous Improvement, Sustainability, Community Engagement.

Another way to think about core values is to ask:

"When customers think about our business or work with our team, what qualities do we want them to remember us for?"

Embedding Core Values into Your Products/Services

Ensure your core values are more than just words on a wall. Incorporate them into your decision-making and product planning. Let your values guide your strategies and choices. Make sure all employees understand and embrace these values, especially during meetings where a decision is taking place. For example, a local bakery whose purpose is to nourish the local community may choose to buy flour from nearby farmers even if it costs more.

And finally, lead by example. Management should exemplify the company values in their actions. If one of your core values is integrity and a decision is being made to let customers know about a product defect, take the lead in crafting a transparent and responsible communication that puts customers first. This will go a long way towards helping your employees make similar decisions in the future.

Serving Your Purpose Through Your Products/Services

Your products should be a direct reflection of your company's purpose, mission and vision.

Ask yourself, does this product help fulfill our fundamental reason for existing? Does it reflect our core competencies and values? Many times, we offer product line extensions or additional service without considering how our customers might perceive our brand. For example, if your purpose is to promote sustainable living, your products should be eco-friendly and support that goal. Adding a less expensive, but non-sustainable product may send the wrong message to your buyers, even if it is available at a lower price point.

Building on Your Strengths into Your Products

Once you've identified your core values and core competencies, product/service development becomes clearer. Use your strengths as the foundation for new offerings—building on what you already do best. This not only makes you more competitive but also creates barriers for competitors. For instance, if your core competency is technological innovation, ensure your products incorporate the latest tech advancements.

Bringing Values in Design and Marketing

Your organization's values should show up in both how products are created and how they're marketed. Apple's commitment to design excellence is a good example: it shaped not only their products but also their packaging, advertising, and even their retail stores. Everything communicated the same message—excellence in design.

In contrast, a company whose values are low prices and affordability should use plain packaging to avoid the perception that they are "wasting" money on expensive packaging.

Maintain consistency to build trust and brand loyalty. Once you've determined your core values, your core competencies, and core purpose, ensure they are reflected across every customer touchpoint, from product fulfillment, packaging to advertising.

Product/Service Alignment Examples

Patagonia: Aligning Products with Purpose and Values

- **Purpose and Mission:** Patagonia aims to build the best product without causing unnecessary harm and uses business to inspire environmental solutions.
- **Core Competency:** Expertise in creating durable, high-quality outdoor clothing.
- **Core Values:** Environmental stewardship, integrity.
- **Alignment:** All products are designed with sustainability in mind, using recycled materials and promoting repair over replacement.

Southwest Airlines: Aligning Products with Purpose and Values

- **Mission:** Dedication to the highest quality of customer service delivered with warmth and friendliness.

- **Core Competency:** Efficient, low-cost operations.

- **Core Values:** Customer service, operational excellence.

- **Alignment:** Products (flights) are offered at competitive prices with exceptional service, reflecting their mission and values.

Local It Support Provider: Aligning Products/Services with Purpose and Values

- **Mission:** Help small businesses run smoothly by making technology reliable and stress-free.

- **Core Competency:** Responsive, personalized service with deep knowledge of SMB systems.

- **Core Values:** Reliability, trust, partnership customer service.

- **Alignment:** Services focuses on proactive monitoring and fast response times, reducing downtime and frustration. Customers stay loyal because service consistently delivers peace of mind.

Key Takeaways Chapter 17 – Align Your Product/Service

You can build a stronger, more sustainable, and purpose-driven business by ensuring your products align with your company's core purpose, competencies, and values.

Aligning your products with your company's foundational elements is not just a strategic move—it's essential for long-term success. It ensures that every product you bring to market is a true reflection of what your company stands for, leveraging your unique strengths and staying true to your core values. This alignment builds stronger relationships with customers, fosters loyalty, and differentiates you in the marketplace.

As an SMB owner, take the time to evaluate your current products. Are they serving your purpose? Do they reflect your mission and vision? Are they leveraging your core competencies and embodying your core values? If the answer to any of these questions is no, it's time to make some adjustments.

Remember, purpose-driven alignment isn't a one and done activity but an ongoing process. Continually assess and refine to ensure that as your company evolves, your products remain aligned with the very foundation of your business. Aligning your products with your company's mission, vision, core competencies, and values is essential for achieving sustained success.

By taking the time to ensure this alignment, SMB owners can create products that not only meet market demands but also resonate with customers on a deeper level, driving loyalty and growth. Engage with your team, leverage your strengths, and stay true to your core principles to build a thriving, purpose-driven business.

Key Takeaways: Chapter 17 - Align Your Product/Service

1. **Your Products and Services Must Reflect Your Core Purpose**

   Your offerings should be a direct extension of your company's **mission and vision**—not just a way to generate revenue. Customers resonate more deeply with businesses that have a **clear and compelling purpose** behind their products.

2. **Leverage Your Core Competencies to Strengthen Product Differentiation**

   Identify and capitalize on **what your business does best**— whether it's technological innovation, superior customer service, or efficient delivery. A strong product/service strategy should be built around these strengths to create a competitive edge that is difficult to replicate.

3. **Ensure Every Product Embodies Your Core Values**

   Customers expect consistency between what a company stands for and what it delivers. If sustainability, innovation, or customer-centricity are core values, they should be evident in product design, marketing, and customer experience. This alignment builds brand trust and customer loyalty.

4. **Align Product Development with Customer Needs**

   Evaluate how well your offerings solve real problems for your target customers. Products should:

   o   Address your customers' most pressing needs.

   o   Enhance the user experience.

   o   Provide clear and measurable value.

5. **Evaluate and Adjust for Long-Term Alignment**

   Product alignment isn't a one-time exercise—it's an ongoing process. As your business grows, regularly review and refine your offerings to ensure they continue to serve your purpose while staying competitive in the market.

6. **Involve Your Team in Ensuring Product-Purpose Alignment**

   Employees should understand how your products reflect your company's purpose, competencies, and values. Engaging your team in this process ensures greater consistency and commitment across all levels of the organization.

7. **Marketing and Messaging Should Reinforce Purpose Alignment**

   Customers should instantly recognize your company's purpose and values through your product positioning, branding, and marketing. Every touchpoint, from your website to packaging, should communicate the unique value proposition that differentiates you from competitors.

8. **Purpose-Driven Products Drive Stronger Customer Loyalty**

   Customers increasingly prefer to buy from brands that align with their own values. By staying true to your purpose, you create emotional connections that result in higher retention, stronger word-of-mouth marketing, and long-term brand advocates.

9. **Be Selective About Expanding Product Lines**

   Not every product extension aligns with your mission. Avoid adding offerings that dilute your brand or send mixed messages to customers. Evaluate potential new products through the lens of purpose, core competencies, and values before launching.

10. **Consistently Communicate Product Alignment Internally and Externally**

    Make sure both your team and customers understand how your products reflect your company's purpose. Use storytelling, case studies, and real-world examples to reinforce this connection. The better aligned your team is, the more consistent your brand message will be in the marketplace.

Reflection Questions Chapter 17: Align Your Product/Service

On Purpose and Core Competencies

1. Do our current products and services clearly reflect our company's core purpose: mission, and vision?

2. Are we fully leveraging our unique strengths to differentiate our products from competitors?

On Core Values and Customer Experience

3. Do our products and services consistently align with our company's core values in both design and delivery?

4. Are there any aspects of our offerings that might conflict with or dilute our company's values?

5. Do our products and services effectively solve real problems for our customers? How can we improve the value we provide?

On Product Positioning and Branding

6. Does our marketing clearly communicate how our products reflect our purpose and values?

7. Do customers recognize and appreciate the deeper purpose behind what we offer? If not, how can we make this clearer?

On Continuous Improvement and Future Alignment

8. When was the last time we evaluated whether our product offerings align with our mission?

9. What steps can we take to ensure future product development remains in alignment with our core purpose?

10. Are there any product lines or services we should reconsider because they no longer align with our core competencies or values?

On Team Engagement and Internal Alignment

11. Does our team fully understand how our products align with our company's purpose, values, and competencies?

12. What steps can we take to involve our employees more in the process of aligning products with purpose?

Final Reflection: Taking Action

13. What stood out most to you in this chapter?

14. What is one specific action you will take to better align your products/services with your company's purpose, core values and core competencies?

CHAPTER 18

OPTIMIZE YOUR PRODUCT/SERVICE

In our retail business, we know that
customers want low prices, fast delivery,
and vast selection. It's impossible to imagine
a future where a customer says, 'I love
Amazon, but I wish the prices were higher,'
or 'I love Amazon, but I wish you'd deliver
more slowly.'[1] *— Jeff Bezos, Amazon*

Why Optimization Matters

In today's competitive business world, simply having a good product or service isn't enough.[2] Small and medium-sized business (SMB) owners must continuously strive to improve their offerings to meet evolving customer needs and stay ahead of the competition.

This is where product and service optimization come into play. By deliberately improving what you offer, you not only increase customer value but also strengthen the connection between your products and your company's larger purpose.

Optimization is more than cutting costs or adding features. Done well, it aligns what you sell with the core mission and values of your business. Every refinement whether in design, delivery, or process should bring you closer to fulfilling your purpose while making life better for both your customers and employees.

Customers benefit from more reliable, relevant, and satisfying experiences, while employees benefit from clearer processes, fewer frustrations, and the tools to perform their work effectively.

 In this chapter, we'll explore the essentials of product and service optimization. We'll share practical strategies, real-world examples, and actionable steps to help you enhance your offerings. Whether you're looking to improve customer satisfaction, increase profitability, or streamline operations, optimizing your products or services is critical to achieving sustainable purpose-driven growth.

What Is Product/Service Optimization?

Product and service optimization is the process of deliberately improving your offerings to better meet customer needs, reduce costs, and enhance overall performance. It's about fine-tuning features, processes, and delivery methods to provide the highest possible value to your customers.

Key Aspects of Optimization:

- **Customer-Centric Improvements:** Adjusting based feedback and preferences.
- **Efficiency Enhancements:** Streamlining processes to reduce waste and costs.
- **Quality Upgrades:** Improving reliability, durability, or functionality.
- **Adding Features:** Incorporating new technologies or methodologies to stay current and competitive.

Making the Most of Limited Resources

For SMB owners, resources are often tight. Every dollar, hour, and resources dedicated to product/service optimization, refining what you already offer, is one of the best ways to make the most of what you have. By targeting specific, strategic improvements, you can stretch resources further and drive impactful results without requiring a large budget. Optimization doesn't necessarily mean a total overhaul; it's about focused adjustments that improve efficiency, customer satisfaction, and a healthy bottom line.

Benefits of Optimization

Maximizing Return on Investment (ROI):

Optimization increases the value of your investments. By focusing on both efficiency and effectiveness, every dollar you spend contributes more to your bottom line. Small changes can add up, ensuring that your investments yield the highest possible returns.

Enhancing Customer Satisfaction:

Satisfied customers are more likely to return, and optimizing your products or services helps meet and exceed their expectations. Studies have shown that much of a company's business comes from repeat customers and happy and satisfied customers are more likely to purchase upgrades and new services. In fact, even a small increase in customer retention can considerably impact profitability.[3] Focusing on customer satisfaction translates into stronger customer relationships, higher retention, and valuable word-of-mouth referrals which are all vital for growth.

Staying Competitive:

In today's fast-moving market, continuous improvement is key to staying relevant. Optimization enables you to keep pace with competitors or even gain an edge, especially when they may offer similar products or services. A focus on fine-tuning can help your business stand out in a crowded landscape.

Adapting to Market Changes:

Customer needs and market trends are constantly evolving. Optimization helps your business stay flexible and respond effectively, positioning you to quickly meet new demands and adjust to shifting trends. This agility is a competitive advantage in any industry.

Common Challenges in Optimization

While the benefits of optimization are clear, SMBs often face unique challenges in this process. Recognizing these hurdles upfront can help you approach optimization with a strategic mindset.

Limited Resources:

Resource scarcity whether in budget or personnel can make significant changes seem daunting. However, even small adjustments can yield meaningful results. Prioritizing high-impact improvements and focusing on feasible changes within your means can make optimization manageable, regardless of budget.

Resistance to Change:

Change can be difficult, especially when employees or management are comfortable with established processes. Building a culture that values growth and improvement can ease this resistance, making optimization a natural part of your business's evolution rather than a disruptive shift.

Insufficient Data:

Without solid insights into customer preferences or product performance, it can be difficult to know where to focus. Even small steps in data collection and analysis can provide clarity, helping you pinpoint areas for improvement and allowing you to make more informed, impactful decisions.

Balancing Quality and Cost:

Improving quality often comes with higher costs, making it challenging to maintain a balance that meets or exceeds your customers' expectations while also delivering that in a cost effective and sustainable manner. We need to learn how to prioritize upgrades that offer the most value and resonate with customer needs to achieve meaningful growth without overspending.

Making Incremental Gains for Long-Term Success

F For SMB owners, optimization is about doing more of what works best—using fewer resources and less wasted effort. Instead of chasing big, risky overhauls, you can focus on small, deliberate improvements that compound over time. This approach not only helps you stretch limited resources but also strengthens your market position and delivers greater value to your customers. In the end, a commitment to optimization is a commitment to sustainable growth built one strategic step at a time.

For SMB owners, resources are often limited, making it vital to get the most out of what you have. Optimization helps you:

- **Maximize Return on Investment (ROI):** By improving efficiency and effectiveness, you get more value from your investments.

- **Enhance Customer Satisfaction:** Better products or services lead to happier customers and repeat business.

- **Stay Competitive:** Continuous improvement keeps you ahead of competitors who may be offering similar products.

- **Adapt to Market Changes:** Optimization enables you to respond quickly to evolving customer needs and industry trends.

Practical Strategies for Product/Service Optimization

1. Gather and Analyze Customer Feedback

Understanding your customers' needs and preferences is the cornerstone of driving effective optimization.

Actions to Take:

- **Surveys and Questionnaires:** Regularly collect feedback on customer satisfaction and suggestions for improvement.

- **Customer Interviews:** Engage directly with customers to gain deeper insights.

- **Monitor Reviews and Social Media:** Keep an eye on what customers are saying about your products or services online.

Benefits:

- **Identify Pain Points:** Discover areas where customers are experiencing issues.

- **Uncover Opportunities:** Find out what additional features or services customers desire.

- **Enhance Customer Relationships:** Show customers that you value their opinions.

2. Analyze Sales and Performance Data

Leverage data to pinpoint what's working and what's not.

Actions to Take:

- **Sales Trends:** Track which products or services are selling well and which aren't.

- **Profit Margins:** Analyze profitability to identify areas needing cost reduction or price adjustment.
- **Usage Patterns:** For service-based offerings, understand how customers are using your services.

Benefits:

- **Data-Driven Decisions:** Base your optimization efforts on solid evidence rather than assumptions.
- **Resource Allocation:** Invest more in high-performing areas and reconsider under performing ones.

3. Streamline Processes for Efficiency

Improving the way you produce and deliver your products or services can significantly impact quality and cost.

Actions to Take:

- **Process Mapping:** Document each step in your production or service delivery process.
- **Identify Bottlenecks:** Look for stages that cause delays or errors.
- **Implement Lean Principles:** Adopt methodologies like Lean or Six Sigma to reduce waste and improve efficiency.

Benefits:

- **Cost Reduction:** More efficient processes often lead to lower operational costs.
- **Improved Quality:** Consistency and precision in processes enhance the end product or service.
- **Faster Delivery:** Streamlined operations can reduce lead times, improving customer satisfaction.

4. Invest in Employee Training and Development

Your team plays a crucial role in delivering optimized products and services.

Actions to Take:

- **Skill Assessments:** Evaluate the current skill levels of your employees.

- **Training Programs:** Provide training to address gaps and enhance expertise.
- **Encourage Continuous Improvement:** Create an environment where employees feel comfortable suggesting improvements.

Benefits:

- **Enhanced Productivity:** Skilled employees perform tasks more efficiently and accurately.
- **Employee Engagement:** Investing in your team boosts morale and retention.
- **Fresh Ideas:** Employees on the front lines often have valuable insights into potential improvements.

5. Leverage Technology and Automation

Embracing modern technology can offer significant optimization opportunities.

Actions to Take:

- **Software Solutions:** For example implement tools for project management, customer relationship management (CRM), or inventory control.
- **Automation:** Use automation for repetitive tasks to reduce errors and free up staff time.
- **Data Analytics:** Employ analytics tools to gain deeper insights into business performance.

Benefits:

- **Increased Efficiency:** Technology can handle tasks faster and more accurately than manual processes.
- **Better Decision-Making:** Analytics provide actionable insights to guide optimization efforts.
- **Scalability:** Technology solutions often allow for easy scaling as your business grows.

6. Offer Customization and Personalization

Tailoring your products or services to individual customer needs can significantly enhance perceived value.

Actions to Take:

- **Flexible Options:** Provide choices in features, sizes, or service levels.

- **Personalized Experiences:** Use customer data to personalize interactions and recommendations.

- **Feedback Implementation:** Adjust offerings based on individual customer feedback.

Benefits:

- **Increased Customer Satisfaction:** Customers appreciate offerings that meet their specific needs.

- **Higher Conversion Rates:** Personalized recommendations can lead to more sales.

- **Customer Loyalty:** Personalization fosters a stronger connection between the customer and your brand.

7. Monitor Competitor Offerings

Keeping an eye on what your competitors are doing helps you stay competitive.

Actions to Take:

- **Market Research:** Regularly review competitors' products, services, and pricing.

- **Benchmarking:** Compare your offerings against industry standards.

- **Adapt and Innovate:** Use insights to inform your own optimization strategies.

Benefits:

- **Identify Gaps:** Spot areas where competitors may be outperforming you.

- **Stay Relevant:** Ensure your offerings meet or exceed market expectations.

- **Innovative Edge:** Differentiating your products or services can attract new customers.

Real-World Examples of Successful Optimization

Example 1: A Local Cafe Streamlines Operations

Challenge: A small cafe noticed long wait times during peak hours, leading to customer complaints.

Optimization Actions:

- **Process Analysis:** Mapped out the order-taking and preparation processes to identify bottlenecks.
- **Benchmark** the average service time.
- **Technology Implementation:** Introduced a point-of-sale system with mobile ordering capabilities.
- **Staff Training:** Trained baristas on efficient drink preparation techniques.

Results:

- **Reduced Wait Times:** Average wait times decreased by 30%.
- **Increased Sales:** Improved customer satisfaction led to a 15% increase in repeat business.
- **Employee Efficiency:** Staff felt more capable and less stressed during busy periods.

Example 2: An Online Retailer Enhances Customer Experience

Challenge: An SMB e-commerce store faced high cart abandonment rates.

Optimization Actions:

- **Customer Journey Mapping:** Identified that the checkout process was cumbersome.
- **User Experience Improvements:** Simplified the checkout to require fewer steps and offered guest checkout.
- **Personalization:** Implemented product recommendations based on browsing history.

Results:

- **Lower Abandonment Rates:** Cart abandonment dropped by 25%.

- **Higher Conversion Rates:** Sales increased due to a smoother purchasing process.
- **Customer Engagement:** Personalized recommendations boosted average order value.

Example 3: A Manufacturing SMB Reduces Production Costs

Challenge: Rising material costs were squeezing profit margins.

Optimization Actions:

- **Supplier Review:** Negotiated better rates with existing suppliers and explored alternatives.
- **Process Efficiency:** Adopted Lean manufacturing principles to reduce waste.
- **Automation:** Invested in machinery to automate repetitive tasks.

Results:

- **Cost Reduction:** Production costs decreased by 20%.
- **Improved Quality:** Automation led to more consistent product quality.
- **Competitive Pricing:** Lower costs allowed for more competitive pricing strategies.

Action Plan for SMB Owners

Step 1: Set Clear Optimization Goals

Define what you want to achieve with your optimization efforts.

- **Examples:** Increase customer satisfaction scores by 10%, reduce production costs by 15%, or improve delivery times by 20%.

Step 2: Conduct a Comprehensive Assessment

Evaluate your current products or services thoroughly.

- **Customer Feedback:** Collect and analyze customer input to ensure optimization goals are aligned with what matters to the customer.

- **Performance Metrics:** Review sales data, profitability, and operational efficiency.
- **Market Analysis:** Understand industry trends and competitor offerings.

Step 3: Prioritize Areas for Improvement

Focus on areas that will have the most significant impact.

- **High Impact, Low Effort:** Quick wins that are easy to implement.
- **Strategic Importance:** Changes that align with long-term business goals.

Step 4: Develop an Optimization Strategy

Create a plan outlining the actions to take.

- **Resources Required:** Identify necessary investments in time, money, or personnel.
- **Timeline:** Set realistic deadlines for each action item.
- **Responsibility Assignment:** Delegate tasks to team members.

Step 5: Implement Changes Incrementally

Avoid overwhelming your team by introducing changes gradually.

- **Pilot Programs:** Test new processes or features on a small scale first.
- **Monitor Progress:** Keep track of how changes are impacting performance.

Step 6: Measure and Adjust

Regularly assess the effectiveness of your optimization efforts.

- **KPIs Tracking:** Use key performance indicators to measure success.
- **Feedback Loops:** Continue gathering input from customers and employees.
- **Flexibility:** Be prepared to adjust strategies based on results.

Step 7: Foster a Culture of Continuous Improvement

Encourage ongoing optimization as part of your company's ethos.

- **Open Communication:** Keep channels open for suggestions and ideas.
- **Recognition:** Acknowledge and reward team members who contribute to improvements.
- **Learning Opportunities:** Provide training and resources to support skill development.

Tips for Sustaining Optimization Efforts

- **Stay Informed:** Keep up with industry developments and technological advancements.
- **Network with Peers:** Engage with other SMB owners to share experiences and strategies.
- **Regularly Review Goals:** Revisit your optimization objectives to ensure they remain relevant.
- **Invest in Relationships:** Strong relationships with suppliers, customers, and employees can provide valuable insights and support.

Key Takeaways Chapter 18: Optimize Your Products/Services

1. **Optimization is an Ongoing Process, Not a One-Time Fix**

   Product and service optimization should be a **continuous effort** to refine and improve your offerings based on customer feedback, market trends, and business goals. Companies that regularly evaluate and improve their products stay competitive and better serve their customers.

2. **Customer-Centric Optimization Drives Business Growth**

   Your optimization efforts should start with the customer. Actively gather and analyze customer feedback to identify areas for improvement. Small adjustments based on customer needs can lead to higher satisfaction, retention, and referrals.

3. **Process Efficiency Enhances Profitability and Quality**

   Streamlining production, reducing waste, and eliminating inefficiencies allow SMBs to improve product quality while cutting costs. Optimizing workflows through automation, process mapping, and data-driven decision-making increases profitability without sacrificing value.

4. **Technology and Innovation Are Key Enablers of Optimization**

Leveraging automation, digital tools, and data analytics can enhance service delivery, improve accuracy, and reduce operational costs. SMBs should invest in the right technology to optimize processes and enhance customer experience.

5. **Employee Training and Development Strengthen Optimization Efforts**

Employees play a critical role in product and service optimization. Investing in training, skill development, and empowerment fosters innovation and ensures that employees can identify and implement improvements effectively.

6. **Incremental Changes Lead to Long-Term Success**

Small, strategic improvements can yield significant long-term benefits. Rather than overhauling everything at once, focus on high-impact areas, test small changes, and gradually refine your offerings.

7. **Data-Driven Decision Making Reduces Guesswork**

Optimization should be based on measurable insights rather than assumptions. Analyze sales data, customer trends, and performance metrics to make informed decisions about where to focus optimization efforts.

8. **Balancing Cost and Quality is Essential**

Enhancing product or service quality should be financially sustainable. Businesses should assess how improvements impact the bottom line and find ways to add value without overextending resources.

9. **Market Awareness Helps Maintain a Competitive Edge**

Keeping an eye on competitors allows SMBs to identify market trends, anticipate customer expectations, and adjust accordingly. Benchmarking against industry standards ensures that products and services remain relevant.

10. **A Culture of Continuous Improvement is a Competitive Advantage**

    Companies that embrace a mindset of ongoing optimization are more adaptable and resilient. Creating a work culture that values continuous learning and innovation, helps SMBs sustain long-term growth and success.

Reflection Questions Chapter 18: Optimize Your Products/Services

On Customer-Centric Optimization

1. What are the most frequent complaints, pain points, or improvement requests from our customers?

2. Are we effectively gathering and acting on customer feedback to enhance our products and services?

On Efficiency and Process Improvements

3. Where are the inefficiencies or bottlenecks in our production or service delivery processes?

4. Have we mapped out our key workflows? What steps can be automated or streamlined?

5. What specific areas could we optimize to reduce costs while maintaining or improving quality?

On Leveraging Technology and Innovation

6. Are we utilizing the right technology to optimize our products/services and improve efficiency?

7. What tools or systems could help us enhance automation, track performance, or better serve customers?

On Employee Engagement in Optimization

8. How well does our team understand their role in improving products and services?

9. What training, skill development, or tools could empower employees to contribute to optimization efforts?

10. Are we encouraging a culture of continuous improvement where employees feel comfortable suggesting and implementing changes? If not what steps can we take to encourage and surface improvement suggestions from our team?

On Competitive Positioning and Market Awareness

11. How do our products/services compare to competitors in terms of quality, pricing, and customer experience?

12. What can we learn from competitor strategies that might inform our own optimization efforts?

On Measuring Success and Continuous Improvement

13. What key performance indicators (KPIs) are we tracking to measure the success of our optimization efforts?

14. How often do we review and adjust our optimization strategies based on data and results?

Final Reflection: Taking Action

15. What stood out most to you in this chapter?

16. What is one specific action you will take to improve and optimize your products or services starting this month?

CHAPTER 19

INNOVATE YOUR PRODUCT/SERVICE

"Innovation is a change that creates a new dimension of performance"[1] *–Peter Drucker*

Understanding True Innovation vs. Incremental Improvement

Drucker's quote reminds us that true innovation goes beyond simply doing things better but creating a new dimension of performance. Instead of incremental improvements, it redefines what's possible.

As a business owner, you already know the importance of constant improvement and in the last chapter on Product Optimization, we provided methods and questions to facilitate your ongoing improvement efforts. These changes primarily consist of adjustments that enhance what already exists, e.g., faster delivery, a more user-friendly interface, or better customer service.

While these are all meaningful and often necessary for staying competitive, innovation can help you stand out from your competitors in different and better ways that you even thought was possible.

This chapter will explore how you can step beyond incremental improvements and reshape how you deliver value to your customers by asking bolder questions and exploring entirely new ways to solve problems. Innovation isn't just a better version of what you already do—it's a "new dimension of performance" that has the power to disrupt, redefine standards of excellence in ways you may never have imagined.

Defining a New Dimension of Performance

A "new dimension of performance" is more than just improving metrics, but changing how people experience value altogether. Where optimization might speed up a workflow or improve a feature, innovation introduces a breakthrough: something customers didn't even know they needed until they saw it.

Innovation often comes from combining existing technologies, tools, or processes in creative ways that unlock unique value. It challenges assumptions, disrupts norms, and creates solutions that stand out not just because they're better, but because they're different in kind.

Whether you're reimagining a customer experience, developing a new business model, or launching a product that changes expectations, the goal is the same: to move beyond incremental improvement and into what redefines what's possible for your business and your industry.

Example: Purpose Matters and the 7P Business Alignment Model™

An example of purpose-driven innovation is how Purpose Matters developed the 7P Business Alignment Model™—and, through it, this book. Seeing that many small and mid-sized businesses struggled to connect purpose with practical execution, we set out to rethink what strategic consulting and coaching could look like.

Most business owners we serve often face two persistent challenges: the inability to consistently focus on what matters most, and the lack of execution support and expertise to translate that focus into meaningful progress.

They're pulled in too many directions, forced to make important decisions without enough structure, and expected to drive growth without the senior leadership capacity required to sustain it.

The 7P Business Alignment Model™ directly addresses this underserved need by combining alignment coaching with fractional executive support in a flexible, affordable format—often for less than the cost of a part-time employee.

This innovation introduced a new dimension of performance—providing a holistic and integrated way to align people, operations, marketing, and finances around purpose and then operationalize that purpose into measurable progress, greater fulfillment, and meaningful growth.

This book *Focus on What Matters* emerged directly from this innovation, introducing the 7P BAM framework and a practical guide for business owners ready to innovate in their own way.

Just as our work at Purpose Matters combines existing disciplines in new ways to create value, many of the world's most recognized innovations were born from reimagining what already existed.

The following are well known examples illustrating how combining ideas, tools, or existing technologies in unique ways creates value— and a new dimension of performance.

Example 1: Apple iPhone

Before the iPhone was introduced in 2007, cell phones were primarily used for calls, texts, and basic web browsing. A product improvement in this space would have been changing the size of the phone, adding a better camera to an existing phone or extending the battery life, an optimization that doesn't transform the user experience but marginally improves the product.

Then came the iPhone—a breakthrough that added a new dimension of performance. It didn't just improve existing features; it completely reimagined what a phone could do by combining a phone, an iPod, and a fully functional internet browser into one sleek device with a multi-touch interface. This was not an optimization. It was a fundamental shift that reshaped an entire industry, creating a product that millions couldn't imagine living without.

Example 2: Netflix's Transition to Streaming

Another example of innovation is Netflix's transformation from a DVD rental company to a streaming service. Initially, Netflix was competing with companies like Blockbuster by offering DVD rentals by mail, which provided greater convenience than driving to a local Blockbuster store and picking up video and/or DVD rentals. However, when Netflix introduced streaming, it created a new dimension of performance—completely changing how people consumed media. Instead of waiting for DVDs in the mail, users could now instantly stream content. This wasn't just an incremental improvement in their existing business model but a fundamental shift in how people accessed entertainment.

In contrast, an incremental improvement in Netflix's original model might have been faster DVD delivery or a more extensive selection of movies, but it wouldn't have fundamentally altered how customers experienced their service.

Example 3: Uber

Uber disrupted the taxi industry by creating a platform where customers could hail rides directly from their smartphones, track their drivers' arrival in real time, and pay digitally. This transformed the taxi industry and created a whole new segment—ride sharing that added greater convenience, transparency, and ease of use, not just by improving the existing taxi service model. In addition, individuals working as independent contractors even on a part-time basis became a source of drivers for the platform without necessarily having to be employed by a traditional taxi company.

In contrast, a minor improvement in the taxi industry might have been equipping cabs with GPS navigation to ensure better route management or installing credit card readers to offer more payment options—upgrades that improve the service but don't fundamentally change the customer's experience.

Example 4: Tesla's Electric Cars: Tesla's success didn't come from merely improving existing car technologies; instead, the company redefined what a car could be. By focusing on electric power trains, high-performance software, and autonomous driving capabilities, Tesla didn't just improve on the status quo; it introduced an entirely new vision for what personal transportation could be, challenging traditional automotive manufacturers and creating an entirely new dimension of performance in the auto industry while still at an affordable price.

In contrast, an incremental improvement in the automotive sector would be for traditional manufacturers to improve fuel efficiency in their gas-powered vehicles or offer hybrid options. While beneficial, these steps don't fundamentally change the user experience. They improve upon existing technology without redefining what a car can offer.[2]

Restaurant Example: Incremental Improvements vs. True Innovation

Not all progress is created equal. Some changes fine-tune what already exists and others redefine what's possible. Understanding the difference can help business owners decide whether they're refining their current model or reimagining it entirely.

Incremental Improvement: Small, gradual enhancements that improve the customer experience without altering the core business model.

Example: A restaurant might expand its menu, introduce online reservations, improve food quality, or streamline service to reduce wait times. These upgrades boost customer satisfaction and operational efficiency—but the dining experience itself remains largely unchanged. It's still the same restaurant, just a bit better.

True Innovation: A transformative shift that reimagines the customer experience, delivers new value, and creates a competitive edge.

Example: Instead of just optimizing what already exists, imagine a restaurant that leverages AI and customer data to deliver personalized dining at scale. Customers use a dedicated app to set preferences—dietary restrictions, favorite ingredients, and even past orders. Based on this profile, the restaurant recommends tailored meals, offers precise nutritional insights, and even curates suggested pairings or seasonal dishes. The experience feels customized and deeply personal—far beyond what a traditional restaurant offers.

This kind of innovation doesn't just improve the business—it redefines it. It changes how customers interact with the brand, raises expectations, and sets a new industry standard. It's not about doing the same thing better—it's about doing something meaningfully different. Netflix didn't invent DVDs or streaming, but combined them in a new way to produce a powerful new model. Their innovation combined existing tools or technologies in a new way that created unique value for their customers.

Why Innovation Matters

For small and medium-sized business (SMB) owners, embracing true innovation means more than just keeping pace with competitors. It's about creating a competitive advantage that differentiates you in the market. Innovation can lead to:

1. **Increased Customer Satisfaction:** Innovation often creates more value for customers, which in turn can drive loyalty. For example, if you own a gym equipment business and introduce a new line of smart equipment that tracks progress via an app, you've added a new dimension of value to your customer's fitness experience, leading to increased satisfaction.

2. **Business Growth:** Innovation opens new revenue streams and markets. By developing products that solve customer problems in fresh, new ways, you can capture market share from competitors who are still optimizing existing solutions.

3. **Loyalty and Referrals:** Offering something revolutionary can turn customers into brand advocates. People love to talk about game-changing products and experiences, and those referrals are often more valuable than any marketing campaign.

Small and medium sized businesses should take advantage of the fact that due to their size and less bureaucratic hurdles to overcome, they are typically more nimble than larger companies and often better positioned to innovate. This of course depends on the mindset of the owner and the degree to which innovation culture is present or absent in his/her company. Small and medium-sized businesses can take advantage of new technologies and emerging opportunities faster than their larger counterparts.

A smaller company whose decision making consists of the owner and partners don't have to get approval from a leadership executive team or board of directors to adapt a new strategy. Innovative companies like Apple, Tesla, Microsoft, and others began as small companies that could adapt faster than their larger competitors (IBM, GM, etc.) because their larger competitors were already deeply entrenched and invested in existing infrastructure, technology and traditional ways of doing things. History has shown repeatedly numerous examples of small firms successfully competing against Fortune 500 companies and overtaking them. [3]

How to Distinguish Innovation from Incremental Improvements

As an SMB owner, it's crucial to know when you're truly innovating and when you're merely optimizing. Here are some key distinctions:

1. **Scope of Impact:** Is the change merely improving an existing feature, or is it fundamentally changing how your product or service delivers value? For example, adding mobile payment to your service might be considered an optimization, but creating a whole new platform that revolutionizes customer interaction (like Uber did) is an innovation.

2. **Customer Experience:** Does this change enhance a current experience, or does it create an entirely new experience that your customers couldn't have imagined? Innovative changes often make customers rethink how they engage with a product or service entirely.

3. **Market Impact:** Incremental improvements help you stay competitive, but innovations change the competitive landscape. They can create new markets, customer segments, or even disrupt an entire industry.

4. **Sustainability:** Ongoing incremental improvements are necessary to stay competitive yet innovation has the potential to build long-term, sustainable competitive advantages that are harder for competitors to replicate.

Aligning Innovation with Purpose

Innovation is essential for SMB owners to stay ahead of the competition and drive sustainable growth. However, as crucial as innovation is, it must be strategically aligned with the company's core purpose, which includes its mission, vision, core values, and core competencies. Simply chasing innovation for the sake of novelty can lead businesses astray, wasting valuable resources and diluting the focus that should remain aligned with the organization's overall purpose and strategic objectives.

- **Mission:** Innovation must contribute to the business's reason for existence.

- **Vision:** This is the company's long-term aspiration. Any innovation should help bring the company closer to realizing its vision.

- **Core Values:** Innovation should not undermine core values. For example, a company focused on sustainability should avoid innovations that produce a negative environmental impact.

- **Core Competencies and Capabilities:** Innovation should leverage and build upon the company's existing strengths. Businesses that innovate in areas outside their core competencies risk overextending themselves.

- **Resources:** SMBs have limited financial, human, and technological resources. Innovation efforts need to be realistic and sustainable, considering the available resources.

Framework for Innovative Thinking

To foster innovation thinking, SMB owners can ask themselves the following questions:

1. **Customer-Centric Innovation:**
   o What are the biggest pain points our customers face today?
   o How can we solve those problems in a way that fundamentally changes how they experience our product or service?

2. **Market and Industry Trends:**
   o What changes are occurring in our industry that could disrupt or make obsolete our business model?

3. **Internal Competencies and Processes:**
   o Which areas of our operations consistently underperform or are least efficient?

o How can we leverage our core competencies in new, creative ways to provide a new dimension of performance and value to customers?

4. **Radical Differentiation:**

o What assumptions are we making about our business model that we could challenge?

5. **Innovation with Limited Resources:**

o What small, incremental steps could we take now that have the potential to become a larger innovation later?

Methodologies to Facilitate Innovation

Innovation doesn't happen by accident. These methodologies help SMBs approach innovation in a structured, cost-effective way:

1. Design Thinking

Design Thinking is a human-centered approach that prioritizes understanding customer needs and creatively solving their problems. It follows five stages:

- **Empathize**: Understand customers' needs and pain points through observation and interviews.

- **Define**: Articulate the core problem based on insights from the empathize phase.

- **Ideate**: Brainstorm solutions without restrictions, exploring both small and big ideas.

- **Prototype**: Develop low-cost prototypes to test ideas quickly.

- **Test**: Gather feedback from real customers, using insights to refine or pivot as needed.[4]

Example: A gym equipment company might use Design Thinking to explore space-saving solutions, leading to innovative foldable designs.

2. Lean Startup Methodology

The Lean Startup Methodology, popularized by Eric Ries, emphasizes rapid testing with minimal upfront investment. It follows a Build-Measure-Learn cycle:

- **Build**: Create a Minimum Viable Product (MVP) that focuses on core features.

- **Measure**: Collect customer feedback to assess functionality and interest.

- **Learn**: Use insights to refine or pivot the product before significant investment.[5]

Example: A software company could release a simplified MVP to test market interest, gathering data before scaling up.

Key Takeaways Chapter 19: Product/Service Innovation

1. **Innovation Goes Beyond Incremental Improvements**

   True innovation creates a new dimension of performance, fundamentally changing how value is delivered to customers. While optimization improves what already exists, innovation redefines the experience and can create new competitive advantages.

2. **Innovation Disrupts the Status Quo and Redefines Industries**

   Game-changing innovations like the iPhone, Netflix's streaming model, and Uber's ride-sharing platform introduced new ways of creating customer value, not just better versions of existing models. SMBs can use innovation to stand out and disrupt their industries by reimagining customer experiences.

3. **SMBs Have a Unique Advantage in Innovation**

   Small and medium-sized businesses can pivot faster, adapt quicker, and experiment with new ideas more freely than large corporations. While big companies are slower to shift due to bureaucracy and legacy investments, SMBs can leverage their agility to lead in innovation.

4. **A New Dimension of Performance Involves Customer Experience, Market Impact, and Sustainability**

   o Customer Experience: True innovation doesn't just enhance the existing customer journey—it creates a new way of engaging with a product or service.

o Market Impact: Incremental improvements help stay competitive, but innovations can disrupt an industry, create new customer segments, or eliminate traditional competitors.

o **Sustainability**: While minor upgrades are temporary, true innovation builds long-term differentiation that is harder for competitors to replicate.

5. **Innovation Must Align with Business Purpose and Core Competencies**

Pursuing innovation just for the sake of novelty can lead businesses off course. Innovative products and services should align with:

o Mission: Contribute to the company's fundamental reason for existing.

o Vision: Move the business closer to its long-term aspiration.

o Core Competencies: Build upon the company's strengths to maximize impact.

o Resources: SMBs have limited budgets and teams, so innovation should be strategically viable and sustainable.

6. **Innovation Opens New Revenue Streams and Strengthens Customer Loyalty**

o Creating new value through innovation can expand market reach, build brand advocates, and generate long-term loyalty.

o Customers love businesses that solve problems in new, unexpected ways, and these companies are more likely to create a following of loyal raving fans, repeat business and word-of-mouth referrals.

7. **Frameworks Like Design Thinking and Lean Startup Facilitate Innovation**

SMB owners can use structured approaches to develop and test new ideas efficiently without massive investment:

o Design Thinking: A customer-first approach that focuses on problem-solving through iteration and feedback.

o Lean Startup Methodology: A rapid experimentation method that minimizes risk by developing Minimum Viable Products (MVPs) to test ideas before full-scale launch.

8. **Radical Differentiation Requires Challenging Business Assumptions**

Many groundbreaking innovations come from questioning industry norms. SMB owners should ask bold questions, such as:

o What if we removed the most expensive step in our process?

o What if we replaced traditional customer interactions with a self-service model?

o How can we solve the biggest customer pain point in a way no one has before?

9. **True Innovation Focuses on Customer-Centric Problem Solving**

Businesses that redefine how they deliver value win customer loyalty. Instead of focusing on competitors, focus on deeply understanding customer frustrations and needs—then design solutions that radically improve their experience.

10. **Successful Innovation Requires a Culture of Experimentation**

• Encourage employees to suggest new ideas without fear of failure.

• Invest in small tests and prototypes before committing to large changes.

• Measure results, learn from failures, and refine innovations based on real-world feedback.

• Stay adaptable—great ideas may not emerge immediately, but persistence can lead to breakthroughs.

Reflection Questions Chapter 19: Product/ Service Innovation

On Defining True Innovation

1. Does our business focus primarily on incremental improvements, or are we exploring innovations that could redefine our industry?

2. Are there existing technologies or industry practices we could combine in new ways to create unique value for our customers?

On Aligning Innovation with Purpose

3. How does our innovation strategy align with our company's mission, vision, and core competencies?

4. Are we pursuing innovation that truly serves our customers, or are we chasing trends that don't align with our business purpose or strategic goals?

On Customer-Centric Innovation

5. What are the biggest customer pain points that no one in our industry has effectively solved?

6. If we could design a product or service from scratch to serve our customers in the best way possible, what would it look like?

On Market and Industry Trends

7. What industry trends are emerging that could disrupt our current business model?

8. Are there overlooked customer segments that could benefit from a new or improved version of our offerings?

On Differentiation and Competitive Edge

9. What assumptions do we hold about our business that could be challenged to create something radically different?

10. Are we competing in the same way as our competitors, or are we offering a fundamentally different experience?

On Testing and Implementing Innovation

11. Have we considered using methodologies like Design Thinking or Lean Startup to test new ideas with minimal risk?

12. What small, low-cost experiments can we run to validate our innovation ideas before making significant investments?

On Embracing a Culture of Experimentation

13. How can we create an internal culture that encourages employees to share new ideas and take calculated risks?

14. How do we currently handle failures in innovation, and how can we create an environment where mistakes lead to learning and better ideas?

Final Reflection: Taking Action

15. What stood out most to you in this chapter?

16. What is one bold idea you will explore to push your business beyond incremental improvements into true innovation?

CHAPTER 20

MEASURE WHAT MATTERS TO YOUR CUSTOMER

"What the customer buys and considers value is never a product. It is always utility, what a product or service does for him." [1]
—Peter Drucker

This insight is echoed by innovation expert and Harvard professor Clayton Christensen, who explained:

> "When we buy a product, we essentially "hire" it to help us do a job. If it does the job well, the next time we're confronted with the same job, we tend to hire that product again. And if it does a crummy job, we "fire" it and look for an alternative. (We're using the word "product" here as shorthand for any solution that companies can sell; of course, the full set of "candidates" we consider hiring can often go well beyond just offerings from companies.) [2]

Both Drucker and Christensen emphasize the importance of focusing on the value and utility your products or services provide to the customer rather than simply the product itself.

Measuring Product/Service Benefits:

Utilizing Net Promoter Score (NPS) to Drive Customer Loyalty and Business Growth

For small and medium-sized businesses (SMBs), aligning products and services with your core purpose and ensuring that they perform the job that customers expect is critical for building customer satisfaction and loyalty. In this section, we'll discuss how tools like the **Net Promoter Score (NPS)** can help you better understand what matters to your customer and increase customer loyalty. By doing so you can determine to what extent your products and services are fulfilling what matters to your customer and fulfilling their needs and expectations in ways that drive word of mouth referrals and recommendations.

Understanding the Net Promoter Score (NPS)

NPS is a straightforward metric that ranges from -100 to 100, assessing customer satisfaction through a single question: *"How likely are you to recommend our product/service to a friend or colleague?"* [3]

Respondents rate their likelihood on a scale of 0-10, which categorizes them into three distinct groups:

- **Promoters (9-10):** Loyal customers who drive growth by continuously buying and referring others.

- **Passives (7-8):** Satisfied customers but unenthusiastic and vulnerable to competitive offerings.

- **Detractors (0-6):** Unhappy customers who may damage your brand through negative word-of-mouth.

Calculating NPS Scores

Net Promoter Score (NPS) Range

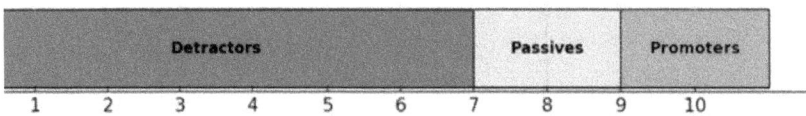

1. **Calculate the Percentage:**
   - Percentage of Promoters = (Number of Promoters / Total Responses) × 100
   - Percentage of Detractors = (Number of Detractors / Total Responses) × 100

2. **Calculate NPS:**
   - **NPS = Percentage of Promoters - Percentage of Detractors**

Example Calculation

- Suppose you have surveyed 100 customers and received the following responses:
  - o 50 Promoters
  - o 30 Passives
  - o 20 Detractors
- Percentage of Promoters = (50 / 100) × 100 = 50%
- Percentage of Detractors = (20 / 100) × 100 = 20%
- **NPS = 50% - 20% = 30**

An NPS score of 30 indicates a positive sentiment among customers, with more Promoters than Detractors. NPS scores can range from -100 (if every customer is a Detractor) to +100 (if every customer is a Promoter.

NET PROMOTER SCORE

How likely is it that you would recommend our company to a friend?

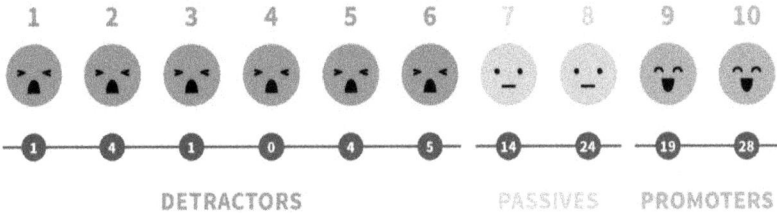

Behaviors, such as buying more, remaining customers for longer, and making more positive, such as

NPS = %PROMOTERS - %DETRACTORS

NPS = % 😊 - % 😠 = 47% - 15 % = 32%

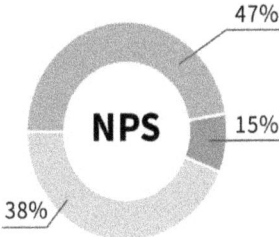

NPS

Detractors - 15% - 156

Passives - 38% - 388

Promoters - 47% - 471

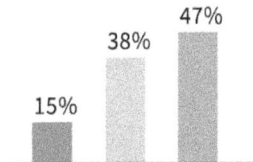

Benefits of NPS for SMBs:

- **Ease of Use:** NPS surveys are simple to implement and analyze, making them accessible for businesses of any size. The straightforward format increases response rates and provides clear, quantifiable data that can be translated into meaningful actions for improving customer experience.

- **Customer-Centric Insights:** NPS provides you with a better understanding of how your customers perceive your products and services. By focusing on the customer's perspective, you can identify key areas that drive loyalty and satisfaction, allowing you to make targeted improvements that resonate with your audience.

- **Benchmarking Performance:** NPS allows you to gauge your performance against industry benchmarks, providing valuable context to understand where you stand relative to competitors and identify areas for improvement. This comparison helps you set realistic goals and prioritize strategic initiatives to enhance customer satisfaction.

- **Predictive Power:** High NPS scores correlate with strong business growth, while low scores may signal a risk of losing customers or declining loyalty.[4]

Best Practices for Implementing NPS

- **Define Clear Objectives**: Before launching your NPS survey, establish what you aim to achieve. Do you want to measure overall customer satisfaction, assess specific product performance, or gauge loyalty after a particular interaction? Clear objectives will guide the design and timing of your survey.

- **Keep the Survey Simple**: The key strength of NPS is its simplicity. Use the standard NPS question: "How likely are you to recommend us to a friend or colleague?" Follow it up with an open-ended question, such as, "What's the main reason for your score?" This keeps the survey brief and encourages participation.

- **Segment Your Audience**: Consider segmenting your customers based on factors such as demographics, purchase history, or product usage. Segmenting helps tailor insights to different groups, making the feedback more actionable. For example, newer customers may have different experiences than long-term clients.

- **Ensure Timely Follow-Up**: One of the most important aspects of NPS is acting on the feedback you receive. Implement a process for following up with Promoters, Passives, and Detractors. Engage Promoters by asking for referrals, while addressing the concerns of Detractors with personalized solutions.

- **Leverage Multiple Channels**: Distribute NPS surveys through a variety of channels, including email, SMS, in-app prompts, and website pop-ups. Using different channels increases the likelihood of getting a representative sample of feedback.

- **Act on Open-Ended Feedback**: While the NPS score is helpful, the true value often lies in the qualitative feedback from customers. Use AI to summarize and analyze feedback to identify common themes and opportunities for improvement.

- **Close the Loop**: Share the feedback and results with your team to ensure everyone understands the customer's voice. Implement changes based on this feedback and communicate these improvements back to customers to demonstrate that their opinions are valued.

- **Benchmark and Track Progress**: Regularly benchmark your NPS against industry standards to see how you stack up. Internally, compare scores across different time periods or customer segments to monitor progress and identify trends.

- **Identify Trends:** Collect customer feedback over time to identify recurring patterns or areas for improvement.[5]

How Frequently Should NPS Be Administered?

- **Quarterly for Ongoing Feedback**: Administering NPS every three to six months provides a steady stream of customer insights without overwhelming your audience. It allows you to track trends and address issues proactively.

- **After Key Interactions**: For more focused insights, send NPS surveys after significant customer interactions, such as after a product purchase, a support ticket resolution, or service delivery. This approach provides timely, relevant feedback tied to specific experiences.

- **Annually for Holistic Feedback**: An annual NPS survey can give you a broader view of customer loyalty and satisfaction over the long term. It's a good opportunity to measure overall brand perception and performance.

- **Customize Frequency Based on Customer Cycle**: Adjust your NPS survey frequency to match your industry and customer engagement cycle. For example, subscription-based businesses may send surveys after every renewal, while product-based companies might use post-purchase surveys.[6]

Using NPS to Improve Products and Services
Identify Areas for Improvement:

- **Promoters:** Learn what you're doing right and leverage that insight to further strengthen your offerings.

- **Detractors:** Focus on pain points to resolve dissatisfaction and prevent customer churn.

- **Passives:** Look for ways to turn Passives into Promoters by addressing their concerns and adding value.

Creating Action Plans:

Once you've identified key insights, it's time to act:

1. **Prioritize Issues:** Focus on areas with the highest impact.

2. **Develop Concrete Steps:** Break down improvements into actionable steps.

3. **Assign Responsibilities:** Ensure accountability by assigning tasks to team members.

4. **Set Timelines:** Establish deadlines to monitor progress effectively.

Case Study 1: Retail Business Enhancing Customer Experience

A local boutique retail store noticed that while customers loved their products, feedback from NPS surveys revealed mixed reactions about the checkout process. **Detractors** frequently cited long lines and a confusing payment system as major pain points, while **Passives** were generally satisfied but not thrilled, indicating the process was serviceable but not seamless. On the other hand, **Promoters** loved the boutique experience overall but subtly mentioned that a quicker checkout process would make their visits even better.

Key Insight for SMB Owners: The checkout process is often the final interaction a customer has with your business, and a poor experience can overshadow all the positive moments leading up to it.

Solution:

- The store implemented a more efficient point-of-sale (POS) system that included mobile payment options and self-checkout kiosks. This reduced wait times by 40% and provided customers with multiple payment options.

- In addition to upgrading the technology, the business trained staff to assist with these new systems, ensuring a smooth transition and positive customer experience.

FOCUS ON WHAT MATTERS

Results:

- **Promoters** continued to spread positive word-of-mouth, praising the improved checkout experience as aligning with the high-quality boutique atmosphere they already loved.

- **Passives** were converted to Promoters as they noticed the checkout process had become faster and more convenient, which significantly improved their overall experience.

- Many **Detractors** moved into the Passive category as their frustrations were addressed. NPS increased by 25 points over six months, resulting in a 20% rise in repeat business and a 15% boost in overall sales.

This case demonstrates how improving operational efficiency at critical touch points like checkout can not only eliminate pain points for Detractors but also build on what Promoters already appreciate. By making the necessary operational improvements, they significantly boosted customer satisfaction and loyalty, translating to higher repeat business and increased revenue.

Case Study 2: IT Service Company Optimizing Client Relationships

A small IT service provider was highly regarded for its technical expertise. However, NPS feedback revealed communication gaps that led to dissatisfaction among many clients. **Detractors** cited poor communication and delays in project updates as their primary reasons for dissatisfaction. **Passives**, while satisfied with the technical solutions provided, felt that communication could be improved, and this lack of engagement kept them from becoming fully loyal. **Promoters** were content with the technical expertise but suggested more proactive updates would enhance their confidence in the service.

Key Insight for SMB Owners: Technical expertise alone is not enough to retain clients. Regular, transparent communication is equally important for maintaining strong client relationships.

Solution:

- The company implemented a structured communication plan, including scheduled update calls, a customer portal for real-time project tracking, and a dedicated account manager for each client.

- Additionally, they launched post-project follow-up surveys to gather feedback and address lingering concerns, ensuring that no issues were left unresolved.

Results:

- **Promoters** became even more engaged, appreciating enhanced communication and proactive updates, which reinforced their trust in the company's ability to deliver.

- **Passives** were converted into Promoters as the communication improvements closed the gap between the technical quality of the service and the client relationship experience.

- Many **Detractors** moved into the Passive category as their frustrations with communication were addressed. NPS improved by 30 points within three months, leading to a 35% increase in client retention. Several clients also upgraded their service contracts, citing enhanced trust and better communication.

This case underscores the importance of communication and client engagement, especially for service-based businesses. While technical skills are crucial, the client relationship is equally important. By improving communication, even highly technical businesses can significantly strengthen their client relationships, boosting loyalty and long-term business success.

By addressing both **Promoters** and **Detractors**, these case studies provide a comprehensive look at how to enhance strengths while resolving pain points. SMB owners can learn from these examples to focus on what's working, while strategically improving areas of weakness to build a stronger, more loyal customer base.

NPS Categories for Fortune 500 Companies

1. **World Class (Best): 70 and above**

   Companies in this range exhibit exceptional customer loyalty and satisfaction. They have a high proportion of promoters, indicating strong customer advocacy and minimal detractors. An example is **Tesla**, which boasts an NPS of 95, compared to the average automotive industry's NPS of 50 reflecting its strong loyal customer base and innovative products. This category indicates that the company consistently delivers outstanding customer experiences.

2. **Excellent: 50 to 69**

   This range signifies very positive customer experiences, with a significant number of promoters and relatively few detractors. Companies in this category are highly regarded in their industries and enjoy robust customer loyalty. For instance, **Amazon**, with an NPS of 73, often falls just beyond this range into the world-class category, highlighting its exceptional customer focus.

3. **Good: 30 to 49**

   Companies with scores in this range have a mix of promoters and passives, with fewer detractors. This range indicates good customer satisfaction but suggests room for improvement. **Microsoft**, with an NPS of 45, exemplifies a company with solid customer loyalty but also areas that may need enhancement.

4. **Average: 0 to 29**

   Scores in this range reflect a mixed customer experience. Companies may have a balanced distribution of promoters, passives, and detractors, indicating inconsistent customer experience. This range suggests that while some customers are satisfied, there is a significant portion that may not be, highlighting areas needing attention.

5. **Poor: Below 0**

A negative NPS score indicates more detractors than promoters. This suggests significant customer dissatisfaction, which can negatively impact the company's reputation and growth potential. Companies in this range face considerable challenges in maintaining customer loyalty and positive word-of-mouth.

These categories provide a useful benchmark for understanding how companies are perceived by their customers. A higher NPS score generally correlates with strong customer loyalty and positive brand perception, while lower scores indicate the need for substantial improvements in customer experience.[7]

NPS Score: Good Profit Measure

In his seminal book The Ultimate Questions 2.0: How Net Promoter Companies Thrive in a Customer-Driven World, Reichheld introduces the concept of "good profits," which he defines as economic gains earned by genuinely "delighting" customers and cultivating their loyalty as a result.

He argues that achieving these "good profits" requires a business to embrace and embed the Golden Rule by treating others as you would want to be treated into every aspect of its operations, from leadership to front-line interactions. By doing so, businesses can foster trust, satisfaction, and long-term loyalty, creating a sustainable foundation for success.[8]

At Purpose Matters, we aim to go beyond the Golden Rule to the "Platinum Rule" treating our customers even better than how we would want to be treated ourselves. This mindset challenges us to anticipate needs, exceed expectations, and create memorable moments and experiences that turn satisfied clients into loyal raving fans.

Key Takeaways Chapter 20: Measure What Matters to Your Customer

Measuring Product/Service Benefits: Utilizing Net Promoter Score (NPS) to Drive Customer Loyalty and Business Growth

1. **Focus on Customer Value:**

   o Customers "hire" your product or service to solve a problem or create value. Knowing what problem you solve helps you deliver better value and grow loyalty.

2. **Understanding Net Promoter Score (NPS):**

   o **NPS is a simple way to measure customer satisfaction and loyalty** by asking how likely customers are to recommend you. It helps categorize customers as **Promoters, Passives, or Detractors.**

3. **Using NPS to Grow Your Business:**

   o High NPS scores mean stronger customer loyalty, repeat business, and referrals. Low scores show areas that need urgent improvement to prevent losing customers.

4. **Leveraging Feedback for Improvement:**

   o **NPS feedback gives real, actionable insights.** Listening to what customers say (especially Detractors) helps improve your product, service, and customer experience.

5. **Follow Best Practices to Get Better Feedback:**

   o Keep surveys short, target the right customers, and follow up on what they say to close the feedback loop.

6. **Benchmark and Track Progress:**

   o Regularly compare your NPS over time and against competitors to see how you're doing and where you need to improve.

7. **Act on Customer Insights:**

   o Fix issues for Detractors, turn Passives into Promoters, and reinforce what Promoters already love.

8. **Improve the Whole Customer Journey:**

o   Use NPS insights to improve processes, customer touch-points, and communication that impact satisfaction.

9. **Consistency Matters:**

o   **Run NPS surveys regularly** (e.g., quarterly, post-service, or annually) to gather ongoing feedback and spot trends.

10. **Create a Customer Centric Culture:**

o   Involve your team in improving customer satisfaction and celebrate wins when customers share positive feedback.

Reflection Questions Chapter 20: Measure What Matters to Your Customer

1. **Understanding Customer Value:**

o   How well do I understand what my customers value most about my product or service?

o   What problem or "job" are customers hiring us to solve, and how well are we meeting that need?

2. **Implementing and Using NPS:**

o   Do we currently measure customer satisfaction with NPS? If so, how often are we reviewing the results?

o   What can I do to simplify and improve how we collect NPS feedback to get more meaningful responses?

3. **Acting on Customer Feedback:**

o   How effectively do we respond to and address concerns from Detractors?

o   What recurring issues or themes show up in customer feedback, and what's one action I can take to address them?

4. **Strengthening Customer Loyalty:**

o   What are specific actions I can take to turn Passives into Promoters?

o   How can I reward or engage Promoters to deepen loyalty and encourage referrals?

5. **Benchmarking and Analyzing Results:**

   o   How does our NPS compare to others in our industry? What does this say about our customer relationships?

   o   Are there customer groups (segments) where our NPS is lower? What can we do to improve their experience?

6. **Improving Customer Touch points:**

   o   What are the key moments (touch points) in the customer journey that need improvement (e.g., onboarding, checkout, customer service)?

   o   How can we integrate customer feedback into ongoing product/service improvements?

7. **Creating a Customer-Centric Team:**

   o   How can I involve my team in reviewing NPS feedback and brainstorming solutions?

   o   How do we communicate back to customers so they know we're listening and acting on their input?

8. **Regularly Tracking Trends:**

   o   Are we collecting NPS feedback often enough to identify patterns and trends?

   o   How can I build a routine for reviewing NPS results and acting on them regularly?

9. **What stood out to you in this chapter or resonated most with you?**

   o   What's one insight or idea that feels especially relevant to improving customer satisfaction?

   o   What specific action will you take to apply these insights and strengthen customer loyalty and satisfaction?

PROCESS—ALIGNING HOW YOU OPERATE WITH WHAT MATTERS

CHAPTER 21

ALIGN YOUR PROCESS WITH PURPOSE

"If the ladder is not leaning against the right
wall, every step we take just gets us to
the wrong place faster."[1]
—Stephen R. Covey

Process Alignment with Purpose

Aligning your business processes with your core purpose—encompassing your company mission and vision— is crucial to ensuring that your business is moving in the right direction. Before tackling process alignment, however, it's best to have a clearly defined and documented mission and vision statement that authentically reflects who you are and your aspirations.

If you haven't completed Section 1: Purpose, it is highly recommended that you do so before starting the four chapters in the Process section. The first step toward strategic alignment of processes, especially those critical to delivering your core customer benefits, is to clearly understand your company's mission (the purpose of your existence) and vision (what you aspire to become). These are the guiding stars for your strategic decisions and process alignment efforts.[2] If your ladder (process) is leaning against the right wall (purpose), you'll be satisfied with the view once you reach the top because you've achieved your overarching goals and objectives.

But, if it's leaning against the wrong wall, even if you have the right ladder and the right people climbing it, you may end up on top of the "wrong building" and perhaps not enjoying the view, one that's far different from what you had initially envisioned. This chapter introduces ways to improve and align your processes with your purpose to ensure that you are climbing up the right wall. In other words, you are both "doing things right" and, most importantly, "doing the right things" that align with your purpose and what matters most. To reiterate, Peter Drucker advises us that "Efficiency is doing things right; effectiveness is doing the right things." [3] And when your process is misaligned with your purpose, Drucker emphasizes that *"There is nothing so useless as doing efficiently that which should not be done at all."* [4] This highlights the critical importance of not just executing tasks well, but ensuring that the tasks themselves are purposeful and aligned with your overarching goals.

Defining Core Processes

In any business, processes are the backbone of operations. Once these processes are aligned with your core purpose, every step, decision, and action work toward achieving your strategic objectives. Clarity about your core purpose enables you to identify the key processes that directly support it, delivering value to your customers. With this understanding, we can then work on making our core processes more effective and productive.

Core Processes vs. Non-Core Processes

Not all processes have the same impact on your business. **Core processes** are those that directly create value for your customers and contribute to achieving your core purpose consisting of your mission and vision. **Non-core processes**, while important, serve a supportive function and don't directly impact value creation. Understanding the difference helps you prioritize where to focus your optimization efforts.

Examples of Core vs Non-Core Processes

Business Type	Core Process	Non-Core Process
Manufacturing Company	The production line, as it directly impacts product quality and delivery.	Payroll processing is necessary but do not directly contribute to product value.
Consulting Firm	Diagnosing client problems and delivering insights, implementing recommendations.	Office administration, such as managing contracts, is essential but not directly related to client outcomes.

Business Type	Core Process	Non-Core Process
Pre-K Education Provider	Teacher-student interactions and curriculum delivery are directly aligned with providing quality education.	School maintenance is necessary but is not core to student learning.
E-Commerce Business	Order fulfillment, including inventory management, packing, and shipping, which directly affects customer satisfaction.	Accounting is necessary but does not directly impact product delivery.

By distinguishing between core and non-core processes, you ensure your resources are efficiently allocated. Your core processes should be the focus of improvement since they directly impact customer experience and your ability to deliver on your mission. Non-core processes, while still necessary, can often be streamlined, automated, or outsourced to free up resources for your core processes.

Streamlining and Aligning for Efficiency

Identifying, reducing, or eliminating non-value-added steps in the value chain is an important part of streamlining your processes to maximize efficiency. A value chain refers to all the key activities your business performs to create value for your customers. It's a way to look at your operations and identify how each step—such as sourcing materials, creating products or services, marketing, selling, and providing customer support—contributes to delivering something valuable to your customers.

Non-value-added steps consume resources but do not contribute to the customer's value perception or the product/service's quality. These principles draw from the lean manufacturing mindset: to provide what is needed, when it is needed, with the minimum amount of materials, equipment, labor, and space. This helps us think about ways to minimize or eliminate wasteful activities, resulting in greater efficiency and cost reduction.

Examples: Non-Value Added Steps

Manufacturing:

- Over processing: Adding features that do not increase the product's or service's value to the customer.

- Excess Motion: Unnecessary movements by workers or machines.

- Overproduction: Producing more products than demanded.

- Bottlenecks: Waiting and idle time when materials, information, equipment, or people are not ready.

- Transportation: Unnecessary movement of materials or products.

- Rework: Correcting defects or failures.

Services:

- Excessive Paperwork: Creating, handling, and storing unnecessary documents.

- Redundant Approvals: Multiple layers of approvals that slow down service delivery without adding any value.

- Customer Waiting Time: Making customers wait unnecessarily.

- Unnecessary Service Steps: Steps that do not enhance the customer's experience.

Administrative and Office Work:

- Data Entry Redundancy: Entering the same data into multiple systems.

- Manual Information Processing: Handling information manually when automation is possible.

- Unproductive Meetings: Meetings without clear objectives.

- Email Overload: Spending excessive time on irrelevant emails.

Streamlining or eliminating these non-value-added steps can significantly improve productivity, cost efficiency, customer satisfaction, and even employee satisfaction while improving overall operational effectiveness. Identifying and addressing these steps requires detailed process analysis and a commitment to continuous improvement.[5]

Reflection Questions: Identifying Core vs. Non-Core Processes

1. What core activities directly contribute to delivering value to your customers?

2. How do they align with your purpose?

3. Which processes support your business but don't directly impact the customer experience?

4. How can these be streamlined or outsourced?

Strategic Process Alignment: Driving Customer Value and Efficiency

The ultimate goal of aligning your business processes with your core purpose is to ensure that every step in your value chain meaningfully contributes to delivering core customer benefits and contributing to your core purpose. Each stage whether in production, delivery, or support should create value from the customer's perspective.[6] This means that every activity must justify the time and resources invested, ensuring your business remains focused on what matters most and operates efficiently to deliver value.

When processes are well-aligned with your purpose, your entire organization is working toward the same objective. However, when processes are misaligned, inefficiencies arise, with team members metaphorically "rowing in different directions." This misalignment weakens focus, dilutes efforts, and prevents your business from cohesively moving toward its goals and ultimately compromises your ability to deliver exceptional customer value and achieve your mission.

In the next chapter, we'll explore **Process Mapping**, a powerful tool that helps you visualize and document your processes. Through this exercise, you'll be able to identify inefficiencies and realign operations with your company's purpose. This tool will provide you with a clear, strategic view of your business, ensuring that every process plays a role in delivering exceptional value to your customers while keeping you aligned with your mission.

Key Takeaways Chapter 21: Align Your Process with Purpose

1. **Processes Must Align with Purpose and Vision:**

   o If your processes aren't aligned with your mission, vision, and purpose, they drain time and money. Aligned processes move you closer to your goals and improve how you serve customers.

2. **Focus on Core Processes, Streamline or Outsource the Rest:**

   o **Core processes** directly impact customers and drive value.

   o **Non-core processes** should be simplified, automated, or outsourced to free up time and resources.

3. **Eliminate Waste and Focus on What Matters:**

   o Get rid of unnecessary steps that don't add value. Streamlining workflows makes your business more efficient and reduces frustration for both employees and customers.

4. **Think in Terms of Value Chains:**

   o Every step in your process should add value for customers — from start to finish. If a step doesn't add value, it may be time to rethink it.

5. **Make Process Review a Regular Habit:**

   o Don't wait for problems to arise. Regularly evaluate and adjust processes to stay aligned with your goals and evolving customer needs.

Reflection Questions Chapter 21: Align Your Process with Purpose

1. **Aligning Processes with Purpose:**
   o Do our current processes clearly support our mission, vision, and purpose — or are there steps that no longer make sense?
   o What is **one process we could adjust** to better align with what matters most in our business?

2. **Focusing on Core Value-Driving Processes:**
   o Which of our processes are critical for creating value and delivering great customer experiences?
   o Are there processes that are non-essential and could be streamlined, automated, or outsourced to save time?

3. **Improving Customer Experience:**
   o Are our processes helping or hurting the customer experience?
   o Where do customers experience delays, confusion, or frustration — and what could we do to fix that?

4. **Cutting Out Waste and Inefficiencies:**
   o Are there steps in our workflows that don't add value and should be eliminated?
   o What's one step we could simplify or remove this month to improve efficiency?

5. **Building a Habit of Continuous Improvement:**
   o When was the last time we reviewed our key processes for alignment and efficiency?
   o How can we schedule regular process reviews — quarterly or biannually — to keep things running smoothly?

6. **What stood out to you in this chapter or resonated most with you?**

   o   What insight, story, or idea felt especially relevant to your business right now?

   o   What is **one thing you feel motivated to act on** because of this chapter?

7. **What are your top 1-2 takeaways from this chapter?**

   o   What **specific action** will you take to start applying these insights and better align your processes for growth and impact?

CHAPTER 22

OPTIMIZE AND MAP YOUR PROCESS

"You don't learn to process map; you process map to learn." [1] *—Dr Myron Tribus*

Introduction to Process Mapping

Process mapping is a practical framework for understanding, improving, and optimizing how your business operates especially when it comes to your **core processes**.

A process is simply a series of actions or steps taken to achieve a specific outcome. When these steps are aligned with your company's core purpose—your mission and vision—they move you closer to what matters most. The more clearly you understand these processes, the more effectively you can lead your team toward strategic goals.

Process mapping involves creating diagrams or flowcharts that show the sequence of steps in a workflow. These visual tools help teams spot inefficiencies, eliminate bottlenecks, and uncover opportunities for improvement. As quality expert W. Edwards Deming famously said:

"If you can't describe what you are doing as a process, you don't know what you're doing." [2]

This quote gets to the heart of why process mapping matters. You can't improve what you haven't defined. Mapping a process forces you to slow down, document the reality of how work gets done, and bring hidden assumptions or inefficiencies to the surface. In this way, process mapping becomes more than just a tool but also becomes a learning process.

You don't need to be an expert to get started. In fact, as Dr. Myron Tribus reminds us, the very act of mapping is how we learn:

"You don't learn to process map; you process map to learn." [3]

Why Use Process Mapping?

1. **See the Big Picture**: It's like zooming out on a map to see the whole journey from start to finish. This helps everyone understand what they're supposed to do and how their part fits into the larger goal.

2. **Find and Fix Problems**: Sometimes, a step in the process might be unnecessary or take too long. Seeing the whole "map" makes it easier to spot these issues and figure out how to fix them. It provides an opportunity to learn about how work is currently performed so you can identify inefficiencies and make improvements.

3. **Improve Teamwork**: When everyone knows what the map looks like, it's easier for them to work together because they understand how their work affects others. This ensures that everyone is singing on the same sheet of music. It can also help identify any redundancies or overlapping work that may create inefficiencies and confusion arising from 'too many cooks in the kitchen'.

4. **Make Things Faster and Better**: By streamlining steps and removing unnecessary work, work can be done quicker and with fewer mistakes, which ultimately makes customers happy and can save you money.

5. **Documentation**: Process maps provide a way to document the "recipe" of steps in a process, creating a user-friendly visual format that simplifies communication and ensures greater consistency of results.

6. **Compliance**: Process mapping helps businesses comply with standards such as ISO 9000 and ISO 9001. It ensures processes are documented, standardized, and aligned with regulatory requirements, facilitating easier audits and certifications.[3]

Additional Benefits of Process Mapping

1. **Understanding**: Process maps help teams understand and communicate their processes. They clarify what needs to be done and in what order, reducing confusion and increasing comprehension.

2. **Roles and Responsibilities**: They identify the people involved in the process and what they do, ensuring everyone knows who does what.

3. **Troubleshooting**: They help identify problems and bottle-necks, allowing a team to see where improvements might be made. This helps identify inefficiencies, gaps, and other issues in the process flow.

4. **Better Onboarding**: Process maps are valuable for training new employees, offering a quick reference to help them understand how work gets done.

5. **Efficiency and KPI (Key Performance Indicators) Measurement**: Consistent, well-mapped processes are more accessible to measure and track. They help measure the efficiency of work processes and KPIs. Inconsistent processes are challenging to measure reliably.

6. **ERP Implementation:** Process Mapping is invaluable for the successful implementation of new technologies, such as ERP implementations.[4]

By mapping out a process from start to finish, you can better understand how the entire process works, identify inefficiencies, and make improvements. Additionally, process maps allow for contingency planning and provide problem-solving guidance, breaking down complex workflows into smaller, more manageable steps. Also, when integrating new technology such as a CRM or ERP, a good process map is critical to a successful implementation.

Steps to Create a Process Map

1. **Identify a Problem/Opportunity or Process to Map**: First, determine the process you want to map out. Is there an inefficient process that needs improvement? Is there a new process you'd like to communicate to your team? A complex process that employees often have questions about? Identify what you want to map and name it.

2. **Gather Your Team**: Gather the people involved in the process, including those who do the work, supervise it, and rely on its outcomes.

3. **Define the Start and End Points**: Decide where the process begins and ends. For example, if you're mapping your manufacturing process, you might start with a request for a proposal/bid and end with a product delivered to the customer.

4. **List the Steps**: Work as a team to list every step in the process in order. It may be helpful to prepare a narrative of each step and not leave anything out, even if it seems small or obvious.

5. **Draw the Map**: You can use Post-it notes, dry-erase markers, and a whiteboard to represent the steps and how they connect. There are also computer programs that can help with this. Each shape, like a rectangle for a task, a diamond for a decision point, and an oval for the start or end, helps make the map easier to understand.

6. **Future State Improvements**: Look at the map with your team and ask questions like: "Can we remove any steps?" "Can we do things better or in a better order?" "Is there anything missing?" Be mindful that quality improvement consists of both doing things right and doing the right things.

Tips for Effective Process Mapping

- **Keep It Simple**: Start with a basic map. You can always add details later. Agree on which process you wish to process map and the desired outcomes.

- **Use Common Language**: Provide a common point of reference and language to discuss how things get done so everyone understands the terms used on the map. Avoid jargon that might confuse some team members. This also provides an opportunity to standardize naming conventions for files and folders, so employees do not refer to the same document in different ways, which causes confusion.

- **Update Regularly**: As your business changes, update the map. New tools, employees, or goals might mean your process needs to change, too. It can now serve as a framework to help analyze and generate ideas for improving current and future processes.

- **Be Flexible**: There is no single right way to process map.

- **Current State**: Initially process map what is, not what you would like it to be.

- **Future State**: After you've documented the current state, you can then work on designing the future state.

- **Involve Everyone**: Get feedback from people at all levels of the process. The best ideas often come from those who do the work daily. Share it with everyone involved.[5]

Commonly Used Process Mapping Symbols

Process Map Legend of Symbols:	Name	Purpose/Use
○ Oval	Start/End	Represents the beginning or end of a process.
■ Rectangle	Process Step	Represents a task, activity, or operation within the process.
◆ Diamond	Decision Point	Indicates a decision that needs to be made, often leading to different paths in the process.
▰ Parallelogram	Input/Output	Represents inputs to or outputs from a process, such as a document, materials, data, or reports.
→ Arrow	Flow/Direction	Shows the sequence or flow of steps within the process.

How to Use This Legend in Your Process Map:

- Begin with an **oval** to represent the start or end of the process.

- Use **rectangles** to depict the steps or actions within the workflow.

- Incorporate **diamonds** for decision points that might lead to alternate paths or actions.

- Connect steps with **arrows** to show the sequence and direction of actions.

- Include **parallelograms** to identify inputs (e.g., documents, data, materials) or outputs (e.g., results, reports).

Types of Process Maps

Process maps come in various forms, each suited to specific purposes and projects. While they all aim to visualize a process, selecting the right type of map can improve understanding, efficiency, and clarity for a particular task. Below are some of the most common types of process maps:

Flowchart: The Simplest Process Map

A flowchart is the most basic form of a process map. Using standard process mapping symbols, it illustrates the inputs, outputs, and steps involved in completing a process. Its simplicity makes it a versatile tool for numerous scenarios.

Uses of a Flowchart:

- Planning new projects by visually laying out steps.

- Improving communication between team members by providing a shared reference point.

- Modeling and documenting processes for better understanding.

- Solving problems in current workflows by identifying bottlenecks or redundancies.

- Analyzing and managing workflows for smoother operations.

Best For: Demonstrating how a process unfolds from start to finish in a sequential, easy-to-follow order.

A Swimlane Map, also referred to as a Cross-Functional Process Map, is particularly effective when a process involves multiple roles, teams, or stakeholders. The visual structure divides the map into distinct "swim lanes," with each lane representing a specific role, function, or stakeholder.

Key Features of Swimlane Maps:

- **Clarification of Roles:** Clearly defines where one role ends and another begins, reducing ambiguity.

- **Activity Organization:** Each activity is listed within the appropriate swim lane for the responsible role or stakeholder.

- **Interaction Visibility:** Highlights how various roles interact and hand off tasks, ensuring smoother collaboration.

Uses of Swimlane Maps:

- Training employees by clearly illustrating their responsibilities within a process.

- Increasing accountability by explicitly assigning tasks to specific roles.

- Identifying inefficiencies, such as delays, redundancies, or potential failure points.

Best For: Clarifying the roles of multiple stakeholders in a process, especially in collaborative or multi-team workflows.

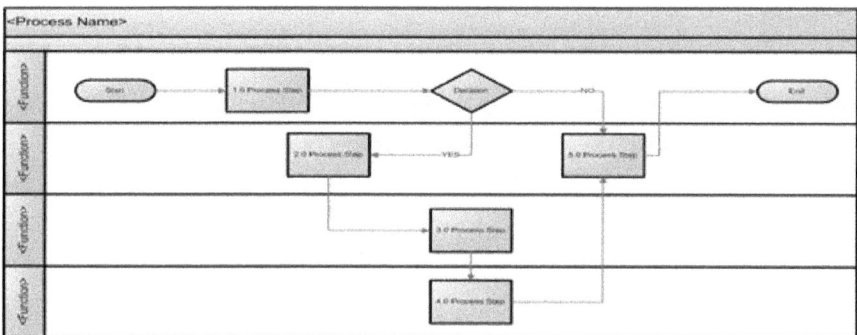

Example: Process Mapping for a Landscape Design-Build Firm

Background:

GreenScape Solutions, a small landscape design-build firm, specializes in creating custom outdoor spaces for residential and commercial clients. With a growing client base, the owner, John, started noticing inefficiencies in their project workflows. Projects were taking longer than expected, and clients were occasionally dissatisfied with the delays, even though the final results met their expectations.

John decided to implement process mapping to identify where the inefficiencies were happening and to streamline their operations.

Problem:

John's team had multiple steps involved in each project—client consultation, design development, material sourcing, construction, and final hand-off. While the quality of work was high, there were bottlenecks, especially in coordinating between the design and construction teams. Projects would often be delayed due to miscommunication or rework because of unclear hand-offs between phases.

Solution:

John brought his team together to create a process map for a typical project, from the initial client consultation through project completion. The goal was to visualize each step, understand the flow, and identify inefficiencies.

Key Steps in the Process Mapping Exercise:

1. **Define Start and End Points:**

   The team mapped the process from the first client inquiry to the final inspection and approval of the project.

2. **List All Steps Involved:**

   Every task, from client meetings to ordering materials and scheduling construction, was broken down step-by-step. The team realized there were overlapping responsibilities and unclear deadlines between the design and build phases.

3. **Identify Bottlenecks and Inefficiencies:**

The process map highlighted two major bottlenecks:

o Delays in material sourcing because the purchasing department was unclear on the timelines.

o Miscommunication between designers and construction teams, leading to rework when design changes weren't properly communicated.

4. **Implement Changes:**

After reviewing the map, John and his team made several key adjustments:

o They created a streamlined communication protocol between the design and construction teams, ensuring all changes were documented and shared in real time.

o They adjusted the material ordering process, giving the purchasing team a clearer timeline for when items were needed to avoid last-minute rushes.

Results:

- **Improved Efficiency:** The process changes reduced project timelines by an average of 15%, allowing the team to take on more jobs without compromising quality.

- **Enhanced Communication:** With clearer hand-offs between phases, miscommunications were reduced, and the need for rework dropped significantly.

- **Higher Client Satisfaction:** Clients were happier with the shorter project timelines, and the business received more referrals due to the improved customer experience.

By using process mapping, GreenScape Solutions was able to visualize their workflow, identify problem areas, and make improvements that boosted efficiency and client satisfaction. For SMB owners like John, process mapping provided a simple but powerful way to optimize operations and improve business outcomes.

Process Mapping for Greater Efficiency and Improvement

Involve key team members in process discussions to gather input and foster collaboration. Understanding how one's role impacts others is critical to improving workflow productivity. For instance, in a process mapping session, the production crew learned they were unnecessarily packaging products for the shipping department, who then ended up often unpackaging and then repackaging them according to customer needs.

Both groups were performing extra work based on incorrect assumptions: the production crew assumed the shipping department wanted the products pre-packaged. The shipping team assumed that was part of the production process even though they didn't want it already packaged. Simply by putting all relevant parties in the same room, they were able to communicate with one another and figure out the disconnect in their process. By coming together instead of operating out of their silos, they were able to improve productivity by eliminating unnecessary work —saving time and money.

By using process mapping, teams can see how the work gets done in their business using a powerful visual tool to identify better what's working and not working and what could be improved.

Oftentimes our business owners and managers will print out the process map and tape it on their desks to have an accessible, visual reference. By doing so, they can better identify opportunities for improvement and recurring trouble spots. Process mapping exercise can also help identify and clarify areas of complexity and where rework is happening while also being able to document process improvement ideas.[6] When everyone is united on how to complete tasks effectively, the business can operate like a well-coordinated team rowing efficiently to get the them to their destination.

Key Takeaways Chapter 22: Map and Optimize Your Processes

1. **Visualize Your Business Processes:** Process mapping provides a clear, visual representation of workflows, helping you and your team identify inefficiencies and opportunities for

improvement. This clarity enhances understanding and communication across the organization.

2. **Align Processes with Purpose:** By aligning your processes with your mission and goals, you ensure that every step contributes to achieving your "what matters most" objectives, ultimately improving efficiency and outcomes.

3. **Identify and Eliminate Bottlenecks:** Process mapping allows you to pinpoint areas of inefficiency, complexity, and rework that slow down your operations. Addressing these bottlenecks leads to smoother workflows and better resource allocation.

4. **Enhance Training and Onboarding:** A well-documented process map serves as a practical tool for onboarding new employees, offering a clear understanding of workflows, expectations, and responsibilities.

5. **Adapt to Changing Needs:** Regularly updating your process maps ensures they remain relevant in a dynamic business environment. This adaptability helps your business stay agile and maintain high performance.

6. **Drive Continuous Improvement:** Process mapping fosters a culture of learning and optimization, enabling your team to refine workflows, improve customer satisfaction, and achieve better business results.

7. **Document Success:** Mapping your processes helps standardize workflows and establish a "recipe for success" that can be replicated consistently across teams, ensuring quality and compliance with standards.

Reflection Questions for Chapter 22: Map and Optimize Your Processes

1. **Core Process Alignment:**

   o What are the core processes in your business that directly deliver value to your customers? Are these processes fully aligned with your mission and goals?

2. **Identifying Inefficiencies:**

o Where do delays, rework, or inefficiencies most frequently occur in your workflows? What specific steps or hand-offs seem to slow things down or cause confusion?

3. **Role Clarity and Collaboration:**

   o Do your team members clearly understand their responsibilities and how their roles interact with others? Are there overlaps, gaps, or hand-off issues that could be improved?

4. **Customer Experience Impact:**

   o How do your current processes impact the customer experience? Are there specific steps you could optimize to better meet customer expectations and improve satisfaction?

5. **Team Input and Feedback:**

   o How often do you involve your team in identifying inefficiencies and brainstorming solutions? Could collaborating on process maps help uncover valuable insights?

6. **Value-Added vs. Non-Value-Added Activities:**

   o Are there steps in your processes that consume resources but do not directly add value for customers or your business goals? How can these be streamlined or removed?

7. **Frequency of Process Reviews:**

   o How often do you review and update your workflows or process maps to keep up with changes in tools, technology, or customer needs? What improvements could you prioritize today?

8. **What stood out to you in this chapter or resonated most with you?**

   o What insight, story, or idea felt especially relevant to your business right now?

9. **What are your top 1-2 takeaways from this chapter?**

CHAPTER 23

SYSTEMATIZE WHAT MATTERS: PROCESS PLAYBOOK

"A system must be managed. It will not manage itself...components become selfish, competitive, independent profit centres, and thus destroy the system. . . . The secret is cooperation between components toward the aim of the organization."
—Edward Deming ."[1]

From Insights to Action: Process Mapping and Creating the Playbook

In Chapter 22, we introduced process mapping as a tool to visualize better, understand, and optimize your workflows. Process mapping gives you a bird's-eye view of your business operations, allowing you to identify inefficiencies and troubleshoot recurring problem areas more easily. As part of one's ongoing learning and improvement efforts, process mapping enables us to simplify complex operations by breaking them down into smaller, more manageable steps. By doing so we can better identify and implement improvement recommendations while ensuring team members are more aligned.

But understanding the map is just the beginning. To turn insights into action, you also need a guide—a practical tool to standardize, document, and execute these improved processes effectively. That's where the Process Mapping Playbook comes in.

This playbook builds on the foundation of process mapping by operationalizing and documenting these improvements as part of your Standard Operating Procedures (SOPs). It equips you with the tools, frameworks, and step-by-step guidance to move from identifying inefficiencies to creating streamlined, standardized workflows. In this chapter, we'll explore how the Process Mapping Playbook can help you optimize your processes and sustain these improvements through clear documentation, role definition, and accountability.

Playbook Benefits

With a focus on accountability and results, this playbook equips SMBs to:

1. **Standardize Core Processes**: Establish repeatable workflows that reduce inefficiencies and errors.

2. **Define Roles and Responsibilities**: Clarify who is responsible, accountable, consulted, and informed (RASCI) for each task.

3. **Enhance Training and On-boarding**: Provide new employees with a clear understanding of operational expectations, which will shorten the training time and enable them to hit the ground running sooner.

4. **Uncover Improvement Opportunities**: Identify bottlenecks, redundant steps, and areas for optimization.

5. **Improve Decision-Making**: Use process improvement insights to allocate resources more effectively.

By leveraging tools such as activity detail sheets and the RASCI framework, this playbook empowers SMB owners and their teams to streamline operations, improve collaboration, and achieve greater business outcomes. Whether on-boarding new employees, managing day-to-day workflows, or planning long-term improvements, the Process Mapping Playbook is your road map to operational success. The following is an example of a process mapping playbook.

Playbook Example Overview

Purpose	This Playbook is to be used by A&B Aerospace team members as a document that establishes what, who, how, and when activities should take place to ensure the success and integrity of the A&B Aerospace order acknowledgment, procurement, and production process. The A&B Aerospace, Inc *Playbook v1.0* (SP 340-1) provides team members with the following:
	Clear depiction and narrative of the steps and key decision points
	Information on tools, resources, and documents used in each step
	"On-boarding" training document for new personnel
	Reference document for management and process stakeholders
	Standardized and ongoing repeatable set of processes
	Accountability across the cross-functional teams
	A methodology for discovering improvement opportunities in processes, tools, procedures, and policies.
Version Control	The Playbook's version and date of release are noted on the cover. Please check with your management team to ensure you use the most current version.
Use of Documents	The tools, process steps, inputs, and outputs reflect current practices but may require changes, combinations, or adaptation to achieve specific results. Use the Playbook as a "living document" – a compilation of the most current standards, tools, and procedures.
Organization	This Process Playbook accompanies the process map and delves deeper into the details, timing, and duration of each step in the process, the stakeholders involved, and recommendations for improvements.

Acronym Definitions for Key Roles

- **CSM**: Customer Service Manager
- **PLAN**: Planner (General Manager)
- **PM**: Project Manager
- **SM**: Shop Manager (Shop)
- **QCM**: Quality Control Manager
- **QCI**: Quality Control Inspector
- **S&R**: Shipping and Receiving
- **M**: Machinist

Roles and Responsibilities within the RASCI Matrix

The RASCI Matrix helps clarify roles and responsibilities in cross-functional processes and projects that require collaboration between multiple departments, teams, or individuals within an organization to achieve a common goal or outcome. RASCI is the acronym that defines who is Responsible, Accountable, Supporting, Consulted, or Informed in a given process or task.

- **Responsible (R):** The responsible person(s) perform the activity. They are responsible for implementation and action. The degree of responsibility is defined by the accountable person and can be shared or delegated.

- **Accountable (A):** The accountable person is responsible for the correct and thorough completion of the activity. There is only one accountable person per activity to ensure clear ownership and decision-making authority. Accountability cannot be delegated.

- **Supporting (S):** The supporting person(s) provide resources and assistance to the responsible person(s). Unlike consulted roles, supporting roles may be tasked with work.

- **Consulted (C):** Consulted individuals provide input and feedback before a final decision or action is taken. This role involves two-way communication.

- **Informed (I):** Informed individuals are kept updated on progress, decisions, and actions. This role involves one-way communication.[2]

Using the RASCI Matrix

The RASCI Matrix identifies activities within a process or project as rows of a table. The columns identify the involved individuals. Each row includes one accountable person and one or more responsible, supporting, consulted, or informed individuals. This tool is particularly useful when there is confusion over who is responsible and accountable. It prevents duplicate efforts and ensures clear ownership. It also clarifies who needs to be consulted or informed, enhancing communication and decision-making.

Activity	Person A (R)	Person B (A)	Person C (S)	Person D (C)	Person E (I)
Activity	R	A	S	C	I

In summary, the RASCI Matrix provide ways to document, understand, and improve processes by clearly defining roles and responsibilities, thereby enhancing organizational efficiency and effectiveness.

Activity Detail Sheet and RASCI Framework

The Activity Detail Sheet, when paired with the RASCI Framework, provides a detailed overview of each step in a process. It documents the following:

Who is in charge: Identifies the person accountable or for overseeing the step.

Who is involved and the degree of their responsibility: Specifies individuals involved and their respective levels of responsibility.

The primary purpose of the step: Clarifies the main objective of the step.

The key activities of the step: Lists the essential actions that make up the step.

Success factors and obstacles encountered on this step: Identifies what contributes to the step's success and any challenges faced.

Documents and tools involved in this step: List any relevant documents or tools used.

Opportunities for improvement: Highlights potential areas for enhancing the step.

Concurrent and Dependent Steps:

Understanding concurrent and dependent steps is essential in process mapping and creating a playbook for an SMB owner. However, identifying the critical path—the sequence of dependent steps that determines the minimum time required to complete a project—is also essential. The critical path highlights the tasks critical to project completion; any delay in these steps will directly delay the entire project.

Concurrent Steps: These tasks can happen simultaneously without affecting each other. For example, in a landscape design firm, ordering materials and preparing the site for installation can often be done concurrently. Running these steps in parallel reduces idle time and speeds up the overall workflow.

Dependent Steps: These steps must be done in sequence—one step relies on the completion of another before it can begin. For instance, installing irrigation pipes can only happen after the ground has been excavated. Mapping these dependencies help operations run smoothly by planning the right order of operations so you can allocate labor and materials accordingly, and avoid starting tasks prematurely and thus creating bottlenecks.

Critical Path: Prioritizing What Moves the Project Forward. In process mapping, the *critical path* refers to the sequence of dependent tasks that directly determine the project's overall timeline. If any step on this path is delayed, the entire project gets pushed back. For example, in a landscape design project, excavation, installing the irrigation system, and laying sod may all be on the critical path. The entire project will be delayed if any of these tasks are delayed. By focusing on the critical path, SMB owners can prioritize resources and attention on the most time-sensitive and essential steps.

By mapping concurrent, dependent, and critical-path steps, SMB owners can optimize workflows, direct resources to the right place, and keep projects on schedule. In the Activity Detail Sheet, each step is flagged:

• **Concurrent?** (Yes/No) – can this task run in parallel?

• **Dependent?** (Yes/No) – does it wait on another task?

Example – Order Acknowledgment (Dependent Step-since it happens only after customer enters an order)

Trigger: Customer order received

Actions: Confirm details - communicate with customer-release next workflow step (procurement or production)

KEY TIME METRICS

Processing Time (PT)

- The active time spent working on a task or step. This excludes any waiting, delays, or idle time.

- Purpose: To evaluate the efficiency of the individual task or step.

Lead Time (LT)

- The total time taken for a task or step to be completed, including both active processing time and waiting/delay time.

- Purpose: To assess overall process efficiency, including delays, waiting, and external factors slowing the step.

QUALITY METRICS: Complete % / Correct %

- The average % that the item or form is complete and % correct when it arrives at this step.

Activity Detail Sheet Example of Process Steps:

1. Order Acknowledgment

Primary purpose of this step	To receive and acknowledge incoming purchase orders from customers.
Concurrent Step	No
Dependent Step	Yes
Who is in charge?	Customer Service Manager

Who is involved?	CSM	Plan	Project Manager	Prod (shop) Mgr	QC Manager	Shipping & Rec	Other	*Responsible Accountable Supporting Consulted Informed*
	RA	S	C					

Key activities	Confirms that the price on the Purchase Order is correct.
	Confirms that the Quantity is correct based on any minimums agreed upon.
	Confirms that the Delivery date is obtainable based on standard lead time.
	Pulls previous ran traveler
	Complete Contract Review
What helps/hinders (delays)	PO Changes
Documents/ tools	Purchase Orders are given via phone, fax HASP, Portal or email.
	Some Purchase orders are given in conjunction with a forecast.
	Pulls Previous ran job traveler to verify there are no changes
	VMI Parts List

Performance measures/ metrics	Process Time	Lead Time	% Complete & % Accurate
	60 minutes	24 hours	87%/70%

Opportunities for improvement	

1.2 **New Order, Regular or Stock Order**

Primary purpose of this step	Customer Service Manager determines if the Purchase order is a New, Regular or Stock Order.
Concurrent Step	No
Dependent Step	1.1
Who is in charge?	CSM – Customer Service Manager

Who is involved?	CSM	Plan	Project Manager	Prod (shop) Mgr	QC Manager	Shipping & Rec	*Responsible Accountable Supporting Consulted Informed*
	RA	C-New I- Reg	S				

Key activities	If Part number has never been manufactured, this would classify as a "New Order"
	Enter Acknowledgment and give to Planner
	If Part has been manufactured before, this would classify as a "Regular Order".
	If Part has been manufactured and CSM verifies E2 stock on hand, this would classify as a "Stock Order".
What helps/hinders/ delays	Having incorrect data in E2 stock inventory hinders task.
	Not being able to find last ran job traveler.
Documents/tools	E2 – Estimating
	RFQ information on E2
	Correct and updated Rev Print / Spec

Performance measures/metrics	Process Time	Lead Time	% Complete & % Correct (CAC)
	10 minutes - New 45 minutes – Regular 10 minutes – Stock	**24 hours**	87%

Opportunities for improvement	Make sure all prints are in the system.

1.3 **Stock Order Fulfillment**

Primary purpose of this step	To fulfill the Stock Purchase Order and deliver the order to the customer for completion.
Concurrent Step	N/A
Dependent Step	1.2
Who is in charge?	Shipping & Receiving

Who is involved?	CSM	Plan	Project Manager	Prod (shop) Mgr	QC Manager	Shipping & Rec	Responsible Accountable Supporting
	S		I		C	RA	Consulted Informed

Key activities	Receive Purchase Order
	Locates last Job traveler ran
	Pulls stock from Bin location
	Counts out correct Quantity
	Prepares and packs parts for shipment
	Creates shipper on E2
	Schedules pickup for FEDEX or UPS
What helps and hinders?	Some stock may have to be reviewed by QC to make sure Rev is current to ship out.
Documents/tools	Purchase Order
	E2 for traceability
	Old Job Traveler for documentation on the back page / Certification document.

Performance measures/metrics	Process Time	Lead Time	% Complete & % Correct (CAC)
	60 minutes	**24 hours**	**80%**

Opportunities for improvement	

Example: Implementing the RASCI Framework in a manufacturing company

The RASCI framework helps define roles and responsibilities within any organizational project or operational process. Originating from project management best practices, RASCI stands as an acronym for Responsible, Accountable, Supportive, Consulted, and Informed. Each of these roles is critical for ensuring the execution of tasks and effective communication across different levels of an organization. Implementing the RASCI framework can significantly benefit Small and Medium-sized Enterprises (SMEs), especially those navigating the complexities of growth and scalability.

Responsible

This category identifies individuals or teams tasked with executing specific actions or decisions. In a manufacturing setting, for instance, production line workers responsible for assembling products fall into this category. They are the hands-on workforce executing the daily tasks that culminate into the company's output.

Accountable

The person who is ultimately answerable for the completion and success of a task. This role involves making critical decisions and providing final approvals. Within a manufacturing company, the plant manager often holds this accountability, ensuring that production targets are met, quality standards are upheld, and resources are allocated efficiently. There is only one accountable person per task or decision to ensure clear ownership and decision-making authority.

Support

These are the roles that provide assistance or resources to those responsible for tasks. In our manufacturing example, the maintenance team that ensures machinery is running correctly provides support. They play a crucial role in enabling the responsible workers to perform their duties without interruption.

Consulted

Individuals or groups with specialized knowledge or expertise who are consulted to provide guidance or solve specific issues. This involves two-way communication, where the consulted parties provide input and feedback that influence the decision-making process. For a manufacturing SME, this could involve managers or external consultants who advise on lean manufacturing techniques to optimize production processes. Their input is sought to make informed decisions, leveraging their expertise to enhance efficiency and effectiveness.

Informed

Stakeholders who need to be kept in the loop regarding project progress or decisions but do not have a direct role in its execution. This is typically one-way communication, where information is disseminated to keep these stakeholders updated. For example, sales and marketing teams might need updates on production schedules to plan their campaigns accordingly.

Benefits of Implementing RASCI

1. **Enhanced Clarity and Efficiency**: By clearly defining roles and responsibilities, the RASCI framework eliminates ambiguity around task ownership and processes. This clarity fosters an environment where employees understand their roles and the expectations placed upon them, leading to improved efficiency and productivity.

2. **Improved Communication and Collaboration**: RASCI facilitates better communication by establishing clear channels and protocols for consultation and information sharing. This structured approach promotes more effective teamwork and cooperation.

3. **Increased Accountability and Ownership**: By specifying who is accountable for each task, the framework ensures that there is always a clear point of responsibility. This accountability encourages a sense of ownership among employees, motivating them to perform their duties to the best of their abilities.

4. **Strategic Allocation of Resources**: Understanding who needs to be consulted or informed about specific decisions enables more strategic use of resources. For instance, by involving external experts only when their specialized knowledge is required, one can optimize consulting expenses while still benefiting from expert advice.

5. **Facilitation of Decision-Making**: With clear delineation of roles, decision-making becomes more streamlined and efficient. The accountable individuals have the authority to make final decisions, supported by input from those responsible and consulted. This can lead to quicker resolutions and more agile responses to challenges.[3]

Summary of RASCI Application in manufacturing company:

- **Responsible**: Production line workers who assemble the products.

- **Accountable**: Plant manager ensuring production targets and quality standards.

- **Support**: Maintenance team ensuring machinery is operational.

- **Consulted**: External consultants advising on lean manufacturing techniques.

- **Informed**: Sales and marketing teams updated on production schedules.

Implementing the RASCI framework can lead to significant operational improvements. By clarifying roles and responsibilities, enhancing communication, and fostering a culture of accountability, organizations can achieve greater efficiency, productivity, and adaptability. This strategic approach to project and process management supports both current operational needs and positions the company for sustainable growth and success.

Key Takeaways Chapter 23: Systematize What Matters: Process Playbook

1. **From Mapping to Action:**
   o Process mapping gives you a clear, big-picture view of how work gets done. A Process Mapping Playbook helps turn those insights into real action steps to improve efficiency, consistency, and accountability.

2. **Standardized Processes Save Time and Reduce Errors:**
   o A playbook creates repeatable workflows that reduce mistakes, prevent confusion, and improve accountability.

3. **Clarifying Roles with RASCI:**

   o The **RASCI framework** clearly defines who is Responsible, Accountable, Supporting, Consulted, and Informed for every step in a workflow, preventing overlap and missed steps.

4. **Better Training and On-boarding:**

   o Documented workflows give new employees a clear road map, helping them get up to speed faster and reducing training time.

5. **Spotting Inefficiencies:**

   o Mapping processes helps identify bottlenecks, redundancies, and gaps that slow you down — and shows where improvements are needed.

6. **Critical Path Awareness:**

   o Knowing which steps must happen on time helps you allocate resources wisely and avoid delays.

7. **Stronger Decision-Making:**

   o Clear processes make it easier to prioritize, allocate resources, and focus on high-impact tasks that move the business forward.

Reflection Questions for Chapter 23: Systematize What Matters: Process Playbook

1. **Documented and Clear Processes:**

   o Are your processes written down and clear enough so that any team member could follow them if someone is out?

   o If a key employee left today, would their processes still run smoothly — or would there be gaps?

2. **Role Clarity and Accountability:**

   o Does everyone on your team know what they are accountable for in critical workflows?

o Are there areas where responsibilities overlap or no one is clearly in charge? How could using a **RASCI chart** help clarify these roles?

3. **Training and On-boarding:**

   o Are your processes clear enough to help a new hire contribute effectively within the first 30 days?

   o What's one process you could document into a playbook to speed up on-boarding and training while maintaining quality?

4. **Identifying Bottlenecks and Inefficiencies:**

   o What recurring delays or inefficiencies do you keep seeing?

   o Are you addressing the root causes or just managing symptoms?

   o What are **two workflows** in your business that would benefit most from being standardized?

5. **Understanding Critical Path and Dependencies:**

   o Do you know which tasks must be done on time to prevent delays?

   o How could mapping dependencies help you focus on what truly drives results?

6. **Resource Allocation:**

   o Are you putting your time and resources into the parts of your processes that create the most value?

   o Where might you be wasting time on low-impact steps?

7. **Continuous Process Improvement:**

   o When was the last time you reviewed and updated a key process?

   o How can you build regular process reviews into your business — instead of waiting until something goes wrong?

8. **What stood out to you in this chapter or resonated most with you?**

   o   What insight or idea felt especially relevant to how you're currently running your business?

   o   What is one thing you feel motivated to act on because of this chapter?

9. **What are your top 1-2 takeaways from this chapter?**

   o   What **specific action** will you take to start applying these insights and improve how your business runs day to day?

CHAPTER 24

PROBLEM SOLVING MATTERS

*"If you want to go fast, go alone, and if you want
to go far, go together"[1]*
–African Proverb

Problem-Solving Matters

We all know that challenges are inevitable in business or life, but how we go about solving them matters, of course, to achieving desired outcomes. Many organizations may struggle to resolve recurring issues because they rely on isolated perspectives or reactive, short-term solutions. Instead, we believe that effective problem-solving can benefit from a more collaborative approach that harnesses the collective intelligence of your team and, when possible external advisors such as a mastermind group.[2]

Mastermind groups can provide invaluable external perspectives, including peers from other industries and Subject Matter Experts (SMEs). These groups can challenge assumptions, act as a sounding board for ideas, and provide accountability support. When we can utilize our client's understanding of their business along with insights of a mastermind group, they can develop even more creative and effective solutions. This chapter introduces group-based collaborative problem-solving methodologies to help you overcome problems and challenges while maximizing opportunities.

Integrative Consultation: Harnessing Collective Wisdom

The first problem-solving or opportunity-maximizing methodology that we've developed over the years of working with client organizations is Integrative Consultation[TM3]. Integrative Consultation (IC) is a collaborative problem-solving approach that involves constructively utilizing the diverse perspectives typically from two to five individuals in a focused session. The goal is to see the challenge or opportunity from multiple angles so you can make better-informed, higher-quality decisions.

The ancient parable of the blind men and the elephant illustrates the opposite of this collaborative approach when we are limited to just a single perspective: Isolated from one another, each blind man, depending on the part of the elephant he's touching, forms a different, and incomplete understanding of what an elephant is.

When asked to describe the elephant, the one touching the leg believes it to be a tree trunk; another, grasping the tail, thinks it's a rope. Naturally, they each think the others are wrong, leading to disagreements and possibly even reacting with hostility. Yet, if they could consider and listen to each other's perspectives, they might conclude that each touches a different part of the same elephant.[4] When we can see beyond the limited perspectives of any individual, we can form a more complete, accurate view of the "elephant"—the problem or opportunity. Only then are we in a position to come up with better solutions.

Reflection Question

Have you ever encountered a situation where different perspectives clashed, only to realize later that everyone had part of the truth?"

Similarly, in a business setting, encouraging communication and considering diverse perspectives relevant to the problem can empower you and your team to make better, more informed decisions. However, having these discussions in a manner that is constructive can be challenging without an effective facilitator or structured approach. Without it, some participants may keep their point of view to themselves, even though their unique vantage point can meaningfully contribute to solving or at least better understanding the problem.

On the other hand, you may have participants who hijack the meeting and take up a disproportionate amount of the meeting time expressing their views without giving adequate time for others to contribute. As trained facilitators, Business Alignment Coaches can guide and coach you and your leadership team how to have a more balanced, inclusive, and productive session.

Creating a Safe Space for Idea-Sharing

Our approach to facilitating constructive dialogue in a group setting comes from our practice of Integrative Consultation (IC). IC teaches a mindset and rules of engagement that seek to minimize destructive conflict and protect team morale. Destructive and negative conflict, resulting in lower morale, often arises from contentious disagreements when people feel attacked and compelled to defend their ideas to avoid looking "bad." When someone criticizes our idea, one may take it personally, feeling as though our idea, our "baby" has been labeled "ugly."

However, in a facilitated session practicing Integrative Consultation, differing perspectives can be shared in a respectful, open exchange where participants can disagree without being disagreeable.

IC encourages participants to adopt a more neutral, detached mindset when expressing views to create this respectful and open environment. For example, rather than feeling personally invested in an idea, we ask participants to imagine themselves as a radio transmitter tuning into various frequencies—thoughts, and perspectives that are in the ether coming through them.

When you share an idea that's been transmitted to you, think of it as placing a piece of fruit into a shared bowl at the center of a round table where all of the participants are seated around it. Once the idea is put forth and placed there, it no longer belongs to you or anyone else; instead, it becomes a shared resource for the group to examine. With this detachment, participants can discuss the idea frankly and even tear it apart without fear of offending anyone since the idea is now owned by the group and part of the collective contribution rather than just a personal one.[5]

Facilitating the Clashing of Perspectives vs Egos

Instead of allowing egos to clash, this method facilitates the idea put forth by 'Abdu'l-Bahá, the Perfect Exemplar of the Bahá'í Faith, that "The shining spark of truth cometh forth only after the clash of differing opinions."[6] When self-centered ego and pride is set aside or at least minimized, the team is more likely to experience open and candid discussions that allow for the best ideas and solutions to surface. In this environment, participants don't care about receiving individual credit but are focused on ideas and approaches that can promote and advance the organization's objectives and greater good.

Prioritizing Relevant Perspectives

When evaluating perspectives, it is crucial to prioritize those of individuals who are directly "touching the elephant"—those with firsthand experience and expertise. These perspectives, rooted in direct evidence and observable facts, are more reliable than secondhand accounts or opinions from individuals with limited knowledge of the situation. Firsthand insights often serve as the foundation for better decision-making and problem-solving.

In today's information-saturated world, where content is available at the click of a mouse, the ability to critically evaluate the accuracy of information is more important than ever. We all know that simply encountering something online or hearing it repeated in the media does not mean it's true. It's a good practice whenever possible to cross-reference information from at least two or three reliable, trustworthy sources to validate its accuracy. Having accurate facts, is the foundation to practicing evidence-based decision-making.

Through **Integrative Consultation**™, we emphasize an evidence-based approach that values the contributions of those with firsthand knowledge. By giving proper weight to direct observations and experiences within your team, you create a clearer, more accurate understanding of the situation at hand. This approach minimizes the risk of being misled by secondhand or less-informed opinions and ensures a higher quality of decision-making.

Reflection Questions:

1. **Leveraging Expertise:** Are you fully utilizing the insights of the "elephant touchers" on your team—those with firsthand experience? How can you better integrate their perspectives into your decision-making processes?

2. **Validating Information:** How often do you challenge the accuracy of the information you rely on? What steps can you take to cross-check and validate critical data before making decisions?

Example: Prioritizing Relevant Perspectives in Retail

A family-owned furniture retail business faced declining sales in one of its key product categories: outdoor furniture. The management team, eager to reverse the trend, gathers to brainstorm solutions. During the meeting, the store's general manager, a long-time family member, suggested that competitors are underpricing similar products, and the team considered slashing prices to compete.

However, the sales associates, who interact directly with customers on a daily basis offer a different perspective. They note that customers often mention dissatisfaction with the outdated designs and request more modern, space-saving options. A few even share examples of customers walking out after commenting on the lack of new inventory. Based on firsthand interactions, the sales team's insights indicate that pricing might not be the issue, but the product relevancy to customer wants and needs.

Applying the IC Framework:

1. **Prioritizing Firsthand Perspectives:** By recognizing that the sales team is "touching the elephant" directly through daily customer interactions, the business prioritizes its input over the incorrect assumptions the general manager is making regarding pricing-driven sales.

2. **Evidence-Based Decision-Making:** Management reviews customer feedback forms and online reviews to validate the sales team's observations. The survey data confirms a recurring and increased demand for modern, space-efficient designs.

3. **Collaborative Problem-Solving:** Utilizing these insights, the business shifts its focus from competing on price to updating its product line. The purchasing team brings in a selection of modern outdoor furniture, and the marketing team highlights the new styles in a targeted campaign.

4. **Results:** Sales of outdoor furniture rebound within months, and the business builds a reputation for listening to customer needs, ultimately creating a competitive advantage in the local market.

This example illustrates the value of applying Integrative Consultation, prioritizing relevant perspectives, and how aligning decision-making with firsthand evidence can lead to more effective outcomes.

Reflection Questions:

- How well does your organization capture and prioritize input from team members closest to the customer?

- What can you implement to ensure that direct insights are heard and acted upon in your decision-making processes?

Utilizing the Power of Purposeful Meetings

Once we understand the power of combining diverse perspectives through Integrative Consultation, the next step is ensuring these discussions occur within structured, purposeful, and effective meetings. As the saying goes, "An hour of planning can save ten hours of execution." We all know that the ability to have an effective "hour of planning" in the form of a well run purposeful meetings can save time and unnecessary headaches down the road.

However conducting a well-organized meeting isn't easy. We need to learn how to have effective meetings and utilize the tools that enable us to do so. By doing so, we can create the space for proactive problem-solving and collaboration to provide solutions as issues arise or escalate. Effective meetings can also uncover new opportunities for growth, and harness your team's collective intelligence.

The Power of Purposeful Communication

To make meetings truly impactful, communication must be purposeful. This means clearly stating the meeting's purpose, setting specific objectives, and defining what needs to be accomplished. Purposeful communication goes beyond ensuring everyone has a chance to contribute; it also involves listening for what's left unsaid—unvoiced concerns, hesitations, or insights that may hold valuable perspectives.

Drucker's approach to purposeful communication includes embracing a mindset of curiosity and humility. He advised consultants to "be ignorant" and to "ask a few questions." [7]

This technique can be broken down into two steps:

1. **Be ignorant**: Assume you don't know the answer. Even if you think you do, approaching conversations with curiosity allows you to ask more insightful questions and uncover valuable information that you otherwise would not have gotten.

2. **Explore**: A curious leader listens not just to confirm their own beliefs but to explore other perspectives. Listening with an open mind leads to a deeper understanding of issues and opportunities.

By improving our ability to listen and ask questions, we develop the foundation of effective communication and conducting effective meetings. By doing so, your team can move from simply discussing issues to collaboratively solving them. When meetings are conducted purposefully, they become a proactive tool for problem-solving, and participants can come away feeling more engaged and motivated.

Planning Effective Meetings

Effective meetings don't just happen; they need to be thoughtfully planned ahead of time and have a clear outcome. Meetings can be a forum for decision-making, resource optimization, and problem-solving within any organization. They provide a platform where each member's perspective and unique problem-solving abilities can be leveraged, and they facilitate both the distribution of information and the discussion of plans and directives. Below are some key elements of effective meetings. We've also included a meeting agenda template in the Appendix.

1. **Prepare and Share the Agenda in Advance**: Distribute a clear and detailed agenda at least 72 hours before the meeting. This gives participants time to review the topics, prepare, and align their contributions with the meeting's goals. The agenda should outline key topics, allocate time for each, and specify the meeting's objectives.

2. **Establish Clear Objectives**: Begin each meeting by articulating its purpose and objectives. This ensures all participants are aligned and maintain focus throughout the session.

3. **Stick to a Focused Agenda**: Address agenda items systematically, discussing each topic in order. Defer unrelated issues to future meetings to maximize efficiency and keep discussions on track.

4. **Maintain Regular Scheduling**: Set consistent meeting times and durations—ideally no longer than one hour. Routine scheduling creates predictability, prioritizes attendance, and ensures meetings are integral to the company standard operating practices SOP's.

5. **Facilitate Effectively**: The facilitator guides the meeting, keeps discussions focused, and effectively manages time. They should ensure all agenda items are addressed and encourage balanced participation.

6. **Document Key Outcomes**: Assign someone to take minutes or use an AI-assisted tool, such as Fathom, for Zoom meetings to record key discussions, decisions, and follow-up actions. Clear documentation ensures accountability and provides a reliable reference for team members regarding the next steps.

7. **Make the first topic: Review and modify agenda as needed.** Even if you and your team have jointly developed the agenda before the meeting, take a minute to see if anything needs to be changed due to late-breaking events.

8. **End the meeting with a plus/delta:** If your team meets regularly, two questions form a simple continuous improvement process: What did we do well (+) ? What do we want to do differently (delta) for the next meeting? Investing five or ten minutes discussing this will enable the team to improve performance, their working relationships and overall satisfaction.

9. **Begin the meeting with a review of the prior plus/delta:** To ensure that your team follows through, review the results of the plus/delta at the beginning of the next meeting.[8]

Here are some questions to consider when identifying what the team has done well and what it wants to do differently:

1. Was the agenda distributed in time for everyone to prepare?

2. How well did team members prepare for the meeting?

3. How well did we estimate the time needed for each agenda item?

4. How well did we allocate our time for decision-making and discussion?

5. How well did everyone stay on topic? How well did team members speak up when they thought someone was off topic?

6. How effective was the process for each agenda item?

When structured and purposeful, meetings become an invaluable tool for your team. By fostering open communication, following a clear agenda, and documenting outcomes, you'll ensure your team's collective intelligence is put to work effectively. When everyone rows in the same direction, aligned by purpose, meetings can serve as a proactive means of driving your organization forward.

Types of Meetings That Drive Organizational Success

It's essential to structure meetings around specific purposes to meet varying business needs. Examples include:

1. **Planning Meetings**: Bring together key team members to clarify goals, define priorities, assign responsibilities, and outline upcoming activities. These meetings are ideal for launching new initiatives or realigning around strategic objectives.

2. **Tactical Meetings**: Shorter, focused sessions aimed at addressing immediate needs—whether operational issues, customer concerns, or emerging opportunities. These help teams stay agile and responsive in fast-moving environments.

3. **Review Meetings**: Held regularly (weekly, monthly, or quarterly), review meetings evaluate what's working, what's not, and where adjustments are needed. Use these to track performance metrics, review OKRs, and implement course corrections.

4. **Problem-Solving Meetings**: Structured around a specific challenge, these sessions invite collaborative thinking to uncover root causes and generate actionable solutions. Encourage open dialogue, cross-functional input, and clear next steps.[9]

Offsite meetings can also be invaluable opportunities to have more reflective and strategic discussions away from the day-to-day noise of operational concerns. Consider having them one to two times a year to reassess long-term goals and strategies.

Adhering to these principles makes meetings invaluable tools for planning, problem-solving, decision-making, performance improvement, and enhancing organizational communication. Conducted in a disciplined, focused, and consistent manner, effective meetings align the team with business goals and drive collective success.

Problem-Solving Methodologies: The Pareto Principle

In business, ongoing challenges and unexpected outcomes may derail progress, but your approach to navigating these challenges ultimately determines one's long-term success or failure. SMB owners often face severe constraints on time, resources, and manpower, making effective problem-solving critical. A structured problem-solving approach ensures that these challenges are resolved efficiently, with the greatest probability of success and positive impact on your organization.

This section will explore additional well-known problem-solving methodologies that allow you to prioritize and address core issues and make the best use of your resources and capabilities to achieve your desired outcomes.

Problem-Solving Methodology: The 5 Whys

The 5-Why problem-solving technique is straightforward and effective for identifying the root cause of a problem. By repeatedly asking "why," you can drill down to uncover the underlying issue behind an event or observed behavior. While the name suggests asking "why" five times, the actual number depends on the complexity of the situation and may require more or fewer iterations. The key is to continue asking until the true root cause is revealed.

The process is highly adaptable and can be applied in various contexts, from a one-on-one discussion to a group meeting. For example, it can be used to explore why an error occurred or to investigate the causes of an accident or defect. Despite its simplicity, the 5-Why approach benefits from structure and visualization. Every effect has a cause, and understanding these relationships is crucial to solving problems effectively.

To enhance clarity, use tools such as a notepad, chart, or whiteboard to map out the problem (effect) and its causes. Visualizing these cause-and-effect connections with arrows helps focus the discussion and ensures the root cause is accurately identified. This structured approach makes the 5-Why technique a powerful tool for uncovering deeper insights and resolving issues at their source.[10]

Applying Pareto and the 5 Whys

Because we face limited resources and time, it's essential we focus on the most impactful issues. One way to do this is by applying the Pareto Principle, also known as the 80/20 rule, which suggests that roughly 80% of effects come from 20% of the causes. For example, 80% of traffic typically occurs on 20% of the streets, and 80% of your sales are generated by 20% of your customers. The Pareto Principle helps you prioritize problems and opportunities based on their potential impact, ensuring you focus your limited resources on issues that will yield the most significant benefits when resolved. The following example will explore how the Pareto Principle can be integrated into problem-solving methodologies, such as the "5 Whys" applied in a manufacturing setting to address customer late deliveries.

Example: Applying the Pareto Principle and the 5 Whys in Manufacturing

Scenario

You own a small manufacturing company that has been experiencing late deliveries to customers. Upon reviewing customer complaints and delivery records, you find that 80% of the late deliveries occur in just 20% of your product lines.

Step 1: Identify the Vital Few

- **Focus**: Concentrate on the specific product lines causing the majority of late deliveries.

Step 2: Apply the "5 Whys" to Uncover Root Causes

Problem: Late deliveries in Product Line A.

1. **Why** are we delivering Product Line A orders late?
    o Because production of Product Line A is frequently delayed.

2. **Why** is production of Product Line A frequently delayed?
    o Because the specialized machine used for Product Line A experiences frequent breakdowns.

3. **Why** does the specialized machine experience frequent breakdowns?

   o   Because it has not been maintained regularly.

4. **Why** has the machine not been maintained regularly?

   o   Because there is no preventive maintenance schedule in place for this machine.

5. **Why** is there no preventive maintenance schedule in place?

   o   Because the maintenance team was unaware of the machine's critical role and lacked clear directives.

Root Cause: Lack of a preventive maintenance schedule for the critical machine used in Product Line A due to insufficient communication and planning.

Step 3: Develop a Solution

- **Implement a Preventive Maintenance Schedule**: Establish regular maintenance for the specialized machine.

- **Improve Communication**: Ensure that the maintenance team is aware of critical machinery and its impact on production schedules.

- **Monitor and Review**: Track machine performance and delivery times to assess the effectiveness of the maintenance schedule.

Step 4: Allocate Resources Effectively

- **Time**: Prioritize scheduling maintenance during off-peak hours to minimize disruption.

- **Budget**: Allocate funds for maintenance without significant strain on finances.

Outcome: By focusing on the vital few—the specific product line causing most late deliveries—and addressing the root cause through the "5 Whys," you efficiently use your limited resources to make a significant improvement in on-time deliveries.

Integrating the Pareto Principle into your problem-solving approach allows you to concentrate on the most impactful issues. Combining this with methodologies like the "5 Whys" helps you uncover root causes efficiently, enabling you to implement solutions that yield the greatest benefits with available resources.

Another Example: Addressing Late Deliveries

Problem: Customers are complaining about late deliveries.

1. **Why** are customers complaining about late deliveries?
    o   Because deliveries are arriving later than the promised time.
2. **Why** are deliveries arriving later than promised?
    o   Because the final packaging process is taking longer than expected.
3. **Why** is the final packaging process taking longer?
    o   Because we often run out of packaging materials.
4. **Why** do we run out of packaging materials?
    o   Because the inventory system doesn't accurately track usage and stock levels.
5. **Why** doesn't the inventory system track usage accurately?
    o   Because it's outdated and relies on manual data entry, leading to errors.

Root Cause: An outdated, manual inventory system leading to inaccurate tracking of packaging materials.

Solution: Implement a modern, automated inventory management system to ensure accurate tracking and timely reordering of packaging materials.

By applying the "5 Whys," you identify that upgrading the inventory system can prevent delays, improve efficiency, and improve customer satisfaction.

Problem Solving Methodology: Brainstorming and Prioritization Framework

Another problem-solving methodology is the brainstorming and prioritization framework, which encourages creative thinking to generate a wide range of ideas for solving a problem. After you have created a list of possible ideas, the team can begin the process of rank ordering or prioritizing these ideas based on what is most feasible to implement given the current constraints of resources, time, talent, and capabilities.[11] By doing so, you can select and then implement the most effective solutions that are more likely to succeed.

Example: Solving Late Deliveries

Problem: Customers are unhappy because their orders are arriving late.

Steps:

1. **Gather the Team**: Include members from different departments to provide diverse perspectives.

2. **Brainstorm Solutions**: Encourage free thinking without criticism. Ideas might include:

   o   Hiring additional staff for packing and shipping.

   o   Upgrading the inventory management system.

   o   Implementing more efficient scheduling.

   o   Improving supplier relationships to ensure timely receipt of materials.

3. **Document All Ideas**: Write down every suggestion to ensure all voices are heard.

4. **Group Similar Ideas**: Organize ideas into categories for easier analysis.

5. **Prioritize Solutions**:

   o   **Impact**: Which solutions will have the greatest effect on the problem?

   o   **Feasibility**: Consider cost, resources, and time required.

   o   **Urgency**: Determine which actions need immediate attention.

6. **Develop an Action Plan**: Assign responsibilities, set timelines, and define success metrics.

Brainstorming and prioritization enable the team to collaboratively generate and select the most effective solutions, fostering a sense of ownership and encouraging innovative thinking.[14]

Next Steps Practical Application:

1. **Facilitate a Problem-Solving Meeting**:
   - o Identify a current challenge your business is facing.
   - o Organize a meeting with key team members using the principles of effective meetings.
   - o Apply the principles of IC, the 5 Whys, or brainstorming techniques to explore the problem and develop solutions.

2. **Reflect on Team Dynamics**:
   - o Observe how differing perspectives are shared during team discussions.
   - o Encourage an environment where clashing perspectives are viewed as opportunities to uncover the "spark of truth."

3. **Evaluate Your Meeting Structure**:
   - o Review your current meeting schedules, agendas, and formats.
   - o Implement changes to align with the best practices outlined in this chapter.

Humble Posture of Learning

In today's rapidly changing and complex world, no single person or team can claim to fully grasp every dimension of a problem. That's why effective problem-solving begins with a humble posture of learning: recognizing the limits of your own knowledge, staying open to new information, and valuing the perspectives of others.

This posture doesn't weaken leadership—it strengthens it by creating space for better insights, stronger solutions, and more sustainable outcomes.

Reflection Question:

- How might adopting a humble posture of learning improve the quality of your decisions?

- How can you encourage your team to share their perspectives openly and respectfully?

Key Takeaways Chapter 24: Problem Solving Matters

- **Integrative Consultation Enhances Problem-Solving**: Leveraging the collective wisdom of your team through shared leadership leads to more effective and innovative solutions.

- **Effective Meetings are Crucial**: Regular, well-structured meetings with clear agendas and objectives facilitate better communication, decision-making, and problem-solving.

- **Harness Diverse Perspectives**: Encouraging open dialogue and valuing differing viewpoints uncovers deeper insights and fosters a collaborative culture.

- **Utilize Problem-Solving Methodologies**: Tools like the "5 Whys" and brainstorming techniques help identify root causes and generate effective solutions.

- **Focus on the Vital Few**: Apply the Pareto Principle to identify and prioritize the most impactful problems, optimizing the use of limited resources and time.

- **Use the "5 Whys" for Root Cause Analysis**: This simple technique helps uncover the underlying causes of problems efficiently, ensuring that solutions address the core issues rather than just the symptoms.

- **Align with Business Strategy**: Integrating problem-solving efforts with your overall business goals ensures that solutions contribute to long-term success.

- **Empower Your Team**: Involving the right team members in problem-solving increases engagement, ownership, and strengthens team cohesion.

Reflection Questions Chapter 24: Problem Solving Matters

1. **Team Perspectives and Problem-Solving**

   o How often do you actively seek input from team members closest to the issue or opportunity?

   o What specific action can you take this week to ensure diverse perspectives are shared in your next team discussion?

2. **Root Cause Analysis**

   o When was the last time you paused to dig into the *real* cause of a recurring issue?

   o What steps can you put in place (5 Whys) to consistently identify and address the root causes of problems rather than just treating symptoms?

3. **Effective Meetings**

   o Are your meetings structured with clear goals and outcomes, or do they often feel like unproductive check-ins?

   o What one thing could you add to or remove from your meeting format to make them more focused and effective?

4. **Prioritizing Resources**

   o How do you currently prioritize where to allocate your limited resources—time, money, and talent?

   o Could using a framework like the 80/20 rule help you focus on the problems and opportunities that will create the greatest results?

5. **Creating a Culture of Improvement**

   o Do your team members feel safe sharing differing opinions or challenging assumptions?

   o How can you model humility and curiosity to create a culture where clashing perspectives lead to better ideas?

6. **Leveraging Firsthand Insights**

   o Are the insights from team members who interact directly with customers being captured and acted upon?

   o What's one simple way you can ensure these insights are brought to decision-making meetings?

7. **Time and Resources**

   o Are you spending enough time working *on* your business instead of just reacting to daily fires?

   o How can you reallocate even one hour this week to focus on long-term solutions rather than immediate tasks?

8. **Leadership Style**

   o How often do you listen openly to others' ideas without jumping in to share your own?

   o What is one habit you could practice this week to lead with more curiosity and less certainty?

9. **What stood out to you in this chapter or resonated most with you?**

   o What insight, story, or idea felt especially relevant to your business right now?

10. **What are your top 1-2 takeaways from this chapter?**

   o What is one specific action you can take to start applying these insights and improve how your team solves problems together?

PROFIT—ALIGNING YOUR PROFIT WITH PURPOSE

CHAPTER 25

PROFIT ON PURPOSE

"Profit for a company is like oxygen for a person.
If you don't have enough of it, you're out of the
game. But if you think your life is about breathing,
you're really missing something."[1]
— *Peter F. Drucker*

Purpose-Driven Business Model: A New Perspective

Aligning your business model and profits with your core purpose, which consists of your mission and vision, is essential for unlocking more of your potential and creating an enduring sense of fulfillment. In this chapter, we'll explore what a business model is and the key components that make up a business model so you can better align those components with your purpose. As a result, purpose-driven profits become a by-product of working toward that purpose.

For purpose-driven leaders and organizations, realizing profits and earning a livelihood, although critically important, is not the sole reason and ultimate goal as to why they exist but also a means of ensuring a sustainable enterprise that enables it to fulfill its purpose.

Companies with a clear purpose whether it's a construction firm building safe, lasting homes for families, an IT services company protecting small businesses from cyber-threats, or a retail shop promoting eco-friendly products can create enduring value propositions that build stronger customer loyalty, especially among those who share their values and purpose.

In a Deloitte article, *Purpose is everything: How brands that authentically lead with purpose are changing the nature of business today;* it cites that Purpose-driven companies witness higher market share gains and grow on average three times faster than their competitors, all the while achieving higher employee and customer satisfaction.[2]

One company that exemplifies this alignment of purpose and profitability is Patagonia. Patagonia aligns with its mission of promoting environmental sustainability through initiatives like the Worn Wear program, even though it could adversely impact revenues and profits. This program encourages customers to buy used Patagonia gear, repair their existing items, and extend the life of their products rather than buy new ones.

In addition, Patagonia also invests in eco-friendly materials such as organic cotton and recycled fabrics, minimizing its environmental footprint.[3] This commitment to sustainable practices can resonate with environmentally conscious customers, building stronger loyalty as they see their purchases as supporting a company and contributing to broader environmental preservation efforts. Every dollar earned supports Patagonia's profitability and aligns with its mission to protect the planet.

Patagonia's alignment between purpose and profits strengthens customer loyalty from those who resonate with their purpose and demonstrates how a business can thrive while staying true to its values.

Understanding Business Models

To ensure this alignment between profit and purpose, it's important to have a well-defined business/profit model that supports your purpose-driven approach. A business model is the blueprint for how your company creates, delivers, and captures value. It answers essential questions like "Who is the customer?" and "What does the customer value?" According to Peter Drucker, answers to these questions shape behavior, guide decisions, and define meaningful results—forming the "theory of the business."[4] This "theory of the business" also addresses fundamental questions of how we make money in this business and what is the underlying economic logic that explains how we can deliver value to customers at an appropriate cost.[5]

The Scientific Approach: Starting with a Business Hypothesis

In science and business, forming a hypothesis is the first step towards understanding and explaining how things work. In scientific reasoning, a hypothesis is a testable and falsifiable statement or explanation proposed to account for observations, often informed by prior research or existing knowledge, which guides further investigation.[6] Similarly, in business, your hypothesis is your initial idea about how your company will create value and succeed in the marketplace.

Joan Magretta writes in her HBR article *Why Business Models Matter* that "Business modeling is the managerial equivalent of the scientific method—you start with a hypothesis, which you then test in action and revise when necessary."[7] In business, a hypothesis becomes more credible and potentially forms the basis of a working theory when it's backed and supported by real-world data. A theory is substantiated by evidence—proof that the underlying assumptions hold true. In business, evidence comes from real-world results in the form of satisfied, repeat customers. Paying customers supports the validity of your business theory and demonstrates that your product or service meets a market need. When customers generate an adequate and reasonable profit, it indicates the viability and sustainability of the enterprise.

Aligning the key components of your business model with your purpose

To align one's business model with purpose, it's important to examine each component of your business model through the lens of your core purpose, which is supported by your core values and competencies. This section breaks down the key components of a business model and offers examples and reflection questions to help you evaluate each one to better align them with your core purpose and differentiate yourself from your competitors.

Key Components of a Business (Profit) Model

1. Customer Segments: Who you are serving

This defines the specific groups of people or organizations your business is built to serve. Different customer segments might require distinct approaches, products, or services depending on their needs. Aligning customer segments with purpose means ensuring that the customers you choose to serve value what you offer and resonate with your mission and values.

- **Example:** A local accounting firm may need to choose between two customer segments: small business taxpayers who are looking for a more transactional relationship, needing help only with completing annual tax returns, or small business owners who prefer assistance not only with tax returns but also value an ongoing relationship that includes additional services like bookkeeping and accounting.

- If its mission is to serve growth-oriented small business owners who value higher levels of service and more of a trusted advisor relationship, then it would seek to prioritize the segment of small business owners who also appreciate and value that level of personalized service. By doing so, the firm ensures it serves clients who resonate with and align with their purpose.

Customer Key Questions:

- Who are the key customer segments your business serves?
- Are there untapped customer segments that align with your mission?
- How well do you understand the needs and desires of each customer group, and how do these align with your purpose?

2. Value Proposition: Why Customers Choose You

Your value proposition explains the unique benefit your business provides and why customers should choose your product or service over their next best alternative. A business model describes how the parts fit together to create and capture value, while strategy explains how to deliver that value in ways that are better and different than competitors—especially for the customers you're meant to serve.[10]

- **Example:** A boutique marketing agency might offer strategic data-driven marketing services for small businesses, providing customized solutions on a scale that larger agencies may not offer. Their value proposition could be, "We help small businesses grow with tailored, data-driven marketing strategies that promote long-term sustainability and community impact."

Value Key Questions:

- What makes your value proposition different and better for your ideal customer?

- Does your offer solve a meaningful customer problem in a way that reflects your values?

- How well does your message communicate the deeper impact you aim to create and contributes to your purpose?

3. Channels: How you deliver your value to customers

Channels are how your business reaches and delivers value to customers. For instance, a retail clothing store might sell through its brick-and-mortar locations, an e-commerce website, and third-party platforms like Amazon. A professional services firm could offer services via in-person meetings, workshops, online meetings/webinars, and downloadable resources from its website. Aligning channels with your purpose means ensuring that the ways you engage with customers reflect your mission and provide the best possible experience without compromising your values.

- **Example:** A coffee roastery might deliver value through direct online sales, wholesale to local coffee shops, and a storefront cafe. To promote sustainability, it might ensure that packaging for online orders is eco-friendly and prioritize partnerships with local businesses that share similar environmental values.

Channel Key Questions:

- Through which channels do your customers prefer to engage with your business?

- Are there other channels you could explore to better align with your customer's needs and your mission?

4. Customer Relationships: How You Interact with Customers to Retain Them

- Customer relationships are about building and maintaining meaningful connections that can result in greater loyalty and repeat business. When these relationships align with your purpose, your interactions with customers foster trust and can reinforce the deeper connection they feel with your mission.

- **Example:** A boutique fitness studio that prioritizes holistic wellness goes beyond offering workout sessions. They build lasting relationships by providing personalized wellness plans, regular client progress check-ins, and hosting community-building events such as mindfulness workshops and wellness retreats.

- By creating a supportive, purpose-driven community, the studio ensures clients feel valued and connected to the broader mission of promoting mental and physical well-being. This personalized approach, combined with fostering a sense of community, encourages long-term loyalty while staying true to the studio's mission of promoting holistic wellness.

Customer Engagement Questions:

- How do you currently engage with your customers to build stronger loyalty?

- Are your interactions fostering meaningful relationships that reflect your mission and purpose?

- How can you use technology, including artificial intelligence AI or other tools to enhance customer engagement while staying aligned with your purpose?

5. Revenue Streams: How your company makes money

Revenue streams represent how your business generates income, such as gym membership fees, project-based revenue for a construction firm, or software subscription plans. Aligning revenue streams with your purpose ensures that your sources of revenue reflect your mission and values rather than conflict with them.

- **Example:** A fitness center might generate revenue through membership fees, classes, and personal training services. To align with its purpose of holistic wellness, it may introduce wellness coaching packages or classes focused on mental health and stress management, creating an additional revenue stream that supports its mission.

Revenue Questions:

- What are the primary revenue streams for your business?
- How can you diversify your revenue streams to reduce dependence on one source, while still aligning with your purpose?

6. Key Resources: The assets needed to deliver value (people, technology, capital)

Key resources are your business's vital assets for operating and delivering customer value. Aligning key resources with your purpose ensures you're investing in resources—people, technology, or capital—supporting your mission.

- **Example:** A software development company requires skilled software engineers, development tools, and intellectual property to build its products. The company might also invest in employee training and development to align with its mission, which includes developing employee growth.

Key Resource Questions:

- What are the most important resources your business relies on to deliver its value?
- How can you better utilize your existing resources to align with your purpose?

7. Key Activities: The actions your business needs to take to succeed

Key activities are the essential tasks and processes your business must undertake to deliver on its value proposition. Aligning these activities with purpose ensures that your business's day-to-day operations support your mission.

- **Example:** A bakery must consistently produce high-quality baked goods, market them through various channels, and handle customer orders efficiently. To promote their mission of enhancing health and community well-being, they may incorporate locally sourced, organic ingredients and offer community-based baking classes.

Key Activities Questions:

- What are the critical activities your business needs to deliver value? And are they aligned with your purpose?

- Can some or parts of these activities be improved or automated for efficiency while staying true to your mission?

8. Key Partners: External organizations or individuals that help your business succeed

Key partners include external organizations, suppliers, or individuals who assist your business in delivering its value proposition. Aligning your partners with your purpose ensures your collaborators share your mission and values.

- **Example:** A home renovation business might partner with local suppliers for building materials, subcontractors for specialized tasks, and architects for design collaboration. To align with its purpose of promoting green living, it may partner exclusively with suppliers of eco-friendly materials.

Key Partners Questions:

- Who are the most important partners your business relies on to succeed?
- Are there any new partnerships you could form to enhance your business in alignment with your mission?

9. Cost Structure: The costs associated with running your business

The cost structure refers to all the expenses involved in operating your business. Aligning your cost structure with your purpose ensures that your spending supports your mission and values. It's about optimizing your costs while maintaining quality and integrity.

- **Example:** A restaurant's cost structure might include fixed costs such as rent, wages, and insurance, as well as variable costs like food ingredients and utilities. To align with its mission, which includes supporting local agriculture, the restaurant may absorb slightly higher costs by sourcing locally, knowing it's aligned with its values.

While many business owners believe that they should maximize their company's profits in order to be successful, you might want to evaluate whether squeezing as much as possible from your costs is an advisable strategy. Depending on your defined purpose, you might want to "right-size" your profit margin instead of maximizing it. Sometimes, chasing the lowest possible cost may go against your company's stated purpose.

Example:

- An irrigation company's product manager suggested reducing the price per unit of each sprinkler by replacing the current steel spring with another, less costly spring. The lower gauge spring would save around $0.05 per unit, thereby increasing margins from 20% to 25%.

- However, after reviewing the test results, the directors decided that the increased failure risk of the product would result in tarnishing the company's reputation, going against their purpose of providing high-quality products.

This doesn't mean that lowering costs isn't a goal, only that you should also look at the trade offs of the lower costs and see whether it conflicts with your core values and purpose.

Cost Structure Questions:

- What are your major fixed and variable costs?

- Are there opportunities to streamline your cost structure without compromising quality or purpose?

- What is your break-even sales volume based on current overhead expense and gross profit %? Monthly, annually?[7]

The Role of Profit in Ensuring Sustainability

Profit is the lifeblood of any business, ensuring its survival and growth. As Peter Drucker emphasized: "Businessmen these days tend to be apologetic about profit... No apology is needed for profit as a necessity of economy and society. Profit and profitability are, however, crucial—for society even more than for the individual business... Profit is not the explanation, cause, or rationale of business behavior and business decisions, but the test of their validity."[9]

This underscores that profit is not only a byproduct of purpose-driven operations; it validates sound business decisions, the theory of your business, and the means to sustain it so it can make a long-term impact.

The 7P BAM: Aligning Your Business Model with Purpose

We've developed the 7P Business Alignment Model™ to provide practical frameworks to help clarify the components and assumptions that make up the "theory of your business."[10] By aligning and analyzing these components through the lens of purpose, you can create a purpose-driven business model that not only generates profit but also ensures that your business makes the impact you intend on the world.

Key Takeaways Chapter 25: Profit on Purpose

1. **Profit Supports Purpose — It's Not the End Goal:**

   o Profit is essential to sustain and grow your business, but profit alone isn't enough. When your profits are aligned with your purpose, you can build a business that is both financially sustainable and impactful.

2. **Your Business Model Should Reflect Your Purpose:**

   o A business model is the blueprint for how you create, deliver, and capture value. Aligning your business model with your purpose ensures that every part of your business — from who you serve to how you deliver value — is working towards fulfilling what matters most.

3. **Clear Purpose Builds Loyalty and Trust:**

   o Businesses with a strong purpose grow faster and keep customers and employees longer. When people connect with what you stand for, they want to do business with you and work for you.

4. **Align All Parts of Your Business with Your Purpose:**

   o Every part of your business — customer segments, value propositions, marketing channels, revenue streams, operations, and partnerships — should reflect your purpose. A purpose-driven business isn't just about marketing — it's built into how you operate every day.

5. **Strategic Alignment Creates Sustainable Success:**

   o While profit can validate good business decisions, alignment with one's purpose ensures the profits are put to its best use. When you align your strategy and operations with your purpose, you can also create a business that's resilient and able to thrive over time.

6. **Use the 7P Business Alignment Model™ to Put Purpose into Action:**

   The **7P Business Alignment Model™** gives you practical tools and frameworks to align the 7Ps, e.g your people, processes, and profits with your purpose — helping you operationalize your purpose in the day-to-day work of your business.

Reflection Questions Chapter 25: Profit on Purpose

1. **Does every part of my business model from who we serve to how we deliver clearly reflect our purpose?**

   o **Example:** Are there offerings or clients that don't fit who you want to serve or how you want to make an impact?

2. **Are we attracting the types of customers who truly value and resonate with our mission or just the ones who pay?**

3. **What specific problem do we solve better and more meaningfully than anyone else and is that benefit connected to our purpose?**

o How well do your current customers "fit" with your business's mission? What can you do to attract more right-fit customers who believe in what you stand for?

4. **Are any of our revenue streams or cost-cutting decisions pulling us away from our purpose?**

5. **To what extent do our partners, vendors, and technology utilized help us deliver on our purpose or are they just convenient?**

6. **If I mapped out our key business activities today, how may directly support our purpose and are there any that may detract from our purpose?**

    o What's one small step you could take to improve that alignment?

7. **Have we validated our business model with actual results from aligned, repeat customers or are we still working off assumptions?**

8. **What stood out to you in this chapter or resonated most with you?**

    o What insight, story, or idea felt especially relevant to your current business situation?

9. **What are your top 1-2 takeaways from this chapter?**

10. **What is one specific action you can take to start applying these insights?**

CHAPTER 26

OPTIMIZE PROFIT DECISIONS

"Business is all about solving people's
problems—at a profit."[1]
— Paul Marsden

Understanding Accounting Profit vs. Economic Profit

Although profit is typically understood as the difference between sales revenue and the cost of generating that revenue, this chapter will explore the idea of economic profit which also factors in opportunity costs, the value of foregone alternatives. By doing so we can improve our decision making and better utilize our time and money to produce the desired outcomes aligned with our purpose.

Opportunity Cost

When economists refer to a resource's 'opportunity cost,' they mean the foregone value of the next-highest-valued alternative use of that resource.[2] In other words, opportunity cost refers to the value of the next-best alternative that you give up when you make a choice. It includes both the resources spent on the chosen activity and the benefits you forego from the alternative.

For example, if you spend time and money going to a movie, you cannot spend that time at home reading a book or doing something else. If your next-best alternative to seeing the movie is reading the book, then the opportunity cost is the money spent on the movie ticket plus the pleasure you forgo by not reading the book.[3] However, measuring one's pleasure is hardly straightforward, especially when comparing different types of satisfaction, such as watching a movie versus reading a book. Despite the difficulty in measuring these satisfactions or values, it's still helpful to consider to the extent that we are able to do so, the trade-offs (the idea that to gain some advantage, one must incur a cost or give up another advantage) we face when making decisions so we can improve the probability of success of achieving a desired outcome.

Viewing Opportunity Costs through Multiple Perspectives

Consider a simpler, more general example to further illustrate the importance of opportunity costs. If you spend money on a vacation instead of investing in a business opportunity, the opportunity cost is the profit you might have earned from that investment. Conversely, if you spend time pursuing a business opportunity, you may miss out on the enjoyment and rejuvenation of the vacation. Evaluating these trade-offs from multiple perspectives—both financial and qualitative—can help you make better choices that hopefully improve overall benefits while also minimizing decision regrets.

Evaluating Opportunity Costs in a Business Decision:

Imagine you own a small bakery and have $100,000 in available funds. You're deciding between two options:

Option 1: Upgrade your bakery's equipment. This could reduce labor costs and improve efficiency, allowing you to serve more customers. Projected result: $150,000 in additional profits over the next year.

Option 2: Expand your menu with new offerings. This might attract new customers and increase sales. Projected result: $300,000 in additional sales, with $120,000 in additional profits over the next year.

Opportunity Cost Analysis:

If you choose to upgrade your equipment, your opportunity cost is the $120,000 in profits you could have earned by expanding the menu.

If you choose to expand your menu, your opportunity cost is the $150,000 in profits you could have earned by upgrading the equipment. In both cases, the opportunity cost is the profit from the option you didn't choose—the next best alternative. A smart business decision requires not only looking at potential gains but also under-standing what you're giving up by choosing one path over another.

Although in the real world it's difficult to precisely determine in ad-vance how one's option may play out, by thinking about opportunity costs, you can better evaluate potential trade-offs and make a more informed decisions.

Economic Profit: An important distinction to improve busi-ness decisions is understanding and considering the economic profit vs. the accounting profit of a decision. Economic profit, often called "excess profits," is the surplus achieved when net income—or account-ing profits—exceeds the potential earnings from the best alternative opportunities available if resources were allocated differently.[4]

Economic Profit Example: Peach Stand vs. Apple Stand

Imagine two stands: one selling peaches and one selling apples. Both have the same overhead costs, and all other conditions are equal (though this is rarely the case in real life). However, the peach stand earns $1 per peach, and the apple stand earns $2 per apple. The oppor-tunity cost of choosing to operate the peach stand is the $2 you could have earned from operating the apple stand. Thus, while the account-ing profit for peaches is positive, the economic profit is negative when factoring in the lost potential profit of the apple stand.

Accounting Profit – Opportunity Cost (Foregone Alternative) = Economic Profit

Stand	Accounting Profit	Opportunity Cost (Foregone Alternative)	Economic Profit
Peach Stand	$1 from peaches	$2 profit from Apple stand	-$1
Apple Stand	$2 from apples	$1 profit from Peach stand	$1

We can infer from the Apple stand's higher economic profit of $1, com-pared to the Peach stand's negative economic profit of -$1, that operat-ing the Apple stand is a more optimal and profitable use of resources. Conversely, the Peach stand's negative economic profit indicates sub-optimal resource utilization compared to its next best alternative, in this case the apple stand.

Opportunity Costs in Action: Balancing Risk, Reward, and Personal Growth

Understanding economic profit and opportunity costs can help us better evaluate business opportunities. For instance, my eldest son, Jaden, was excited to join his best friend in Florida for two weeks to earn "big money" by door-knocking residential homes. His job involved making short pitches to homeowners to set up appointments with solar consultants who would then present solar panels' benefits and cost savings. Jaden would earn a sizable commission if a sale was made, and the panels were installed.

His two-week, 100% commission-driven venture earned him $2,200. After accounting for flight and other expenses incurred during those two weeks, his net earnings (accounting profit) were $1,700.

To evaluate his **economic profit**, we considered the opportunity cost of his next best alternative—staying home and working his regular jobs as a server at a high-end Brazilian steakhouse and as a part-time Sales Development Representative. Had he stayed home, he could have earned $1,700 over those same two weeks from those jobs.

Accounting Profit – Opportunity Cost = Economic Profit

- **$1,700** (accounting profit from solar sales)
- **$1,700** (opportunity cost from regular jobs)
- **= $0** economic profit earned from selling solar

Thus, his economic profit from selling solar panels ended up being zero compared to what he could have earned staying home. Moreover, the risk and uncertainty he took by selling solar didn't justify making the same amount of money he could have earned with nearly 100% certainty from his regular jobs. Although he managed to set up enough appointments that resulted in one sale, he could have just as easily earned nothing for his two weeks of effort.

To assume the risk of not earning any money to be worthwhile, his upside would need to be much greater. For example, if the two-week sales venture had a 50% probability of success in closing a sale, he would need to earn twice the amount—**$3,400**—to justify the risk compared to staying home. If the probability of success drops to 20%, he would need to achieve five times $1,700, or $8,500, to justify the risk and compensate for the increased uncertainty.

Given the uncertainties of commission-based work, one must have significantly higher potential earnings to compensate for the increased risk uncertainty. To give up a job with consistent and predictable earnings for a commission-based sales job, there must be a much higher upside to make it worthwhile.

However, another side of this story is worth mentioning when evaluating opportunity costs beyond monetary considerations. As a result of the challenges he endured and the life lessons learned, Jaden returned a "new man" with a greater appreciation and know-how of how to communicate with different types of people under pressure. It galvanized him and increased his motivation to further hone his sales abilities. The mental fortitude Jaden gained from going door to door and enduring repeated "no's" can become a valuable asset as he moves forward and is difficult to pin down in just monetary terms.

With that said, it's also worth asking: What might be the opportunity costs of staying home and remaining in his comfort zone compared to the valuable life lessons he would have missed by not going on the trip?

Understanding opportunity cost helps business owners evaluate options from multiple perspectives, considering the potential cost or value of the next best available foregone alternatives. By doing so, we can improve our ability to make better decisions that result in more fulfilling outcomes.

Making Better Decisions by Understanding Opportunity Costs

When clients face tough decisions about allocating and optimizing resources among competing options, we help them make better choices by considering potential opportunity costs. Opportunity cost is a fundamental concept in economics that aids individuals and businesses in making more informed and efficient decisions. As previously stated, it involves considering what you must give up when pursuing a certain course of action. Evaluating opportunity costs can be difficult because alternatives aren't always obvious. However, considering opportunity costs can still improve decision-making.

The Value of Intelligent Decision-Making

As Charlie Munger reminds us, "Intelligent people make decisions based on opportunity costs,"[5] considering the value of foregone alternatives when making decisions. By doing so, we can better allocate and optimize resources—such as time, talent, and capital—resulting in better outcomes and greater profit or ROI. Moreover, evaluating outcomes and opportunity costs can extend beyond financial considerations to include quantitative and qualitative factors.

Our clients have found it helpful when we guide them through thought experiments and "what-if" scenarios to evaluate the costs of foregone alternatives in both quantitative and qualitative terms. This process increases the likelihood of making better decisions, leading to improved outcomes. Evaluating all potential alternatives can be challenging, and some might argue that it's futile since no one can know all the available options or determine which is truly "best." We can't run simulations in parallel universes to see the outcome of each decision. To complicate matters further, what does "best" even mean in terms of—financial gain, KPIs, quality of relationships, health, peace of mind, or happiness? This complexity can lead to analysis paralysis, where the sheer number of options and the difficulty of weighing potential outcomes can overwhelm decision-makers and hinder them from taking a course of action.

While we may not always have a grasp of all possible alternatives, we can improve our decision-making by better understanding the pertinent facts, available options, and exercise our ability to reason within the confines of our current understanding and knowledge.

Even within the constraints of limited information and resources, evaluating opportunity costs can improve our ability to think critically and strategically. By considering the implications of our decisions by factoring in the value of the next best alternatives we forgo, both quantitatively and qualitatively, we can strive to make better choices. This practice not only increases the likelihood of achieving better outcomes but also contributes to a more purposeful and fulfilling life.

Avoiding Foolish Choices Over Striving for Perfection

It may be helpful, however, instead of striving to make "better choices" to simply avoid making foolish or irrational ones. Charlie Munger wisely points out, "It is remarkable how much long-term advantage people like us have gotten by trying to be consistently not stupid, instead of trying to be very intelligent."[6]

This quote reinforces the idea that practical decision-making involves reducing irrationality and avoiding mistakes rather than striving for unattainable brilliance. It also helps us overcome analysis paralysis since avoiding the obvious foolish choices is usually easier than making brilliant ones, resulting in better decisions over time.

Intelligent Decision Making:

As part of our effort to clarify key terms, here are different ways to understand the concept of intelligence. (One of my personal frustrations is how often terms like "intelligence" are used without clear definitions, which can lead to confusion or misinterpretation)These perspectives also provide insights into what Charlie Munger may mean by an "intelligent individual" in the context of making better business decisions and evaluating opportunity costs.

Intelligence is a multifaceted concept that encompasses an individual's ability to learn from experience, adapt to new situations, understand complex ideas, and apply knowledge effectively.[7] According to the American Psychological Association (APA), intelligence is defined as: "The global capacity to act purposefully, to think rationally, and to deal effectively with the environment."[8]

Another perspective comes from the Oxford Learner's Dictionaries, which defines intelligence as: "The ability to learn, understand, and think about things."[9]

Intelligent Decision Making Involves:

1. **Critical Thinking:**

    o   Assessing options and their potential outcomes.

    o   Analyzing both the seen—explicit, immediate consequences—and the unseen—implicit, longer-term consequences of a decision.

2. **Opportunity Cost Evaluation:**

    o   Recognizing that choosing one option inherently means giving up others.

    o   Considering the potential benefits that are sacrificed when selecting a particular path.

3. **Rational Decision-Making:**

    o   Applying logical reasoning to maximize value and efficiency.

    o   Avoid cognitive biases that might cloud judgment by excluding relevant facts that don't fit into preconceived ideas or beliefs.

The Relativity of Intelligence: Context Matters

Expanding on the APA's definition, it's essential to recognize that intelligence can manifest differently depending on the context or environment. This idea is encapsulated in a famous quote often attributed to Albert Einstein: "Everybody is a genius. But if you judge a fish by its ability to climb a tree, it will live its whole life believing that it is stupid."[10]

This perspective emphasizes that assessing intelligence should also consider an individual's unique strengths, talents, and the specific environment in which they operate. Just as a fish is naturally adept at swimming but not climbing trees, humans possess diverse abilities that may excel in particular contexts but not others.

For example, you or one of your employees may excel in communicating with and relating to people in a customer service role. Another may shine in a role requiring data analytical skills and attention to detail, and another may be adept at working with tools and doing things requiring manual dexterity, spatial awareness, and hand-to-eye coordination. These are just a few domains of many areas where humans can be competent, and their talents can be made productive.

Understanding intelligence as context-specific and relative to one's environment becomes crucial to making effective decisions and better utilizing your team's collective strengths. Intelligent individuals consider their strengths and specific circumstances when evaluating opportunity costs. They recognize that an optimal decision for one person may not be the best for another due to differing abilities and situational factors.

Reflection Questions for Leveraging Your Strengths

As an SMB owner, understanding what you're good at and where you thrive can help your business grow and make your work more enjoyable. Ask yourself these three questions:

1. **What tasks in your business have you found relatively easy for you compared to others and also energize you?**

   o Think about the things you're naturally good at and enjoy doing. These are your strengths.

2. **When do you feel most productive and happy at work?**

   o Look at the situations where you do your best—like working with a team, solving problems alone, or handling tough challenges. How do these moments demonstrate your strengths and make you effective?

3. **How can you focus more on your strengths in your business?**

   o Think about ways to spend less time or delegate some parts of tasks you're not great at while spending more time doing what you're good at. How can you make more productive the collective strengths of your team to complement your own.

Answering these questions can help you focus on what you do best, make a bigger impact in your business, and feel more fulfilled in your work.[14]

Key Takeaways Chapter 26: Optimize Profit Decisions

Profit is not merely the difference between revenue and costs—it's the lifeblood that fuels sustainable growth. By understanding economic profit, which accounts for opportunity costs, SMB owners can make smarter, purpose-driven decisions.

1. **Opportunity Costs Drive Better Choices**

   Every decision involves trade-offs. Evaluating the opportunity cost—what is sacrificed by choosing one option over another—enables you to optimize resources like time, money, and talent.

2. **Economic Profit vs. Accounting Profit**

   Economic profit accounts for the value of foregone alternatives, offering a clearer picture of how well resources are utilized compared to their next-best use.

3. **Avoid Analysis Paralysis**

   While evaluating every alternative is impossible, avoiding irrational decisions rather than striving for perfection can lead to consistent, better outcomes.

4. **Relativity of Intelligence and Decision-Making**

   Intelligent decisions come from leveraging your unique strengths and recognizing that optimal choices vary depending on context and resources.

5. **Align Decisions with Long-Term Purpose**

   Smarter decisions aren't just about maximizing immediate gains. Aligning business operations with your mission and values ensures a sustainable and fulfilling path.

Reflection Questions Chapter 26: Optimize Profit Decisions

1. **How do you currently evaluate opportunity costs when making business decisions?**

- o What steps could you take to better consider what you might be giving up when choosing one option over another?

- o Example: Are you thinking about how time, money, or talent could be better used elsewhere?

2. **Are there areas in your business where time, money, or effort is being spent without clear results?**

    - o How could you reallocate those resources toward activities that have a higher impact on your business growth and profitability?

    - o Example: Are there tasks or projects that could be paused, delegated, or eliminated to free up time and money for what matters most?

3. **Are you focusing on the tasks and activities that align with your greatest strengths and highest value?**

    - o What lower-value tasks are pulling you away from working on the parts of your business where you add the most value?

    - o Example: Are there routine or administrative tasks that someone else could do so you can focus on strategic priorities?

4. **Are your team members working in roles that play to their strengths?**

    - o How could you better align their tasks and responsibilities to match what they do best?

    - o Example: Is there someone on your team doing work that doesn't fit their natural skills — and how can that be adjusted?

5. **Are the customers you serve aligned with your business's purpose and values?**

    - o If not, what changes could you make to attract more of the right-fit customers who value what you uniquely offer?

o Example: Could you refine your marketing, services, or pricing to better attract customers who appreciate your purpose and approach?

6. **When making tough decisions, do you focus more on avoiding mistakes or trying to find the perfect answer?**

    o How can you strike a better balance by making smart, timely decisions without getting stuck in overthinking or perfectionism?

    o Example: What would making a "good enough" decision look like that still moves you forward?

7. **Are your profit and business decisions aligned with your long-term purpose and mission?**

    o How do you ensure that the way you make money reflects your deeper goals and values?

    o Example: Are there decisions you've made recently that prioritized short-term gains over long-term purpose — and how might you adjust for the future?

8. **What stood out to you in this chapter or resonated most with you?**

    o What insight, story, or concept felt especially relevant to your current business situation?

    o What is one thing you feel motivated to act on because of this chapter?

9. **What are your top 1-2 takeaways from this chapter?**

CHAPTER 27

MAXIMIZE ROI OF WHAT MATTERS

"The key is not spending time, but investing it"[1]
— *Stephen Covey*

Aligning Time, Money and Purpose:

Opportunity Cost and Financial Performance

Opportunity cost plays an important role in evaluating financial performance especially when assessing whether your business is generating a true return above what your capital could have earned elsewhere.

One way to express opportunity cost is by comparing your Return on Equity (ROE) to a reasonable benchmark return. For example, if your opportunity cost of capital is 10%, meaning you could reasonably expect to earn 10% by investing that capital elsewhere—your business would need to earn more than 10% ROE to generate an economic profit.

If your business earns an ROE of 8%, it hasn't lost money in accounting terms but it has underperformed relative to the opportunity cost. That gap reflects value left on the table because those resources could have generated a higher return if allocated differently.

Return on Equity (ROE) Guide:

- **Opportunity Cost Benchmarking:** ROE shows whether your business is earning more than the expected rate of return based on market conditions and investment alternatives.

- **Comparative Measure:** ROE allows you to compare your business to others in the same industry, helping assess relative financial strength and operational efficiency.

- **Performance Indicator:** While ROE expectations vary by industry, a sustained ROE of 15-20% is often considered a sign of strong financial performance and effective resource use.[2]

Bottom Line: ROE isn't just a finance metric—it's a lens for evaluating how well your business turns equity into profit relative to what else you could have done with that capital. When ROE consistently exceeds your opportunity cost, your business is generating real economic value.

Maximizing the ROI of Your Time

The principle of opportunity cost helps you evaluate which option could offer more significant economic benefits, given your understanding of the best alternatives within your consideration set. Remember, you can only choose from options you know, which vary depending on the individual and the context. For instance, someone unemployed or only able to secure a minimum-wage job may be willing to wait in line for several hours because the pay foregone for those hours isn't as high as it is for someone earning a higher wage. If the person waiting in that same line is an attorney or surgeon capable of earning hundreds of dollars per hour, the opportunity cost—the foregone income from not working during those hours—is much higher than that of someone unemployed or earning a low wage.

This could explain why people of means and wealth tend to be more conscious about how they utilize their time and will delegate tasks, especially routine ones that would be costly in terms of opportunity cost if they did those tasks themselves. To illustrate, If a surgeon mows his lawn—a task that could be performed by someone else for $15 an hour—it could be argued that he's effectively valuing his time at $15 an hour instead of earning $200+ per hour as a surgeon during those same hours. However, evaluating opportunity costs is rarely as straightforward as only the hourly wages foregone.

Weighing Opportunity Costs Beyond Money

When making decisions, it's crucial to remember that monetary factors are rarely the sole criteria. Personal satisfaction and well-being are also important. For example, a surgeon might mow his lawn on a Saturday afternoon instead of working because he enjoys the activity.

It offers therapeutic benefits, such as outdoor physical activity and much-needed sunlight, which he doesn't get in his usual indoor hospital environment. Sometimes, the non-financial benefits of an activity make it worthwhile, even despite the potential economic loss.

By considering the opportunity cost of something—what you must give up or the foregone benefits of the next best alternative—you can make more informed and efficient decisions, resulting in better utilization of time and resources. However, while financial considerations are important, personal satisfaction and well-being are also crucial factors when evaluating the cost of what you give up when making decisions.

Considering individual preferences and values requires thoughtful reflection and wisdom to weigh these factors appropriately on a case-by-case basis. No one said this was easy. However, by being more aware of these factors, we can strive to balance quantitative and qualitative considerations while taking a more holistic approach that enables you to better align with your purpose and create a greater sense of fulfillment.

Establishing Your Hourly Worth

Establishing a baseline for your time's worth can help you better evaluate the opportunity cost of your time. A straightforward method is dividing your current or desired annual earnings by 2,000 hours (the approximate number of full-time work hours per year).

- **$100,000 per year:** $100,000 / 2,000 hours = **$50/hour**
- **$150,000 per year:** $150,000 / 2,000 hours = **$75/hour**
- **$300,000 per year:** $300,000 / 2,000 hours = **$150/hour**

Understanding your hourly worth can help you allocate your time more effectively. For instance, if you aim to earn $300,000 annually, you should focus on activities worth at least $150 per hour. Spending time on $25-$50 per hour tasks could undermine your ability to achieve your income target.

Maximizing the ROI of Your Time

Most business owners typically pay themselves a salary and benefits commensurate with their role but also leverage other people's time

(OPT) to generate additional business earnings in the form of profits. Regardless of the mix in total compensation (wages or profits), it may be useful to evaluate one's time based on the desired or required "hourly rate" to achieve one's earnings goals.

Generally, it's better to leverage your skills and strengths on the highest-value activities you're qualified for. For instance, a CNC programmer should focus on programming at $30 per hour rather than operating machines at $22 per hour. If the programmer spends time as a machine operator earning $22 per hour, the economic profit is negative $8—the difference between the $22 earned and the $30 that could have been earned (assuming programming work is available). It makes sense to maximize the ROI of your time by spending time on higher-value activities.

However, assigning an hourly value to executive-level strategic planning can be more complex. An hour of planning and thinking can significantly impact the company's trajectory and create shareholder value beyond the executive's hourly salary. For example, during this time, an executive might develop an innovative product or service idea that better meets customer needs and redefines what's considered excellent or possible.

Thus, for an owner or higher-level manager/executive the opportunity cost of not focusing on tasks that maximize your strengths, resources, and capabilities for the greater benefit to your organization can be enormous. This is why its so crucial for SMB leaders and owners to develop the habit of concentrating on tasks that make the most of your strengths and resources for the highest good of your organization.

Applying the Law of Diminishing Returns to Improve Resource Allocation

In addition to opportunity cost, one of the most enduring economic principles that has stuck with me is the law of diminishing returns. This concept, which I first encountered in my economics courses as an undergrad, has proven relevant in both personal and professional decision-making. It explains that after a certain threshold of "good enough," pouring in more effort, money, or resources yields diminishing benefits—and sometimes, can even lead to negative outcomes.

Although this chapter primarily focuses on the concept of opportunity cost as a tool for making better business decisions, understanding the law of diminishing returns can also improve decision-making and enable us to allocate our time, money, and personnel more effectively.

The law of diminishing returns is an economic principle that states that beyond a certain point, adding more of one input—such as labor, capital, or time—to a fixed amount of other inputs results in progressively smaller increases in output. Eventually, adding even more may lead to a decrease in overall output.[3]

In simpler terms, there comes a point where putting in additional effort, money, or resources no longer yields proportional benefits. Sometimes, these excess inputs can even make things worse, turning what began as an improvement into a liability. Recognizing and applying this principle can help business owners avoid waste, make more informed choices, and identify the optimal point at which further investment is no longer advantageous.

Example: Quenching Thirst with Water

Imagine you've been hiking on a hot day, dehydrated and thirsty. Drinking the first glass of water provides great satisfaction and replenishment, giving you energy and relief. This initial input (the first glass of water) provides a high return in terms of physical well-being and satisfaction.

As you continue drinking a second and third glass, the benefit begins to diminish compared to the first. While these additional glasses might still be enjoyable, they are not as satisfying as the first glass, as your thirst has already been largely quenched.

Now, if you keep drinking water beyond what your body needs or can comfortably hold, you may start to feel discomfort or even nausea. At this point, the input (additional glasses of water) leads to negative returns, as drinking more water causes harm instead of benefit.

Business Examples:

1. **Hiring Additional Staff:**

    - **Initial Benefit:** Let's say you run a small manufacturing business. Hiring more workers at first boosts your production.

    - **Diminishing Returns:** However, your factory space is limited. As you keep adding workers, the space becomes crowded. Employees start getting in each other's way, mistakes happen more frequently, and productivity per worker declines.

    - **Negative Returns:** If you continue adding workers beyond this point, the overcrowding could lead to accidents or significantly slowed production, causing total output to decrease despite more people on the job.

2. **Marketing Spend:**

    - **Initial Benefit:** Investing $1,000 in online advertising brings in a good number of new customers.

    - **Diminishing Returns:** Increasing your ad spend to $2,000 brings in additional customers, but not twice as many as before.

    - **Negative Returns:** Pushing the budget to $10,000 might oversaturate your market segment, leading to ad fatigue, where people start ignoring your ads, and the cost per new customer becomes unsustainably high.

Why Diminishing Returns Matters for Your Business:

- **Optimal Use of Resources:** Understanding this law helps you identify the most efficient level of resource allocation. There's an optimal point where your inputs (time, money, and labor) maximize outputs (products/services, customer satisfaction, sales, profits). More isn't necessarily better, and simply increasing inputs doesn't guarantee proportional increases in output and may not be cost-effective.

- **Avoiding Waste:** Recognizing when you're hitting diminishing returns prevents you from wasting resources that could be better used elsewhere in your business.

- **Find the Sweet Spot:** Aim to identify the level at which additional inputs result in additional improvements or benefits that become negligible. At that point, trying to improve it or putting more time, effort, or resources into it doesn't make sense.

- **Focus on Efficiency:** Instead of adding more resources, you might need to improve processes, invest in training, or adopt new technology to achieve better results.

By integrating this principle into your decision-making, you can avoid unnecessary expenditures and ensure your resources are focused where they can create the most meaningful impact. Whether deciding how much to invest in marketing, how many employees to hire, or how to allocate your time, understanding diminishing returns can help us improve the ROI of our time and money spent.

Connecting Opportunity Cost and the Law of Diminishing Returns

Both opportunity cost and the law of diminishing returns offer valuable insights into optimizing resource allocation. While opportunity cost helps you decide where to allocate resources, the law of diminishing returns tells you when to stop adding resources. Together, they ensure that you're not just allocating resources but doing so optimally.

Key Insights:

- **Economic Profit:** Incorporate opportunity costs into decision-making to achieve better outcomes.

- **Evaluate Opportunity Costs:** Balance potential benefits of alternatives to optimize resources.

- **Apply Diminishing Returns:** Identify and avoid points where committing additional resources yield negligible or even negative value.

What is a Good Profit Margin?

When evaluating financial performance in light of its opportunity costs—the value of foregone alternatives—it is helpful to contextualize based on your particular industry since metrics such as healthy profit margins can vary significantly across industries. Here are some benchmarks:

- **Grocery Stores & Retailers:** Typically operate on low margins due to high inventory and labor costs, averaging 2-5%.

- **Technology Companies:** Enjoy higher margins, particularly in software, with Software-as-a-Service (SaaS) companies achieving 20-40%.

- **Consulting Firms:** Often see 15-30% margins due to low capital investment and high labor dependency.

- **Manufacturing:** High-tech manufacturing might have margins between 5-10%, while traditional sectors often see 5%.

- **Construction & Specialty Contractors:** Typically range from 5-10%, driven by material and labor costs.

- **Wholesale/Distribution:** Usually operate on thin margins of 2-5%, emphasizing high-volume sales.[4]

Actionable Steps to Optimize Financial Metrics:

Benchmarking: Compare your profit margins and financial metrics with industry standards to identify areas for improvement. For example:

- What is your Gross Profit % (GP%), Cost of Goods Sold % (COGS%), Overhead % (OH%), and Operating Profit %?

- How do these figures compare to industry benchmarks for businesses of your size?

- Are there specific cost areas where you're over- or under-spending compared to competitors?

Cost Management: Compare your fixed and variable costs with similar businesses to identify cost-saving opportunities.

- What percentage of your revenue is spent on materials, labor, and overhead?

- Are there areas where expenses have increased without a clear return?

- Have you negotiated better rates with suppliers or vendors in the last 12 months?

Value Pricing: Ensure your pricing strategy reflects the unique value of your purpose-driven offerings.

- How do your prices compare to competitors offering similar products/services?

- Have you calculated your true break-even point and optimal pricing margins?

- Are you pricing based on value (differentiation) or cost-plus pricing (commodity pricing)?

Revenue Diversification: Explore multiple revenue streams that align with your purpose to reduce dependency on one source.

- What percentage of revenue comes from your top 5, 10 or 20 clients? Does it look top-heavy or are you overly reliant on them?

- Are there new services, products, or partnerships that align with your mission and could generate additional revenue?

- What percentage of your revenue is recurring (e.g., subscriptions, contracts) versus one-time transactions?

By optimizing these financial metrics, you can drive sustainable growth, increase profitability, and ensure that every aspect of your business remains aligned with your core purpose.

Profit Sharing and Employee Alignment

Another way to better align your profits with your purpose is through profit-sharing programs that incentivize employees to align their interests with the overall health and success of the business. Profit sharing can create a win/win culture where linking employee total compensation to company performance and profitability fosters a sense of employee ownership, encouraging them to be mindful of both revenues and expenses.[5]

Impact on Productivity

Employees participating in a profit-sharing plan are more likely to take ownership of business results since their work product and total compensation becomes more defined by their contribution. "A plan that rewards employees with a share of the fruits of their labor draws a direct connection between work and reward," [6] writes Stu Watson for the Edward Lowe Foundation. Productivity often reaches higher levels when employees have the opportunity to share in the profit margins they help create through their efforts, rather than being compensated solely for their time on the job.

Actionable Steps for Implementing Profit Sharing

- **Design the Plan:** Determine how profits will be shared among employees and establish clear criteria for distribution. One scenario is for the company to take 20-25% of the profits realized, provided a minimum threshold of profitability has been achieved, and put it in a profit-sharing pool to be divided among the employees based on both quantitative and qualitative criteria. An example of a purely quantitative approach would be a minimum of one year of employment and profit share based on a pro-rata share of each person's wages compared to the total company payroll.

- **Communicate Clearly:** Ensure employees understand how the profit-sharing plan works and how their contributions impact overall profitability.

- **Monitor and Adjust:** Review the effectiveness of the profit-sharing plan regularly and make adjustments as necessary to maintain alignment with business goals and purpose.

- **Maintain Flexibility:** In addition, we've found it helpful to frame any profit sharing plan to your employees as a we will adjust and learn as we go so we can apply it for the overall good of the company and employees. By doing so you're not locked into the initial set up or expectations.

Key Takeaways Chapter 27: Maximize ROI of What Matters

1. **Profit is a Means, Not the End — Align Profit with Purpose:**

   o Profit is essential for sustaining and growing a business, but it should serve your broader purpose and vision. Profit should enable you to better serve your customers, employees, and community — not become the sole focus of the business.

2. **Opportunity Cost Defines True Profitability:**

   o **Opportunity cost** is what you give up when choosing one course of action over another. True profitability means generating a return that exceeds what you could reasonably earn from other opportunities. Evaluating decisions based on opportunity costs leads to smarter resource allocation and better business outcomes.

3. **Return on Equity (ROE) as a Strategic Performance Indicator:**

   o ROE measures how efficiently your business generates profits relative to equity. Aim for a ROE that exceeds your opportunity cost of capital — often 15-20% — to ensure that you're creating real economic value. ROE helps you compare your business performance to industry peers and assess whether you're making the most of shareholder investment.

4. **Calculating and Maximizing the ROI of Your Time:**

   o Understanding the **true value of your time** helps prioritize high-impact activities and avoid low-value tasks. Assigning a baseline "hourly worth" to your time clarifies what tasks you should delegate, outsource, or eliminate to focus on what matters most. Leverage other people's time (OPT) and focus on strategic decisions and actions that align with your highest value.

5. **Recognizing and Applying the Law of Diminishing Returns:**

   o More effort, money, or resources do not always lead to proportional benefits. At some point, adding more becomes wasteful or even harmful. Learn to identify the optimal level of resource allocation and avoid overinvestment. This applies to areas like staffing, marketing, and operations.

6. **Integrating Opportunity Cost and Diminishing Returns to Optimize Resource Allocation:**

   o Use opportunity cost to decide where to allocate resources and diminishing returns to decide when to stop adding resources. Together, these principles help ensure you're investing wisely and not over spending or over committing in areas with limited payoff.

7. **Benchmarking Profit Margins and Financial Performance:**

   o Understand profit margin benchmarks for your industry to set realistic targets and identify areas for improvement. Regularly review metrics like Gross Profit %, Cost of Goods Sold (COGS %), Overhead %, and Operating Profit % to monitor financial health. Align pricing and cost structures with your business's value proposition and purpose.

8. **Align Profit with Employee Engagement through Profit Sharing:**

   o Profit sharing helps aligns employee interests with business success, motivating them to improve performance, reduce costs, and contribute to long-term growth. A well-designed plan promotes ownership culture, improves retention, and rewards contributions.

9. **Balancing Financial and Non-Financial Opportunity Costs:**

    o   Not all opportunity costs are about money. Personal fulfillment, well-being, and values matter too. Sometimes, activities that bring joy or relaxation, even if not financially optimal in the short term, may contribute to long-term sustainability and greater fulfillment. Balance ROI considering both financial and personal and team well-being for sustainable success.

10. **Focus on Purpose-Driven Profitability:**

    o   When profit and purpose work together, both can grow. Profit supports your mission, and purpose builds trust with customers and employees — leading to greater success and fulfillment.

Reflection Questions for Chapter 27: Maximize ROI of What Matters

1. **How do you currently evaluate opportunity costs when making business decisions?**

    o   What steps could you take to more effectively assess what you are giving up when you choose one investment, project, or customer over another?

    o   Example: Are you considering the true value of your time, money, and energy when deciding where to focus?

2. **Does your Return on Equity (ROE) meet or exceed your expectations and industry standards?**

    o   If not, where could you improve how you're using your resources to generate stronger returns?

    o   Example: Could better pricing, cost controls, or focusing on higher-margin work help boost returns?

3. **Are you focusing your time and energy on high-value, strategic activities that align with your highest hourly worth?**

   o What lower-value tasks could you delegate or outsource to free up time for what matters most?

   o Example: What are some routine or administrative tasks you're still doing that could be handled by others?

4. **Are there areas in your business where adding more time, money, or resources is producing smaller and smaller (negligible) returns?**

   o How can you identify and operate at the optimal level of input — avoiding waste or overinvestment?

   o Example: Are you over-hiring, over-spending on marketing, or over-serving clients without a clear return?

5. **Are your profit goals aligned with your broader purpose and mission?**

   o How do you ensure that decisions to grow profit also reflect the kind of business you want to be?

   o Example: How does your pricing, customer selection, or product/service offering align with what you stand for?

6. **How do your current profit margins compare to benchmarks in your industry?**

   o What specific adjustments could help you improve margins — whether through pricing, cost controls, or efficiency?

   o Example: Are you underpricing your services? Do you need to re-evaluate supplier agreements or overhead costs?

7. **How might a profit-sharing plan positively impact employee morale, engagement, and ownership?**

   o What steps could you take to explore or implement a profit-sharing model that rewards employees for contributing to profitability?

- o Example: How would employees behave differently if they had a share in the profits?

8. **How do you currently evaluate the return on investment (ROI) for your time and business improvement efforts?**

    - o What specific metrics or benchmarks could help you assess whether your time and money are being invested wisely?

    - o Example: Could you track revenue, profit margins, customer growth, or other KPIs tied to improvement efforts?

9. **Are you balancing financial opportunity costs with non-financial values like personal well-being, family, and fulfillment?**

    - o What's one way you can make better decisions that consider both money and what matters to you personally?

    - o Example: Are there times you sacrifice personal well-being for financial gains — and how could you shift that?

10. **What stood out to you in this chapter or resonated most with you?**

    - o What insight, story, or concept felt especially relevant to your current business situation?

11. **What are your top 1-2 takeaways from this chapter?**

    - o What is one specific action you can take to start applying these insights and improve ROI of time and money while aligned with your purpose and business goals?

CHAPTER 28

KEEP IMPROVING WHAT MATTERS

"Without continual growth and progress,
such words as improvement, achievement,
and success have no meaning."[1]
— *Benjamin Franklin*

The Key to Meaningful Success: A Continuous Process

Benjamin Franklin emphasized that for success, achievement, and improvement to be meaningful, they must stem from continual growth and progress. The operative word here is *continual*. Progress isn't a single event—it's a steady process of small improvements that build over time.

Success in any endeavor—whether losing weight, improving health, developing better relationships, or building a business—is never the result of a single event. It comes from a process of consistently making small improvements that drive growth and progress. Yet, to keep progressing, we must also be willing to change. However, we often resist change even though growth, learning, and progress are always preceded by some type of change—oftentimes a letting go of what no longer serves us to make space for something better.

This truth is beautifully illustrated by 'Abdu'l-Bahá, one of the central figures of the Bahá'í Faith:

"If you plant a seed in the ground, a tree will become manifest from that seed. The seed sacrifices itself to the tree that will come from it. The seed is outwardly lost, destroyed; but the same seed which is sacrificed will be absorbed and embodied in the tree, its blossoms, fruit, and branches. If the identity of that seed had not been sacrificed to the tree which became manifest

from it, no branches, blossoms, or fruits would have been forthcoming."[2]
— *The Promulgation of Universal Peace*

Just as a seed transforms into a tree, we too must allow old ways to fall away so that new growth can occur. Everyone desires growth and learning, yet few are willing to release the habits, beliefs, or systems that keep them in their comfort zone and prevent them from becoming who they are capable of being. Growth and progress for both individuals and businesses requires moving beyond that comfort zone and embracing the discomfort of change. And as Leo Buscaglia observed, *"Change is the end result of all true learning."*[3]

The Power of Small, Manageable Steps

However, making changes including the degree of discomfort that inevitably may come with it requires manageable and practical steps. To make the change process manageable and practical, its helpful to break it down into small steps. By doing so, we can increase engagement and consistency, ultimately setting us on a trajectory toward sustainable success. You've probably heard sayings like, "How do you eat an elephant? One bite at a time,"[4] or "A journey of a thousand miles begins with a single step."[5] These well known aphorisms remind us that big goals are best achieved through small, steady steps.

For example, someone who has been sedentary for years might find that jumping into an intensive workout routine three times a week feels unsustainable and overwhelming. A more reasonable first step could be walking for 10 minutes a day, three times a week, gradually increasing the intensity as they build it into a daily routine. Taking smaller, sustainable steps also has the benefit of requiring less motivation and is more achievable, leading to greater consistency.

We've learned from working with our clients that they often overestimate what a manageable next step looks like and subsequently, we need to make adjustments to smaller steps in order for them to maintain consistency.

Steady effort over time, with gradual progression, is among the most important factors contributing to progress and achieving desired outcomes. Helping our clients take manageable next steps consistently is where our Business Alignment Coaches can serve as invaluable guides.

They help you customize a manageable action plan to implement the Purpose Matters 7P Business Alignment Model™, considering your current resources and capabilities. They get you moving based on meeting you where you are and then helping you utilize and implement the power of consistent, manageable next steps to progress safely and sustainably toward your desired outcomes. Our coaches collaborate with you on an ongoing basis, providing the expertise to determine the minimum level of activity, effort, and progression required to achieve your goals based on your desired time frames.

Overcoming Inertia

Inertia is defined as the tendency of an object to remain in its current state either at rest or in motion unless acted upon by an external force. Without this "external force" we can't engage in an improvement process that we don't even start. One of the biggest challenges our clients face is overcoming the inertia of remaining stuck in the status quo. Our clients begin working with us when they have a desire and willingness to "do something" and engage an external force like implementing the 7P BAM to finally overcome this inertia. They realize that the status quo is no longer acceptable and are open to exploring how to make changes, even if they're unsure exactly where to start.

Consistency of Showing Up

One of the most effective ways to overcome inertia is simply the act of *showing up* for the new behavior or way of doing things. As Woody Allen famously said, *"80% of success is showing up."* [6] Learning to show up consistently may be the single most important factor in beginning the process of growth and eventually achieving your desired outcomes. Fore example, if you can manage to show up at the gym, you're more likely to engage in exercise, even if you didn't feel like it initially. Similarly, putting on your running shoes and stepping outside makes it more likely you'll at least do some minimal activity before heading back in.

By consistently showing up and doing something versus nothing, you begin taking small steps that compound over time, setting you on the path toward achieving your goals. The importance of movement and action is captured in sayings like, you can't steer a parked car. [7] Our clients have found that our Business Alignment Coaches provide invaluable assistance by serving as accountability partners and sources of encouragement, ensuring they're more likely to show up consistently and act on their commitments.

Course Corrections and Achieving Desired Outcomes with the 7P BAM

An effective process not only enables you to take the next steps but also allows for course corrections, ensuring a sustainable trajectory toward your desired outcomes. Like the coxswain in a boat, our Business Alignment Coaches help you steer and make necessary adjustments, ensuring the six Ps (Prioritization, People, Pipeline, Product, Process, Profit) are aligned and moving you toward the seventh P—*Purpose*. This alignment enables you to achieve your goals in a way that realizes more of your potential and brings a greater sense of fulfillment for you and those around you.

Embrace a Progress-Growth Mindset

Developing a progress-growth mindset, rooted in Kaizen principles—a philosophy of continuous improvement through small, incremental changes—equips you to achieve meaningful and lasting success. The Purpose Matters 7P Business Alignment Model™ simplifies the journey by breaking down the improvement process into more manageable and sustainable steps. By prioritizing continuous growth through the lens of Ongoing Performance Improvement (OPI) efforts, you establish a foundation for your business to thrive, adapt, and achieve its most meaningful goals.

Recognize the Evolving Nature of Improvement

It's important to understand that the definition and criteria of "improvement and progress" may change over time, depending on personal and business contexts. For instance, someone who lifted heavy weights in their 20s and 30s may no longer be able to do so in their 50s and 60s. The definition of "success" that was relevant in the earlier stages of life may no longer be applicable for their later stages of life. Success may now be viewed as simply maintaining a regular workout regimen and feeling energized and healthy, rather than the amount of weight lifted. Similarly, your business goals may evolve. Perhaps you're in a season where rapid growth is no longer the primary objective. Instead of seeking 30-40% year-over-year growth, a steady 5-8% growth might fit your current criteria of progress, allowing more time to spend with family. Perhaps a stronger sense of purpose and fulfillment may now play a greater role in determining what progress and improvement means to you.

Investing in Your Business for Ongoing Growth

Most business owners agree that spending time and money *working on* the business, rather than being consumed *in* the daily operations, is a sound idea. However, few intentionally budget for this purpose. Imagine looking at a P&L statement of a pharmaceutical company and seeing they invest little to nothing in R&D. It's reasonable to assume that this lack of investment would negatively impact their future sustainability and growth. Without new or improved products in their pipeline, the company would struggle to stay competitive or even survive. Similarly, for SMBs, not investing in business improvement activities can hinder long-term growth, sustainability, and competitiveness.

The Importance of OPI in Your Budget

Think of your "OPI" (Ongoing Performance Improvement) line item as serving a similar function to the R&D line item in a pharmaceutical company's P&L. Investing in OPI ensures your business remains viable, profitable, and competitive. Unlike R&D, OPI has a broader scope, impacting every aspect of your business, including sales, cost of goods sold (COGS), labor, and overhead expenses.

Consider adding a specific budget line for OPI in your income statement. For example, our clients allocate anywhere from 1% to 3% of their total revenues to activities that drive improvement across the board. They know that the ROI on that investment which can include implementing the 7P Business Alignment Model™, training and development, organizational coaching, process improvement, technology upgrades, etc., will more than pay for itself.

The 7 Ps of the Business Alignment Model

The word "performance" in Ongoing "P" Improvements also encompasses the other 7 Ps within the Business Alignment Model:

1. **Ongoing Purpose Improvement:** Aligning your business with your mission and vision.

2. **Ongoing Prioritization Improvement:** Ensuring that objectives and key results are aligned with your purpose, and critical tasks are effectively prioritized.

3. **Ongoing People Improvement:** Attracting, aligning, and retaining the right fit employees to build a winning team.

4. **Ongoing Pipeline Improvement:** Aligning your sales and marketing efforts with your purpose and attracting the right fit customers to enable profitable growth.

5. **Ongoing Product Improvement:** Continuously enhancing your products or services to better serve your customers.

6. **Ongoing Process Improvement:** Streamlining your processes to improve efficiency and productivity.

7. **Ongoing Profit Improvement:** Optimizing profit and profitability while aligning with your purpose.

Reducing Risks and Ensuring Long term viability

Investing in Ongoing Performance Improvement (OPI) can significantly reduce the risk of declining revenues or even going out of business by ensuring you respond effectively and in a timely manner to changes in your competitive marketplace. By regularly evaluating and adapting your business strategies based on evolving market trends, you not only stay ahead of competitors but also improve the probability of surviving and sustainably growing your business for years to come.

Analyzing Expenses for Better ROI

To analyze expenses effectively for better ROI, consider each expense line item not just as a cost, but as an investment in creating value for your customer. This means evaluating how each expense contributes to the revenue it helps generate and how it compares to industry benchmarks to ensure a sustainable and healthy ROI. Here's a breakdown of how to implement this approach:

Value Perspective on Expenses:

Think of each expense as a contribution towards delivering a product or service that your customer is willing to pay for. This helps you prioritize spending on items that directly impact customer satisfaction and perceived value.

Revenue Relationship

Calculate each expense as a percentage of total revenue. This provides a clear picture of how much of your sales is being used to cover specific costs. A high percentage for certain expenses might indicate areas for potential improvement and optimization.

Industry Benchmarking:

Compare your expense ratios to industry benchmarks. This gives you a sense of whether your costs are in line with competitors and if there are areas where you can potentially improve. Industry reports, professional associations, and online databases can provide benchmark data.

Sustainable ROI:

A sustainable ROI implies that your profits are sufficient to cover your costs and reinvest in future growth. If your expense ratios are significantly higher than industry averages, it might indicate the need for adjustments to improve long term sustainability.

Specific Examples:

Direct Labor and Material Costs:

Analyzing these costs as a percentage of revenue can reveal if your production process is efficient. High percentages might suggest opportunities for cost reduction through improved efficiency, sourcing, or negotiating with suppliers.

Marketing and Advertising:

While these are essential for customer acquisition and retention, their ROI should be carefully monitored. If the cost of marketing continues to exceed the incremental revenue generated or produces an inadequate return, it needs to be re-evaluated to better allocate marketing spend.

Overhead Expenses:

General administrative and operational costs should also be considered in relation to revenue. High overhead can indicate inefficiencies that need to be addressed.

Actionable Steps:

Identify High-Impact Expenses:

Focus on the expense line items with the largest impact on profitability and revenue. Prioritize efforts to optimize these areas first.

Cost Reduction Strategies:

Explore ways to reduce costs without compromising quality or customer value. This could involve negotiating better supplier prices, improving efficiency, or streamlining operations.

Regular Monitoring and Adjustment:

Regularly review your expense ratios and other KPIs like revenues, gross margin %, sales and margin mix, cash runway (how long can we operate) DSOs days on average to collect, DPO days to pay, win rate %, OTIF On-time, In-Full delivery %, CAC (customer acquisition costs) CSAT (customer satisfaction) or NPS: % Promoters - % Detractors, etc. and compare actual vs budgeted and industry benchmarks.

By regularly monitoring your expenses and KPIs through the lens of both customer value and business performance, you can make more informed decisions that improve ROI, reduce waste, and support sustainable growth.

OPI ROI-Impact on Bottom-Line Results

A common concern among our clients is understanding how investments in Ongoing Performance Improvement (OPI) will benefit their bottom-line results and overall peace of mind. Here's a simple example showing how a small boost in productivity can significantly improve profitability and peace of mind.

Example Assumptions:

- **Total Sales:** 100% (used as a baseline)
- **Current Labor Costs:** 30% of total sales
- **OPI Investment** 1% of total sales

- **Productivity Improvement:** 10% increase
- **Current Net Operating Profit (EBITDA):** 10% of total sales

Productivity Impact:

- **Labor Costs Reduction:** A 10% productivity improvement reduces labor costs.

Calculation: 10% of 30% labor costs = 3% reduction

  o **New Labor Costs:** 30% - 3% = **27%** of total sales

- **Net Operating Profit Increase:** Savings from reduced labor costs directly increase net operating profit.

  o **New Net Operating Profit:** 10% + 3% - 1% (OPI)= **12%** of total sales

Metrics	Before OPI Improvement	After OPI Improvement
Total Sales	100%	100%
Labor Costs	30%	27%
Other Costs	60%	60%
Net Operating Profit (EBITDA)	10%	12%

Key Takeaways:

- **Labor Costs Decrease:** Labor costs drop from **30%** to **27%** of total sales due to improved productivity.

- **Profit Increase:** Net operating profit increases from **10%** to **12%** of total sales after deduction of 1% OPI investment.

- **Percentage Improvement:** This is a **20% increase** in net operating profit

  o **Calculation:** (12% - 10%) / 10% = **20%**

Explanation:

By investing 1% in OPI and achieving a 10% improvement in productivity, you reduce labor costs without changing sales or other expenses.

- The reduction in labor costs directly enhances your net operating profit.

- Even modest improvements in productivity can lead to significant increases in profitability.

This example demonstrates how investing in OPI can have a substantial positive impact on your bottom line. If your current net operating profit (EBITDA) is 10%, this 2% increase boosts your profit to 12%, representing a 20% increase in net operating profit.

Reducing Waste to Increase Productivity

Increasing productivity often involves reducing waste—activities that don't add value to your product or service. Lean Manufacturing principles provide management practices aimed at improving efficiency by eliminating waste. The core principle is to reduce non-value-adding activities from the business.

Many business owners acknowledge that a focused effort to identify and reduce wasteful practices could realistically improve productivity by 10%. Reducing waste by just an additional 1% each month could lead to a cumulative 12% improvement in productivity over a year.

Real-World Example:

Consider a small bakery that implemented the *Process* P of the 7Ps, applying lean principles to reduce waste.

They used to bake extra bread daily, often throwing away unsold loaves. Now, they track sales closely and bake only what they expect to sell, significantly cutting waste. They also reorganized their workspace, streamlining how dough and ingredients move through production, saving both time and effort.

As a result, they now produce the same amount of bread faster and with less waste—reducing costs and improving efficiency. Their labor cost, which was originally 30% of total sales, decreased by 3 percentage points, representing roughly a 10% increase in productivity. This improvement directly boosted profitability: if their profit margin (EBITDA) was previously 10%, the reduction in labor cost raised it to 13%—a 30% increase in net operating profit.

By focusing on eliminating non-value-adding activities and optimizing core processes, they didn't just save money—they began developing a new mindset and habit of operational excellence.

The Power of OPI Consistency:

Small, consistent investments in improving your business processes can yield significant financial returns. By integrating OPI into your operations, you're not only cutting costs but also setting the stage for sustainable growth and success:

- **Small Improvements, Big Impact:** Focusing on improving just one of the 7Ps in your business can lead to significant gains. For instance, achieving a modest **10% increase in labor productivity** over a year can substantially boost your profitability.

- **Direct Profit Increase:** When productivity improves, your labor costs decrease relative to your sales. This reduction in costs directly increases your net operating profit. Even a small percentage improvement in productivity can lead to a disproportionately larger increase in profits.

- **Enhanced Profit Margins:** If your business currently operates with a certain profit margin, improving productivity can raise this margin without increasing sales or prices. This means more profit from the same level of business activity.

In summary, investing in OPI enables you to do more with the same or even less resources, directly enhancing your productivity and profitability. Even modest improvements can have a significant positive effect on your bottom line, providing not only financial benefits but also greater peace of mind knowing your business is operating more efficiently.

Cumulative Benefits of OPI Investments

The cumulative impact of OPI efforts across all 7 Ps can lead to substantial increases in your profits and profitability. Many of our clients would be delighted to invest 1% of their total revenues if it produced a 2:1 ROI year after year. The improvement in the owner's peace of mind and level of fulfillment, while difficult to quantify, is also a significant added benefit. Even though the bakery example focused on improving the P-process what if you could make improvements in the P-Pipeline dimension, resulting in more profitable sales? What if you could also enhance the product-service dimension, leading to happier customers and more repeat purchases?

Continual Progress: The Path to Sustainable Growth and Success

By prioritizing continual progress, learning, and growth, you set yourself and your business on a path to sustainable success and achieving more of your potential. When you consistently apply the right processes and embrace the mindset of ongoing improvement, the cumulative effects of small, manageable steps compounded over time will create a significant impact. This approach not only ensures that your business remains competitive and viable but also fosters a culture of continuous improvement that enables you to better adapt to changing circumstances and market conditions.

Developing the Growth Mindset for Success

One of the most effective mindsets to achieve sustainable success is adopting a growth mindset, one that strives for continual, incremental improvements. These small changes, compounded over time, can significantly enhance performance and peace of mind. While occasional large improvements may occur, we've found that applying smaller, manageable changes is a more sustainable approach.

Realizing more of your potential and creating a greater sense of fulfillment while engaging in continuous improvement requires a growth mindset. Carol Dweck, in her book *"Mindset: The New Psychology of Success,"* shares her research on the belief in one's abilities and potential for growth. She identifies two primary mindsets: fixed and growth. Those with a fixed mindset view qualities like intelligence as static traits, while those with a growth mindset believe that abilities can develop through dedication, perseverance, and learning.

Dweck explains that *"People with growth mindsets take charge of their learning and continuously seek opportunities to improve."*[8] Cultivating a growth mindset can profoundly affect how we approach challenges and learning opportunities, influencing our ability to succeed and live fulfilling lives.

Embracing Challenges

Individuals with a growth mindset embrace challenges rather than avoiding them. For SMB owners, this means approaching business obstacles as opportunities to learn and grow rather than threats to be feared.

Example:

Imagine your business is facing increased competition. Instead of viewing this as a threat, consider it an opportunity to innovate and improve your offerings. By analyzing competitors, gathering customer feedback, and investing in new technologies or processes, you can turn this challenge into a growth opportunity.

Learning from Feedback

Viewing feedback as constructive rather than a personal attack is essential. SMB owners can apply this by actively seeking and valuing feedback from employees, customers, and mentors.

Example:

Suppose you receive negative feedback from a customer about your product or service. Instead of becoming defensive, use this feedback to make necessary improvements. By treating feedback as part of the improvement process, you can create a culture of continuous learning within your organization.

Fostering a Learning Environment

A growth mindset encourages a learning environment where experimentation and development are valued. This means creating a culture where employees feel safe to try new ideas and learn from their experiences.

Example:

Implement regular "innovation meetings" where employees are encouraged to share new ideas. Provide resources and support to experiment, even if it means risking failure. Celebrate efforts and learnings, regardless of the outcome.

Developing Resilience

A key aspect of a growth mindset is resilience—the ability to recover from setbacks and keep moving forward. SMB owners can cultivate resilience by viewing failures as temporary setbacks rather than permanent defeats.

Example:

If a new product launch doesn't go as planned, analyze what went wrong and what can be improved. Use the experience to adjust your strategy and try again with a better-informed approach. Encourage your team to adopt the same resilience.

Key Takeaways Chapter 28: Keep Improving What Matters

1. **Success is a Continuous Process, Not a One-Time Event**

   o   Meaningful success comes from ongoing growth and progress, not isolated achievements.

   o   Change is required for progress—resisting change prevents growth.

2. **Small, Manageable Steps Drive Sustainable Improvement**

   o   Breaking improvements into small, consistent actions increases engagement and ensures long-term success.

   o   Progress happens when change is sustainable—not overwhelming.

   o   Avoid overestimating initial efforts; start smaller to build momentum.

3. **Overcome Inertia by Simply Showing Up**

   o   Action leads to improvement—you can't improve if you don't start.

   o   Consistency matters more than intensity—showing up regularly leads to long-term results.

   o   An accountability partner (like a Business Alignment Coach) can help sustain motivation and consistency.

4. **Course Corrections Keep You on Track**

   o Progress is not linear—adjustments along the way are necessary.

   o The 7P Business Alignment Model™ helps realign priorities, people, and processes to keep your business moving toward its purpose.

5. **A Growth Mindset is Essential for Continuous Improvement**

   o Learning leads to change—if you're learning, you're growing, and if you're growing, you're changing.

   o Embrace Kaizen principles (continuous improvement through small, incremental changes).

   o Challenges and feedback are opportunities for growth, not setbacks.

6. **Invest in Ongoing Performance Improvement (OPI) as a Business Priority**

   o Businesses that fail to invest in improvement stagnate and lose competitiveness.

   o Just as pharmaceutical companies invest in R&D, SMBs must invest in OPI to stay competitive.

   o Allocate 1-3% of revenue toward OPI efforts, including coaching, process enhancements, and strategic realignment.

7. **Measure ROI and Optimize Performance**

   o Analyze expenses and productivity—small efficiency gains (e.g., 10% labor productivity improvement) can increase net profit in some instances by up to 30% or more.

   o Identify wasteful activities that don't add value and eliminate them.

   o Regularly compare business performance to industry benchmarks.

8. **Align the 7P's for Ongoing Business Success**

   o **Purpose:** Keep your business mission at the center of decisions.

   o **Prioritization:** Focus on what truly moves the needle.

   o **People:** Continuously improve hiring, training, and retention to build a high-performing team.

   o **Pipeline:** Enhance sales and marketing efforts to attract right-fit customers.

   o **Product:** Innovate and refine your product or service for maximum value.

   o **Process:** Optimize workflows for efficiency and scalability.

   o **Profit:** Ensure profitability aligns with purpose-driven growth.

9. **Success Criteria Evolve Over Time**

   o Business goals shift over time—growth today may mean expansion, while later it might focus more on self sufficiency, more freedom of time and/or greater or fulfillment.

   o Regularly redefine success to match your business's current stage and personal priorities.

10. **Foster a Culture of Continuous Improvement**

    o Encourage innovation, employee feedback and experimentation.

    o Make process improvement a habit, not just a reaction to problems.

    o Recognize and celebrate small wins to sustain motivation and engagement.

Summary of Takeaways: Continuous improvement is not just a best practice—it's a necessity for long-term success. By consistently refining and aligning the 7Ps, investing in ongoing improvement, and fostering a growth-oriented culture, you can build a business that is resilient, adaptable, and purpose-driven while achieving sustainable profitability.

Reflection Questions Chapter 28: Keep Improving What Matters

1. **What small, manageable step can you take today to improve one area of your business?**

   o   How can breaking this improvement into smaller steps help you stay consistent and engaged?

2. **What is one thing you've been putting off in your business that you can start today, even in a small way?**

   o   What would be the benefit of simply starting, even if it's not perfect?

3. **How can you ensure you show up consistently for the things that matter most to your business growth?**

   o   What habits, routines, or accountability can you put in place to stay on track?

4. **Do you have a budget or plan for ongoing performance improvement in your business?**

   o   If not, what resources — time, money, or support — can you begin to allocate to invest in improvement efforts?

      Examples: Implementing the 7P Business Alignment Model, investing in training, coaching, process improvement, or leveraging better technology.

5. **How do you typically respond to challenges or setbacks in your business?**

   o What can you do to reframe these as opportunities for growth rather than obstacles?

   Examples:

   - Instead of viewing a lost client as a failure, use it as a chance to review your customer experience process and identify improvements that could prevent similar losses in the future.

   - When a project runs over budget or timeline, treat it as a learning opportunity to improve your scoping and planning process for next time.

   - After receiving negative feedback from a customer or employee, reflect on what can be learned from the feedback to strengthen your business and leadership.

6. **How do you encourage your team to share new ideas and take initiative in creating improvements?**

   o What can you do to foster a culture of learning, innovation, and continuous improvement?

7. **How can you better evaluate the return on investment (ROI) for the resources and time you dedicate to business improvements?**

   o What measures or benchmarks could help you assess whether your improvement efforts are paying off?

8. What stood out to you in this chapter or resonated most with you?

9. What are your top 1-2 takeaways from this chapter?

10. What specific action can you take to apply these insights to achieve better outcomes and align your business with your purpose?

RENEWAL— REALIGNING WITH WHAT MATTERS

CHAPTER 29

ENJOYING THE VIEW?

"Remember to celebrate milestones as you prepare for the road ahead"[1] —Nelson Mandela

Enjoying the View

Once you've reached the top of the proverbial mountain, are you actually enjoying the view? If you've been aligned with your purpose throughout the climb, the view should feel both fulfilling and meaningful.

Consider the classic story of the three bricklayers. When asked what they were doing, the first replied, "I'm laying bricks." The second said, "I'm building a wall." But the third, with enthusiasm, said, "I'm building the world's greatest cathedral."

This simple parable illustrates how three people doing the exact same task can experience their work in entirely different ways depending on their mindset and connection to a larger purpose.

What sets the third bricklayer apart is not the task itself, but how he sees the task. He sees his daily actions connected to and in the context of something greater, visionary and deeply meaningful to him.

As a business owner, when your work is aligned with your purpose and connected to your mission and vision, each step forward becomes more than just progress. It becomes part of the reward. The climb itself, the process, becomes meaningful. The view from the top becomes even more satisfying when it reflects not just what you've accomplished, but why it matters.

The Importance of Celebrating Achievements and Avoiding Burnout

As you already know the climb of successfully growing a business takes hard work, perseverance, vision, a bit of luck, timing, and other factors beyond one's control. Many business owners are strongly goal-driven and future-oriented, continuously striving toward the next goal, the next peak to climb and conquer.

However, if we only focus on the gap between where we are and where we want to be, we may experience more frustration and misery than necessary. For instance, let's say you are trying to get in shape and have lost the first ten pounds of your weight loss goal of forty pounds. Only focusing on what's left to achieve—the remaining thirty pounds—without giving yourself kudos for losing the first ten pounds could feel unsatisfying or even discouraging.

Similarly, if your goal is to grow your customer base by a hundred, and you've gained ten new customers, you may feel frustrated if you only focus on the goal of the remaining ninety customers without acknowledging the accomplishment of acquiring the first ten.

This is why it's important to balance celebrating and acknowledging the progress made while striving towards and keeping the end goal in sight. After winning a game or round in the playoffs, professional athletes and their coaches often say, "We'll enjoy this win tonight and then prepare for the next round." They acknowledge the value of enjoying the victory, even for that one night.

We've found in our experience that most business owners, could benefit from becoming more intentional when celebrating progress made and milestones achieved. Doing so can also lessen the likelihood of that dreaded feeling of burnout and eventually not wanting to come to work. This doesn't preclude company celebrations of birthdays, major holidays, and work anniversaries; however, try to connect celebrations with meaningful progress and performance achieved.

For example:

- Organize a company BBQ or team outing to acknowledge reaching a significant milestone.

- Offer performance bonuses or extra time off as rewards for a well-done job.

- Host a special team dinner to recognize exceptional effort or progress made.

- Encourage employees to share their small victories as appropriate on a public "Wins" board where folks can see it or even digitally to foster collective celebration.

These intentional celebrations create moments of joy and recognition, which can encourage the behaviors and attitudes you want to instill in your culture while also recharging your team for future challenges. Of course, one of the most important ways to celebrate meaningful progress is in the context of OKRs and the achievement of the (KR's) key results and milestones that have been set as part of your overall strategic company (O) objectives.

Another way to become more intentional about celebrating smaller successes personally is to journal daily about one to three steps taken or tasks completed that are moving the needle in a positive way for which you can be grateful for. This will also encourage a more positive mindset. Learn to acknowledge the effort when appropriate so long as the unit of effort is meaningful and progresses over time. (For example, as part of a get healthier plan, you may determine that the effort of simply putting on your running shoes may not be worth acknowledging unless you at least walk for a few minutes afterwards).

Reflection Questions:

- What are 1-3 things you are proud of, feel good about, and/or grateful for having accomplished so far in this phase of your business? (Consider making this a daily exercise as part of a gratitude journal)

- How did you celebrate your most recent accomplishment or significant milestone?

- If not, why not?

- Could you go out to a nice dinner, maybe take a weekend getaway with your spouse, significant other, or family?

- Perhaps find a way to treat yourself to an evening out doing something you enjoy and find relaxing that you otherwise wouldn't normally do.

Celebratory occasions usually won't happen until a date, time, and place is scheduled with the required people or significant other(s) in your calendar.

Growing a business is not a linear journey. It involves peaks and valleys, moments of triumph, and times of struggle. It's easy to get caught up in the relentless pursuit of the next goal or milestone. But it's also important to pause and appreciate the journey, the progress made, and the challenges overcome along the way. By doing so, one can better enjoy the journey while maintaining a sustainable pace that prevents burnout.

Avoiding Burnout: "Burnout" is a state of emotional, mental, and physical exhaustion caused by prolonged and excessive stress, particularly related to work. It often occurs when someone feels overwhelmed, emotionally drained, and unable to meet constant demands. Burnout can lead to feelings of detachment, reduced performance, and a loss of motivation. Over time, it can affect one's health, well-being, and relationships. Symptoms include chronic fatigue, irritability, lack of focus, and decreased job satisfaction or engagement.

Reflection Questions:

- Am I experiencing any of the burnout symptoms described, e.g., chronic fatigue or emotional exhaustion at work?
- If so, what specific factors might be contributing to these feelings, and how can I manage or reduce them?
- Do I feel a greater sense of detachment or feel less engaged in my business than before?
- How can I reconnect with my initial passion and sense of purpose?
- To what extent or degree am I feeling overwhelmed by the demands of my business?
- What steps can I take to effectively delegate tasks and establish healthier boundaries to prevent burnout?

The Celebration Motivation Achievement-Positive Feedback Loop

By taking time to acknowledge and celebrate your achievements, you can create a positive feedback loop that fuels future success. A positive feedback loop is a process where the outcome of an action reinforces that same action, creating a cycle that amplifies itself over time. For example, celebrating a win boosts morale and motivation, which encourages more effort and drive toward achieving new wins. As you accomplish more, these new wins give you even greater reason to celebrate, leading to a continuous cycle of motivation and success. In this way, each part of the loop fuels the next, creating ongoing positive reinforcement.

1. **Celebrate Wins**: Acknowledging achievements boosts morale and provides a sense of accomplishment, reinforcing positive behavior.

2. **Increase Motivation**: This sense of achievement energizes individuals and teams, increasing their drive to work harder and stay focused on future goals.

3. **Achieve More Wins**: Increased motivation leads to further successes that can be celebrated. This creates a continuous cycle of achieving more wins, resulting in celebrating more wins, which increases motivation to achieve more wins.

For example, imagine your team closing a major deal or successfully completing a challenging project. Taking the time to celebrate this win—whether through recognition, rewards, or a team event—improves morale and makes everyone feel valued. This positivity energizes the team, inspiring them to tackle the next big challenge with renewed enthusiasm. When they achieve another success, the celebration can start the cycle again, creating a continuous loop of progress and achievement.

In this way, the **celebration-motivation-achievement loop** contributes to your ability to drive ongoing progress and success. By making celebration an intentional part of your business culture, you not only reinforce positive behaviors but also build a motivated, high-performing team that thrives on its accomplishments.

Key Takeaways: Enjoying the View?

For goal-driven action oriented personalities typical of many business owners, pausing to celebrate progress doesn't always come naturally. In our experience, they bristle at the idea of participation trophies handed out to youth for simply showing up.

While the intent may be well-meaning, sadly, this practice may set the bar "too low" and risk creating a sense of entitlement based on minimal effort. That is not the way the real world works. No working adult gets a "participation trophy" for showing up to work and doing their job. Special recognition and perhaps even a promotion would be warranted when they have a demonstrated track record of exceeding expectations given their job role and commensurate pay.

To achieve a balance between acknowledging real, measurable achievements rather than rewarding mere participation, we've found that business owners and their leadership teams can use more practice celebrating and acknowledging their progress.

Of course, this must be done appropriately and proportionate to measurable and meaningful business outcomes and milestones achieved. Just as professional athletes celebrate their victories but quickly refocus on the next challenge, business owners must also find joy in their accomplishments while preparing for the next milestones.

Why Intentional Celebration Matters

1. **Maintains Motivation**: Regularly celebrating successes—both big and small—rewards effort and reinforces positive behaviors that contribute to long-term results.

2. **Prevents Burnout**: Reflection and acknowledgment allow leaders and teams to recharge, recognize progress, and stay energized for the road ahead.

3. **Builds Team Morale**: Recognizing achievements creates a sense of shared purpose, motivating employees to stay engaged and aligned with the business's goals.

Practical Ways to Celebrate Achievements

- **Reflect Regularly**: Schedule time to review progress and acknowledge both team and individual contributions.

- **Celebrate Wins Thoughtfully**: Tailor celebrations to the size of the achievement where small milestones may warrant a team lunch, while larger successes could involve public recognition, bonuses, or team events.

- **Connect to the Bigger Picture**: Use celebrations as an opportunity to reinforce how achievements align with the company's purpose, vision, and goals.

Business like life is a journey and by taking time to "enjoy the view," you acknowledge how far you've come while preparing for what lies ahead. When done intentionally and meaningfully, celebrating achievements can positively contribute to both performance and fulfillment along the way.

CHAPTER 30

SLOW DOWN, BE STILL, AND LISTEN

> *"Almost everything will work again*
> *if you unplug it for a few minutes,*
> *including you."[1]—Anne Lamott*

Feeling Overwhelm?

In today's fast-paced world, constant demands and endless to-do lists often push us into "redlining"—operating at maximum capacity for too long. The result? Our bodies eventually force us to stop, whether through illness, exhaustion, or burnout. The real challenge is learning to recognize the warning signs before we hit that breaking point.

Common signals of approaching burnout include: trouble sleeping, irritability, brain fog, constant fatigue, skipping meals or exercise, or feeling increasingly resentful toward your work. Left unchecked, these patterns can harm not just your health but also your business and relationships.

Reflective Questions

- What early warning signs show up for you—physically, mentally, or emotionally—when you're stretched too thin?

- When have you ignored those signals, and what was the cost to your health, business, or relationships?

- What simple practices could you put in place to reset before exhaustion forces you to stop? (Examples: a daily walk without checking your phone, a weekly pause for quiet reflection, or a quarterly Alignment Reset day to step back from the grind.)

The Power of Slowing Down

This chapter title is inspired by Norwegian Soprano, Sissel's beautiful rendition of *"Slow Down"* performed with the Mormon Tabernacle Choir in 2019.[2] If you're in front of your computer or have your smartphone, pause and take a few minutes right now and treat yourself to a refreshing respite in your busy day by listening to "Sissel Slow Down" on YouTube.

The song connects me to a deeper, heart-inspired awareness that often gets drowned out in the busyness of our day-to-day lives. Slowing down I believe can create moments that help us reconnect with this spiritual aspect of ourselves. Whether listening to music, spending time in nature, or sitting in meditative silence, these moments can revitalize us, and leave us feeling refreshed and renewed.

Personal Reflection and Awareness

I was at a friend's house when she casually asked me how I was doing. I answered in my default, perfunctory manner like many of us do when asked questions like "How was everything?" at a restaurant, with a habitual response like, "Fine... everything's fine."

However, she asked again, "How are you *really* doing?" I paused to reconsider her question and tried to come up with something more authentic than my initial response. I answered, "I don't know... fine, I guess."

My hesitation puzzled me. I realized I had no idea how I was doing beyond the surface level of my being. It's like asking someone how their car is doing. "Fine, it seems to be running fine." But unless you check the dipstick to see if you're low on oil or have a mechanic look under the hood and perform diagnostic tests, how do you know how your car is doing? Too often, we don't find out until something breaks down, and by then, it may be too late or much more costly to fix than if we had addressed it sooner.

Similarly, periodic health check-ups allow a doctor to "check under the hood" and perform tests to assess how we're doing beyond the superficial. If we want to move beyond a habituated way of answering the question "How are you doing?", we need to learn how to check our own internal "dipstick" from time to time to see if we're "low on oil" and assess how we're truly doing, feeling, and being.

Checking in: Reflective Questions and Best Practices:

- When was the last time you checked in with yourself on how you're really feeling? What did you notice?

- How do you check in with yourself? If not, what simple habit could you adopt to help you periodically check your internal "dipstick" to assess your energy and emotional well-being?

Best Practices for Checking in (Self-Awareness)

- Journaling: Writing down your thoughts and feelings can help you understand your emotions and become more aware of recurring negative or positive behavioral and thought patterns.

- Reflecting on your day: Consider how you're feeling, what challenges you've faced, and how those feelings impact your thoughts and actions.

- Talking to someone: Share your feelings with a trusted person for clarity and support.

- Listening to your intuition: Your gut feelings can reflect your true thoughts and values.

- Are you getting enough sleep? For most of us, getting at least seven to eight hours of sleep every night helps your body restore itself and keep emotions in check.

- Check in on your relationships: Consider whether your relationships are moving forward as you would like and whether any friction needs to be resolved.

The Wisdom of Slowing Down: A Lesson from Indigenous Cultures

A Westerner was on an African expedition with local tribesmen transporting his equipment for a work project. For several days, they made rapid progress, covering great distances and checking off many items on his daily to-do list. Everything seemed on track, and since he was eager to keep moving, it felt like a productive journey so far.

Then, unexpectedly, the tribesmen stopped, sat under a tree to rest, and refused to go further. The Westerner became frustrated with this stoppage, perceiving it as a waste of time. Anxious to get moving again, he asked the interpreter to find out what was causing the delay. The interpreter replied, "We had been moving too fast and had to wait for our souls to catch up."

Versions of this story have been told about South African tribesmen, Himalayan Sherpas, and even Inca guides. Despite the different settings, the message is universal: slowing down is not laziness, but wisdom. It's how we allow our energy and purpose to realign before we move forward again. We need to occasionally slow down to catch our breaths, reconnect with ourselves, and *let our souls catch up.*[3]

In our modern, hyper-busy lives, we often rush from task to task, filling our schedules with seemingly endless commitments, goals, and to-do lists, barely allowing ourselves time to breathe. The result? Burnout, exhaustion, and a sense that we're always behind, even when we are constantly pressing forward. The habitual busyness that pervades today's society often prevents us from stopping, reflecting, and allowing ourselves the space to reconnect with what truly matters.

Reflective Pause: Letting Your Soul Catch Up—A Moment to Reconnect Within

The phrase "let your soul catch up" speaks to something deeper than just physical rest. It's about making time to reconnect with your inner self—your values, emotions, purpose, and the quiet voice of wisdom that often gets drowned out in the noise of day-to-day demands.

Letting your soul catch up doesn't always require hours of silence or a retreat into the mountains. It might mean taking a quiet walk without your phone, journaling for 10 minutes before your day begins, or simply pausing between meetings to breathe and reset. These small moments of intentional stillness can create space to listen inward, reconnect with your purpose, and bring a sense of groundedness and clarity back into your life and business.

Reflective Questions for Slowing Down with Purpose:

- When was the last time you created space to slow down—not just to rest, but to reconnect with yourself? What did you notice in your mind, body, or spirit afterward?
- Which of the following best describes your current practice of slowing down to reflect and recharge?
  Regularly (daily or almost daily)
  Occasionally (once or twice a week)
  Rarely (a few times per month or less)
  Almost never
- What are some small ways you could begin making space in your weekly routine to slow down—without guilt—and reconnect with what matters most to you? (e.g., stepping away for a midday walk, journaling, scheduling a quiet hour on Fridays)
- What tends to get in the way of giving yourself permission to slow down? Is it urgency, expectations, fear of falling behind—or something else?
- If you created even 10 more minutes of stillness per day, how might that impact your clarity, energy, or decision-making?

The Necessity of Sacred Space

One way to ensure we pause long enough to let our *souls catch up with our bodies* is by intentionally creating time and space to do so. Joseph Campbell refers to this space as sacred and an integral part of what I believe makes life worth living. He says,

"Sacred space is an absolute necessity for anybody today. You must have a room or a certain hour or so a day where you don't know what was in the newspapers that morning, you don't know who your friends are, you don't know what you owe anybody, you don't know what anybody owes to you. This is a place where you can simply experience and bring forth what you are and what you might be. This is the place of creative

incubation. At first, you may find that nothing happens there. But if you have a sacred place and use it, something eventually will happen."[4]

For SMB owners, sacred space isn't necessarily mystical—it's practical. It means blocking time in your calendar that's not tethered to meetings, calls, or urgent tasks. It's time to reflect, re-center, and think without pressure. You might begin with just one hour a week and gradually increase it depending on your circumstances.

Unlike traditional time management practices that focus on maximizing productivity, Campbell's idea of "sacred space" encourages us to make time and space for being vs doing. In this space, free from external distractions, "nothing is getting done" on the surface. Yet, when practiced regularly, it cultivates the clarity, creativity and calm required to lead effectively while also refreshing and rejuvenating one's spirit.

Practical Tips on Applying the Concept of Sacred Space

1. Creating a Dedicated Time and Space

Identify a Space: Choose a quiet, comfortable place where you won't be interrupted. This could be a designated space in your home office, a quiet corner in your workplace, or even a local park.

Set a Time: Allocate a specific time each day or week to spend in this space. Preferably, it's a time that can be consistently adhered to and eventually turned into a routine or habit. It could be the first hour of your morning or a set time after lunch.

2. Disconnect from External Distractions

Digital Detox: Turn off notifications on your phone and computer. Avoid checking emails, social media, or the news during this time.

Different ways this time and sacred space can be utilized:

1. Focus on Personal and Business Reflection

Journaling: Use this time to journal—capture ideas, surface insights, and notice patterns in your thinking in both your business and personal life.

2. Foster Creativity

Idea Generation: Allow your mind to wander and explore new ideas without the pressure of immediate implementation. This can lead to innovative solutions and creative strategies for your business.

Strategic Planning: Reflect on your business goals, strategies, and long-term vision. Use this time to think deeply about the direction you want your business to take.

3. Evaluate and Adjust

Regular Review: Periodically review the insights and ideas generated during your sacred space time. Assess which ideas can be implemented and develop action plans for them.

Adjust Routine as Needed: As you become more accustomed to this practice, adjust the routine and environment to better suit your needs and preferences.

4. Encourage a Company-Wide Practice

Lead by Example: Share the benefits of having a sacred space with your leadership team. Encourage them to create their own time for stillness and reflection.

If conditions permit, companies have been known to even set aside a separate room, e.g. a "quiet room" for their employees to decompress even for a few minutes. Whether or not employees actually use the space, the fact that you have an intentional space like that signal to employees that the company values their well-being and creating a culture of "sharpening the saw" beyond the just the daily grind.

These practices not only benefit you as a leader but can also positively impact your entire organization. By integrating Joseph Campbell's concept of sacred space into your routine, you create more than quiet time—you build a practice of inner alignment, reconnecting your thoughts, emotions, and actions with your deeper purpose. This isn't about retreating from your business; it's about returning to it renewed. Over time, the stillness you cultivate becomes the source of clearer thinking and wiser decisions resulting in meaningful growth and greater fulfillment.

The CEO's Role: Paid to Think

In fact, setting aside this sacred space is essential for fulfilling your primary role as a CEO—being paid to think. Victor Cheng, a former McKinsey consultant, renowned author, and business advisor, explains that the CEO's job is not about doing everything but about making critical decisions. CEOs must focus on "what" is important and "who" should execute it. To make these decisions effectively, leaders must carve out time to think, evaluate, and prioritize. As the owner and top leader of your organization, you must have time to think. You are ultimately "paid" to think—to prioritize, evaluate, learn from feedback, adjust, re-prioritize, and communicate effectively. Victor Cheng emphasizes this point

> *"An engineer engineers. A marketer markets. A salesperson sells. A finance professional finances. A CEO ... 'CEOs?' Unlike all other roles in a company, the word 'CEO' is not a function. There is no CEO department. The engineer thinks about how to engineer a solution to a problem. A marketer thinks about how to market a product to a target customer. A salesperson thinks about how to sell a deal to a particular account. A CEO doesn't think about any of this. The CEO has two primary roles: 1) What, and 2) Who. The CEO decides on what is important enough for the company to focus on. Then, the CEO decides who should get the 'what' done. What ... and who ... these are the principal things CEOs focus on.*[5]

To properly fulfill your CEO function, you must intentionally set aside time each day and each week to develop and exercise your "what and who" evaluation and decision-making skills. By doing so you can better effectively utilize your organization's strengths, resources, and capabilities to achieve your strategic goals. Unlike larger organizations, where they have the luxury of having just one person filling that functional CEO "paid-to-think" role, in smaller organizations, the owner needs to do more than serve as the leader—coxswain. They will, as needed, step into the other day-to-day rowing roles.

However, when they take time to implement the 7P BAM, it empowers them to really focus on the strategic "paid to think" role that decides the who and the whats of their business. By instilling the discipline to take the time and space to think, you can develop a more productive, fulfilling, and sustainable approach to running your business. Remember, as the CEO, you're paid to think—so give yourself the time and space to do it well.

Paid to Think Reflective Questions

- How often do I regularly set aside dedicated time for strategic thinking and reflection, free from meetings and tasks?

- If not, how can I begin incorporating this "reflective thinking time" into my schedule to improve my decision-making as a CEO?

- How can I better focus on the "what" and the "who" in my business rather than getting caught up in the "how?"

Develop a Mindfulness Practice

By consciously allocating time for strategic thinking, you're taking a crucial step toward effective leadership. However, maximizing this time requires a clear and focused mind. We've found that developing a mindfulness practice can help reduce stress and enhance mental clarity.[6]

Mindfulness or meditation can help clear your mind and help you focus on the present moment. You might try setting aside five minutes daily to begin a mindfulness practice. This can consist of sitting quietly and noticing your breathing. We've found that having a designated chair—next to your bed or in your office—and cultivating your practice at a set time that piggybacks on an existing habit or routine works best.

For example, BJ Fogg explains that if you already have the habit of brushing your teeth every morning, you might add to that action by doing a single push-up right afterward to start an exercise routine.[7] Similarly, you could incorporate a brief mindfulness session after an existing daily habit. I recommend starting the practice before you check your emails and get the day going.

You can also use a guided meditation app like Headspace, Calm, or others; there are a plethora of resources out there. It's just one approach to becoming more present and mindful while also developing the ability to check your "internal dipstick" consistently.

Mindfulness Reflection Questions:

- Can I set aside five minutes daily to begin a mindfulness practice? How might this enhance my clarity and effectiveness as a leader? As you experience the benefits, work up to 10-20 minutes daily to de-stress
- What existing daily habits (like brushing my teeth or having morning coffee) can I use as a trigger to incorporate a moment of mindfulness or meditation?

Preventing Burnout: Acting Sooner Rather Than Later

There's a saying that if you drink water when you feel thirsty, you're already dehydrated and have gone too far beyond the time when you should have had a drink.[8] Similarly, if you're feeling burned out, you may have passed the point where you should have stopped to let your "soul catch up to your body."

Like so many others, it often takes me a while to notice and pay attention before I do something about it. So, this little phrase—letting your soul catch up—can serve as a gentle reminder, challenging us to catch up sooner rather than later.

Key Takeaways Chapter 30: Slow Down, Be Still and Listen

It's easy to lose sight of what matters when moving too fast. Slowing down allows you to reconnect with yourself, your values, and your priorities. Taking time to slow down and "let your soul catch up" enables you to *be still and listen*. By doing so, you can reduce chronic stress and the feeling of being overwhelmed while empowering yourself to better align with what matters most, creating a greater sense of fulfillment.

1. **The Importance of Slowing Down:**

   Slowing down isn't wasted time—it's how you regain clarity, protect your health, and focus on what truly matters.

It creates space for meaningful reflection and alignment with what truly matters.

2. **Checking Your "Internal Dipstick":**

Periodically assessing your mental, emotional, and physical well-being helps prevent breakdowns and ensures you're functioning at your best, both personally and professionally.

3. **Sacred Space and Mindfulness:**

Creating dedicated time and space for reflection and mindfulness can enhance clarity, creativity, and decision-making. Even a few minutes daily can yield significant benefits.

4. **The CEO's Role – Paid to Think:**

As a leader, your role is to focus on the "what" and "who," not just the "how." Strategic thinking and intentional reflection are essential for making sound decisions and guiding your business effectively.

5. **Preventing Burnout:**

Recognizing the signs of overwhelm early and taking proactive steps, such as slowing down and creating reflective practices, can prevent burnout and improve overall well-being.

Reflection Questions Chapter 30: Slow Down, Be Still, and Listen

1. **When was the last time I slowed down to check in with myself — mentally, emotionally, and physically?**

   o What did I notice about how I'm really doing, beyond just "busy"?

   o How might this self-awareness affect the way I lead, make decisions, or interact with my team?

   Examples:

   ▪ I realized I'm feeling drained and short-tempered, which may cause me to be impatient or dismissive with my team.

- I noticed I'm anxious about cash flow, which might lead me to avoid important but difficult conversations with my leadership team.

- I'm feeling physically exhausted, which could affect the quality of decisions I'm making and how I show up for my employees and customers.

2. **Do I have a dedicated time or space for reflection and mindfulness?**

   o If not, what's one simple way I could start creating that space in my routine?

   o How could even five minutes of stillness help me gain more clarity and calm?

3. **Am I allocating enough time to think strategically as a CEO — focusing on the "what" and "who," not just the "how"?**

   o Where am I spending too much time on tasks that could be delegated?

   o What would carving out more time to think and reflect do for my business and leadership?

4. **Can I commit to starting a mindfulness or reflection practice, even for five minutes a day?**

   o What existing habit could I pair it with to make it easier to stick with? (e.g., before checking email, after lunch)

5. **Am I recognizing and addressing signs of stress or overwhelm early enough, or do I wait until it's too late?**

   o What's one action I can take sooner to protect my well-being and prevent burnout?

   Examples:

- **Set a hard stop to the workday** (e.g., finish by 6 PM and disconnect from work).

- **Block out 30 minutes a day** of "What Matters Time" for reflection, strategy, or quiet thinking — and treat it like an important meeting.

- **Delegate or drop** at least one low-value task this week that's draining your time and energy — something a team member could handle or that doesn't need to be done.

6. **What stood out to you in this chapter or resonated most with you?**

   o What insight, story, or idea felt especially relevant to your business or leadership right now?

   o What is one thing you feel motivated to act on because of this chapter?

7. **What are your top 1-2 takeaways from this chapter?**

   o What is one specific action you can take to start applying these insights and better align your business and leadership with what matters most?

Reflective Questions After Practicing Slowing Down, Being Still and Listening:

- How do you feel after taking time to slow down? What changes, if any, do you notice in your stress levels and clarity?

- How has practicing mindfulness impacted your ability to lead and make decisions?

- What positive changes have you observed in your well-being and productivity since incorporating sacred space into your routine?

CHAPTER 31

THE HERO'S JOURNEY TO WHAT ULTIMATELY MATTERS

The Entrepreneurial Journey

The Hero's Journey, a concept popularized by Joseph Campbell, introduces a storytelling pattern found in myths, literature, and cinema around the world and across cultures dating back thousands of years. It describes an individual's journey, responding to a call to adventure, facing tests and challenges, and ultimately transforming into a stronger, wiser version of themselves. Along the way, the hero often discovers a broader purpose that transcends his personal or selfish ambitions.[1]

For our small and medium-sized business (SMB) owners, we've found the idea of the Hero's journey resonating with their own entrepreneurial journeys filled with challenges, growth, failures, and triumphs. Through these experiences, one can tap into something more profound—the quest for meaning and purpose in both life and business. By recognizing the stages of the Hero's Journey, we can connect with a greater sense of purpose shared by countless entrepreneurial "heroes and heroines" who have walked similar paths before us.

Embarking on an Adventure: The Call to Entrepreneurship

For many SMB owners, the call to entrepreneurship comes unexpectedly perhaps they got laid off or found a way to turn a side hustle while working into more of a full-time endeavor, or maybe someone approached them about an opportunity to get into or purchase a business. Like heroes summoned to adventure, entrepreneurs find themselves pulled out of their comfort zones into a world of risk, uncertainty, and opportunity. This often marks the beginning of a journey into the unknown, where new challenges and possibilities await them.

Crossing the Threshold: Taking the Leap

Stepping into the entrepreneurial journey requires courage to face potential failure, financial uncertainty, and personal sacrifice. Yet, this very act of embracing the unknown sets the stage for personal and professional growth.

Facing Challenges: The Road of Trials

Like any hero, the SMB owner faces numerous trials. Challenges come in many forms, e.g. market competition, financial hurdles, operational difficulties, and personnel issues that test one's resolve. However, through these trials, the hero gains strength and wisdom. Each obstacle overcome presents an opportunity to learn, adapt, and grow stronger.

Allies and Mentors: Finding Support

No hero journeys alone. Along the way, allies and mentors provide wisdom, guidance, and support. For SMB owners, mentors might be business advisors, seasoned entrepreneurs, or trusted friends and family. Allies could include loyal employees, partners, or collaborators who share the vision. For an SMB owner, this might involve securing initial funding, obtaining the resources to develop a first product, or assembling a dedicated team. These relationships are crucial, offering critical support and resources.

The Abyss: The Darkest Hour

In every Hero's Journey, there's a moment of crisis—the abyss. For SMB owners, this might be a financial downturn, losing a major client or key employees, or personal hardships threatening the business. During this darkest hour, the hero must find inner strength, relying on their purpose to persevere. As Thomas Fuller said, "It is always darkest just before the dawn."[2] Similarly, Confucius reminds us, "Our greatest glory is not in never falling, but in rising every time we fall."[3]

These insights reinforce the idea that achieving success is not about falling or failure per se, but the perseverance required that enables us to get up after each failure and overcome the challenges that inevitably face us throughout our journey. As notable actress, formerly known as America's sweetheart, Mary Pickford, says, "You may have a fresh start any moment you choose, for this thing that we call 'failure' is not the falling down, but the staying down."[4]

Transformation and Revelation: Emerging Stronger

After facing the abyss and repeatedly getting knocked down and falling down, heroes rise up again and again by refusing to give up. Our hero overcomes the abyss to become a stronger, more resilient, and wiser version of himself. By overcoming, he becomes and undergoes a transformation that enables him to be even better equipped for future challenges.

The Return: Bringing Back the Elixir

At the journey's end, the hero returns home with the elixir—knowledge, wisdom, and achievements gained. For SMB owners, this could represent the maturation of their own character and their business, where success benefits not only themselves but also their employees and community. Having grown through their journey, they can share wisdom and help others, adding value beyond profit and leaving a lasting legacy.

Continuation: The Next Adventure

Even after achieving success, the journey isn't over. There's always a new challenge, another goal to pursue. This continual striving represents the ongoing cycle of renewal, learning, growth, and change. In business, this means constant adaptation and realignment with one's evolving sense of purpose.

The Purpose of the Hero's Journey and One's Life Pie

The Hero's Journey transcends business success—it's about aligning one's life with a deeper sense of purpose. Picture your life as a *"Life Pie,"* divided into slices representing personal, professional, financial, spiritual, and relational dimensions. Each slice is interconnected and vital to your overall well-being and fulfillment. But beyond balancing these individual slices, what gives one's Life Pie its ultimate purpose?

Perhaps we can turn to religion for how it has inspired and guided humanity in this regard. In its truest sense, religion, derived from the Latin *religio*, meaning "to bind together" was intended to bind humanity back to God, drawing us nearer to Him in accordance with His will and teachings. While over time man-made dogmas and traditions have often distorted and strayed away from this original intent, the foundational teachings of the world's major religions have provided guidance on life's greater meaning and purpose to billions of people.

Though perspectives vary widely and are beyond the scope of this or any single book when it comes to exploring the subject of religion, there can be no denying the profound impact that religion has had on humanity. According to Population Education, over six billion people, 85% of the global population identifies with a religion, and the four largest ones—Christianity, Islam, Hinduism, and Buddhism—represent over 75% of humanity. And despite perceived differences, at their core these faiths share a recurring theme: knowing, loving, and aligning with a higher power while striving to live ethically and contribute positively to the world. The following offer perspectives on the purpose of one's Life Pie, as expressed in the sacred writings of several of the world's major religions:

Christianity: Purpose of Life

In Christianity, life's purpose is to know, love, and serve God. Believers are called to live in harmony with God, follow His commandments, and seek eternal life through Jesus Christ.

Scripture Reference:

"And you shall love the Lord your God with all your heart, with all your soul, and with all your mind. This is the first and great commandment. And the second is like it: 'You shall love your neighbor as yourself.'[6]

— Matthew 22:37-39 (NKJV)

Islam: Purpose of Life

In Islam, life's purpose is to worship Allah (God) and live according to His guidance as revealed in the Quran. Life is viewed as a test, with success achieved through fulfilling duties to Allah and serving humanity.

Scripture Reference:

"And I did not create the jinn and mankind except to worship Me... Indeed, Allah commands justice, the doing of good, and generosity to relatives; and He forbids immorality, wrongdoing, and oppression."[7]

— Quran 51:56 , Quran 16:90 (Sahih International)

Bahá'í Faith: Purpose of Life

The Bahá'í Faith teaches that life's purpose is to know and worship God, develop spiritual virtues, and contribute to the progress of society. Life is a journey of spiritual growth and service to the betterment of humanity.

Bahá'í Writings:

"The purpose underlying the revelation of every heavenly Book... is to endue all men with righteousness and understanding, so that peace and tranquility may be firmly established amongst them.[8]

— Bahá'u'lláh, *Gleanings from the Writings of Bahá'u'lláh*

Judaism: Purpose of Life

In Judaism, life's purpose is to live according to God's will as revealed in the Torah. This includes fulfilling mitzvot (commandments), pursuing righteousness, and contributing to *tikkun olam*—repairing and improving the world.

Scripture Reference:

"He has told you, O man, what is good; and what does the Lord require of you but to do justice, to love kindness, and to walk humbly with your God?"[9]

— Micah 6:8 (ESV)

Hinduism: Purpose of Life

Hinduism identifies four goals: Dharma (righteous duty), Artha (prosperity), Kama (pleasure), and Moksha (liberation). The ultimate purpose is attaining Moksha, or unity with Brahman, the supreme spirit.

Scripture Reference:

"When a man renounces all the desires of the heart and is satisfied with the Self alone, then he is said to be one steadfast in wisdom."[10]

— Bhagavad Gita 2:55

Buddhism: Purpose of Life

In Buddhism, the purpose of life is to overcome suffering (dukkha) and attain Nirvana—freedom from the cycle of birth and rebirth. This is achieved through the Eightfold Path, which cultivates wisdom, ethical conduct, and mental discipline.

Teaching:

"He who has gone for refuge to the Buddha, the Teaching and his Order, penetrates with transcendental wisdom the Four Noble Truths—suffering, the cause of suffering, the cessation of suffering, and the Noble Eightfold Path leading to the cessation of suffering." [11]

— *Dhammapada 14:190–191*

A Universal Message: Beyond Individual Success

Across these faith traditions, a universal message emerges: life is not just about achieving personal success or material gain. It reminds us that the Hero's Journey whether in business or life is not just about achieving goals but about who we become in the process and the positive impact we can make. True fulfillment lies in leaving a positive legacy, making the world a better place, and even inspiring others to embark on their own transformational journeys.

At its deepest level, the Hero's Journey perhaps mirrors our Soul's journey: a call to unlock more of our potential, cultivate our connection with the Divine (or the transcendent), and align our lives with a greater purpose. In this light, success is redefined—not by what we accumulate, but by how we are transformed and how that transformation contributes to the well-being of others and the greater good.

Key Takeaways Chapter 31: The Hero's Journey to What Ultimately Matters

By viewing your own entrepreneurial journey through the lens of the Hero's Journey, you can find greater meaning and a sense of purpose by recognizing that you are part of a universal narrative—a story shared by many others who have gone before you. Embracing these universal themes can generate greater motivation and resolve and serve as a guidepost for your own personal and professional growth. Remember, it's not always about reaching the destination but also about the person you become and the impact you make along the way.

1. **The Hero's Journey in Business:** Your entrepreneurial path often mirrors the stages of the Hero's Journey. Each challenge, transformation, and triumph is a step toward personal growth, transformation and an opportunity to align with a purpose greater than yourself.

2. **Resilience and Renewal:** The journey of an SMB owner is marked by constant challenges. Embrace these as opportunities to learn and grow by overcoming these obstacles.

3. **Mentors and Allies Matter:** Building strong relationships with mentors, advisors, and allies is crucial for overcoming challenges and sustaining success.

4. **Alignment with Purpose:** True success comes from aligning your business with core values, competencies, and a purpose that empowers you to achieve your potential and create greater fulfillment.

5. **The Spiritual Dimension of the Journey:** Just as religious teachings guide life's purpose, you can draw from these perspectives to align your business with values that contribute positively to the world, creating a legacy that transcends financial success.

Reflection Questions Chapter 31: The Hero's Journey to What Ultimately Matters

1. How do I want to be remembered—as a leader and as a person—and what parts of my current behavior already reflect that?

2. What impact do you want to have made on your employees, customers, and the broader community through your business?

   o Consider how your business aligns with your core values and how it contributes to the greater good.

3. If your family, friends, employees, and business partners were giving a eulogy about you, what would you want them to say?

   o Reflect on the qualities, values, and achievements you hope others will celebrate about your character, leadership, and life's work.

4. If others described the way I lead, what do I hope they would say about my character, my leadership, and the way I treat people?

   o How can you live out those qualities more intentionally today?

5. Where am I on my own Hero's Journey right now—and what is the next small step that would move me forward with more courage, clarity, or purpose?

6. What are my top 1-2 takeaways from this reflection?

   o What is one specific action I can take to begin shaping the legacy I want to leave — in my leadership, business, and life?

CHAPTER 32

PREPARING FOR WHAT MATTERS NEXT

"When one door of happiness closes, another opens; but often we look so long at the closed door that we do not see the one which has been opened for us."[1]
— Helen Keller

Preparing for Life after Business: Understanding Exit vs. Succession Planning

As you approach the latter stages of your business journey, considering and preparing for what comes next in life's retirement or rather post-working phase can be daunting. However, retirement doesn't mean sitting in a rocking chair and watching time pass, which is a sure way to hasten one's decline. For many, retirement represents a new phase of life filled with opportunities to travel, spend time with grandchildren, or give back to their church, community, or other causes they feel passionate about. (I've known many retirees who are as busy or busier now than when they were working!)

Others look forward to having the space and time to reflect on what truly matters in this next chapter of life. In this phase, ideally you will have the health, resources, and freedom to choose how you want to spend your time and with whom while no longer being tethered to the daily demands of your business.

This chapter explores the two paths business owners can take when considering the future of their business: exit planning and succession planning. It is essential to understand their differences and how to prepare for each. By understanding the nuances of exit and succession planning, owners can better position their business and themselves for success and greater fulfillment in this new chapter of life. Exit planning generally involves preparing the business for sale to an outside buyer or transferring ownership to employees or family members. Succession planning, on the other hand, may or may not involve a transfer of ownership and typically focuses on ensuring the business continues to operate smoothly after the current owner steps down, often by training and empowering a new generation of leaders.[2]

The Holy Grail of SMB Ownership: A Business That Grows Into a Saleable Asset

Growing a successful business involves hard work, vision, and a bit of luck. Many SMB owners dream of creating a sustainable business that is attractive enough to sell. However, growing a business that is attractive enough for someone to buy requires sustainable and predictable cash flow and the infrastructure in place to ensure its continuity. Very few SMB enterprises can get sold, especially since the business is over-reliant on the owner to sustain itself.[3] In contrast, if you own several Subway franchises where the customers have no idea who the owner is and have the systems and personnel to run the systems that in turn runs the business, those businesses are naturally much more sellable.

In addition, pricing to sell a small to mid-sized business is often challenging due to much smaller set of comparable sales data.[4] Unlike real estate, where similar homes in a neighborhood provide a basis for valuation, such as dollars per square foot, many small businesses do not have this level of comparability. Ultimately, the value of a business comes down to what two parties—the buyer and the seller—are willing to agree upon: "The price at which the property would change hands between a willing buyer and a willing seller when the former is not under any compulsion to buy and the latter is not under any compulsion to sell, both parties having reasonable knowledge of the relevant facts."[5]

Exit Strategies: Selling, Delaying, or Closing Shop

Closing Shop: A Last Resort in Exit Planning

"Closing shop" refers to the decision to shut down a business entirely, often selling off inventory, equipment, and assets and ceasing operations. This option is usually considered a last resort for business owners when other exit strategies—selling the business or passing it on through a succession plan—are not viable or attractive.

When closing a business, the owner liquidates assets, paying off debts and liabilities, with any remaining value being the final proceeds. Unfortunately, closing shop often means the loss of intangible assets like goodwill—the business's reputation, brand value, and customer relationships—which are typically not transferable or sellable in this scenario.

Owners who choose this route may walk away with significantly less value than if they had sold the business as a going concern. This option is common in cases where the business relies heavily on the owner's presence or expertise, making it less attractive or feasible for a buyer to take over. While closing shop may be necessary and inevitable under certain circumstances, careful planning and exploring alternatives—such as selling to employees or family members who are willing and capable of running the business—can help SMB owners avoid the financial and emotional toll of simply closing shop.

Selling the Business: Maximizing Value Through a Sale

Selling the business is often the preferred exit strategy for many SMB owners looking to retire or move on to new ventures. This involves transferring ownership of the business to an outside buyer, employees, or family members. The key goal in selling a business is to maximize its value, ensuring that the owner can "harvest" the wealth built over the years.

Selling to an outside buyer may offer the highest potential financial return, as it can attract a larger pool of interested parties. However, this often requires careful preparation, such as ensuring the business is profitable, has a stable customer base, and operates independently of the owner. To create a seamless transition for the outside buyer, the business must document operational processes, develop strong management, and position the business for continued success under new ownership.

Alternatively, selling the business to employees or family members can provide continuity and preserve the business's legacy. A structured buyout or gradual ownership transfer may be set up in these cases. While this may not always garner the highest financial return, it can ensure business continuity while also potentially rewarding the loyalty of those employees and family members that have worked and contributed to the business and wish to continue to do so now as owners of the business. Regardless of the selling strategy, seeking professional advice, conducting a thorough business valuation, and preparing well in advance are crucial steps to ensuring a smooth and successful sale.

Delaying the Decision: Postponing Transition While Earning Income

"Delaying the decision" refers to an exit strategy where the owner maintains ownership of the business while stepping away from day-to-day operations. The business continues to run with a full management team, allowing the owner to collect income from the business without being directly involved. This approach can provide financial stability in the short term and delay the need for an immediate transition.

However, this strategy is often not sustainable in the long run unless the management team can have an opportunity to gain equity or ownership stakes in the business. Without such incentives, the business may struggle with leadership continuity and motivation, leading to potential operational inefficiencies or loss of key personnel.

Additionally, delaying the decision postpones the inevitable need for a formal exit plan, which could reduce the business's overall value over time. Market conditions may change, the business may become more reliant on key employees, or the owner may face health or other personal challenges that make a sudden exit more difficult. While this option may offer temporary financial comfort, it's essential to have a long-term plan in place, with considerations for management succession, fluctuating business value, and if selling, eventual ownership transfer.

The Reality of Selling a Business

Many business owners aim to sell their business for its full value to fund retirement. However, Christopher Snider, CEO of the Exit

Planning Institute (EPI), notes that many owners aren't taking the necessary steps to achieve this goal. Snider conducted a survey that shows many owners aren't positioned well because they're not maximizing the transferable value of the business and/or they're not positioning it to transfer successfully so that they can "harvest wealth locked in the business."[6]

For example, he said, "If 80 to 90 percent of owner wealth is in the business, how can these estate plans be effective if two-thirds of them don't incorporate a recent business valuation or plans for the transition of the business?"[7]

Snider suggests owners seek help from accountants and other advisors to get an accurate picture of the business value—a picture that tax returns cannot provide. He also suggested that owners should stop viewing the business transition plan as important but not urgent. Instead, they should become educated about the process and carve out time for planning. Snider advises, "You can't start working on the asset until you know what it's worth."[8]

An EPI survey of San Diego business owners also highlights several challenges:

- **Minimal Mindshare**: 53% have given little to no attention to their transition plan despite most being over 51 years old.

- **No Transition Plan**: 88% lack a written transition plan.

- **Going it Alone**: 80% have never sought advice about a transition.

- **Uncertain Financial Needs**: 70% don't know their after-tax income needs for retirement.

- **Estate Planning Gaps**: Only 58% have an estate plan, with many lacking updated business values or provisions for sale.

- **Unknown Business Value**: Less than 40% have had a formal valuation in the last three years, and 65% have never had their financial statements audited.

- **Lack of Buy-Sell Agreements**: Less than 48% of businesses with multiple partners have a buy-sell agreement.

- **Management Succession Concerns**: One-third have not considered management succession, and only 25% are confident in their management team's ability without the owner.[9]

Understanding Risk and Risk-Adjusted Returns

Brian Hamilton, co-founder of Sageworks, highlights that many business owners overestimate their business's value, much like the discrepancies often seen on *Shark Tank* when founders pitch the sharks valuations of their companies that far exceed what the sharks feel it's worth. Owners tend to value their businesses based on projections, while investors focus on current cash flow and the risk or uncertainty of achieving those anticipated returns.[10]

Defining Risk and Risk-Adjusted Return

Risk refers to the likelihood or probability of losing part or all of your investment or earning less than the expected return. Simply put, the higher the risk, the greater the uncertainty of receiving your money back or achieving the anticipated results.

A risk-adjusted return accounts for this uncertainty, measuring the potential return relative to the risk taken. Investors ask themselves: *"How much return do I need to justify this level of risk?"*

- **Low-risk investments** provide lower returns because they carry minimal uncertainty.

- **High-risk investments** require higher returns to compensate for the greater chance of losing money.

For example, let's assume you have $1 million to invest.

1. **Low-Risk Option**: You invest in an S&P 500 index fund, which historically provides an 8% annual return with relatively low risk. Over a 5–10 year period, it's unlikely you'll lose all your money—unless every major company in the S&P 500 fails (and if that happens, we're all in trouble).

2. **High-Risk Option**: You invest in a small business, where the likelihood of losing your money is much higher due to operational challenges, market uncertainty, and competition.

To compensate for this added risk, investors expect significantly higher returns:

- If you aim for a 20% annual return, it will still take 5 years to recover your $1 million investment.

- At a 33% annual return, it would take 3 years to break even.

This illustrates why buyers and investors typically look for 20–30% or greater annualized returns when investing in riskier ventures like small businesses. The higher the uncertainty (risk), the greater the return required to justify the investment.

Why This Matters for Business Valuation

When assessing the value of your business, it's critical to consider the risk-adjusted return from an investor's perspective. Comparing your business to safer investments—such as a government bond offering a 5% return—provides a useful benchmark. While bonds carry nearly zero risk, your business represents a far riskier venture, and any investor will factor that risk into their required returns. In other words, buyers will need higher than 5-8% return for a business that is nowhere as safe as the next best alternative, such as Government bonds or the S&P 500 Index.

For business owners, this means two things:

1. **Reduce Uncertainty**: Demonstrating consistent cash flow, operational stability, and growth potential can reduce perceived risk and make your business more attractive.

2. **Understand Investor Expectations**: Investors aren't just buying potential—they're evaluating the risk as measured by the degree of certainty or uncertainty of realizing projected returns.

By understanding these concepts of **risk** and **risk-adjusted returns**, business owners can approach valuations and negotiations more in line with market realities and take steps to improve their business's appeal to potential buyers or investors.

Calculating Seller's Discretionary Earnings (SDE)

Seller's Discretionary Earnings (SDE) is a common starting point for valuation. SDE is the total financial benefit a full-time owner-operator derives from the business. It includes the company's net income before interest, taxes, depreciation, and amortization (EBITDA), as well as adjustments for the owner's salary, one-time expenses, personal expenses, and non-operational income or expenses.

For example, SDE will account for the owner's salary and benefits (health insurance, vehicle expenses, etc.), non-recurring expenses (one-time legal fees, repairs, etc.), and discretionary spending (expenses that aren't crucial to running the business, such as entertainment or travel). To calculate the business's earning potential, a buyer will typically average the past three years of SDE. However, more weight is usually given to the most recent year, as it most accurately reflects a business's current state. [11]

Determining the Right Multiple

Once you have determined the SDE, the next step is to apply a valuation multiple to calculate the business's potential sale price. This multiple depends on factors such as the business's size, growth potential, industry, customer base, and market conditions. For smaller, riskier businesses, the multiple might range between 1.5 to 3 times the SDE.[12] For example, if your business generates $200,000 in SDE, it might sell for $300,000 to $600,000. The higher the risk, the lower the multiple. For businesses with more stability and higher growth prospects, the multiple might be higher, ranging from 3 to 6 times SDE, e.g., SMB generating $1 million in SDE might sell for $3 million to $6 million.

Factors that influence the multiple:

- Consistent profitability and positive cash flow
- Strong customer base with long-term contracts
- Growth potential and scalability
- Industry trends and market demand
- Well-documented financials and operational transparency
- Management team strength and operational autonomy without the owner

The more favorable these factors, the higher the multiple, ultimately leading to a better sale price. [13] Smaller, riskier businesses like a cafe might sell for 1-2 times annual cash flow, whereas more established businesses with long-term contracts might see 3-6 times EBITDA. (For comparison, the average S&P 500 price-to-earnings P/E-price to earnings multiple is around 25 as of July 2024).

Emotional Challenges in Transitioning

While the financial aspects of selling a business are crucial, addressing the transition's emotional challenges is equally important. Many business owners struggle with letting go—an emotional hurdle that can be more difficult to overcome than the logistical and financial factors of the sale.

- **Identity and Attachment**: For many business owners, their business is a reflection of who they are. They've poured years, sometimes decades, of time, energy, and passion into building the company. Letting go of such a significant part of their life can feel like losing a piece of their identity. Owners can emotionally prepare for the transition by identifying new ways to channel their energy and passion and mapping out their post-business life.
- **Fear of the Unknown**: Transitioning into retirement or a new phase of life can be daunting. Many business owners fear the unknown, wondering what their days will look like without the structure and purpose that running a business provides. This uncertainty can cause procrastination or denial when planning the exit.
- **Concern for Employees**: Business owners often feel a strong sense of responsibility toward their employees, who have helped build the company. They worry about how the transition will affect their teams and whether the new owner will treat them with the same respect and care.

Addressing these emotional factors is essential for a smoother transition. Owners should seek support from family, peers, or professional advisors to help them navigate both the financial and emotional complexities of exiting the business.

Actionable Steps for SMB Owners

Here are some practical steps SMB owners can take to prepare for a smooth transition:

1. Assess and Plan Early

- **Develop a Written Transition Plan**: Outline your exit strategy, financial goals, timelines, and succession planning.

- **Seek Professional Advice**: Consult accountants, business brokers, and financial planners to understand your business's value and transition options.

- **Conduct Regular Valuations**: Assess your business's value through formal valuations.

2. Financial and Estate Planning

- **Clarify Financial Needs**: Understand the after-tax income needed for retirement or the next phase of life.

- **Update Estate Plans**: Ensure your estate plan reflects current business valuations and includes provisions for sale or transfer of ownership.

- **Plan for Taxes**: Work with a tax advisor to minimize the tax burden from the sale.

3. Prepare Your Management Team

- **Develop a Succession Plan**: Ensure there's a clear succession plan involving the training and empowerment of your management team.

- **Implement Buy-Sell Agreements**: Establish buy-sell agreements with partners to facilitate smooth transitions in case of retirement, disability, or death.

4. Prepare the Business for Sale

- **Document Operational Procedures**: Buyers value businesses with well-documented processes and systems. Create manuals, SOPs, and documentation to ensure a smooth transition.

- **Increase Transferable Value**: Make the business less dependent on you, the owner, which increases its appeal to potential buyers.

5. Plan for Post-Business Life

- **Create a Personal Plan**: Reflect on how you'll spend your time after the sale—whether it's traveling, volunteering, mentoring, or pursuing new ventures.

- **Build New Passions**: Start thinking now about how you can stay engaged and purposeful in your post-business life.

Key Takeaways Chapter 32: Preparing for What Matters Next

Transitioning out of a business can be a complex and emotionally daunting process. By understanding the differences between exit and succession planning, conducting regular valuations, and preparing your management team, you can ensure a smoother transition.

This chapter is not an exhaustive treatment of all the intricacies of selling or preparing a business for sale, which can take three to five years of preparation with adequate documentation, e.g., three years of tax returns demonstrating positive and growing income of the business. Therefore, we encourage you to consult a professional business broker or exit planning expert for guidance on maximizing the value of your life's work and achieving your long-term financial goals.

1. **Know the difference between exit and succession planning.** Exit planning focuses on selling or transferring ownership of the business, while succession planning ensures the business runs smoothly by developing future leaders.

2. **Plan early.** Having a written transition plan and conducting regular business valuations are essential to maximize value and ensure a successful exit when you're ready.

3. **Build a business that can survive without you.** Increase transferable value by creating systems, documenting processes, and reducing reliance on you, the owner.

4. **Prepare emotionally, not just financially.** Letting go of a business is one of the biggest emotional transitions you'll face. Start thinking about what will give you purpose and fulfillment after the sale.

5. **Understand your financial needs.** Work with advisors to determine your after-tax income requirements and ensure your estate plan is updated to reflect your retirement goals.

6. **Develop and empower your leadership team.** A well-trained management team is crucial for the business to thrive without you — and it makes the business more attractive to buyers.

7. **Explore all exit options.** Selling to an outside buyer, transferring to family or employees, or postponing a sale are all valid paths — what matters is picking the right fit for your goals.

8. **Get professional help.** Advisors such as accountants, brokers, and exit planning specialists can help you increase value, minimize taxes, and ensure a smooth process.

9. **Think beyond the business.** Start planning now for a meaningful life after the business — whether that's traveling, giving back, mentoring, or pursuing a new passion.

10. **Address both the financial and emotional risks.** A thoughtful exit plan reduces risks and gives you peace of mind — for both you and your employees.

Reflection Questions Chapter 32: Preparing for What Matters Next

1. Transition Planning

- Do I have a written exit or succession plan in place?
- Have I sought professional advice to guide this process?

2. Financial Preparedness

- Have I assessed my after-tax income needs for retirement?
- Is my estate plan up to date and aligned with my long-term goals?

3. Business Value

- Do I have a current business valuation?
- What steps am I taking to increase the transferable value of my business?

4. Succession Planning

- Have I identified and developed a leadership team capable of running the business without me?
- What training or support do they still need?

5. Emotional Preparation

- What would letting go of my business mean to me emotionally?
- How can I prepare for that transition and find a fulfilling purpose post-business?

6. Exploring Exit Options

- Which exit option best fits my personal and financial goals: selling to an outside buyer, transferring to family or employees, or delaying the decision?
- What are the pros and cons of each option in my situation?

7. Documentation and Systems

- Are my financial statements, operational procedures, and business systems up to date and ready for a potential buyer?
- What documentation still needs to be created or improved?

8. Valuation and Market Readiness

- Have I considered how current market conditions and industry trends affect my business's value and saleability?
- What could I do to make my business more attractive in today's market?

9. Employees and Continuity

- How can I ensure my employees are protected and valued during the transition process?
- What steps can I take to prepare them for leadership or changes in ownership?

10. Timing and Urgency

- Am I treating my transition plan as something to do "someday," or am I actively working on it now?
- What is one step I can take this month to move this process forward?

11. What stood out to me as I reflected on these questions?

- What surprised me most about my current level of readiness?
- What is one insight I gained that I want to act on right away?

12. What are my top 1-2 takeaways from this chapter?

- What's one specific action I can take to move closer to being ready for life after business?

SECTION 9

IMPLEMENTATION—TRANSLATING PURPOSE INTO REALITY

CHAPTER 33

IMPLEMENTING WHAT MATTERS:THE 7P BAM

"Vision without execution is delusion.
The joy is in the results."[1] —Peter Drucker

Turning Alignment Into Action

The concepts and strategies in this book are only as useful as your ability to put them into action. This Implementation section is designed to help you apply the 7P Business Alignment Model™ to your business so you can close the gap between where you are today and where you want to be.

What makes the 7P Business Alignment Model™ particularly valuable for small and mid-sized businesses is its flexibility. It adapts to your resources, capabilities, and goals. In the chapters ahead, we explore common implementation challenges and how to overcome them, the importance of defining scope, and the different levels of implementation support available to you.

Translating Ideas into Meaningful Results

At Purpose Matters, we live by a simple motto: *"We are in the business of creating meaningful results for our clients."* Everything we do focuses on learning, adapting, and finding better ways to help our clients achieve the outcomes that matter most.

What counts as a meaningful result varies from business to business. For some, it means increasing revenue and market share. For others, it's preparing for a future exit—selling the business or passing it on to the next generation. Some owners want more personal freedom: more time with family, more space for passions outside of work, or simply fewer fires to put out. Many dream of the holy grail—a self-sufficient business that runs well, grows sustainably, and is attractive enough for someone to buy. Others want to balance profitability with growth and finally take a vacation without worrying that everything will fall apart in their absence.

Regardless of what meaningful results look like for you, we've found that most business owners value peace of mind and a sense of fulfillment above all.

Reflection Question: Which outcome resonates most with you right now?

The Growth Mindset

Creating meaningful results requires a structured change process and adopting a growth mindset. In *Mindset: The New Psychology of Success*, Carol Dweck, a renowned psychologist, explains that mindset change goes beyond surface-level adjustments. She writes:

"Mindset change is not about picking up a few pointers here and there. It's about seeing things in a new way. When people...change to a growth mindset, they change from a judge-and-be-judged framework to a learn-and-help-learn framework. Their commitment is to growth, and growth takes plenty of time, effort, and mutual support."[2]

This is not about quick fixes but about creating a culture of learning where growth, reflection, and improvement become embedded in your business processes.

Business Applications of a Growth Mindset

1. **Reframing Performance Reviews**

   Traditional performance reviews often focus on what's missing—what didn't go well, what wasn't delivered, where someone fell short. This focus on judgment and criticism leaves employees feeling anxious and defensive.

   A better approach is to adopt Dweck's "learn-and-help-learn" mindset and turn reviews into **collaborative development conversations** rather than grading sessions.

   o **Example**: A manager and employee sit down together to identify strengths, discuss one or two areas for growth, and agree on specific skills to develop next. The tone shifts from "evaluating performance" to "building capability."

- o **Impact**: When reviews feel safe, fair, and focused on growth, employees become far more open to feedback—leading to better performance, higher trust, and a stronger working relationship.

2. **Turning Problems into Learning Opportunities**

In many businesses, problems trigger blame, defensiveness, or finger-pointing. A growth mindset replaces that reaction with curiosity and learning.

- o **Example**: Instead of asking, *"Who caused this?"* ask, *"What can we learn from this, and how can we improve moving forward?"* Encourage teams to analyze what went wrong, share their learnings openly, and brainstorm better solutions.

- o **Impact**: When mistakes are treated as information instead of failures, people stop hiding them. Issues come to the surface sooner, solutions happen faster, and performance improves because the team feels safe being honest and not on who to blame.

3. **Celebrating the Learning Process**

Encouraging a growth mindset means valuing the learning process—not just the final outcome. When leaders recognize progress, effort, and lessons learned, especially during challenging work, it reinforces the behaviors that lead to long-term improvement.

- o **Example**: After resolving a recurring customer service issue, the team might share what they tried, what didn't work at first, and what finally did.

- o **Impact**: Celebrating learning boosts morale and strengthens trust. Teams become more open about problems, more willing to take initiative, and more focused on improving the work and not just avoiding mistakes.

The Power of Growth Mindset for SMBs

For SMB owners, adopting a growth mindset is not just an abstract concept—it's a practical way to run a better, healthier business. By embracing humility, curiosity, and a commitment to continuous learning, leaders can empower their teams to:

- View challenges as opportunities for growth.
- Use feedback as a stepping stone for improvement.
- Collaborate on solving problems creatively and effectively.

As Carol Dweck's research demonstrates, the real transformation happens when businesses move from a *judge-and-be-judged* mentality to a *learn-and-help-learn* mindset.

Understanding the Implementation Process

As we covered in the prior chapter 28-Keep Improving What Matters, and Ongoing "P" Improvement, growth and success in any endeavor is a process, not a single check-the-box task or one-time activity. The most successful client outcomes result from an iterative and ongoing process of making sustainable, incremental improvements over time.

At the beginning of this journey especially during the first two to three months you may not notice dramatic changes immediately. However, consistent small steps toward improvement across the 7Ps—**Purpose, Prioritization, People, Product/Service, Pipeline, Process, and Profit**—compound over time, ultimately delivering a positive and lasting impact on your organizational productivity, profitability and overall performance.

The Power of Consistency

Consistency in efforts, execution, and follow-through is essential for turning plans into reality. This consistency is often a byproduct of daily habits and routines developed to ensure continuous efforts. Maintaining these habits creates a foundation for a more empowering mindset, leading to sustainable growth and success. Your Business Alignment Coach can be an invaluable accountability partner, helping you stay on track and make quicker course corrections by not letting a bad day spiral into a bad week, a bad week turn into a bad month, or worse—a bad year.

For example, let's say you are determined to set aside 30 minutes of daily strategic self-reflection. You begin on Monday with great enthusiasm and continue your practice on Tuesday, but on Wednesday, something derails your plan, and the rest of the week goes by without conducting your daily self-reflection. At this point, one may "fall off the wagon" entirely, and the self-reflection exercise becomes forgotten like many New Year's resolutions set and never followed up to completion.

The Power of Consistent Course Corrections

However, if the following week you can "course correct" and get back on track by starting again on Monday, and this time around, you can improve and sustain your efforts from Monday through Wednesday before veering off course and only missing Thursday and Friday, you have in fact improved the overall consistency of your effort as compared to the prior week.

Over time, consistency can improve to the point where you complete your daily self-reflection Monday through Friday with an occasional day missed every couple of months. One key difference between those who succeed, whether it's sticking to a diet or exercise program or making a certain number of outbound sales calls each week, is the degree of consistency that results from their ability to get back on track, course correct quickly, and even immediately when they start to drift. It's been said that the Apollo mission was off course 90% of the time and yet through constant and timely course corrections, it reached its intended destination, the moon.

- **Reflection Question**: Where in my business am I starting to drift—and what small, immediate course correction would help me get back on track this week?

Developing Consistency Through Habits

One of the best ways to develop this consistency of effort is by developing daily routines that over time become productive and healthier habits. A routine refers to a regular or repeated sequence of actions. It's typically a set of activities or procedures that you can carry out consistently. For example, a morning routine may included waking up, a shower, brushing your teeth and drinking a cup of coffee - things you do the same way most days. When you have a structured repeatable process in place, it's easier to act on.

However, if the routine is too difficult, time-consuming, or unrealistic, it likely won't be repeated enough to become a habit. For example, if you're not used to running and you want to develop the routine of jogging 5 miles every morning that's probably not a good starting point for most folks as a way to develop a routine of jogging. Starting a routine that is too difficult and far from where we are starting from will make it unlikely that we will consistently apply and exert the required focused effort over time to build into habits that ultimately produce our desired outcomes.

Of course, progress eventually requires stretching our capacity. The principle of progressive overload—gradually increasing effort, distance, or intensity—helps us adapt and grow stronger. But this must be done intentionally and incrementally.

In his book *Tiny Habits: The Small Changes that Change Everything*, BJ Fogg explains in his behavior change model that the right balance of motivation, ability, and triggers can empower us and improve the probability of success when it comes to creating new habits.

He also offers a critical insight into developing these habits that goes beyond sustained effort and repetition by incorporating the power of positive emotions: "Celebrating tiny successes wires in new habits." Emotions create habits, not repetition."[3]

At Purpose Matters, our Business Alignment Coaches draw on BJ Fogg's behavior change strategies and tactics to help our clients improve the "do-ability" of the change process. We help break large goals into bite-sized, sustainable steps, tailored to each client's business, capacity and starting point.

By doing so, this improves the probability that positive and enduring changes will occur. The often-quoted aphorism of "How do you eat an elephant? One bite at a time," and understanding that "you don't feed steak to a newborn" applies when we meet clients where they are so they don't take on too much too soon and can take the next step safely and sustainably.

Personalizing the Change Process

Consistency is key but it must be built around what's realistic and repeatable for your situation. Growth isn't an event or a single burst of energy; it's a process. I've heard it said that the best exercise or diet is the one that you'll stick to, given that the exercise and diet programs follow sound principles.

However, what someone will stick with, and what is "doable" and "sustainable" will vary according to each person's unique circumstances, capacity, and competing responsibilities. The key is finding an approach that fits you not forcing yourself into an approach that isn't sustainable.

Starting Small: Overcoming Barriers to Change

Let's say you're a 55-year-old working professional who's been mostly sedentary for the past decade. You've reached a point where the current lifestyle is no longer acceptable—maybe you're feeling sluggish, unhealthy, and tired of feeling that way. Living healthier, losing weight, and getting fit have now become urgent.

But where do you begin?

A program that requires two to four hours of exercise per day is clearly unrealistic. That might work for a full-time athlete but not for someone balancing work, family, and life. And frankly, it's unnecessary. You don't need Olympic level effort to make meaningful progress to becoming healthy. You just need the next right step, one that's aligned with your goals, your reality, and your ability to stay consistent.

Sustainable and Sufficient Effort

A more sustainable level of effort in terms of do-ability could be one hour a week. However, this level of effort may not be sufficient to achieve your desired fitness goals. A more appropriate and effective level of effort to achieve your goals may be more in line with four to six hours a week.

A qualified fitness trainer can be invaluable in helping you determine the right balance of time and effort according to your goals and needs. They can design an appropriate and effective exercise program that fits your schedule and life circumstances. For example, if you want to gain strength and build muscle, doing a bicep curl using a pencil isn't enough weight for muscle growth. On the other hand, trying to curl a weight that you can't budge may not be safe or effective either. A knowledgeable weight training coach can be instrumental in determining a reasonable rep range and weight appropriate to your goals and available time while also considering where you are starting from.

We also know that exercising four hours one day per week is not as optimal as one hour daily for four days a week. Perhaps walking 10-20 minutes a day to start would be even more effective. Our Business Alignment Coaches, analogous to a qualified fitness trainer, can help you optimize and develop the appropriate routine and units of effort within a reasonable range of effort and frequency based on your current circumstances to successfully implement the 7P Business Alignment Model™ into your business.

These examples illustrate that between doing nothing and doing too much, there is an optimal range of effort that can produce a desired outcome. If it's too far on the spectrum towards "nothing," the effort expended may not be enough to reach the desired result unless that effort gradually increases to produce a meaningful result.

Collaborative Change Management

Successfully navigating the change process requires a collaborative approach between the client and the BAC (Business Alignment Coach). They can serve as invaluable guides and coaches when helping our clients apply frameworks within the 7P (Purpose, People, Process, Prioritization, Product, Pipeline Profit) Business Alignment Model.

BACs are also critical to ensuring the implementation is conducted in an actionable, "digestible" manner and appropriate to our client's needs. They begin by assessing and meeting clients where they are, and then collaborating to develop a roadmap that empowers them to take the next step —one that's practical, sustainable, and fulfilling.

Practical Strategic Alignment

We've designed our methodology while considering the limited time and resource constraints of busy business owners already spread too thin. We know that most SMB owners typically don't have the ability to take the time and incur the expense of an offsite week-long retreat at a luxury hotel with their leadership team to work on their strategic planning, including developing their Mission, Vision, and Core Values. However, somewhere between the range of values of doing nothing and feeling overwhelmed by trying to do too much, we believe there is a unit of effort one can start with that is sustainable and practical while putting you on a path toward achieving your desired outcome. This effort is not just about implementing the 7P Business Alignment Model™ and its frameworks but, more importantly, facilitating a transformational journey where habit and mindset changes empower continuous learning. meaningful growth and greater fulfillment.

Operationalizing Purpose and the 7P BAM

Unlike many traditional business advisory or management consulting services, Purpose Matters goes beyond providing advice or coaching by operationalizing their purpose with the implementation of the 7P Business Alignment Model™. In addition, we provide executive level fractional support and execution in the following areas especially in the People and Pipeline P's of their business:

- **PEOPLE-Improve Hiring and Team Alignment:** Our talent acquisition services help professionalize the hiring process for our clients and alleviate some of the tedious and time-consuming elements associated with the front end of the recruiting process. By sourcing and pre-screening resumes and pre-interviewing potential job seekers, we can deliver a pool of higher-quality candidates for our clients to choose from. As a result, we can save our clients time and money while improving their ability to make better hiring decisions, resulting in attracting and retaining more of the right-fit employees over time.

- **PIPELINE: Improve Marketing and Customer Alignment:** Through strategic, data-driven analysis of your customers and potential customers, we can help you make more informed marketing decisions. This results in attracting and retaining more of the right-fit customers who align with your purpose and are more likely to become loyal advocates of your business.

- **FOCUS and Business Alignment:** Through our alignment coaching, we can provide the tools and accountability to help our clients and their leadership team better focus and align around what matters most to drive the business forward

With the right-fit employees, customers and focus aligned with your purpose, you can build a winning team and a loyal customer base that drives long-term growth and sustainability.

Key Takeaways Chapter 33: Implementing What Matters: The 7P BAM

1. **Ideas + Actions = Results**

   o Ideas are only as good as their implementation. Translating the 7P Business Alignment Model™ into actionable steps bridges the gap between where you are and where you aspire to be.

2. **Defining Meaningful Results**

   o Every SMB owner defines success differently—growth, self-sufficiency, profitability, or work-life balance. Identifying what truly matters to you provides direction and focus for implementing changes.

3. **Embracing a Growth Mindset**

   o Shifting from a "judge-and-be-judged" mentality to a "learn-and-help-learn" framework encourages continuous learning and improvement.

4. **Consistency is Key**

   o Sustainable progress is built through consistent effort and course corrections, even when setbacks occur. Small, steady actions compound over time to create significant, lasting change.

5. **Personalizing the Change Process**

   o Effective implementation depends on starting where you are and scaling efforts appropriately. Incremental, manageable changes tailored to your business's capacity lead to sustainable growth.

6. **Collaborative Change Management**

   o A Business Alignment Coach is a guide and accountability partner, helping you prioritize, execute, and refine your strategies to achieve optimal results.

7. **Balancing Effort and Do-ability**

   o Between doing nothing and doing too much lies an optimal range of sustainable effort. Finding this balance ensures that changes are both impactful and sustainable

8. **Purpose Matters goes beyond traditional advisory services**

   o By actively supporting day-to-day operations, when it comes to professionalizing the hiring process, providing data-driven customer insights, and aligning their team around purpose and what matters, we can empower them to meaningfully grow.

Reflection Questions Chapter 33: Implementing What Matters: The 7P BAM

1. **What does success look like for your business in this phase?**

   o Define what meaningful results mean to you — whether it's growth, profitability, more time, or work-life balance.

   o How would achieving these results positively impact both your business and personal life? How would not achieving these results impact your life?

2. What's one meaningful result you want to make real over the next 90 days?

3. What's one small step you can take this week to move toward that result?

4. What daily or weekly routine would make the biggest positive difference right now?

5. What's one thing you can remove or stop doing that would make progress toward your goal easier?

6. Who can help hold you accountable and guide you through the change process?

   o How would having a trusted advisor or Business Alignment Coach support you in staying focused and following through?

7. What stood out to you as you read this chapter?

8. What are my top 1-2 takeaways you want to remember or act on?

CHAPTER 34

OVERCOMING IMPLEMENTATION CHALLENGES

*"If you want something you have never had,
you must be willing to do something you have
never done."[1] —attributed to Thomas Jefferson*

*If nothing changes, then nothing
changes — Anonymous*

Common Obstacles and Challenges to Implementation:

Even though we've designed the 7P Business Alignment Model™ (BAM) to be implementable within busy business owners' tight time constraints and limited mental-emotional bandwidth, significant obstacles still exist. These challenges must be anticipated and adequately planned for to avoid derailing progress.

- **Time Constraints**: Many SMB owners struggle to find the time to implement new strategies while managing day-to-day operations. Therefore, they must learn to prioritize tasks better and delegate responsibilities to free up time for strategic thinking, planning, and implementation. We'll present tools to help you do this in Chapter 7 Focus on What Matters.

- **Resource Limitations**: Limited financial and human resources can hinder the implementation of new ideas. Therefore, focusing on high-impact areas that align with your core purpose improves your ability to allocate your resources of time and money effectively.

- **Resistance to Change**: Employees and even leadership may resist change, preferring familiar routines and processes. Owners need to learn how to better communicate the benefits of change clearly and involve employees early and often in the process to gain their buy-in and support. In this chapter we'll introduce methods and tools to help facilitate the changes needed to grow and help overcome this resistance.

Overcoming Organizational Inertia

Acknowledging these challenges and symptoms is the first step toward remedying them. However, we've found that many busy business owner-leaders who are open to taking the next steps and recognize these challenges still struggle to break free of this *organizational inertia,* the tendency to stick with familiar, habituated ways of doing things even when they no longer serve the business effectively.

Breaking free from organizational inertia requires more than willpower or better intentions. It requires understanding the forces that actually drive behavior. Most human behavior—including how we act as business owners—is shaped by two complementary forces: the desire to avoid pain and the desire to move toward growth, reward, or fulfillment. These are two sides of the same coin.

When used intentionally, both forces can support meaningful change. Avoiding pain helps us recognize what is no longer working—burnout, chaos, missed opportunities, or stalled growth. Moving toward growth helps us stay motivated by what is possible—greater clarity, progress, fulfillment, and a business that works better for us rather than consuming us. Sustainable implementation happens when leaders learn to work with both forces, rather than relying on one alone.

As "human doings" rather than "human beings," they are like firefighters constantly putting out fires, moving from one urgent task to another. Caught up in the relentless demands of daily operations, they find it challenging to step back and focus on the bigger picture—working *on* the business rather than *in* it.

Dr. Myron Tribus, a distinguished engineer and academic, served as the director of the Center for Advanced Engineering Study at the Massachusetts Institute of Technology (MIT). A pioneer in Total

Quality Management (TQM), he worked alongside industry leaders like W. Edwards Deming to advance quality practices globally. Myron Tribus, drawing on Deming's teachings, writes:

"The job of the manager has changed. People work *in* a system. The job of a manager is to work *on* the system, to improve it continuously with their help…working *in* the system is doing the daily work of the system…working *on* the system is improvement work."[2]

Helping clients work "on" the systems that comprise the business rather than constantly consumed "in" the day-to-day busyness of the business empowers them to achieve break-through transformations. Unburdened by the constant pull of daily tasks, Business Alignment Coaches (BACs) can provide an external perspective that encourages leaders to adopt a much-needed strategic improvement focus. By enabling this shift in focus, clients can accelerate their growth and progress while gaining greater clarity and peace of mind.

The Gravitational Pull of Daily Operations

The gravitational pull of day-to-day operations often keeps business owners "grounded," making it difficult to rise above and see the business from an elevated, more strategic, 30,000-foot view. This broader perspective, which enables you to "see the forest for the trees," is essential to developing a strategic focus. A strategic focus lets you see the bigger picture, "the whole forest," while a tactical focus centers on the individual trees and branches. Both perspectives are necessary for running a successful business and making informed decisions about allocating our time, attention, and money resources.

However, many owners often become mired in and consumed by the individual trees and leaves, losing sight of the whole forest. When owners adopt a broader, more strategic perspective of their business, they can also begin to see their business as part of a larger business ecosystem, unlocking opportunities for growth that may have been previously hidden to them.

Making Time for Strategic Reflection

To develop this strategic perspective, we've found that business owners need to break free from the daily grind by carving out dedicated time for reflection. Setting aside time daily and a larger block of time during the week for "What Matters Time" allows for reassessing priorities, optimizing resources, and ensuring that actions are aligned with long-term goals. This reflective thinking time is critical to making better decisions, leading to better outcomes.

As Peter Drucker says, *"Follow effective action with quiet reflection. From the reflection will come even more effective action."* [3]

Taking time for strategic reflection is key to maximizing productivity and long-term growth.

- What times during the day or week are most likely not to get disrupted so that we can devote ourselves to what matters—strategic reflection?

Unhelpful Generalizations Mistaken as Advice

Familiar sayings like "The definition of insanity is doing the same thing over and over again and expecting different results" or "If you find yourself in a hole, stop digging" oversimplify complex challenges. They may point to a general truth, but they rarely help you figure out what to do next.

These kinds of platitudes—trite, overused statements may feel satisfying in the moment but leave you without a real path forward.

That's where the 7P Business Alignment Model™ comes in. With the help of your Business Alignment Coaches (BACs), you can replace vague generalities with clear, practical solutions tailored to your situation. Each of the frameworks contained within the 7Ps comprising key dimensions of your business provides a series of questions that, when answered, can help clarify your thinking and enable you to make better decisions.

We all know that good decisions drive successful outcomes. Yet learning to make good decisions comes from experience, and, ironically, a lot of experience inevitably comes with making a lot of bad decisions.[4]

By having greater clarity, and developing our powers of discernment: the ability ot perceive, understand, and judge things clearly and wisely—especially when the situation is complex, subtle or emotionally charged— we can reduce the number of "bad" or sub-optimal decisions and produce better outcomes.

Discernment in Action: Making the Right Distinctions

Discernment is the ability to see what truly matters—and filter out what doesn't—so you can make better decisions with confidence. In business, this often means knowing which details are critical and which ones just create noise. Making the right distinctions is about matching the level of detail and focus to the needs of the situation. Distinguishing the appropriate level of detail in any given context allows business owners to make better decisions, prevent wasted time, energy and enable you to better focus on what matters most.

For example, in financial statements, business owners, investors, or financial analysts rarely need revenue figures presented down to the penny when dealing with millions of dollars. Excessive precision or granularity adds unnecessary complexity and level of detail to the analysis for it to be useful. However, in scenarios like auditing credit card transactions, distinctions down to the penny are essential for accuracy and compliance.

Another illustrative example of making distinctions comes from the Inuit people and their understanding of snow. Living in extreme climates, they rely on the ability to make nuanced distinctions when it comes to reading the weather and have over 20 words to describe different types of snow—such as *piqsipoq* (blowing snow), *akimak* (snowdrift that can serve as shelter), and *kanirsiq* (frosty snow) to navigate their environment and survive. In contrast, someone living in downtown Los Angeles has no need for such snow distinctions, as understanding the types of snow is irrelevant to their day-to-day life. Perhaps, instead, the ability to make distinctions related to traffic patterns or commute times would be far more valuable.

Examples of Making the Right Distinctions in a Business Environment

Here are a few practical examples of how making the right distinctions at the right level can lead to better decisions and outcomes in your business:

1. Employee Productivity

In a manufacturing business with limited resources, obsessing over whether a worker produces 99 or 100 units per day adds little value. Instead, focus on broader trends, like removing process bottlenecks that cause unnecessary delays or increasing employee efficiency as measured by % of revenues to identify areas for improvement. This bigger-picture approach allows business owners to optimize labor allocation and increase overall productivity without getting lost in minor details.

2. Marketing Budgets

For a small marketing firm, debating whether to spend an extra $50 on Facebook ads is less impactful than assessing which marketing channels drive the highest return on investment (ROI). Business owners can make smarter decisions about resource allocation by focusing on strategic distinctions such as comparing the effectiveness of content marketing versus pay-per-click ads.

3. Customer Service Processes

For a service-based business, it's important to distinguish between customer satisfaction and customer loyalty. While satisfaction scores measure short-term experiences, customer loyalty drives repeat business and long-term revenue. Shifting your focus from small tactical improvements in satisfaction to strategic efforts that drive loyalty, such as enhancing follow-up processes or offering loyalty rewards, can have a much larger impact on your bottom line.

Improve Focus and Clarity with the 7P Business Alignment Model

The 7P Business Alignment Model™ (BAM) is designed to guide you in making the right distinctions within the context of your business. Whether it's optimizing resource allocation or identifying opportunities for long-term strategic growth, the structured 7P frameworks can help you better focus on what truly matters.

By breaking down your business into its core dimensions—**Purpose, Prioritization, People, Pipeline, Product/Service, Process, and Profit**—the 7P BAM empowers you to ask the **right questions** to gain greater clarity and help navigate the complexities of your business.

Adopting a Learner Mindset

As we've seen, making the right distinctions is essential for identifying what truly matters in your business. But recognizing these distinctions alone is not enough. To create meaningful progress, one must let go of old habits and thinking patterns that may hinder progress and/or adopt new ones that help us grow. Yet, how can we change habitual ways of thinking and learn to make more nuanced distinctions that lead to better outcomes? The answer lies in adopting a learner mindset—a mindset grounded in humble curiosity and a willingness to embrace learning as a continuous, iterative process.[5]

A learner mindset acknowledges that business is always a work in progress. It requires ongoing course corrections and refinement, much like the scientific method, where hypotheses are developed, tested, and adjusted based on evidence. This learner mindset and evidence based approach can be cultivated with the right culture that encourages experimentation, learning, and growth rather than rigid adherence to outdated habits or assumptions.

Making Adjustments: From Tweaks to Transformations

For some, achieving better results may only require a few thoughtful tweaks to existing practices. For others, it might demand a more significant intervention—perhaps a significant reordering of priorities, a reallocation of resources, or a fundamental shift in how you focus your time and energy. The willingness to approach these challenges with a spirit of learning and experimentation distinguishes those who remain stagnant from those who are able to transform themselves and their organizations.

Turning Learning into Action

Adopting a learner mindset is a critical step toward transformation, but the real challenge lies in turning this mindset into consistent action. Change—whether it requires small tweaks or a complete realignment—can feel overwhelming when faced alone. Without the right support, it's easy to lose momentum, become uncertain, or fall back into old patterns.

This is where the journey doesn't have to be taken alone, and having the right support as needed can make all the difference.

The Role of Your Business Alignment Coach

A Business Alignment Coach can serve as your:

- **Critical thinking partner**: Helping you ask better questions, explore options, and uncover blind spots and surface insights that might otherwise be missed.

- **Sounding board**: Providing a space to bounce ideas around, share concerns, and even vent frustrations when needed.

- **Guide and accountability partner**: Supporting you in making decisions, staying on course, and navigating challenges as they arise.

By partnering with a BAC, you can accelerate your progress, build confidence in the changes you're making, and remain aligned with what matters most while unlocking greater potential and fulfillment for yourself and your organization.

Achieving Success Through Alignment and Balance: The 7Ps Framework

As you work through the challenges and obstacles discussed in this chapter, we believe achieving success requires a holistic approach that ensures the critical dimensions of your business are attended to and work together for the overall good of the enterprise.

Each of the 7Ps represents critical dimensions like the oars of your business that need to work together for success, similar to how the vital organs in a human body work holistically for the greater health of the body.

Purpose is the foundational "P," guiding the overall direction of the business, while the other 6Ps, Prioritization, People, Pipeline, Product, Process, and Profit, serve as the core operational elements that need to work together for lasting success.

It's also been said that operating a successful business or any successful endeavor is not unlike cooking a delicious meal. It would help if you had the right mixture and balance of ingredients—too much of one or too little of another can ruin the dish. In other words, you can have the perfect meal ruined by pouring a cup of salt over it.

Similarly, all 7Ps must be properly aligned for optimal business health and achieving your desired outcomes. Pouring too much attention into one "P" at the expense of another, like focusing too heavily on sales or rowing the pipeline oar while ignoring the profit one, can compromise the long-term overall success of the business.

Reflection Question:

- Which of the 7Ps might I be overemphasizing or neglecting?
- How can I create a more harmonious balance across these dimensions to ensure my business operates at its fullest potential?

Achieving alignment across the 7Ps isn't just about solving immediate problems. It's also about creating a unified, well-rounded business capable of sustained success while aligned with your purpose and what matters most.

Key Takeaways Chapter 34: Overcoming Implementation Challenges

1. **Overcoming Inertia**: Recognize the organizational inertia and habitual ways of doing things that hinder strategic thinking and actively work to address them.

2. **Reflective Thinking**: Set aside time daily and weekly for **What Matters Time** to engage in reflective thinking, which allows for more effective strategic decision-making and alignment with long-term goals.

3. **Right Distinctions for Success**: Focus on making the right distinctions in your business so you can effectively allocate

resources, improve customer retention, or optimize processes. Not every detail matters equally but learning to focus on the right ones can make a meaningful difference.

4. **Learner Mindset**: Adopting a learner mindset with humble curiosity is essential for continuous growth and successful transformation. Be open to experimentation, learning, and ongoing improvement.

5. **Holistic Approach:** Use the 7P Business Alignment Model™ to align and balance each of the seven critical dimensions: Purpose, Prioritization, People, Pipeline, Product-Service, Process, and Profit to achieve optimal success and organizational health.

Reflection Questions Chapter 34: Overcoming Implementation Challenges

1. **Where in my week can I block a small, protected window for "What Matters Time" that's least likely to get interrupted?**

   o What's one way you could start protecting time for strategic reflection each week?

2. **What's one simple boundary I can set this week to protect even 20–30 minutes of strategic reflection?**

3. **Are your resources — time, people, and money — directed toward high-impact areas that align with your core purpose and goals?**

   o What adjustments could improve how you allocate resources to better focus on what matters?

4. **What habitual ways of doing things are holding your business back from necessary change?**

   o What's one old pattern or process you need to challenge or rethink to move forward?

5. **How can you adopt more of a learner mindset to embrace change and growth?**

   o What's one area of your business where trying, failing, and learning could lead to real improvements?

6. **Which idea in this chapter hit closest to home right now—and why?**

7. **What are my top 1-2 takeaways from this chapter?**

    o   What is one specific action I can take to start overcoming these obstacles and move closer to my goals?

CHAPTER 35

RIGHT-SIZING THE SUPPORT YOU NEED

"Plans are only good intentions unless they
immediately degenerate into hard work."[1]
– Peter Drucker, The Effective Executive

The Importance of Defining Scope

Amazon founder Jeff Bezos explains another critical obstacle to successful implementation: failing to adequately define and understand the "scope" of what is required. In project management terms, "scope" describes a project's detailed objectives, deliverables, tasks, and boundaries, along with the time and effort required to complete it.[2] This chapter illustrates what we can learn and how we can benefit from his insights on why properly defining scope is so important. And we can gain valuable insights into the key factors that contributed to the success and growth of one of the most valuable companies in the world, Amazon.

In a letter to shareholders, Bezos explained that properly defining scope first requires defining what a "good" result looks like. As Bezos points out, knowing what good looks like or having high standards is "domain-specific" and not universal. He explains, "I believe high standards are domain-specific and that you have to learn high standards separately in every arena of interest. When I started Amazon, I had high standards on inventing, on customer care, and (thankfully) on hiring. But I didn't have high standards on operational processes: how to keep fixed problems fixed, how to eliminate defects at the root, how to inspect processes, and much more. I had to learn and develop high standards on all of that (my colleagues were my tutors)."[3]

Recognizing Limitations and Seeking Guidance

Bezos also points out the necessity of being open, humble, and acknowledging one's limitations and blind spots: "Understanding this point is important because it keeps you humble. You can consider yourself a person of high standards in general and still have debilitating blind spots. There can be whole arenas of endeavor where you may not even know that your standards are low or non-existent and certainly not world-class. It's critical to be open to that likelihood."[4] Recognizing both strengths and limitations with humility opens the door for learning and growth. This mindset encourages business owners to seek guidance and expertise where needed, enabling them to overcome challenges more effectively. As Bezos illustrates, even highly capable individuals and organizations must embrace a willingness to learn and develop high standards in areas where they may initially lack expertise.

He tells a story about a friend who tried to learn how to do a proper handstand. She hired a coach with "handstand domain expertise" who understood the scope of executing a proper handstand. The coach pointed out, "Most people think that if they work hard, they should be able to master a handstand in about two weeks. The reality is that it takes about six months of daily practice. If you think you should be able to do it in two weeks, you're just going to end up quitting." Bezos goes on to say, "Unrealistic beliefs on scope—often hidden and undiscussed—kill high standards. To achieve high standards yourself or as part of a team, you need to form and proactively communicate realistic beliefs about how hard something is going to be—something this coach understood well."[5]

Similarly, our 7P Business Alignment Coaches (BACs) can help identify business owner blind spots and fill in gaps while recognizing high standards in critical domains where the owner may not be as knowledgeable. Our BACs serve as our clients' "handstand coaches" to guide them in successfully executing and implementing the 7P BAM to achieve their desired outcomes.

Reflection Question: What are some areas of my business where I might have blind spots or unknowingly operate below high standards and lack the expertise needed to excel?

Applying Scope at Amazon

Jeff Bezos provides a compelling example of how defining the right scope drives results at Amazon. When presenting ideas, he mandates the use of narratively structured memos, often spanning up to six pages, instead of traditional PowerPoint slide decks. These memos are designed to engage the reader more deeply by framing the information as a coherent narrative rather than a series of bullet points. This approach allows for a richer context, better background understanding, and a logical sequence of ideas. He describes the process:

> "We silently read one at the beginning of each meeting in a kind of 'study hall.' Not surprisingly, the quality of these memos varies widely. Some have the clarity of angels singing. They are brilliant and thoughtful and set up the meeting for high-quality discussion. Sometimes, they come in at the other end of the spectrum."[6] (*2017 Letter to Shareholders*, Amazon.com, Inc.)

Bezos emphasizes that the issue with subpar memos is not usually a lack of high standards but a misunderstanding of scope. Writers often underestimate the time and effort required to craft a compelling memo, assuming it can be completed in one or two days—or even a few hours. In reality, as Bezos explains, crafting an excellent memo can take a week or more.

"The great memos are written and rewritten, shared with colleagues who are asked to improve the work, set aside for a couple of days, and then edited again with a fresh mind. They simply can't be done in a day or two," Bezos says. "The key point here is that you can improve results through the simple act of teaching scope—that a great memo probably should take a week or more."[7]

This insight highlights the importance of setting realistic expectations. Understanding the time and effort required for a task makes individuals less likely to become frustrated or discouraged when immediate results aren't forthcoming. Knowing that a well-crafted memo might take a week helps sustain motivation and persistence, reducing the likelihood of abandoning the task prematurely.

In addition to recognizing high standards and appropriate timelines, Bezos also points out the value of delegation and teamwork. He notes that in a team setting, the leader doesn't necessarily have to be the one writing the memo. Much like a football coach doesn't need to throw a perfect pass or a film director doesn't need to act, leaders "need to recognize high standards for those things and teach realistic expectations on scope."[8]

Leveraging SME (Subject Matter Expertise)

Similarly to Bezos, no single business owner can be expected to have expertise in all domains of running a successful business enterprise, especially one that scales beyond just the owner and a few employees. As businesses grow, successful owners surround themselves with people who have expertise and high standards in areas where they are weak or lacking knowledge.

This may involve enlisting the help of SMEs, subject matter experts with domain-specific high standards, and then partnering with this expertise on an as-needed or part-time basis. The SMEs can provide the necessary knowledge and expertise to fill in gaps or blind spots in the business without the owner having to hire them full-time.

Using a sports team analogy, when an SMB owner taps into fractional executive level support and execution, it's like having access to specialized players—such as a left fielder, catcher, or pitcher—on game day instead of the owner or their staff scrambling to cover multiple positions on their own. By ensuring their "baseball team" is adequately fielded, they can better address any critical gaps or blind spots and position their business team to "win."

Peter Drucker emphasizes, "The task of leadership is to create an alignment of strengths so strong that it makes the system's weaknesses irrelevant."[9]

Implementing the 7P BAM empowers owners of SMBs with access to a team of domain-specific SMEs on a fractional basis: Chief People Officer (CPO), Chief Marketing Officer (CMO), Chief Operations

Officer (COO) HR Generalist, Recruiter, Controller and Alignment Coach.

Instead of adding several hundreds of thousands of dollars in additional payroll annually, clients gain high-value contributions of multiple executives and specialists who are integrated with your management team for a cost comparable to a part-time or even single employee, depending on the needs and size of your organization.

Guiding an Effective Change Process: The Role of Your Business Alignment Coach

Achieving meaningful progress, whether in health, fitness, or business, requires more than just knowledge; it requires consistent execution. For example, many people desire to improve their health, lose weight, and maintain a fit physique. Yet, despite knowing what to do to lose weight— eat less and move more—few act on that knowledge. According to the Centers for Disease Control and Prevention (CDC), 2 of 5 adults in the United States have obesity.[10] This disconnect could indicate that the challenge is often not a lack of knowledge of what to do but consistently applying what we know we should do.

This same challenge applies to business owners. Many know more than they can effectively act on compared to what they know they should do. It's why the adage *ideas are a dime a dozen* is so often referred to since success isn't about just good ideas; it's about translating those ideas into tangible results.

As Peter Drucker is often credited with saying, *"Don't tell me you had a good meeting with me, tell me what you're going to do differently on Monday."* [11] It's this focus on action and what happens after the meeting or the brainstorming session that drives progress. For business owners, bridging this gap between knowing and doing is where our **Business Alignment Coach** can play an important role, providing guidance, accountability, and the tools needed to turn ideas into meaningful results.

The Role of Business Alignment Coaches: Integrating Expertise for Success

The role of the 7P Business Alignment Coaches (BACs) is multifaceted, bridging the gap between strategy and execution. Much like a football coach or film director, BACs can recognize high standards in their area of expertise while also helping clients set realistic expectations for the scope of a successful 7P Business Alignment Model™ (BAM) implementation. However, their value can extend beyond just guidance and coaching—they also serve as consultants and implementers. In other words, our BACs can also perform some aspects of the execution—tackling, blocking, throwing, and catching—essential to the functioning of your business based on their respective domain-specific expertise within the 7P BAM.

BACs can help you tackle real-world challenges while alleviating some of the burdens of the owner and their current staff. In reference to the earlier rowboat metaphor, our BACs can also take on some of the "rowing" duties as needed for actual implementation. As coaches, they can ensure that your team understands the amount of effort "rowing" and aligning required to achieve your desired outcomes. The following explains further the unique role of our Business Alignment Coaches, who combine the traits and capabilities of consultant, coach, and advisor while also explaining the primary differences between the three functions.

Understanding the difference between Coaching, Consulting, and Advising

To fully appreciate the unique value BACs provide, it's essential to understand the distinctions between coaching, consulting, and advising. These three approaches address different needs and situations, and understanding the unique strengths of coaching, consulting, and advising helps business owners determine the right type of support or combination of support for their specific needs. Ed Reece, Chairman of ReeceCorp, provides a helpful way to distinguish between coaching, consulting, and advising, "Consulting leads from the front, coaching leads from behind, and advising walks side by side with the client"[12].

- Coaching: Facilitates growth and reflection (leads from behind).

- Consulting: Provides expertise and solutions (leads from the front).

- Advising: Offers strategic guidance (walks side by side).

Coaching: Facilitating Insight and Growth

Coaching fosters personal and professional development through facilitation, reflection, and accountability. Coaches empower clients by asking insightful questions, enabling them to generate their own solutions and clarify their thinking. Coaches lead from behind, guiding clients to uncover their own insights and solutions rather than prescribing actions.

Consulting: Delivering Expertise and Solutions

Consulting provides Subject Matter Experts (SMEs) who deliver real-world solutions for specific business problems. Consultants focus on achieving tangible outcomes through their expertise, offering project-based solutions and hands-on implementation. In contrast to coaching, consulting typically involves an SME with expertise in a particular domain who recognizes high standards and knows what it takes to achieve them. Like the handstand coach, they can teach you how to execute a "perfect handstand" versus an executive coach or life coach who may not have the specific technical expertise but can hold you accountable, encourage, and even serve as your accountability-thinking partner.

For example, if you are in a manufacturing business and need help getting ISO 9001 certified, a knowledgeable and experienced consultant who is an SME in this area can assist with the process and documentation required to be certified. If you need to implement Enterprise Resource Planning (ERP) software or set up a new accounting system software, you may also outsource the expertise of a consultant with specialized software knowledge.

The level of expertise you bring in often depends on the complexity and scope of your needs. For highly technical or specialized challenges, this might mean temporarily engaging a fractional CFO to strengthen financial oversight, a fractional CMO to sharpen branding and marketing strategy, or even a digital agency to execute a targeted SEO campaign. In cases involving labor law or employee relations, it could mean turning to a labor attorney or HR generalist to provide the right guidance at the right time.

If you need more qualified candidates to fill open positions, you might hire an outside recruiter or temp agency or bring on a fractional CPO (Chief People Officer) who serves as an extension of your management team and handles the day-to-day posting, sourcing, resume screening, and pre-interviewing of candidates.

Advising: Strategic Guidance and Perspective

If coaching "leads from behind and consulting leads from the front," then advising is akin to "walking side by side" with the client. Advising combines elements of coaching and consulting but emphasizes strategic insight. Advisors offer practical recommendations based on their experience and area of expertise while maintaining a broader focus than consultants. Unlike coaching, advising involves direct input, and unlike consulting, it's less implementation focused. They serve as sounding boards for critical decisions, offering practical recommendations based on their expertise without being directly involved in execution.

Summary of Key Differences

	Coaching	Consulting	Advising
Primary Role	Facilitator, accountability partner	SME solution provider, problem-solver	Strategic guide, sounding board
Focus	Personal and professional growth	Targeted solutions for business problems	Strategic decisions and long-term planning
Engagement Type	Long-term, ongoing sessions	Project-based, short to medium-term	Flexible, often ongoing
Delivery	Questions and facilitation	Recommendations and implementation	Recommendations and insight
Outcomes	Improved skills, clarity, and leadership	Tangible results or completed projects	Informed decisions and strategic clarity

The Unique Power of Business Alignment Coaches: Blending Strategy, Support and Execution.

What makes the 7P Business Alignment Coaches truly unique is their ability to integrate all three roles—consultant, coach, and advisor—depending on the moment and the needs of the business in both a holistic and integrative manner. During strategic planning sessions, they may walk beside you as an advisor, helping clarify direction and ensure alignment. When your team hits execution challenges, they may step in like a consultant, offering hands-on support or subject matter expertise in areas like recruiting, operations, or marketing. At other times, they'll serve as a coach—asking the right questions to help you lead with more clarity, confidence, and purpose.

When we combine the integrative and holistic approach of the 7P Business Alignment Model™ and fractional executive-level leadership and execution, this blended approach becomes more than just helpful—it becomes a scalable, flexible, and game-changing solution for SMB owners who are serious about unlocking more of their potential and meaningful growth without carrying the burden alone. It's not one-size-fits-all—it's adaptable, cost-effective and designed specifically for SMBs.

How Long Does Alignment Take?

A Realistic Look at the Journey

A common question we hear from clients is: What's a reasonable timeline for implementing the 7P Business Alignment Model™? The short answer: it's a marathon, not a sprint.

We often say this isn't a "learn to do a handstand in two weeks" kind of project. Lasting alignment takes time. While you may begin to see meaningful improvements within the first few months, building a fully integrated and sustainable 7P BAM foundation typically takes 12 to 18 months, depending on the urgency, level of effort, and resources you're able to commit.

Breaking Down the Time Commitment

We've designed the process to be manageable for busy business own-ers. Most clients participate in twice-monthly 7P implementation (ARAM) sessions, averaging about 1 hour each plus an additional 1hr per month Alignment Reset meetings. Over a year, that adds up to roughly 36 hours of focused alignment practice.

As a result of these sessions, owners will usually find time to focus an additional 3 hours or so per month strategically working on their business. This comes out to approximately 6 hours a month which is 1.5 hours on average per week and 72 hours annually.

To put that in perspective: 72 hours divided by a typical 2000 hour work year (we know most owners work many more hours per year) is a little more than 3% of total time spent—a small but high-leverage in-vestment that can yield transformative results for your business, your leadership, and your personal fulfillment.

Why Consistency Matters Most

The most successful business owners we work with realize progress and tangible results occur when they consistently engage with and practice their strategic alignment efforts, little by little, week by week. As this happens, it encourages them to dedicate even more time work-ing *on* their business rather than being consumed *in* the business and chaos of day-to-day operations.

Sustainable change and success require steady, focused effort over time and allocating even a small portion of your weekly time to working "on" the business, can achieve meaningful results leading to greater fulfillment, profitability, and alignment with your purpose.

Reflection Question

- How can you consistently dedicate 1–2 hours each week to working on your business to ensure steady progress and long-term success?

Key Takeaways Chapter 35: Right-Sizing the Support You Need

1. The Knowing-Doing Gap

o   We all know that success is not just about having great ideas; it's about translating ideas into consistent action. Many business owners know what to do but may struggle with execution.

o   *Key Insight*: A Business Alignment Coach can help bridge the gap between knowledge and consistent action, ensuring ideas are turned into meaningful results.

2. **Defining Scope for Success**

o   Achieving high standards requires understanding and defining the scope of an endeavor—what "high standards" or good looks like and how much effort, time, and resources are required.

o   *Key Insight*: Working with your BAC, you can set clear, realistic expectations to sustain motivation and reduce frustration.

3. **Leveraging Subject Matter Expertise**

o   Business owners cannot be experts in all areas. Enlisting fractional SMEs, such as a fractional CFO, CMO, HR generalist, or CPO, helps fill critical knowledge gaps cost-effectively.

o   *Key Insight*: Like a sports team, businesses need the right players in the right positions to "win." A BAC helps ensure your team is equipped with domain-specific expertise to fill in the gaps as needed.

4. **Recognizing Blind Spots**

o   Business owners may have blind spots where their standards or understanding may be insufficient. A BAC acts as a coach to guide improvements efforts and to identify blind spots.

5. **Utilizing Coaching, Consulting, and Advising**

o   Different business challenges require different approaches:

   ▪   **Coaching**: Facilitates growth by helping owners find their own solutions.

- **Consulting**: Provides expert-driven solutions for specific challenges.
- **Advising**: Offers strategic guidance and perspective in a particular area of expertise.

  o *Key Insight*: BACs can utilize coaching, consulting, and advising to offer a multi-faceted approach that meets SMB owners' needs.

6. **Realistic Timelines for Change**

  o Implementing the 7P Business Alignment Model™ (BAM) is not a short-term fix; it's a process that typically takes 12 to 18 months to achieve sustainable, lasting results.

  o *Key Insight*: Allocating just 1–2 hours per week to "work on the business" can drive significant progress over time.

7. **Consistency and Incremental Progress**

  o Sustainable change requires consistent, incremental steps rather than sporadic bursts of effort.

  o *Key Insight*: A BAC helps clients pace themselves, course-correct, and develop consistency to achieve their desired outcomes.

Reflection Questions Chapter 35: Right-Sizing the Support You Need

1. **Have I clearly defined what success looks like for my business over the next 12–18 months—and what "good" actually means?**

  o Given my current resources and priorities, are my expectations for scope and timeline realistic—or do they need to be right-sized?

2. **In which 1–2 areas of my business would outside expertise (BAC or fractional SME) relieve the most pressure or unlock the most progress?**

    o Where might I be operating below "high standards" without realizing it—and who could help me see what I'm missing?

3. **Realistically, how many hours a week am I spending working on the business—not just in it?**

    o What's one practical way I can protect at least 1–2 hours a week for strategic work on the 7P BAM?

4. **Am I trying to do too much at once—or am I pacing myself to make steady, realistic progress?**

    o What would a sustainable weekly effort look like for me and my team—something we could keep doing for the next 12–18 months?

5. **Right now, what kind of support would help me most—coaching, consulting, advising, or a blend—and for which specific issue?**

    o How could a Business Alignment and Growth Advisor help you clarify your next steps, provide expertise, or hold you accountable?

6. **Which idea or story in this chapter felt most relevant to my business or leadership right now—and why?**

7. **What are your top 1-2 takeaways from this chapter for the next 6-12 months?**

CHAPTER 36

CHOOSING THE RIGHT SUPPORT

Good, Fast, Cheap: The Pick Two Principle

When making a purchase, an idea known as "Good, Fast, Cheap—Pick Two" refers to the trade-offs between choosing between the different sets of two of the three picks.

The principle that you can prioritize only two of three attributes—speed, cost, and quality—is a common tenet in project management, often referred to as the Project Management Triangle.[1] In practical terms, you can typically only get two at once: fast and cheap might sacrifice quality; cheap and good might take longer; fast and good usually costs more.

If someone claims to offer all three—fast, cheap, and high-quality—proceed with caution. It might sound appealing, but it often falls into the "too good to be true" category. The following are examples of different "Fast, Cheap, Good" trade-offs in the context of professional or technical service offerings:

Good and Fast (Not Cheap)

If you want something fast and good, it usually won't come "cheap." Good, high-quality services usually require highly skilled professionals, who typically charge higher fees and can complete your project faster and at a higher quality standard than those with less skill and experience. Additional costs may be incurred if they prioritize your project ahead of others to meet a tight deadline.

Example: Imagine you're a highly regarded aerospace machine shop with a specialized skill set, and Boeing needs a quick turnaround (fast) for a complex job. While your expertise and capabilities can produce "good" in the form of quality results, the expedited deadline and shortened time frames mean Boeing will pay a premium (not cheap).

Good and Cheap (Not Fast)

If you want something done well and at a low cost—cheap, it probably won't be "fast." Quality work at a lower price usually means the provider will fit your project into their schedule as time allows, which can lead to longer lead times.

Example: Consider the ubiquitous long lines and relatively longer wait times compared to other fast-food outlets at In and Out Burger. Since their burgers are of higher quality and taste while offered at a relatively low price (cheap), it's no surprise that many folks (including myself) will tolerate a much longer wait time (not fast) compared to other fast-food outlets.

Fast and Cheap (Not Good)

If you want something done quickly and cheaply, you run the higher risk that it will not be "good." In this scenario, the service provider may cut corners to save time and money, resulting in lower-quality outcomes that may or may not meet your needs or standards.

Example: Consider rushing a budget print shop to produce promotional materials overnight (fast). If the price is relatively low (cheap) and the turnaround is fast, the quality of the materials and printing might suffer (not good).

GOOD

FAST

CHEAP

More expensive

Will take time to deliver

They're dreaming

Not the best quality

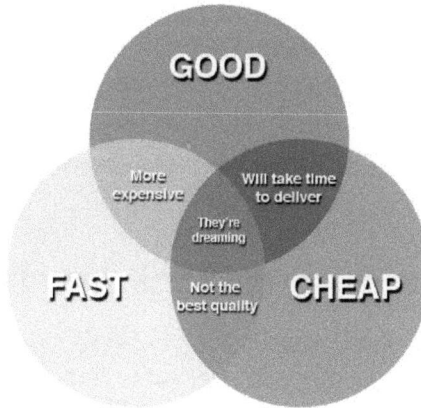

Applying the Pick Two Principle to Purpose Matters

At Purpose Matters, one of our core values is delivering high-quality services that make a meaningful impact. Consequently, our approach always includes "good" as one of the two that you can pick from the Fast, Cheap, and Good options:

- **Good and Fast, Not Cheap**: When clients require quick turn-around times, we allocate our best resources and expertise to meet the deadlines without compromising quality. This typically incurs higher costs when we prioritize your project and utilize talent who can perform the task in an expedited manner while still delivering a good work product.

- **Good and Cheap, Not Fast**: For clients with a smaller budget, we may have to go slower while still maintaining our standards for producing quality deliverables. Clients must be flexible about when we can accommodate them. This still enables us to deliver high-quality client results while effectively managing costs.

- **Cheap and Fast, Not Good—Not a Purpose Matters Option**: We do not offer services in the "cheap and fast" category, nor will we work with clients who expect or want this type of offering. Our success results from working with clients looking to invest in high-quality, ongoing, trusted advisor relationships. We avoid working with clients with a "quick fix" mentality and who are unwilling to invest the money and time required for a sustainable and enduring solution. Quick and "cheap" solutions can lead to incomplete and unsatisfactory results. This also presents a higher risk to the purchaser as it may cost them more in the long run if the job is not done right the first time. Remember, the adage of taking the time to measure twice so you only cut once applies here.

Good, Fast, and Cheap- Pick Two Summary:

Understanding the relative trade-offs between fast, cheap, and good helps set realistic expectations and ensures that the services mutually align with the client's values and ours. At Purpose Matters, we prioritize quality and ensure that every service we deliver is good while still delivering it in a cost-effective and timely manner. If you are primarily focused on fast and cheap solutions, we may not be the right fit for you. However, if you value a more long-term, ongoing, trusted advisor relationship that can deliver higher-quality and cost-effective solutions that are still timely for your needs, we are here to help.

The Advice Utility and Implementation Spectrum

But implementation quality doesn't just depend on speed and cost—it also depends on the kind of support you receive to help you execute. One of the most common frustrations among SMB owners and certainly one of my biggest pet peeves is the prevalence of vague generalizations disguised as advice. While they may sound insightful, these platitudes rarely meet business owners where they are, leaving them unsure how to move forward in a practical, sustainable way.

Effective advice must bridge the gap between broad principles and actionable, personalized guidance—offering clear steps that can actually be implemented to create meaningful results.

To illustrate how advice can evolve from unhelpful generalities to high-impact implementation, the following **Advice Utility Spectrum** uses a simple example from the world of health and fitness. Each level demonstrates how advice becomes more useful as it becomes more specific, relevant, and executable.

Advice Utility Spectrum	Description	Example	Impact
1. Wrong/Bad Advice	Providing recommendations that are the opposite of what is conducive to a healthy lifestyle.	Telling someone who is out of shape and sedentary to exercise less and eat more processed food.	Harmful and counterproductive, worsening the situation.
2. Poor Advice	Offering enabling behavior that suggests no changes are necessary.	Saying, "Keep doing what you're doing—you're fine; it will work itself out."	Negative impact as it ignores the need for improvement.
3. Typically Unhelpful Advice	Giving vague advice without actionable steps.	"Exercise more and eat less."	Lacks breakdown of necessary actions into manageable steps based on where they're at.
4. Could be Helpful Advice	Providing general advice applicable to a healthier lifestyle but lacking personalization.	"Go to the gym or walk more and eat less processed foods."	More specific but still lacks detailed guidance for implementation.
5. Helpful Advice with a Generic Plan for Implementation	Offering a generic workout and eating plan.	Following a diet or exercise plan found in a book or online.	It may not suit personal needs or circumstances and lack support.
6. Guided Advice with a Personalized Implementation Plan	Receiving guidance from an expert who tailors a plan to your needs.	Develop a plan with a fitness trainer or nutritionist, considering your unique situation.	Personalized and more effective but may lack ongoing support and accountability.
7. Guided Advice with a Personalized Plan and Accountability Support	Developing a plan with regular check-ins for accountability and adjustments.	Having a tailored plan with accountability support to track progress.	Increases consistency and the likelihood of implementation.
8. Guided Advice with a Personalized Plan, Accountability Support and Implementation	Comprehensive support with real-time corrections and hands-on implementation.	Acting as a personal trainer who is with you in the gym.	Accelerates progress and ensures consistency, greatly increasing the chances of a successful outcome.

Advice Utility Spectrum	Description	Example	Impact
9. Self-Sufficiency with Ongoing Support as Needed	Achieving self-sufficiency with optional high-level support.	Maintaining healthy habits but still engaging trainers as neeeded for ongoing improvement.	Ensures sustainability and continuous improvement growth.

Summary: The Advice Utility and Implementation Spectrum

The *Advice Utility and Implementation Spectrum* is one way to describe the quality and impact of guidance and support, ranging from harmful or vague advice to hands-on implementation that drives meaningful results. SMB owners often face challenges when navigating generic or impractical advice that fails to provide actionable steps or address their unique needs. At the upper levels of the spectrum, advice moves beyond generalizations to become highly personalized, incorporating customized plans, accountability support, and hands-on implementation.

Where Purpose Matters Fits on the Spectrum

Purpose Matters and the 7P Business Alignment Model™ engage clients at Levels 7 and 8, to help them reach Level 9 on the *Advice Utility and Implementation Spectrum*. Through the implementation of the 7P Business Alignment Model™, Purpose Matters goes beyond traditional consulting to include at the higher levels (8) some of the day-to-day tactical and strategic implementation provided by our fractional executive level support, e.g. CPO (Chief People Officer), CMO (Chief Marketing Officer), COO (Chief Operations/Organization Officer) expertise based on each client's unique circumstances and objectives.

Empowering Clients to Achieve Self-Sufficiency with Strategic Support

While Purpose Matters mostly lives on Levels 7-8, our ultimate goal is to empower our clients to reach Level 9, achieving self-sufficiency with ongoing support as needed. We aim to equip business owners with the tools, processes, and confidence to maintain their purpose-driven success independently. However, we always remain available as an integrated part of your management team to provide high-level executive support as needed to ensure continued purpose-driven growth and fulfillment.

Cultivating your Business to be Fruitful

Once you understand the difference between vague advice and actionable guidance, the next question is: how much support do you really need to grow? Just like tending a garden, the level of care and expertise you bring to your business determines how well it flourishes. The following are the different levels of attention and support for it to grow well.

- **Doing Nothing** → Like an untended garden, inefficiencies (weeds) take over and growth stalls.

- **DIY Approach** → You try to improve on your own, but without expertise, results may be uneven or slow.

- **DIY with Guidance** → With expert tips and advice, you begin to make smarter choices and see healthier growth.

- **Professional Support** → You bring in a landscape designer— someone who customizes, implements, and helps you maintain a high-functioning, fruitful ecosystem.

Just as a garden requires varying levels of care depending on your approach, so does your business. The 7P Business Alignment Model™ provides a structured approach to nurture and grow your business. Hiring a professional landscaper to help design, implement, and maintain it will not necessarily be "cheap." Yet, in return for money spent on professional expertise, you will save time while also producing a better outcome, getting more of both the "good and fast" compared to the DIY approach.

We've found that most of our clients in the latter stages of their business-career journey become increasingly impatient and do not have the luxury of time to waste. The costs of delays have a far greater impact on someone in their forties, fifties or sixties than someone in their twenties, thirties, with far more years ahead of them.

Whether you start on your own, seek guidance, or hire professional support, the key is to act now and continually nurture and invest in what matters most and ensure that investment pays off. Similar to a well-tended garden, a well-aligned and cared-for business will flourish and yield fruitful results.

Example: Fruitful ROI (return on investment)

Just as professional athletes surround themselves with dedicated trainers, nutritionists, and coaches to reach peak performance, successful business owners also invest in the right support to become the best version of themselves. Even the best athletes in the world rely on trainers and support to elevate their performance to world-class levels. For instance, LeBron James reportedly spends over $1 million annually on his health, fitness, and recovery to sustain his elite performance as an NBA player. While that figure may seem astronomical to most of us, it's essential to put it into perspective. LeBron's annual earnings of $100 million means he invests just 1% of his income in maintaining and improving his performance.[2]

If we translate that into more relatable terms for a working professional earning $100,000 annually, spending 1% of your income would amount to $1,000 a year—or about $83 per month—on tools, resources, or coaching to improve one's fitness or overall performance doesn't appear that unreasonable to invest in one's health and personal growth.

What If You Invested in Your Business Health?

Just like a 30-minute daily workout boosts your long-term health, what if you applied that same mindset to your business?

A small, consistent investment in your personal health can yield powerful results over time—and the same is true for your business. Dedicating even a modest percentage of your time and/or money to **Ongoing Performance Improvement (OPI)** can generate a substantial return on investment (ROI).

Example of investing1% of your revenues:

Let's assume a 1% investment in OPI enabled you and your team to better focus on what truly matters and that with each month, that investment helped you become just 1% more focused with each month. By the end of ten months, you would have cumulatively improved focus and productivity by 10% by the end of the year—with even a couple of months off.

Quick Math: 1% Investment and potential Productivity Return

Assumptions:

- Annual Revenue: $3,000,000
- Labor Costs: 25% of revenue → $750,000
- Current Profit Margin: 7% → $210,000
- OPI Investment: 1% of revenue → $30,000/year
- Annual Labor Productivity Gain: 10% through steady monthly improvements (1% per month, cumulative)

ROI Breakdown – Step-by-Step

OPI Investment
1% of $3,000,000 = $30,000

Labor Costs
25% of $3,000,000 = $750,000

Productivity Savings (10%)
10% of $750,000 = $75,000

Net Profit Gain
$75,000 (productivity savings) – $30,000 (OPI investment) = $45,000

Total New Profit
$210,000 (original profit) + $45,000 (net gain) = $255,000

Impact on Profit Margin

- **Profit Before OPI**: $210,000
- **Profit After OPI**: $255,000
- **Profit Margin Before**: 7%
- **Profit Margin After**: 8.5%
- **Profit Increase**: 21% increase in profitability

Beyond Labor Productivity—More ROI Ripple Effects

When you invest in OPI - Ongoing Performance Improvements, the pay off goes well beyond just productivity.

Quality & Reputation

- Fewer product returns and rework, lower warranty costs and h
- Stronger word-of-mouth and reviews

Right-Fit Customers

- Attract more customers who value your work and pay on time.
- Fewer that drain your time and margins

Innovation & Edge

- Free up capacity to create ideas for new offerings
- Stay ahead of competitors

Efficiency beyond labor

- Less waste, smoother operations
- Better vendor terms and inventory flow

Customer Experience

- Higher retention and word of mouth referrals
- Greater Customer Lifetime Value (CLV)

You & Your Team

- Less stress, absenteeism and turnover saving thousands in hiring costs
- More time for family, health, and personal fulfillment

The Power of Concentrated Focus

Scattered light doesn't do much—but when concentrated through a magnifying glass, it can burn through wood. The same is true in business. Even small, steady improvements—just 1% more focus each month—compound into meaningful results. By year's end, that added clarity and execution can significantly strengthen your bottom line.

Question: Where would concentrated focus create the greatest impact in your business over the next 90 days?

OPI and Continuous Improvement:

Just as elite athletes invest in coaches, tools, and recovery systems to stay at their best, high-performing businesses recognize the value of and take time to *work on* their business versus being consumed in the daily grind of just working *in* the business. As part of working "on" their business, they invest in **Ongoing Performance Improvement (OPI)**—making steady, focused progress one step at a time.

Even a small investment of 1% of your revenue into working on the business can make every line item on your P&L more productive and profitable. The key is working *on* your business, not just *in* it.

At the core of OPI is the mindset and practice of continuous improvement across all seven dimensions of your business: Purpose, Prioritization, People, Pipeline, Product, Process, and Profit. using the **7P Business Alignment Model**™:

Our clients have found that even a modest, intentional investment made in OPI helps align these areas more effectively—leading to greater clarity, focus, productivity, and meaningful results while promoting a greater sense of fulfillment with less burnout.

What does purposeful improvement look like for you right now—and where would you most like to see meaningful progress in the next 90 days?

Key Takeaways Chapter 36: Choosing the Right Support

1. The Reality of Trade-Offs: Fast, Cheap, Good – Pick Two

In business, you typically cannot optimize for speed, cost, and quality simultaneously—you must choose two.

At **Purpose Matters, we always prioritize "Good"**:

- o **Good and Fast (Not Cheap):** We deliver high-quality, timely results with prioritized resources—at a reasonable (not cheap) investment.

- o **Good and Cheap (Not Fast):** We maintain our high standards while still delivering cost-effective solutions, though implementation timelines may be longer.

- o **Fast and Cheap (Not Good): We don't offer this.** Cutting corners leads to lower-quality results and costly mistakes.

If you're serious about building a profitable, purpose-driven business, a "quick fix" approach will not get you there. Instead you value the investment of a trusted advisor relationship to ensure lasting impact.

FOCUS ON WHAT MATTERS

2. The Levels of Support: Why Most SMB Owners Struggle Without the Right Help

Many business owners **waste time and money** on generic advice that doesn't address their unique challenges.

The Advice Utility and Implementation Spectrum shows that the best results usually occur when the following elements exist:

o   Guided, customized planning

o   Ongoing coaching and accountability

o   Hands-on implementation with expert support

Purpose Matters operates at Level 8+, where we don't just give advice—we help implement real solutions tailored to your business.

If you're tired of vague advice that doesn't translate into action, working with Purpose Matters gives you the structure, clarity, and expert support to execute, improve, and scale sustainably.

3. Growing Your Business is Like Growing a Garden—Neglect It, and Weeds Take Over

Businesses, like gardens, require ongoing care.

o   **Stage 1 – Doing Nothing:** Leads to inefficiency, stagnation, and lost opportunities.

o   **Stage 2 – Doing It Yourself (DIY):** Can work but is slow, inefficient, and often frustrating.

o   **Stage 3 – DIY with Guidance:** Better, but still requires trial and error to execute properly.

o   **Stage 4 – Professional Design & Implementation: The fastest and most effective path to a thriving and sustainable business.**

Just like professional landscapers ensure a garden flourishes, Purpose Matters helps businesses implement the 7P BAM framework for lasting growth, alignment, and profitability.

4. Investing in Ongoing "P" Improvement (OPI) Delivers ROI

Would you invest 1% of your revenue to increase your profit by 20-30%?

A small investment in Ongoing Performance Improvement (OPI) can significantly enhance productivity, efficiency, and profitability.

Example:

o   Investing 1% of revenue into strategic improvements can yield a 2:1 ROI or higher.

o   A 10% increase in labor productivity alone could raise net profit margins by 20% or more.

Like elite athletes invest in world-class trainers, top SMB owners invest in OPI (Ongoing "P" Improvement) to create meaningful growth and greater fulfillment.

5. The 7P Business Alignment Model™: Your Roadmap for Purpose-Driven Results

To build a scalable, profitable, and fulfilling business, you need alignment across all 7Ps:

Purpose: Keep your mission central in every decision.

Prioritization: Focus on what moves the needle.

People: Attract, align, and retain the right-fit employees.

Pipeline: Optimize sales and marketing to attract right-fit customers.

Product: Continuously improve offerings for maximum value.

Process: Streamline operations for efficiency and scalability.

Profit: Align profit with purpose-driven growth.

6. The Cost of Delaying Action — Time Is Your Most Valuable Asset

Time is often seen as a resource more precious than money—once it's gone, you can't earn it back.

The cost of delay and inefficiency doesn't just add up—it compounds, making it harder to hit your long-term goals the longer you wait.

For SMB owners in their 40s, 50s, and 60s, the margin for error shrinks. There's simply less time to recover from costly missteps or missed opportunities.

That's why investing in expert guidance now doesn't just save money—it saves years of wasted effort, frustration, and unrealized potential.

Every month you delay purpose-driven alignment is a month you reinforce inefficiencies, prolong stress, and leave profits on the table.

The real question isn't "Can I afford to do this?" It's: How much longer can you afford not to?

Reflection Questions Chapter 36: Choosing the Right Support

1. When you think about implementing the **7P Business Alignment Model**™ to achieve meaningful business outcomes, do you lean more toward the "Good and Fast" or "Good and Cheap" approach— and why?

   How Do You Currently Invest in Business Growth and Alignment?

   o Am I investing enough of my time or revenue into improving performance and alignment—or have I treated this as optional?

2. **Where Could Incremental Improvements Yield the Biggest Returns?**

- o If you could improve just one of the 7Ps by at least 10% over the next year, which area would make the biggest impact —and why?

- o How much additional revenue or profitability could that improvement generate?

3. **Are you treating your business like a carefully tended garden?**

   - o Where is my business well-tended—and where might things be "growing wild" or going unattended?
   - o Who could walk alongside me to help bring clearer priorities, sharper insight, and more peace of mind as I grow?

4. **What's the Real Cost of Doing Nothing?**

   - o If nothing changes, where is my business realistically heading over the next 1–3 years—and is that acceptable to me?

Final Thoughts: Investing in What Truly Matters

Building a successful business isn't about quick fixes or one-size-fits-all solutions. It's about making intentional shifts that create lasting growth, clarity, and fulfillment. The 7P Business Alignment Model™ offers a holistic approach—seeing your business as a whole system—and an integrative approach—bringing its parts into alignment as one system. Together, they create a path for aligning your business with its deeper purpose, while also driving profitability, sustainability, and greater peace of mind.

Start small. Stay consistent. Start today

Every owner's journey is different. Your pace, priorities, and timing may not look like anyone else's—and that's okay. But the longer you wait to begin, the harder it usually becomes to start. A well-known Chinese proverb advises us: *The best time to plant a tree was twenty years ago. The second best time is today.*

It's a reminder that action today matters more than regret over missed opportunities. Even if you didn't start earlier, it's never too late to take that first step—no matter how small—and begin reaping the benefits.

Clarity, alignment, and continuous improvement form the foundation of your thriving, purpose-driven business. Whether you take the first steps on your own or seek structured support to accelerate the process, the most important thing is to begin—and to keep going.

When you approach this journey with a learner's mindset—grounded in curiosity, humility, and openness—you position yourself for the kind of meaningful growth and deeper fulfillment that can also create an enduring legacy that impacts future generations.

A fitting close for our purpose-driven leaders is another tree planting analogy drawn from a Greek proverb: *A society grows great when old men (and women) plant trees whose shade they know they shall never sit in.*

May your work plant trees that shape a better world and serve the greater good for generations to come.

APPENDIX

Accelerate Learning and Engagement with the Alternating Reading Aloud Method (ARAM)

At Purpose Matters, we're committed to helping you apply the 7P Business Alignment Model™ in ways that lead to real results without wasted effort. One of the most effective tools we use to deepen engagement and accelerate learning is the Alternating Reading Aloud Method (ARAM).

ARAM involves you, and/or fellow participant along with your Business Alignment Coach taking turns reading from *Focus on What Matters* or related handout in front of you for note-taking and highlighting. Read aloud as much or as little as you like, then say "pass" to switch readers. This method transforms passive reading into active engagement, helping you reflect deeper, retain more, and apply insights faster.

Why ARAM Works

1. Boosts Participation and Focus

Alternating reading keeps both parties engaged and equally invested. It encourages shared attention and accountability, which keeps the conversation moving forward with greater energy and clarity.

2. Improves Comprehension

Reading aloud slows the pace, making it easier to absorb complex ideas and consider how they apply. Slowing down creates space for reflection and understanding, rather than rushing through the material.

3. Sparks Meaningful Dialogue

Reading together also creates natural moments to pause, ask questions, and explore relevance in real time—turning abstract frameworks into practical application. (I recall a time when..or I can see how this applies to my business in this way...)

4. Increases Retention

When you read aloud, your brain engages in what researchers call the "production effect"—you're more likely to remember what you've spoken. It's especially powerful for auditory learners.

5. Builds a Collaborative Learning Experience

Instead of one person teaching and the other just listening, ARAM creates a conversational, back-and-forth learning rhythm. It becomes a shared exploration rather than a one-way download.

6. Breaks Down Complex Ideas

Rather than overwhelming you with information, ARAM allows concepts to be tackled in smaller, digestible parts—one paragraph or page at a time—making it easier to grasp and retain.

7. Encourages Immediate Application

Strategic pauses offer the perfect space to connect your reading to your business and how you can apply it.

8. Supports All Learning Styles

ARAM blends auditory (hearing it), visual (seeing it), and kinesthetic (speaking it, writing it) learning. That multi-sensory approach reinforces understanding and keeps the material engaging.

ARAM Key Takeaways

The Alternating Reading Aloud Method creates a more engaging, interactive, and effective learning experience. It turns complex business frameworks into bite-sized learning moments. With real-time conversation, improved comprehension, and stronger retention, ARAM helps clients move from insight to action—faster and with greater confidence and clarity.

ARAM works because **structured, repeated, facilitated learning rewires how you think** and shapes how you act. It builds new habits through reinforcement, connects insights directly to your business, and helps you make better decisions resulting in better outcomes.

ARAM Reflection Questions

1. Learning Preferences

Which methods help you learn best—reading, listening, doing, or a mix of all three?

2. Preparation and Review

Would you prefer to look over the materials before your Alignment session, or review them afterward? —or receive them afterward?

3. Application to Your Business

What's one challenge in your business right now where you'd like ARAM to help you make better decisions and get different results?

The PRPAH Framework.

Pause → Reflect → Prioritize → Act → Habit

A five-step practice for slowing down, focusing on what matters most, and following through.

The **PRPAH Framework** is a structured alignment practice used within the **Purpose Matters Alignment Coaching** methodology. It helps us shift from reacting to re-aligning —moving from scattered busyness to purposeful focus. Whether applied on your own, with your leadership team, or in coaching sessions, PRPAH creates the reflective space needed for questions to surface, and thoughtful adjustments to take place. This intentional space allows insights to emerge, reframing to occur, and focus to return to what matters most.

The Five Steps

- Pause – Create space before responding. Use mindful breathing, a short clearing exercise, or simply notice what's top of mind—your thoughts, emotions, and surroundings. The pause interrupts autopilot and opens room for awareness.

- Reflect (Look Back to Learn) – Review what has happened, how it felt, and what you've learned. Reflection helps identify patterns, reveal insights, and reframe experiences in ways that can improve decision making in the future.

- Prioritize (Look Forward to Choose) – Decide what matters most right now. Out of all possible options, focus on the one or two actions that will move the needle. Prioritization converts awareness into direction.

• Act – Translate clarity into concrete steps. Define one specific action — or the next indicated step — you will take and commit to a timeline.

• Habit – Repeat meaningful actions until they stick. Reinforce with check-ins, team accountability, and begin with consistent small steps that turn into sustainable habits and routines.

PRPAH is most often used during Alignment Coaching sessions, but it's just as valuable any time you feel stuck, overwhelmed, or reactive. Take a few minutes to move through the five steps— inividually or as a team—to re-center on what truly matters.

Pause. Breathe. Align.

At the beginning of our 7P Alignment sessions, we like to start with a short mindful breathing exercise. It helps us slow down, clear our minds, and focus—starting with our breath.

Sit comfortably and place your cupped hands on your lap. Let your spine be upright but relaxed. Imagine a gentle string pulling upward from the top of your head, lengthening your posture.

Gently rest your tongue on the roof of your mouth. Tuck your chin just slightly to relax your neck. You can close your eyes and let your shoulders drop—soften them if they're holding tension. Now, just begin to notice your breath. No need to change it yet—just observe it. As thoughts come up, that's normal. Acknowledge them and gently bring your attention back to the next inhale and exhale, allowing your breathing to come from your diaphragm (belly), instead of your chest.

You can also try the following breathing pattern. When you're ready, begin a slow inhale through your nose for 4 seconds, pause, and then exhale gently through your mouth for 6 seconds. Let's stay with this rhythm for the next few minutes—giving ourselves permission to pause, set everything else aside, and be fully present.

When you're ready slowly open your eyes and bring your attention to the present moment.

Overcoming Organizational Inertia

Making change possible with those who are ready and seeking.

Inertia refers to the tendency to stick with the status quo or resist change—even when change might be beneficial.

- It can show up as habitual routines, outdated systems, or mental resistance to new ideas.

- In business, inertia often slows down innovation or transformation, as people or organizations prefer the comfort of what's familiar.

Dr Myron Tribus learned about this problem of inertia in the mid-1940s, and his insights may give us much-needed perspective to properly set expectations when attempting to effect change.

Irving Langmuir (1881-1957) was awarded a Nobel Prize in Chemistry in 1932. During his life, he created a long string of diverse inventions in the fields of physics and chemistry.

In 1944 Myron became interested in Langmuir's work on cloud seeding—precipitating changes in structures within clouds, with the possibility of making rain.

When Myron failed in his attempt to attract the interest of the US military in Langmuir's work, Langmuir told Myron:

> *The hardest thing in the world to sell is a new good idea.*
> *If it is new, people will not understand it.*
> *If it is good, they will feel they must act on it.*
> *But, if they are to act on it, they will have to learn, and*
> *they will have to change their ways.*
> *And they simply don't want to do that.*

Myron went on to explain: *You present people with a new idea, and their first reaction is, 'This will change things, and I am comfortable with what exists'*[1]

At Purpose Matters, we work with clients who are not "comfortable" with what exists and willing to engage with the tools, methods and resources that can facilitate the changes and transformation they are looking to achieve.

7P Business Alignment Scorecard

The Purpose Matters 7P Business Alignment Model Scorecard provides a preliminary assessment and alignment check across the 7Ps. These 28 Likert scale statements are designed to help SMB owners identify strengths and uncover gaps across the 7Ps.

Some of the benefits of addressing areas of misalignment are: enhanced operational efficiency, improved team productivity, and long-term sustainable growth. By doing so, this can unlock more of your business's potential while leading to a greater sense of fulfillment for you and your team.

Rating Scale:

1 = Strongly Disagree

2 = Disagree

3 = Neither Agree nor Disagree

4 = Agree

5 = Strongly Agree

Purpose

1. Our company's mission is clearly communicated and actively used to guide decisions.

2. Our mission energizes our leadership and inspires purposeful growth.

3. Our core values and strengths shape how we lead internally and how we serve customers.

4. My business feels personally meaningful and aligned with the impact I want to make long term.

Prioritization

5. Every team member has clearly defined priorities and measurable key results they are accountable for.

6. We regularly revisit and realign priorities as business needs change.

7. We hold consistent check-ins to review and support progress on priorities.

8. Our team spends most of its time on what maters most, not distractions.

People

9. We have a clear profile of the "right-fit employee" for each role.

10. Our hiring process consistently attracts these right-fit employees aligned with our values.

11. Managers provide timely, specific feedback to help employees grow.

12. We have a fair, effective process to address misfit employees or misalignment.

Pipeline

13. We have a well-defined "right-fit customer profile" that guides sales and marketing.

14. Our sales and marketing efforts focus on attracting the right-fit customers.

15. We generate enough right-fit customers to sustain long-term growth.

16. We "weed out" or decline misfit customers who don't align with our purpose.

Product

17. Our products or services align with our core values and core competencies.

18. We gather customer insights to guide product and service improvements.

19. We innovate our products and services to improve performance in ways that stand out from the competition.

20. Our customer satisfaction generates referrals and positive word-of-mouth.

Process

21. Our team follows documented processes that ensure quality and accountability.

22. Our workflows are regularly reviewed and improved to ensure clarity, accountability, and efficiency.

23. We solve problems collaboratively, bringing together different team perspectives, leading to better solutions and faster results.

24. I regularly dedicate time to working on the business (strategic planning, improvement) rather than being consumed by daily tasks.

Profit

25. We regularly review key financial metrics (revenue, margin, cash flow) to guide decisions.

26. We have adequate cash flow to cover daily operations.

27. Our pricing and business model (revenue-cost structure) support sustainable, purpose-aligned growth.

28. Our business is financially healthy and positioned for long-term success.

Rating Assessment Categories:

28-49: Significant Misalignment – Critical Issues

Severe gaps exist across most of the 7Ps, leading to inefficiencies, lack of focus, and potential business risk. Immediate corrective action is needed to stabilize operations and prevent further decline.

50–71: Moderate Misalignment – Improvement Required

Some strengths are present, but multiple dimensions are underperforming. Without focused effort, these gaps will hold back growth, profitability, and alignment.

72–93: Mixed Alignment – Key Opportunities

A balance of strengths and weaknesses exists. Performance is uneven across the 7Ps, requiring targeted improvement in one or more critical areas to fully unlock potential.

94–115: Strong Alignment – Ready for Optimization

The organization is well-aligned overall, with effective pracices in place. Continued focus on refinement and optimization can move the business from good to great.

116–140: Outstanding Alignment – Purpose-Driven Excellence

The business demonstrates exceptional alignment across all 7Ps, reflecting a high-performance, purpose-driven culture. Serves as a benchmark of excellence and a potential model for others.

Next Steps

1. Reflect on Your Scores – Look at your lowest-scoring areas and ask: *What's the cost of leaving these gaps unaddressed?*

2. Prioritize Improvement Areas – Select 1–2 dimensions of the 7Ps to focus on first, rather than spreading effort too thin.

3. Develop a Clear Action Plan – Turn insights into steps. Define ownership, timelines, and success measures for closing alignment gaps.

4. Review and Adjust Regularly – Use this scorecard as a living tool, revisiting it quarterly to track progress and re-align priorities.

RIGHT FIT EMPLOYEE PROFILE (RFEP)

1.0 Purpose

Develop each position's Right Fit Employee Profile (RFEP): What does "right fit" look like using the Baseline–Differentiating Traits/Competencies (BDTC) Framework..

1.1 Developing Position Baseline & Differentiating Traits/Competencies

As part of making your team's strengths more productive, we identify the baseline and differentiating traits/competencies for each position in the company. This allows you to:

1.1.1 Clarify and communicate the key traits/competencies tied to each position's Desired Performance Outcomes (DPO).

1.1.2 Provide on-the-job examples to help employees understand what "good" looks like in the context of your company's values and methods.

1.1.3 Set clearer performance standards for feedback and evaluations.

1.1.4 Hire better by screening for right-fit candidates using job-relevant success factors (traits and competencies).

1.2 Instructions

1.2.1 Initial Selection

After reviewing the definitions of competencies and traits:

- Select up to 10 that seem most important to the role.
- Traits are characteristics (e.g., attention to detail), while competencies are skills or abilities (e.g., ability to delegate).
- It's okay if the line between traits and competencies isn't always clear.

1.2.2 Narrow Down to the Top 5–7

Refine your selection to the 5–7 most relevant and impactful traits/competencies for the position. Exclude "givens" as appropriate (e.g., attendance or basic literacy).

Use the following questions to guide your selection:

- Is the trait/competency essential to job performance?
- Would its absence disqualify someone from succeeding in the role?

1.2.2.1 Example:

- For a baseball pitcher: throwing 95 MPH accurately is a baseline competency; running or catching is a given.
- For a manager: "attendance" may be a given, not a baseline trait.
- For an entry-level admin: "develops others" is not likely to be baseline.

1.2.2.2 Differentiating Traits

- Select up to 2–4 differentiating traits.
- These are traits commonly found in your top performers that help distinguish between adequate and excellent performance.
- You may select a differentiating trait from the baseline list if a top performer demonstrates it at a significantly higher level.

1.2.2.3 Flexibility & Context

- This framework is not exhaustive; different managers and companies may choose different traits for the same role depending on their culture and performance expectations.
- Some traits/competencies may be "higher order" and include others (e.g., "trust builder" may encompass "influencer").

1.2.2.4 Practical Use

- This exercise helps managers and employees co-create a shared vision of success.
- It also clarifies hiring needs if the role were to be filled from scratch.

1.2.3 Summarize

- On Definitions Pages 5–8: Check your top 10 traits/competencies.
- On Summary Page 4: Circle the selected items.

- Number your top 5–7 baseline traits.
- Choose up to 2–4 differentiating traits marked with an asterisk (*), which can overlap with baseline traits.
- Ranking the traits is optional unless helpful.

1.3 Competencies/Traits in Action Using Stories and Examples

1.3.1 Trait Story Worksheet

- Use the "Traits in Action" worksheet (Pages 11–12) to describe how your selected traits appear on the job.
- For each baseline or differentiating trait, describe:
  o A real or realistic example
  o Specific behavior or action tied to success

1.3.2 Example: Service Orientation

Nordstrom Employee:

Stays after closing to help a frantic customer, ensures the suit is delivered by 8 a.m. to a hotel for an important meeting.

Walmart Employee:

Walks a customer to the aisle, helps them load the item into their car—prompt, helpful, and efficient.

The expectations and expressions of the same trait differ depending on company culture and service model.

Final Thoughts

Using the baseline–differentiating traits/competency framework allows your organization to define, measure, and reinforce what matters most in each role. Through shared understanding and examples, teams can align expectations, improve performance evaluations, and create a stronger "Company Way."

2.0 Summary of Traits/Competencies

(Label DR: Direct Report MGR: Manager to compare selections)

Individual Work Style Traits/Competencies			
Achievement Orientation	Communication	Initiative	Quality Orientation
Active Learning	Compliance	Integrity	Coachability
Adaptability	Curiosity	Learning Agility	Stress Tolerance
Attendance	Deadline Driven	Organization	
Attention to Detail	Dependability	Positive Attitude	

Management/Sales Traits/Competencies			
Accountability	Influence	Professional Presence	Verbal Charm
Commitment	Motivator	Resilience	Strategic Resource Mgmt
Decision Making	Negotiation	Strategic Thinking	Adaptive Communication
Delegation	Outreach	Team Leadership	Customer Centric
Develops Others	Persuasion	Trust Builder	Culture Fit

Problem Solving & Process Traits / Competencies		Relational Competencies/Traits	
Analytical Thinking	Prioritization	Collaboration	Service Orientation
Creativity	Problem Sensitivity	Concern for Others	
Innovation	Problem Formulation	Emotional Intelligence	
Optimization	Troubleshooting	Friendliness	
		Rapport	

Required Technical Competencies			
Computer Literacy	Word Proficiency		
Excel Proficiency	Digital Literacy		
Mathematical Aptitude	CAD		
Mechanical Aptitude	Other:		
Quick Books			

1. Definition of Traits/Competencies (excluding technical competencies)

Accountability	Enjoys taking responsibility for accomplishments, developments, and challenges on the job
Achievement Orientation	Desire to work well or to compete against a standard of excellence
Active Learning	Actively observes and requests information from others to understand personnel, customer, and equipment issues and stays abreast of new techniques and product developments
Adaptability	Is open to and comfortable with uncertain, changing, and often fast-paced situations, can thrive under pressure even when thrown into new situations.
Adaptive Communication	Beyond general communication skills, this trait involves adjusting one's communication style to effectively connect with a diverse range of individuals and situations.
Analytical Thinking	Ability to address complex issues by breaking them into manageable components or logical steps, analyzing information and drawing logical conclusions based on evidence-based reasoning.
Attendance	Reports to work on time and ready to work, and is willing to arrive early or stay late as necessary
Attention to Detail	Can focus on details consistently, derives satisfaction from doing thorough and error-free work
Coachability	Desire to implement suggestions, accept feedback with an open mind, and deliberately seek out mentors
Collaboration	Works effectively with coworkers and customers, integrating their capabilities and perspectives
Commitment	Demonstrates and communicates genuine commitment to and enthusiasm for the brand, product, company, and customer
Communication	Has strong verbal and solid written communication skills to effectively convey accurate information to management, personnel, and customers
Compliance	Promptly takes instruction and delegation from superiors and consistently follows through on agreed-upon tasks.
Concern for Others	Is sensitive to others' needs and feelings and takes steps to be helpful on the job
Creativity	Can create innovative, unexpected solutions by drawing inspiration from a variety of sources, including one's intuitive insight
Curiosity	Has a passion for new information and new ideas, enjoys asking and answering questions that will help current and future decision-making and troubleshooting

Customer/ Client-Centric	Focusing not just on service orientation but on deeply understanding customer needs, behaviors, and trends to drive better service and product innovation.
Deadline Driven	Is motivated by meeting scheduled or self-imposed deadlines and gets satisfaction from being "on time."
Decision Making	Can make decisions, considering the costs and benefits, and accept the risks and responsibilities of making choices.
Delegation	Can effectively assign work to others and coordinate their workflow with appropriate follow-up and encouragement
Dependability	Is reliable, responsible, and dependable in fulfilling obligations; is accountable even in the face of obstacles
Develops Others	Places others in situations that will utilize and make most productive their strengths, providing timely constructive feedback
Emotional Intelligence	Understands how emotions factor into motivation, decision-making, and trust, discerning and appropriately responding to emotional dynamics at play in coworkers and customers
Friendliness	Is warm and welcoming toward other employees, customers, and management, genuinely likes other people.
Influence	Uses credibility, expertise, trustworthiness and empathetic understanding to affect how others think, feel and act
Initiative	Self-starter who takes action and does whatever it takes to complete tasks promptly and thoroughly
Innovation	Designs new, unexpected and ingenious solutions to meet potential customers desires and appeal to their needs.
Integrity	Is ethical and accountable in all aspects of work, including staying productive in unsupervised situations and handling sensitive information
Learning Agility	Is able to pick things up quickly in new situations and while learning on the job. A self-learner looks at a challenge and thinks: "Where can I go to learn more about that?
Motivator	Is good at motivating, moving individuals and/or groups of people to take action
Negotiation	Is good at and enjoys reaching mutually beneficial agreements and negotiating favorable terms
Optimization	Passion for making something, a product, process or decision as functional and effective (fully perfect) as possible.

Organization	Takes an efficient and orderly approach to tasks, processes and overall workflow.
Outreach	Enjoys and is good at making customer and industry-relevant connections with people outside of the company, while positively representing the company to the public
Persuasion	Can sway the opinions, decisions and actions of others, selecting the best techniques for each situation
Positive Attitude	Has a good-natured attitude even in the face of stressful job demands and difficult operational or interpersonal issues
Prioritization	Ability to weigh tasks and goals by relative importance and urgency while keeping the big picture or end result in mind.
Problem Formulation	Ability to clearly define and structure complex problems before attempting to solve them. This task involves breaking down larger issues into manageable components,
Problem Sensitivity	Has the ability to foresee when something is wrong or likely to go wrong
Professional Presence	Represents oneself in a confident, respectable, and business-oriented manner
Quality Orientation	Can meticulously assess products and services to ensure that they are assembled as intended, meeting and/or exceeding minimum quality standards
Rapport	Ability to establish a close and harmonious relationship by understanding one another's feelings or ideas and communicating well.
Resilience	Ability to stay motivated in the face of challenges and to "bounce back" after unsuccessful attempts.
Service Orientation	Passion for and seeks ways to help others and to meet their needs.
Strategic Thinking	Ability to develop effective plans aligned with company goals and objectives given its personnel, resources, and capabilities.
Strategic Resource Management	For roles involving resource allocation (like budget, staff, or materials), the ability to strategically manage resources for optimal efficiency and effectiveness.
Team-Leadership	Can effectively motivate, manage, and support a strong and cohesive team
Troubleshooting	Ability to work through and enjoy going through the details of a problem (complex) to solve with the best chance of success while adapting the approach as needed.

Trust Builder	Communicates in ways that inspire trust and confidence—ability to demonstrate a high degree of competency (logic), purity of motive (he/she cares about me), and authenticity-relatability.
Verbal Charm	Ability to "win over" through confident and personable tonality, establishing rapport and influence through voice.

3 Trait Selection

4.0 Traits in Action with Stories & Examples

Baseline Trait	Stories & Examples of How This Trait Looks on this Job
Communication:	Example: Effective communication is paramount for a recruiter. It involves clearly articulating job expectations to candidates and accurately conveying the candidates' qualifications and fit to the hiring team.

Differentiating Trait	Stories & Examples of How This Trait Looks on the Job

TDL: TASK & DUTY LIST FRAMEWORK

1.0 Introduction

Jobs can best be understood as a series of tasks. A **task** is an action designed to contribute a specified end result to the accomplishment of an objective. It has an identifiable beginning and end, serving as a measurable component of the duties and responsibilities of a specific job.

While every job has a title, the actual work expected can vary widely. Tasks offer a detailed description of what the job entails. For example:

- A **doctor** may perform tasks such as operating, conducting physical exams, or providing emergency first aid.Key characteristics of tasks include:

- **Specificity**: A task statement must describe a specific action using a verb and an object. For example, "Measure distances accurately with a tape measure."

- **Structure**: Start each task statement with a verb, describe how it is performed, and state its objective. For example, "Loads pallets using a forklift."

To develop a comprehensive task list, involve employees by having them prepare their own lists, starting with the most critical tasks. Compare and reconcile these with managerial input for accuracy and inclusiveness.

2.0 Task Analysis

A **task analysis** breaks down the job into its component tasks to understand the Knowledge, Skills, and Abilities (KSAs) required to perform them. This analysis helps identify opportunities to:

- Optimize workflows.
- Redesign or reassign tasks.
- Split tasks into smaller, more manageable parts.

Key aspects to analyze:

1. **Task frequency**: How often the task is performed.
2. **Difficulty of learning**: The complexity of acquiring the necessary skill.

3. **Criticality**: The task's importance in terms of urgency and overall impact.

4. **Delegation feasibility**: How easily the task can be assigned to others.

5. **Training needs**: The level of training required.

Example:

- Task: "Update inventory levels."
    - o Frequency: Weekly
    - o Difficulty: Low (requires basic software skills)
    - o Delegation Feasibility: High (can be assigned to a junior employee)

3.0 Task Statements

A **task statement** combines an action and a result to clearly describe what is to be achieved.

Examples:

1. **Firefighter**:
    - o **Task**: "Determines manual ladder type and size needed at incident scene."
        - ▪ Action: "Determines"
        - ▪ Result: "Manual ladder type and size identified."

2. **Retail Store Manager**:
    - o **Task**: "Conducts weekly inventory checks to ensure accurate stock levels."
        - ▪ Action: "Conducts"
        - ▪ Result: "Accurate stock levels identified."

Tips for Writing Good Task Statements:

- Use a clear action verb (e.g., measure, load, calculate).
- Specify the objective or outcome.
- Categorize actions into **People**, **Data**, and **Things** for clarity.

To refine task statements:

- Observe employees performing their tasks.
- Ask them to verbalize their thought processes (especially for mental actions like "analyzing").

4.0 Task Steps

Task steps (or performance steps) are detailed, sequential instructions for completing a task. They are particularly useful for:

- Training purposes.
- Standardizing processes.

Example: **Task**: "Place a purchase order for low-stock items."

Steps:

1. Look up usage for the item over the previous 12 months.
2. Calculate the average monthly use.
3. Add the planned growth rate for the product line.
4. Contact suppliers for the best buy rates.
5. Verify specifications with planned usage tables.
6. Submit the purchase order.

When to Skip Task Steps: Documenting task steps can be time-consuming. Focus on tasks that:

- Require formal training.
- Have a significant impact on workflow efficiency.

The Tree Metaphor: Clarifying Duties, Tasks, and Task Steps

To simplify the distinctions:

- **Trunk**: Represents the **Job Objective**, the core purpose of the role.
- **Major Branches**: Represent **Duties**, broad areas of responsibility.
- **Minor Branches**: Represent Core **Tasks**, key actions that fulfill duties.
- **Leaves**: Represent **Task Steps**, usually found in step by step instructions for completing tasks.

Example: **Job Objective**: Manage a restaurant's operations.

- **Duty**: Ensure food quality.
  - o **Task**: Inspect produce deliveries.
    - ▪ **Task Steps**:
      1. Check delivery logs.
      2. Inspect freshness and temperature.
      3. Approve or reject items.

5.0 Decision Tree for Classification

Use this framework to determine whether an activity is a duty, task, or task step:

1. **Does it involve multiple processes or actions?**
   - o Yes → **Duty**
   - o No → Proceed to Question 2.
2. **Is it a specific action with a measurable result?**
   - o Yes → **Task**
   - o No → Proceed to Question 3.
3. **Does it require detailed, sequential instructions?**
   - o Yes → **Task Step**

6.0 Practical Tools and Resources

- **TDL Excel Framework**: Use this tool to document and analyze duties, tasks, and task steps effectively.

Duty	Task	Task Steps
Ensure food quality	Inspect produce deliveries	1. Check delivery logs.
		2. Inspect freshness and temperature.
		3. Approve or reject items.
Manage inventory	Update stock levels weekly	1. Log in to the inventory system.
		2. Generate stock reports.
		3. Enter new quantities.

7.0 Continuous Improvement

Developing task and duty lists is a dynamic process. Periodically revisit and refine lists to:

- Adjust to evolving business needs.
- Ensure alignment with organizational goals.
- Enhance productivity and efficiency.

Duties

Duties are a combination of related or like tasks. For example, an inventory control specialist might have two duties:

1. Perform shipping duties:
   o Pull items using a letdown. (task)
   o Prepare items for shipment. (task)
2. Perform receiving duties:
   o Unload trailers using a forklift. (task)
   o Receive the items into the computer database. (task)

As mentioned earlier, tasks should have a definite beginning and end and explain a process. This is the main clue for separating tasks from duties. For example, is the following a task or duty for a Fire person?

Stands watch to receive incoming alarms and information, answers phones, and monitors access to the station house.

This would be a duty as it would be extremely hard for someone to identify the process and note when it has started and when it has stopped. Clues that give this off as a duty are the multiple action verbs: stands, receive answer, and monitor. Also, if this was a task, then you would have to see all the actions performed when observing the task, e.g. when an alarm is received then the phone would have to be answered. Remember, a task stands alone as it has a definite start and an end.

The tasks performed while carrying out this duty might include:

o *Receives notification of multiple alarms, downtown alarms, and other significant emergencies through the Fire Alarm Office.* ("Receives" is the action while "being notified of the various alarms" is the result.)

o *Notifies station personnel over public address system of incoming alarms and required response (e.g., everybody goes, truck only, engine only, etc.).*("Notifying" is the action while "the other fire persons being made aware of the required response" is the result.)

Task Example Quiz

Listed below are 12 jobs. Below each job are three statements. Next to each statement, write if it a task, duty, or task step.

EXAMPLE - Truck Driver

o Maintain and operate a truck and trailer. **duty**

o Selects the most direct and expeditious route to destination. **task**

o Obtain weather report before crossing mountain pass. **task step**

1. Administrative Assistant

o Answers department and outside phone. _____

o Performs office duties as needed. _____

o Check spelling. _____

2. Supervisor

o Recognize the smell of marijuana. _____

o Supervise personnel as needed. _____

o Identify a substance abuser. _____

3. Company Driver

- o Drives company employees and other personnel to various functions as directed by dispatcher. _____
- o Checks horn for proper operation. _____
- o Performs preventive maintenance checks and services before operating vehicle. _____

4. Power Plant Operator

- o Open the water valve to increase water flow. _____
- o Adjust the cooling system to prevent overheating. _____
- o Monitor power system for faults. _____

5. Manager

- o Interviews and hires new employees. _____
- o Conducts an interview with a prospective candidate. _____
- o Asks a behavioral question. _____

6. Bulldozer Operator

- o Builds roads. _____
- o Tilt the blade. _____
- o Digs a drainage ditch. _____

7. Search and Rescue Team Member

- o Searches assigned area to locate victims. _____
- o Align map in correct direction using a compass. _____
- o Locates present position using a map and compass. _____

8. Accountant

- o Perform SKU substitutions as needed for positive and negative numbers. _____
- o Reconcile the production department. _____
- o Perform end-of-month closeouts. _____

9. Lifeguard

o Monitors swimming pool area for safety. _____

o Checks for breathing by placing ear next to mouth and listening. _____

o Rescues drowning victims using life-saving techniques. _____

10. Painter

o Prepare, paint, and perform cleanup as required. _____

o Prepares room for painting. _____

o Cover all furniture, appliances, using plastic and canvas covers. _____

11. Barista

o Make a shot of espresso. _____

o Make drinks. _____

o Measure out one serving of coffee grounds. _____

12. Trainer

o Look up the cost of printing materials. _____

o Create training programs. _____

o Estimate the cost of a training program. _____

QUIZ ANSWERS to Task, Task Step and Duties

1. Administrative Assistant

o Answers department and outside phone. (**task**—although there are two phones, the task would be performed the same way)

o Performs office duties as needed. (**duty**—this is often used as a catch-all task)

o Check spelling. (**task step**)

2. Supervisor

o Recognize the smell of marijuana. (**task step**—this could possibly be a task if your target population have never had any substance abuse training)

o Supervise personnel as needed. (**duty**—this is almost never a task)

o Identify a substance abuser. (**task**)

3. Company Driver

o Drives company employees and other personnel to various functions as directed by dispatcher. (**duty**)

o Checks horn for proper operation. (**task step**)

o Performs preventive maintenance checks and services before operating vehicle. (**task**)

4. Power Plant Operator

o Open the water valve to increase water flow. (**task step**—depending upon the type of power plant, this could also be a task)

o Adjust the cooling system to prevent overheating. (**task**—also depending upon the type of power plant, this could be a task step if there are several steps–the important part is that you used deductive reasoning to determine which is a task and which is a step)

o Monitor power system for faults. (**duty**)

5. Manager

o Interviews and hires new employees. (**duty**)

o Conducts an interview with a prospective candidate. (**task**)

o Asks a behavioral question. (**task step**—could possibly be built into a task)

6. Bulldozer Operator

o Builds roads. (**duty**)

o Tilt the blade. (**task step**)

o Digs a drainage ditch. (**task**)

7. Search and Rescue Team Member

- o Searches assigned area to locate victims and to obtain further information about incident, following standard search and operating procedures. (**duty**)
- o Align map in correct direction using a compass. (**task step**)
- o Locates present position using a map and compass. (**task**)

8. Accountant

- o Perform SKU substitutions as needed for positive and negative numbers. (**task step**)
- o Reconcile the production department. (**task**)
- o Perform end-of-month closeouts. (**duty**)

9. Lifeguard

- o Monitors swimming pool area for safety. (**duty**)
- o Checks for breathing by placing ear next to mouth and listening. (**task step**)
- o Rescues drowning victims using life -saving techniques. (**task**)

10. Painter

- o Prepare, paint, and perform cleanup as required. (**duty**)
- o Prepares room for painting. (**task**)
- o Cover all furniture, appliances, using plastic and canvas covers. (**task step**)

11. Barista

- o Make a shot of espresso. (**task**)
- o Make drinks. (**duty**)
- o Measure out one serving of coffee grounds. (**task step**)

12. Trainer

- o Estimate cost of printing materials. (**task step**)
- o Create training programs. (**duty**)
- o Estimate the cost of a training program. (**task**)

PEOPLE DATA THINGS (PDT) Framework

People	Data	Things
advising	accounting	assembling
briefing	auditing	calibrating
communicating	analyzing	constructing
consulting	balancing	controlling
coaching	balancing	cutting
conducting	budgeting	disassembling
critiquing	compiling	driving
delegating	comparing	hammering
demonstrating	coordinating	hand-eye coordination
directing	creating	handling & packaging
explaining	designing	inspecting
facilitating	documenting	lifting
following through	evaluating	loading
giving feedback	forecasting	maneuvering
influencing	identifying	manufacturing
initiating	monitors	mixing
interviewing	organizing	molding
managing	planning	monitoring
mentoring	preparing	operating
motivating	problem-solving	painting
negotiating	researching	preparing
persuading	retrieving information	repairing
promoting	surveying	sanding
public speaking	systematizing	transporting
selling	tracking	typing
sponsoring		
supervising		
teaching		
training		

Position Title: Name:

Definitions of People related Tasks/Duties

Check the top 5 tasks/duties in each applicable section.

Rank order by importance the top two or three if able to do so.

1-5	Key Tasks-Duties Definitions	"PEOPLE" related Tasks- Duties
	advising	To give advice (services rendered, or the state of affairs) or counsel
	briefing	To give a summary of facts, findings, and objectives.
	communicating	To reach mutual understanding through exchange of information and ideas but also create and share meaning.
	consulting	To provide expert knowledge for a fee. For example, a company seeking to sell its products abroad may look for a consultant familiar with the business practices of the target country. The consultant will tell the company what best practices should be followed, what to expect from customers, and how to deal with foreign regulations.
	coaching	To extend traditional training methods to include focus on (1) an individual's needs and accomplishments, (2) close observation, and (3) impartial and non-judgmental feedback on performance.
	conducting	To lead or direct affairs of a business
	counseling	To help client or coworkers see things more clearly, possibly from a different viewpoint.
	critiquing	To evaluate in a detailed and analytical way.
	delegating	To transfer responsibility for a task (usually from a manager to a subordinate).
	demonstrating	To show or display
	directing	When a manager instructs, guides, and oversees the performance of the workers to achieve predetermined goals.
	explaining	To show or express an idea or a process clearly.
	facilitating	To provide a productive or impartial meeting: a process where an individual who is agreed upon and acceptable to group members intervenes to assist the group in solving problems and making decisions to improve productivity and efficiency who may or may not have authority to make decisions
	following through	To take action and see through to commitments until the end.

	giving feedback	To provide information to an entity (individual or a group) about its prior behavior so that the entity may adjust its current and future behavior to achieve the desired result.
	influencing	To have an effect on the character, development, or behavior of someone or something.
	Initiating	To get things going by taking the first step in a course, process, or operation.
	Instructing	To teach a subject or skill, to direct/command
	interviewing	To ask prospective employees questions to see whether they are suitable for a job, and to evaluate their qualifications.
	managing	To oversee, direct, and organize a project or establishment.
	mentoring	To develop a professional relationship in which an experienced person assists another in developing specific skills and knowledge that will enhance the less-experienced person's professional and personal growth.
	motivating	To generate the energy required for an employee to behave in a way that will bring the organization closer to its goal.
	negotiating	To bargain between two or more parties to reach common ground.
	persuading	To change a person's (or a group's) attitude or behavior toward an event, idea, object, or another individual.
	promoting	To present for buyer acceptance through advertising, publicity, or discounting.
	public speaking	To perform a speech to a live audience.
	selling	The last step in the chain of commerce where a buyer exchanges cash for a seller's good or service, or the activity of trying to bring this about.
	sponsoring	To organize and commit to the development of a product, program, or project
	supervising	To monitor and regulate processes, or delegated activities, responsibilities, or tasks
	teaching	To instruct by precept, example, or experience.
	training	To effectively prepare new employees with job-related skills and knowledge.
	welcoming	To greet someone in a kind, friendly and courteous way

1.0 Definitions of "Data" Related Tasks

Check up to the top 5 definitions if applicable. Rank order the top 3 # 1-3 if useful to do so.

1-5	Task/Duties-	"DATA" related Tasks- Duties Definitions
	accounting	To practice methods of recording transactions, bookkeeping
	analytical thinking	The break down complex problems into smaller components, analyze them systematically, and draw logical conclusions. Analytical thinking involves using critical thinking skills, data analysis, and evidence-based reasoning to solve problems, make decisions, and generate insights.
	auditing	To perform a systematic examination and verification of a firm's books of account, transaction records, other relevant documents, and physical inspection of inventory
	analyzing	To take an accounting item and evaluate it for possible reasons for discrepancies.
	balancing	To bring the totals of debit and credit accounts into agreement to determine the profit or loss made during that period.
	budgeting	To allocate resources and estimate revenues and expenses over a specified future period.
	compiling	To condense information by classifying and tabulating data gathered from various sources.
	comparing	To estimate, measure, or note the similarity or dissimilarity between two items.
	coordinating	To synchronize and schedule activities, people and/or resources in an efficient manner.
	creating	To make or bring into existence something new.
	decision analysis	To consider factors such as costs, benefits, probabilities, and preferences to arrive at the most rational and advantageous choice.
	designing	To devise for a specific function or end.
	documenting	To record communication or facts.
	evaluating	To determine the significance, worth, or condition of usually by careful appraisal.
	forecasting	To make a prediction based on study and analysis of available pertinent data.
	identifying	To recognize the abnormalities in trends.
	monitors	To check for consistency or abnormalities daily.
	organizing	To arrange several elements into a purposeful sequential or spatial (or both) order or structure
	planning	To write an account of intended future course of action
	preparing	To work out the details in advance, to make ready for use

	Prioritization	Assessing tasks, projects, or goals to determine their relative importance and urgency.
	Problem Formulation	Clearly defining and structuring complex problems before attempting to solve them. This task involves breaking down larger issues into manageable components, establishing objectives, and determining the scope of analysis to ensure a systematic approach to problem-solving.
	prob-lem-solving	To work through details of a problem to reach a solution.
	researching	To investigate aimed at the interpretation of data, facts, and processes.
	retrieving information	To obtain information resources relevant to the company's business goals. (i.e. searching documents, databases, etc.)
	risk assessment	Evaluating potential risks and uncertainties associated with a decision or course of action. This task involves identifying, quantifying, and prioritizing risks to make informed choices that minimize negative outcomes and maximize opportunities.
	strategic planning	Developing long-term strategies and plans to achieve organizational goals. This task involves analyzing the current state of affairs, forecasting future trends, and devising a comprehensive plan of action that considers various factors, risks, and resources.
	surveying	To investigate the opinions or experiences of a group of people by asking questions.
	synthesize	Systematic combination of otherwise different elements (ideas) to form a coherent whole.
	systematize	Marked by a methodical plan or procedure and repeatability.
	tracking	

2.0 Definition of "Things" Related Tasks

Check up to the top 3-5 definitions if applicable. Rank order the top # 1-3 if useful to do so.

1-5	Task/Duty Definitions	"THINGS" related Tasks- Duties
	agility & speed	To move about quickly and easily
	assembling	To put together a number of parts.
	calibrating	To correlate the readings (of an instrument) with those of a standard to check the instrument's accuracy.
	constructing	To make or form by combining or arranging parts or elements.
	controlling	To exercise restraint or direction over machinery.
	cooking	To practice or skill of preparing food by combining, mixing and heating ingredients

	cutting	To slice/separate raw material (in two parts) into desired final shape and size.
	disassembling	To take apart.
	driving	To operate a motor vehicle, forklift
	hammering	To physically beat a heavy object against another.
	hand-eye coordination	The control of hand movement based on vision.
	handling & packaging	To wrap and handle goods accordingly.
	inspecting	To look at products closely, typically to assess their condition and to identify any shortcomings.
	lifting	To pick up and move to a different position.
	loading	To place a load or order onto a vehicle or container.
	machining	Ability to use machine tools such as lathes, power saws, and presses.
	maneuvering	To move skillfully or carefully.
	manufacturing	To make something on a large scale using machinery.
	mixing	To combine or put together to form one substance.
	molding	To produce a product based on another form.
	monitoring	To observe and check the progress or quality of an item over time.
	operating	To control the functioning of a machine, process, or system.
	painting	To cover the surface with a coat of pigment.
	preparing	To get material ready for usage.
	repairing	To fix or mend an appliance from being damaged.
	sanding	To smooth or polish
	transporting	To take or carry goods from one place to another.
	typing	Typing WPM (Data Entry)

PDT Framework Examples and Applications

If you determine that a particular position requires mostly people-related tasks and competencies, then you would look for someone whose strengths also align with that domain versus someone whose strengths may be more focused on data and relatively weak in people areas.

- **People-Focused Role**: An employee with high emotional intelligence (EQ) and strong communication skills would benefit from a position that requires strong interpersonal skills, such as a customer service representative.

- **Data-Focused Role**: A data analyst role would require someone with strong analytical skills, proficiency in data management tools, and a high disposition toward data-related tasks.

- **Things-Focused Role**: A proficient welder would need to demonstrate a high disposition for and competency in "things" related domain areas of expertise, which require working with their hands in a skilled manner.

Some roles, like a management consultant, require an equal combination of both people and data skills, also referred to as high IQ (Intellectual Quotient) and EQ (Emotional Quotient). This combination is essential for effectively managing and analyzing complex information while also engaging with clients and team members.

By understanding the nature of each role through the PDT Framework and aligning it with the appropriate competencies, you can ensure that you hire and retain the right employees. This approach helps optimize performance and achieve organizational goals.

POSITION GUIDE FRAMEWORK

A clear understanding of the desired performance outcomes for each functional position in your company begins with a well-thought-out, documented position guide (also referred to as a job description) that is consistently and regularly communicated to each employee.

Unlike most job descriptions, which comprise mostly lists of tasks and duties, the Position Guide Framework aims to provide a more useful approach that helps us think through the problem or pain that each position is hired to address while also understanding the desired traits and competencies best suited for the role and desired performance outcome (DPO).

The Position Guide Framework builds on prior frameworks by incorporating the work of the Focus Alignment Framework, which details more of the day-to-day tasks, and the baseline-differentiating-traits-competencies (BDTC) Framework, which highlights the most relevant and required traits and competencies for each role. Additionally, the People, Data, Things (PDT) Framework (see appendix) also gives us more clarity about the nature of the role based on whether the key tasks and duties fall in the competency of people, data, or things.

Documented Position Guides

Position Guides are written to clarify and document specific authorities, responsibilities, duties, traits, and experience levels requisite for each key job in your business. Making these elements explicit allows employees and management to understand the most important outcomes of a given role, where employees fit within the greater organization, and where one person's responsibilities end, and another's begin.

As your small business expands, there is potential for confusion and conflict due to employee role ambiguity unless you take the time to document who is supposed to be doing what, who they report to, what areas of authority they have, and their responsibilities. If these things are not carefully and properly considered, tasks may fall through the cracks, and misunderstandings, dissatisfaction, and loss of employee productivity may ensue.

There should be a written Position Guide for every position in the company, especially those positions that entail managing or supervising others. This helps to ensure that expectations are made explicit and are clearly documented, as it is only possible to perform to meet expectations if they are clearly, mutually understood. Employees can be evaluated by comparing actual performance to the responsibilities, duties, and requirements listed in the position guide.

Position Guides as a Management Tool

The Position Guide is typically drafted by the manager or owner supervising the position. It is essential that each employee clearly understands what is expected of him or her and how to achieve them. The Position Guide is a powerful thinking and management tool for ensuring that this happens, and as Peter Drucker wisely counsels us:

"The largest single source of failed promotions is the failure to think through, and help others think through, what a new job requires. Years ago, a boss of mine challenged me four months after he had advanced me. Until he called me in, I had continued to do what I had done before. To his credit, he understood that it was his responsibility to make me see that a new job means different behavior, a different focus, and different relationships."[2]

Drafting the Position Guides with Employee Input

It is helpful to have employee involvement when developing Position Guides. Employees can provide valuable insight into the day-to-day realities of their positions and by taking a more collaborative approach, the employee's input can increase his or her commitment to performing per the specified guidelines.

Example of Position Guides Components: (see appendix for Position Guide Sample):

- **Introduction**: A brief paragraph stating the name of the position and the company.
- **Company Description**: Ideally, a strong positioning statement that succinctly describes the company's unique selling proposition and should include vision, mission, and values.

- **Functional Role**: This section should include a short paragraph describing the overall desired performance outcome DPO of the position.

- **Position Summary in the form of a Job Posting (Optional)**: Includes basic "specs" of the job, e.g., location, pay usually not included, dress code, job type, employee type, industry, manage others, travel requirements, etc.

- **Tasks and Responsibilities**: An overview of the specific tasks and duties listed in order of importance.

- **Reporting Relationships**: Indicate to whom the individual filling the position reports (use the title of the position, not the individual's name). Also, indicate the titles of any positions that report directly to this position.

- **Experience and Education Requirements**: A list of minimum standards for the education, experience, and skills necessary for satisfactory performance of the position.

- **Baseline Traits and Competencies**: List up to 7 Baseline traits and/or competencies

- **Differentiating Traits and Competencies**: List up to 2-4 Differentiating traits and/or competencies shared among your top performers in this role. These may be used as employee selection criteria or as target areas for the growth of existing employees.

- **Performance Measurement**: If possible, include both quantifiable and qualitative measurement criteria used to evaluate the employee's performance.

- **Acknowledgment:** State that the position guide has been reviewed and understood. The manager and the employee receiving the Position Guide should sign off on it, and then it should be filed in the employee's personnel file, with a copy provided to the employee.

Regular Review and Updates

Position Guides must be reviewed and revised regularly. Best practice to review at least annually to ensure they are current and relevant to changing company needs. Job duties, authorities, and responsibilities will change over time, and Position Guides should be modified accordingly.

It is an integral part of the documentation policy to ensure all revised Position Guides are dated, signed, and filed in each employee's personnel record. These periodic reviews are beneficial as they require you to decide whether all items included in the previous Position Guide are still relevant and represent the best uses of your and your employees' time, talents, and skills. They also provide a tool to organize better what is to be done in your business and by whom.

SAMPLE POSITION GUIDE: Senior Dispatcher

Introduction This procedure establishes the essential functions, authority, responsibilities, reporting relationships, and performance criteria for the Dispatcher position for GSV Transportation.

GSV Transportation GSV Transportation is a family-owned trucking company based in Ontario, CA, that provides trucking and logistics management solutions for business clients primarily in the Midwest, Southeast region, and state of Texas. GSV offers a wide range of transportation solutions, including local, regional, and long-haul truckload services for suppliers, manufacturers, distributors, and retailers.

GSV's continued success depends on attracting, retaining, and developing an enthusiastic team of customer-oriented learners who are passionate about our mission and values. We strive to create a culture of employee engagement that maximizes your strengths, enabling you to thrive while contributing to our sustainable growth and profitability.

The GSV Dispatcher is service-oriented and very organized, working systematically to keep orders moving efficiently. The Dispatcher must be comfortable with constant phone communication with drivers, customers, and other partners and stay focused on main priorities without getting overwhelmed by small tasks. With a service attitude towards our internal customers (drivers) and external end-user customers, the Dispatcher works to stay positive and organized in high-stress environments while keeping the big picture in mind.

GSV Transportation's Mission is "To become a trusted partner while going the 'extra mile' to exceed our customer expectations."

Motto: "Go the extra mile for our customers."

Trusted Partner: Caring and Competent Problem Solver

Functional Role: A trucking dispatcher directs and monitors the movements of trucks and freight while doing it cost-effectively, considering customer satisfaction and driver safety. Dispatchers are also responsible for keeping records, monitoring driver daily logs for errors or violations, and monitoring drivers' remaining hours of service and equipment availability. They must be adept in contingency planning, always thinking of backup plans since something can inevitably go "off the rails." A good dispatcher is more than someone who answers the telephone. They must be excellent communicators, building good relations with both customers and drivers and always keeping the customer informed to prevent any surprises or disappointments.

Job Summary

- **Job Title**: Dispatcher
- **Location**: Ontario, CA
- **Base Pay**: $ hourly salary DOE
- **Benefits**: Include overtime, paid vacation after one year of employment, paid health insurance, and company matching retirement plan
- **Dress Code**: Business Casual
- **Job Type**: Customer Service/Admin
- **Employee Type**: Full time
- **Industry**: Transportation and Logistics
- **Manages Others**: No
- **Reports to**: Transportation Manager

Tasks, Duties, and Responsibilities

- Communicate with Drivers throughout their trips to monitor their progress and address any issues or problems that may arise.
- Monitor personnel and equipment locations to coordinate service and schedules.
- Prepare daily schedule and coordinate efficient scheduling by applying knowledge of customer schedules, peak delivery times, and alternate routes.
- Determine the best delivery methods and make minor changes in a driver's route as necessary to facilitate freight consolidation, conferring with the Driver on the best way to arrange it.
- Utilize knowledge and information about geographical areas, driver schedules, DOT regulations, and vehicle operation capacity to optimize safety and efficiency of delivery.

- Operate dispatch board and update computer system with all pertinent information.

- Operate and manage communication equipment and systems to maintain reliable contact with drivers.

- Advise drivers about traffic problems, construction areas, weather conditions, or other hazards.

- Make calls to customers and update them on their service status according to delivery schedules.

- Ensure a steady backlog of loads and backhauls by proactively communicating with customers.

- Stay up-to-date with current publications and legislation and make pertinent information available to management and drivers when appropriate.

- Review drivers' documentation each day; update and record Trip Reports, BOLs, Logbooks, pre-trip inspections, and receipts for reimbursements.

- Resolve any operations or delivery problems that require immediate attention.

Reporting Relationships the Dispatcher reports directly to the Transportation Manager.

Requirements

Education:

- High school diploma or equivalent

Experience:

- At least 5+ years' experience in dispatching (preferably in the trucking industry)

- Extensive experience in transportation/logistics-related fields

Baseline Requirements:

- **Attention to detail**: Focus on details consistently, deriving satisfaction from thorough, error-free work.

- **Decision Making**: Able to make decisions considering the costs and benefits, accepting the risks and responsibilities of making choices. Reliable, responsible, and dependable in fulfilling obligations, accountable even in the face of obstacles.

- **Communication**: Strong verbal and written communication skills to effectively convey accurate information to management, personnel, and customers.

- **Stress Tolerance**: Ability to perform calmly and effectively in high-stress and ambiguous situations.

- **Positive Attitude**: Good-natured attitude even in stressful job demands and difficult operational or interpersonal issues.

- **Organization**: Efficient and orderly approach to tasks, processes, and workflow.

- **Initiative**: Self-starter who acts and does whatever it takes to complete tasks promptly and thoroughly.

Differentiating Requirements: Traits Shared Among Top Performers

- **Positive Attitude**: Maintains a good-natured attitude despite stressful job demands and complex operational or interpersonal issues.

- **Problem-Solving**: Ability to work through and enjoy going through the details of a complex problem to reach a solution with the best chance of success while adapting the approach as needed.

- **Negotiation**: Skilled and passionate about reaching mutually beneficial agreements and negotiating favorable terms.

Planning and Time Utilization:

- Meet scheduled deadlines for achievement of GSV Transportation goals and objectives.

- Demonstrate the ability to consistently recognize and deal with priorities, focusing on top priorities and your highest payoff activities.

Initiative:

- Institute problem-solving actions as soon as it becomes evident that problems exist.

- Willing to take responsibility to seek guidance, direction, and training for the performance of duties.

- Constantly scan the Customer Service and support environments for new and new-to-the-company opportunities and processes that would improve Administrative, Customer Service, and Support operations.

- Evaluate work practices in the company's office operations; design improved practices and, with your supervisor's approval, implement them.

Attendance and Commitment:

- Complete all work schedules on time and assure quality.

- Serve as a role model for other personnel through personal commitment and enthusiasm.

Performance Measurement:

The Dispatcher shall be deemed to be performing satisfactorily when the following measures of performance are met:

- Successfully meeting or exceeding the goals and objectives of GSV Transportation as they relate to the Dispatcher's functions.

- Achievements address the responsibilities and duties listed in Section 5.0, Tasks, Duties, and Responsibilities.

Acknowledgment:

I have reviewed and understand the above job description and believe it to be accurate and complete. I also agree that the GM retains the right to revise this job description at any time after discussing it with the Dispatcher.

Senior Dispatcher:_____ Date: _____

Transportation GM:_____ Date: _____

PERFORMANCE EVALUATION FRAMEWORK (PEF)

This tool provides a framework for both the manager and direct report to assist in evaluating performance along with documented feedback about employee performance during the review period. Performance can be rated utilizing the following scale:

RATING	PERFORMANCE	Description / Action Required
9-10	Excellent	Track record of performing at a high level, delivering significant positive impact. Should mentor others and serve as a model worth emulating. (A 10 reflects sustained performance that redefines the standard of excellence.)
7-8	Good to Very Good	Consistently meets—and at times exceeds—role expectations. Makes valuable contributions, requires little supervision, and is ready for increased responsibility or new opportunities.
5-6	Needs Improvement	Performance less than that of a fully proficient employee and requires improvement with guidance and support. Acceptable if still in training or adjusting to the role.
3-4	Poor	Performance is inconsistent and results in limited contribution. Requires immediate action to assess role fit and substantial improvement to continue in the role.
1-2	Very Poor	Under performing over an extended period and having a negative impact on the organization—should have been "weeded" out a long time ago (Management should be held accountable)

Employee Name-Title/ Dept	R. Adam	Talent Acquisition Partner/ Recruiting
Position Summary in terms of Desired Results/ Performance Outcome of the Performance Pie)	PRODUCT/SERVICE: Attract "right fit" employees: Help our clients by improving the probability of success of hiring more of the "right fit, A-player" employees by attracting and sourcing a higher quality pool of candidates to interview and choose from. Deliver this service faster and more cost-effectively than our clients can achieve on their own, resulting in better hiring decisions and better hires over time. By doing so, we help owners create a winning team of positive contributors to help them achieve their most important goals and profitably grow their company.	

Performance Criteria (What)

The following provides a framework to help clarify the key (5-7) slices that comprise the overall "performance pie" of a particular position/role. You can also approximate time spent and the relative weight/importance as a percentage of 100% that each "slice" represents. Each slice can also be seen as the major "tree branches" of your role, and the OKR's Objectives with **KR's Key Results** can be viewed as the "fruits" of the branches and your efforts.

OKRs: Provides a goal-setting (critical thinking) framework to enable you to better focus on what matters. The O- Objectives are the overall outcome you want to achieve. Ideally, there should be no more than 3-5 objectives per role, with 1-3 KRs' key results per objective.

KR: Key results: Each objective has ideally 1-3 key results. KRs describe the measurable outcomes X to Y or milestones to be reached that drive the achievement of the Objectives. KRs can also include relevant success factors such as KPIs (Key Performance Indicators). KRs that do not have a KPI or metric per se are what's referred to as milestone goals, such as "launch a new marketing system" or any other similar results that can be measured on whether they've been completed but not necessarily associated with a direct number.

OKR example: Objective-Improve profitability. This is evidenced by KR's (key results) Increase in gross margin % from 27-30%, where gross profit % is the KPI-Key Performance Indicator.

OKR example: Objective—"get in shape fast" as evidenced by KR's (key results) Lower body fat % from 25%-21% where body fat % is the KPI. Another KR example is attending weekly yoga classes, where weekly attendance is the key milestone. You can also use the Comments section to observe and document performance gaps and improvement recommendations to achieve OKR's Objectives and KR's—key results.

PERFORMANCE "SLICE": **XX%** (**XX**% apx time spent)	OKR: OBJECTIVES & KEY RESULTS with KEY PERFORMANCE INDICATORS: e.g. timeliness, accuracy, completeness, efficiency, customer service ratings	SELF RATING 1-10	MGR RATING 1-10
HEALTH & FITNESS	**Objective: Improve my endurance - cardio** Key Results: Increase my cardio fitness-endurance level by reducing my 3 Mile Run Time (KPI) from 30- 27 Min by end of year. **Objective: Increase my flexibility** Key Results: Improve flexibility and core strength via weekly yoga class starting this quarter		
PERFORMANCE "SLICE": **XX%** (**XX**% apx time spent)	OKR: OBJECTIVES & KEY RESULTS with KEY PERFORMANCE INDICATORS: e.g. timeliness, accuracy, completeness, efficiency, customer service ratings	SELF RATING 1-10	MGR RATING 1-10
PRODUCT/SERVICE: (PEOPLE) Help our clients by improving the probability of successfully hiring the "right fit" employees by sourcing and screening for a higher qualifying pool of candidates to interview and choose from resulting in better hiring decisions and hires over time.	**Objective: Help our clients hire the "right fit" employees as evidenced by:** **Key Result:** • Deliver a Sufficient # of Qualified candidates for the Hiring Mgr/Owner to interview in a timely manner, resulting in a qualified/appropriate hiring decision. • At least 80% of placed candidates receive positive performance reviews at 60-day mark."		
COMMENTS			

PERFORMANCE "SLICE": **XX**% (**XX**% apx time spent)	OKR: OBJECTIVES & KEY RESULTS with KEY PERFORMANCE INDICATORS: e.g. timeliness, accuracy, completeness, efficiency, customer service ratings	SELF RATING 1-10	MGR RATING 1-10
PRODUCT/SERVICE: Help our clients by improving the retention or the "right fit" employees	**Objective: Help the client retain the "right fit" employees as evidenced by:** **Key Result:** **• Reduced turnover 20%- 15%, resulting in better right-fit retention.** **• Improve overall employee engagement scores by 10%**		
COMMENTS:			

PERFORMANCE "SLICE": **XX**% (**XX**% apx time spent)	OKR: OBJECTIVES & KEY RESULTS with KEY PERFORMANCE INDICATORS: e.g. timeliness, accuracy, completeness, efficiency, customer service ratings	SELF RATING 1-10	MGR RATING 1-10
	Objective: Key Result:		
COMMENTS:			

PERFORMANCE "SLICE": **XX**% (**XX**% apx time spent)	OKR: OBJECTIVES & KEY RESULTS with KEY PERFORMANCE INDICATORS: e.g. timeliness, accuracy, completeness, efficiency, customer service ratings	SELF RATING 1-10	MGR RATING 1-10
	Objective: Key Result:		
COMMENTS:			

Performance Traits/Competencies (How)

You can evaluate employee performance in terms of both the baseline and differentiating traits/competencies required for the specific position being evaluated. Baseline criteria (beyond the givens) are typically those must-have traits that, if missing, would automatically disqualify him/her from being a good fit for the job. Differentiating traits/competencies are those qualities that top performers in this role seem to have in common compared to those who are "adequate" performers. Performance criteria-expectations regarding the employee's role should be clarified and communicated on an ongoing basis.

PERFORMANCE TRAITS/ COMPETENCIES ☒Baseline ☐Differentiating	To be demonstrated by: (stories, examples, behaviors)	SELF RATING 1-10	MGR RATING 1-10
1-Rapport- Ability to establish a close and harmonious relationship by understanding one another's feelings or ideas and communicating well	Building strong relationships with both candidates and hiring managers is essential. This involves establishing trust, understanding needs, and creating a positive candidate experience		
COMMENTS:			

PERFORMANCE TRAITS/ COMPETENCIES ☒Baseline ☐Differentiating	To be demonstrated by: (stories, examples, behaviors)	SELF RATING 1-10	MGR RATING 1-10
2-Analytical Thinking Is good at addressing complex issues by breaking them into manageable components or logical steps	The ability to analyze job requirements and candidate profiles to make accurate matches. This includes assessing skills, potential cultural fit, and long-term suitability for the role.		
COMMENTS:			

PERFORMANCE TRAITS/ COMPETENCIES ☒Baseline ☐Differentiating	To be demonstrated by: (stories, examples, behaviors)	SELF RATING 1-10	MGR RATING 1-10
3-Achievement Orientation- Desire to work well or to compete against a standard of excellence.	Recruiters with a strong achievement orientation set high-performance standards for themselves. This means they are more driven to meet or exceed recruitment targets, such as the number of qualified candidate interviewees, successful placements, quality of hires, and time-to-fill metrics. Quality of Hire: They are not just focused on filling positions but are committed to finding the best possible match for each role. This involves a deep understanding of the job requirements and the company culture and a keen ability to assess candidates' fit.		
COMMENTS:			

PERFORMANCE TRAITS/ COMPETENCIES ☒Baseline ☐Differentiating	To be demonstrated by: (stories, examples, behaviors)	SELF RATING 1-10	MGR RATING 1-10
4-Communication Has strong verbal and solid written communication skills to effectively convey accurate information to management, personnel, and customers	Effective communication is paramount for a recruiter. It involves clearly articulating job expectations to candidates and accurately conveying the candidates' qualifications and fit to the hiring team.		
COMMENTS:			

PERFORMANCE TRAITS/ COMPETENCIES ☒Baseline ☐Differentiating	To be demonstrated by: (stories, examples, behaviors)	SELF RATING 1-10	MGR RATING 1-10

5-Dependability: Is reliable, responsible, and dependable in fulfilling obligations; is accountable even in the face of obstacles	Consistency of effort in reviewing resumes, setting up initial pre-screening calls/interviews, and setting up interviews with hiring managers. Timely response within the same day or 24 hours to any client or manager communications.		

COMMENTS:

PERFORMANCE TRAITS/ COMPETENCIES ☒Baseline ☐Differentiating	To be demonstrated by: (stories, examples, behaviors)	SELF RATING 1-10	MGR RATING 1-10
6-Initiative Self-starter who takes action and does whatever it takes to complete tasks promptly and thoroughly	Proactively seeking out potential candidates, networking, and staying ahead of industry trends are important for a recruiter in a fast-paced business environment.		

COMMENTS

PERFORMANCE TRAITS/ COMPETENCIES ☐Baseline ☒Differentiating	To be demonstrated by: (stories, examples, behaviors)	SELF RATING 1-10	MGR RATING 1-10
D-Trust Builder			

COMMENTS:

PERFORMANCE TRAITS/ COMPETENCIES ☐Baseline ☒Differentiating	To be demonstrated by: (stories, examples, behaviors)	SELF RATING 1-10	MGR RATING 1-10

D-Initiative	Ability to proactively source resumes via resume(Indeed, ZipRecruiter) database, with alerts…etc.		
COMMENTS:			

Performance Traits/Competencies (PDT- PEOPLE/DATA/THINGS)

PEOPLE	To be demonstrated by: (stories, examples, behaviors)	SELF RATING 1-10	MGR RATING 1-10
Advising: To give advice			
Communicating: To reach mutual understanding through exchanging information and ideas but also create and share meaning.			
Consulting: To provide expert knowledge for a fee			
Influencing: To affect the character, development, or behavior of someone			
Facilitating: To provide a productive or impartial meeting			
COMMENTS:			
DATA	To be demonstrated by: (stories, examples, behaviors)	SELF RATING 1-10	MGR RATING 1-10

Evaluating: To determine the significance, worth, or condition of, usually by
careful appraisal.

Analytical Thinking: The break down
of complex problems into smaller components, analyze them systematically,
and draw logical conclusions. Analytical
thinking involves using critical thinking
skills, data analysis, and evidence-based
reasoning to solve problems, make
decisions, and generate insights.

COMMENTS:

Employee Development (Self-Assessment)

Areas of employee development to focus on between now and the next review period. This section may include specific suggestions to address developmental needs, or it may be used to document discussion of career growth options and next steps

What are your top strengths and how do they help you succeed in your role?
Click here to enter text. Enter N/A if you have no comments.
What areas could you improve to become more effective?
Click here to enter text. Enter N/A if you have no comments.
What type of training, coaching, or support would help you reach the next level of performance?
Click here to enter text. Enter N/A if you have no comments.
What part of your work feels most meaningful or energizing to you?
Click here to enter text. Enter N/A if you have no comments.
Is there a part of your role that feels unclear, repetitive or draining?
Click here to enter text. Enter N/A if you have no comments.
In what ways do you contribute to promoting the culture of the company, .e.g:
Click here to enter text. Enter N/A if you have no comments
What's one idea you have to improve a process, product, or client experience?
Click here to enter text. Enter N/A if you have no comments.
What are some factors or things that your manager does or does not do that either helps or hinders in doing your job more effectively?
Click here to enter text. Enter N/A if you have no comments.
What are your career interests or goals over the next 1-2 years?
Click here to enter text. Enter N/A if you have no comments.
Any other observations or questions?
Click here to enter text. Enter N/A if you have no comments.

Employee Development (Manager-Assessment)

Areas of employee development to focus on between now and the next review period. This section may include specific suggestions to address developmental needs, or it may be used to document discussion of career growth options and next steps

What are the employee's top strengths and how have they positively impacted the team or company?
Click here to enter text. Enter N/A if you have no comments.
What specific areas could the employee improve to grow in their role or prepare for greater responsibility?
Click here to enter text. Enter N/A if you have no comments.
What training, coaching, or support would help this employee reach the next level of performance?
Click here to enter text. Enter N/A if you have no comments.
What adjustments or support could help the employee stay more engaged and effective?
Click here to enter text. Enter N/A if you have no comments.
What are some things that the employee (direct report) does that most help you do your own job more effectively?
Click here to enter text. Enter N/A if you have no comments.
What are some things the employee does/does not do that may hinder you in doing your job effectively?
Click here to enter text. Enter N/A if you have no comments.
In what ways do the employee contribute to promoting the culture of the company
Click here to enter text. Enter N/A if you have no comments
How do you see this employee's role evolving in the next 1–2 years, based on their strengths and interests?
Click here to enter text. Enter N/A if you have no comments.
Other observations
Click here to enter text. Enter N/A if you have no comments.
Other questions
Click here to enter text. Enter N/A if you have no comments.

Overall Performance Rating

In addition to evaluating whether or not individual objectives and performance results were met, we also need to consider the individual's impact and degree of positive contribution to the overall good of the company. This overall rating should reflect the employee's performance ratings in sections 2.0 (what), 3.0 and 4.0 (how), as well take into consideration demonstrated positive workplace attitudes and behaviors.

OVERALL PERFORMANCE RATING 1 - 9	Self:		Manager:	

Acknowledgment

By signing below, both the supervisor/manager and employee agree to having reviewed and clarified the performance criteria for his/her role-position. Mutual discussion pertaining to the above information has taken place, and both parties believe this form to be accurate and complete.

Employee Print Name/Signature   Date

Manager Print Name/Signature   Date

CONFIDENTIAL EMPLOYEE SURVEY

Employee Information

Name: _____

Job Title: _____

Yrs of Service: _____

Hourly Rate: _____

Annual Salary: _____

Dept: _____

Report to: _____

Date: _____

Confidentiality Notice

Your personal thoughts and opinions are extremely important in assisting in the evaluation of your company. Your answers will be kept STRICTLY CONFIDENTIAL. They will be used to get a general idea of the company and under no circumstances will your answers be shown directly to any executive manager, owner, or other employee of the company. Please be as objective as possible in rating (1-5) using .5 increments (e.g., 3.5, 4.5) as needed to describe the situation as you see it. Enter your rating (1-5) in the box provided to the right of the questions.

Survey Questions:

Rate 1-Strongly Disagree, 2- Disagree, 3- Neither agree or disagree, 4- Agree, 5-Strongly Agree

1. My company's most important goals and objectives for this year have been communicated to me.

2. In the last 30 days, I have received recognition or praise for doing good work.

3. I have a clear understanding of the success criteria and desired performance outcomes for my position.

4. My job tasks, duties, and desired performance outcomes are documented in a written job description.

5. My manager-supervisor "manages for results" giving me freedom in how I go about fulfilling my job duties and/or completing a particular task.

6. How pay is determined is a fair and transparent process.

7. Poor employee performance is not tolerated.

8. I have received a company organization chart outlining lines of communication and reporting relationships with each employee having only one boss.

9. I feel my pay is fair given my overall contribution, performance, and time of employment.

10. At work, there is someone who encourages my learning and development.

11. The mission of my company makes me feel my job is important.

12. I have a good relationship with my direct manager, and he/she seems to care about me as a person.

13. I have adequate materials, tools, and equipment to perform my job effectively.

14. At work, my opinions seem to count.

15. My position largely utilizes my strengths, and I can do what I do best every day.

16. An incentive program exists, and it rewards performance.

17. In the last year, my employer has provided me opportunities to learn and grow.

18. In the last six months, I have received feedback from my manager regarding my progress and where I stand relative to performance expectations.

19. I feel confident that my employer has a bright future.

Additional Questions

1. What are your primary job responsibilities?

2. What else is expected of you?

3. Do you often feel overwhelmed with too much to do and not enough time in the day to get it all done? If so, why?

4. What do you like most about working at our company?"

5. What improvements would you suggest?

6. What are some things (your manager does or doesn't do) that help you do your job effectively?

7. What are some things (your manager does or doesn't do) that may hinder you in performing your job effectively?

8. How do you get a raise? When was the last time you received one?

9. How would you like to see your role evolve in ways that are most satisfying to your professional development?

10. Do you give management your thoughts and ideas? Do they listen?

11. If you could trade places with your supervisor (boss), what's one thing you would change and why?

12. Any other observations, feedback, and/or suggestions for improvement?

Your feedback is invaluable for continuous improvement. Thank you for taking the time to complete this survey.

TERMINATING AN EMPLOYEE

Introduction

Terminating an employee is one of the most unpleasant aspects of being a business owner or manager. However, avoiding this task can harm your business as problematic employees can "poison the well" and signal to other employees that poor behavior is tolerated.

This standard procedure provides some guidelines on how to terminate an employee appropriately to avoid escalating issues or legal repercussions. This should not substitute appropriate legal and qualified HR expertise that can take into account your company size, location and laws specific to your locale.

Should You Terminate?

There are many reasons why an employer might want to terminate an employee. As long as those reasons comply with California and Federal law, the decision to terminate depends on the specific facts and circumstances of each situation and the employer's business judgment.

Laws and Policies

California, like most states, is an "at-will" employment state. This means that an employer may hire or fire an employee for almost any reason or no reason at all, including poor job performance. However, ensure that the employee does not fall within the following legal exceptions:

Americans with Disabilities Act

- Is the employee physically or mentally disabled?
- If so, were attempts made to reasonably accommodate the employee's disability?
- Were reasonable accommodation measures well documented?

Title VII / California's Fair Employment and Housing Act

- Is the employee being treated in the same manner as other employees in similar situations?
- Have other employees been given more chances before being terminated for the same or similar reasons as this employee?
- If so, are there legitimate, non-discriminatory reasons for treating this employee differently than other employees?

Pregnancy

- Is the employee pregnant? Employees are entitled to four months off for pregnancy-related disabilities.

Workers' Compensation

- Has the employee filed a workers' compensation claim? Terminating an employee who has filed a claim, intends to file a claim, or has testified in a worker's compensation hearing could be considered workers' compensation discrimination.

Unemployment Insurance

Most terminated employees are legally entitled to unemployment benefits unless the termination was due to serious, willful misconduct. As an SMB owner, your focus should be on documentation and timely responses to unemployment insurance inquiries.

Trying to contest every claim is rarely worth the time or energy. Instead, maintain accurate performance records, provide truthful information when responding to claims, and understand that for most situations—especially poor performance or downsizing—former employees will qualify.

Check Your Past Feedback

- Ensure that you have given fair warning and a period of time to change and improve. Make sure they know that you aren't pleased with their performance ahead of time.

Fire Early in the Week

- Never fire on a Friday; give them time to tap into their network and begin a job hunt.

Keep it Concise

- "Mary, I'm sorry but we have to let you go." Do not get caught up in emotions.

Don't Let the Employee Linger

- Make it clear that they will have a few minutes to grab their things and then they will be expected to leave the premises immediately. Escort the employee to the door to ensure that they do not try to sabotage any aspect of your business by stealing passwords, trashing computer data, or taking company keys or credit cards.

Document Everything

- Maintain records of all performance issues, warnings, and improvement plans.
- Document the termination process thoroughly, including the reasons for termination and any severance packages offered.

Prepare for the Termination Meeting

- Plan the meeting in advance and ensure that a witness (such as an HR representative) is present.
- Have all necessary documents ready, including the termination letter and any information about final pay and benefits.

Communicate Clearly with Remaining Employees

- After the termination, communicate with the remaining team members to address any concerns and maintain morale.
- Emphasize that the decision was made in the best interest of the team and the company.

Provide Support to the Terminated Employee

- Offer support such as outplacement services, career counseling, or references to help them transition to a new job.

Review Company Policies

- Regularly review and update company policies and procedures to ensure compliance with employment laws and best practices.

Final Thoughts

Terminating an employee is never an easy task, but by following these guidelines, you can manage the process with professionalism and empathy. This approach helps protect your business, maintains team morale, and supports the departing employee through their transition.

SAMPLE MEETING AGENDA TEMPLATE:

SAMPLE MEETING AGENDA TEMPLATE (1hr)

Meeting Focus/ Title: [Insert Meeting Name]

Date-Day and Time: [Insert Date-Day and Time]

Location/Platform: [Insert Location or Virtual Meeting Link]

Facilitator: [Insert Name of Facilitator]

Agenda

1. **Welcome and Purpose (5 minutes)**

   - Greet attendees and thank them for their time and contributions.

   - Clearly state the purpose of the meeting, why it matters now, and the desired outcome.

2. **Review of Previous Action Items (10 minutes)**

   - Recap tasks assigned in the last meeting.

   - Discuss progress, challenges, and any unresolved issues.

3. **Main Discussion Topics (30 minutes total)**

Topic 1 (15 minutes): [Insert Topic]

   - Key Questions

   - Talking Points / Key Data

   - Decisions Needed or Blockers to Resolve

Topic 2 (15 minutes): [Insert Topic]

   - Key Questions

   - Talking Points / Key Data

   - Decisions Needed or Blockers to Resolve

4. **Action Plan and Next Steps (10 minutes)**

   - Summarize decisions made and confirm action items.

   - Assign responsibilities with deadlines (consider using RASCI).

   - Confirm alignment on next steps and ensure everyone knows their role and deadlines.

5. **Wrap-Up and Closing (5 minutes)**

   - Reiterate key takeaways.

   - Address any final questions or concerns.

   - Confirm date and time for the next meeting.

Additional Notes

Expected Outcomes:

[List 2–3 specific decisions, updates, or actions expected by the end of the meeting.]

Materials to Prepare:

[List any documents, reports, or metrics attendees should review beforehand.]

PROFIT FIRST SYSTEM by Mike Michalowicz

Profit First is a system of cash management, created by small business finance expert Mike Michalowicz, that prioritizes and allocates profit as your first line of expense before any other expenses are paid. By doing so we can ensure that there are profits remaining in our bank accounts at the end of the month or fiscal year instead of the traditional way of hoping there's profit left after we've paid all the outgoing expenses. We've often heard the adage of paying ourselves first but rarely taught how.

Profit First helps us implement this principle by prioritizing profit as your first line of expense before paying any other expenses. The system allocates a predetermined amount like a percentage of income set aside for profit first and then uses the remaining money to budget for expenses. If there's not enough left, it indicates that expenses need cutting. If Profit First were a formula, it would be: Income – Profit = Expenses.

However, this is not a one size fits all solution for every type of business and in all situations. If you are in an early stage, start-up venture or a company in growth mode making intensive capital investments in lieu of the "profit first" allocation could be a better utilization of resources and money especially considering potential opportunity costs of not making those investments. Profit First for many SMB owners can help change your mind set about finances, making profit something you plan for, rather than hope for.

This method also aligns with Parkinson's Law, which states that demand for a resource adjusts to meet its supply. Essentially, given more time or money, we'll use it, but Profit First forces efficiency by limiting what's available for expenses, and if we become more efficient, we can also become more profitable. In addition, if you can automate the allocation of profit via automatic bank transfers at regular intervals, it's more likely this will occur.

When I worked as a Business Development Manager at ADP, I recall after leaving my employment there after 2 years, I had $4,500 accumulated in my 401k plan resulting from the deductions they made with every paycheck. Interestingly, I had not noticed the small amount getting deducted and it certainly didn't impact my lifestyle. It provided me with a nice surprise windfall and demonstrates the power of Parkinson's law that we can always manage to fit our lifestyle demands based on the budget we give it.

Setting Up the Profit First System

Profit First is a financial management system that flips traditional accounting on its head. Instead of following the conventional formula:

Sales - Expenses = Profit

Profit First advocates for:

Sales - Profit = Expenses

This approach ensures that profit is prioritized, and businesses operate within their means. By allocating profit first, businesses can avoid the common pitfall of overspending and ensure sustainable growth.

The Bank Accounts

The Profit First system works like the cash envelope system. Income is divided into specific bank accounts for different purposes:

- **Income**: All income is deposited here before being distributed to other accounts.
- **Profit**: Acts as a cash cushion and source of quarterly profit distributions.
- **Tax**: Allocates money for taxes.
- **Owner's Pay**: Provides your salary. Always pay yourself a salary!
- **Operating Expenses (OpEx)**: This is your business budget.

This approach simplifies financial management by reconciling deposits and periodic transfers from the Income account, with all expenses coming from the Operating Expense account. The other accounts typically involve just a single transfer in and out on the 10th and 25th of each month.

Getting Started

To determine what percentage goes into each account, start with a trend analysis of your company's operating budget, P&L, and balance sheet. Industry benchmarks are used to establish goals for allocation percentages and create a roadmap for achieving these goals over time.

Profit, Owner Pay, and Tax Uses

Profit, Owner Pay, and Tax benefit the owner(s), but their uses are distinct. Owner's Pay covers your salary, Profit is a quarterly bonus or rainy-day fund, and Tax is reserved for tax payments. Keeping these accounts separate ensures clarity in financial management.

Allocating 15% for Taxes

Allocating 15% for taxes might seem high, but it covers both corporate and personal taxes, ensuring you're prepared when taxes are due.

Who is it for?

Profit First is suitable for businesses at any stage, whether profitable or in debt. Starting early helps instill good financial habits and ensures your business runs efficiently. Even established profitable businesses can benefit from Profit First, accelerating progress towards long-term goals. For businesses in debt, paying off minimum fees from Operating Expenses and using the profit allocation to steadily reduce debt while maintaining profitability is key.

Implementing Profit First: Step-by-Step

Step 1: Set Up Multiple Bank Accounts

To effectively implement Profit First, set up five main bank accounts:

1. **Income Account**: All revenue is deposited into this account. It acts as a holding account from which funds are allocated to other accounts.

2. **Profit Account**: A percentage of revenue is transferred here immediately. This account is only accessed quarterly for profit distributions.

3. **Owner's Pay Account**: This account is for your salary. Ensuring that the business pays you regularly is crucial for personal financial stability.

4. **Tax Account**: Allocate funds for taxes to avoid surprises during tax season. This account ensures you are always prepared for tax liabilities.

5. **Operating Expenses (OpEx) Account**: The remaining funds are allocated here. This is the budget for running the business, covering all operational expenses.

Example: Setting Up Accounts

Imagine you run a small marketing agency. Last month, your total revenue was $50,000. Using the Profit First method, you might allocate as follows:

- Profit Account: 5% ($2,500)
- Owner's Pay Account: 15% ($7,500)
- Tax Account: 15% ($7,500)
- Operating Expenses Account: 65% ($32,500)

Step 2: Determine Your Allocation Percentages

Allocation percentages will vary based on your business size, industry, and financial health. Start with conservative estimates and adjust over time as you get more comfortable with the system.

Example: Adjusting Percentages Over Time

Year 1:

- Profit: 5%
- Owner's Pay: 15%
- Tax: 15%
- OpEx: 65%

Year 2:

- Profit: 10%
- Owner's Pay: 20%
- Tax: 15%
- OpEx: 55%

Step 3: Allocate Funds Twice a Month

On the 10th and 25th of each month, transfer funds from the Income Account to the other accounts based on your predetermined percentages. This creates a consistent rhythm and prevents end-of-month financial surprises.

Example: Bi-Monthly Allocation

If your Income Account has $25,000 on the 10th of the month:

- Profit Account: $1,250
- Owner's Pay Account: $3,750
- Tax Account: $3,750
- OpEx Account: $16,250

Repeat the process on the 25th with any additional income received.

Step 4: Review and Adjust Quarterly

Quarterly reviews are essential to ensure your allocations remain aligned with your business performance and goals. Adjust percentages as needed to reflect growth, market changes, or business priorities.

Example: Quarterly Review and Adjustment

After the first quarter, you realize that your operating expenses are consistently lower than expected, leaving excess funds in the OpEx Account. You decide to adjust your percentages:

- Profit: Increase to 10%
- Owner's Pay: Increase to 20%
- Tax: Maintain at 15%
- OpEx: Decrease to 55%

Benefits of Profit First

1. **Ensures Profitability** By prioritizing profit, businesses ensure they remain profitable, reducing the risk of financial strain.

2. **Promotes Financial Discipline** The system encourages disciplined spending and better financial management, leading to more sustainable business practices.

3. **Provides Financial Clarity** Multiple bank accounts provide clear visibility into different financial areas, making it easier to track and manage funds.

4. **Reduces Financial Stress** Regular allocations and tax planning reduce end-of-year financial stress and surprises.

5. **Improves Cash Flow Management** Consistent bi-monthly allocations help in better managing cash flow, ensuring that funds are available when needed.

Real-World Example: A Small Retail Business

Consider a small retail business that sells handmade jewelry. The owner, Sarah, implemented the Profit First system with the following initial allocations:

- Profit: 5%
- Owner's Pay: 15%
- Tax: 10%
- OpEx: 70%

Sarah's monthly revenue is $20,000. Here's how she allocates her income:

- Profit Account: $1,000
- Owner's Pay Account: $3,000
- Tax Account: $2,000
- OpEx Account: $14,000

By implementing Profit First, Sarah noticed several benefits:

- **Increased Profitability**: By setting aside profit first, Sarah ensured her business remained profitable each month.

- **Improved Cash Flow Management**: Regular allocations helped Sarah manage her cash flow more effectively, ensuring funds were available for operating expenses and taxes.

- **Financial Peace of Mind**: With dedicated accounts for profit, owner's pay, and taxes, Sarah experienced less financial stress and more clarity.

Common Challenges and Solutions

Challenge 1: Resistance to Change

Many business owners are accustomed to traditional financial management practices and may resist changing to the Profit First system. Overcoming this resistance requires understanding the long-term benefits and committing to the process.

Solution: Start small with initial allocations and gradually adjust as you see the benefits. Engage with a Profit First professional to guide you through the transition.

Challenge 2: Cash Flow Constraints

Businesses with tight cash flow may struggle to allocate funds to multiple accounts.

Solution: Begin with smaller percentages and gradually increase them as your financial health improves. Focus on reducing expenses and increasing revenue to create more cash flow.

Challenge 3: Complexity of Managing Multiple Accounts

Managing multiple bank accounts can seem daunting.

Solution: Use online banking tools and automation to simplify transfers and track account balances. Regularly review and reconcile accounts to maintain accuracy.

Conclusion

The Profit First system offers a revolutionary approach to financial management for SMB owners. By prioritizing profit and using multiple bank accounts to manage funds, businesses can ensure sustainable profitability, improved cash flow management, and reduced financial stress. Implementing Profit First requires commitment and discipline, but the long-term benefits far outweigh the initial challenges. By adopting this system, SMB owners can create a financially healthy business that supports growth, stability, and personal fulfillment.

Whether you're just starting or looking to improve your financial management practices, Profit First provides a clear, actionable framework that can transform your business. Start today by setting up your accounts, determining your initial allocation percentages,

and committing to regular bi-monthly allocations. Your future self—
and your business—will thank you.

5 Key Lessons from Profit First

1. **The Importance of Prioritizing Profits** One of the key lessons
   in Profit First is the need to prioritize profits in your business.
   The system argues that profits should be allocated first, before
   any other expenses, to ensure that the business remains profitable and sustainable in the long run.

2. **The Concept of the "Profit First" Mindset** Profit First introduces the concept of adopting a "profit first" mindset, which
   encourages business owners to focus on maximizing profits
   rather than solely focusing on revenue or sales. This mindset
   shift helps business owners make better financial decisions
   that prioritize profitability.

3. **Implementing a Cash Flow Management System** The book
   provides a step-by-step guide on how to implement a cash flow
   management system using separate bank accounts for different purposes. This system involves allocating a percentage of
   income to profit, taxes, operating expenses, and owner's compensation to ensure that all financial obligations are met while
   still achieving profitability.

4. **The Importance of Small, Consistent Profit Allocations**
   Profit First emphasizes the concept of small, regular profit allocations. This approach encourages business owners to allocate
   a small percentage of income to profit regularly, rather than
   waiting for a large profit at the end of the year. By consistently
   allocating profits, businesses can achieve gradual but sustainable growth over time.

5. **The Power of Behavioral Finance** Profit First recognizes the
   role of human behavior in financial management. The book
   suggests using psychological techniques, such as the "envelope
   system" or gamification, to help business owners stick to their
   profit allocations and avoid the temptation of dipping into
   funds reserved for other purposes.

By incorporating these lessons and principles, small and medium-sized business owners can transform their financial management practices, ensuring not only profitability but also long-term growth and stability.

References

- Michalowicz, Mike. "Profit First: Transform Your Business from a Cash-Eating Monster to a Money-Making Machine." Portfolio, 2017.

- Parkinson, C. Northcote. "Parkinson's Law: The Pursuit of Progress." John Murray, 1958.

- "Profit First Professional." Profit First Professionals, www.profitfirstprofessionals.com.

AFTERWORD

It's no surprise that writing this book was much more complicated and harder than I expected. I initially thought it might take 3-4 months, maybe six at the most. It ended up taking up a good chunk of my life—over a period of nearly two years. It also required time to *learn* how to apply myself to dedicate the intense, focused attention to something as daunting as writing a book.

I've heard that AI can now write you a book in a matter of minutes but whether that writing is rooted in an author's lived experiences and authentic to who you are and what value you can actually deliver to others remains to be seen.

From the start, I knew it would be challenging and that I'd have to jump in with both feet, diving into the proverbial deep end, if I wanted to avoid rehashing vague generalities or offering non-actionable advice to our primary readers: busy SMB owners trying to grow without losing their purpose or themselves in the process.

But as the project unfolded, the "deep end" kept getting deeper. At times, I felt like I was treading water in the middle of the ocean with no land in sight. During those moments of uncertainty bordering on despair, I had to remind myself that writing this book aligned with my own purpose—to contribute perhaps even in a small way to the betterment of our clients and the greater good.

That hope kept me going, but really, to be frank, so did the apprehension of disappointing others, myself included, and letting people down, especially my sons, Jaden and Kai. Not finishing would have been embarrassing, and my sense of shame proved to be helpful in this instance, along with the fact that I didn't want to set a bad example.

Completing the book, on the other hand, gave me the satisfaction of finishing something that I had started, and that I could both "talk the talk and walk the walk." And perhaps it could also inspire them to reach higher in their own artistic pursuits.

The experience reminded me of training for the Murph Challenge that I did with my two sons and a good friend of mine during the COVID lock down: 100 pull-ups, 200 push-ups, 300 air squats, sandwiched between a 1-mile run for a total of 2 miles. You can't train for something like that in just few days or weeks, especially if you've been sedentary for a while, like I had been. It takes months of consistent effort, which paid off when we actually completed the Murph Challenge around the time of Memorial Day Weekend.

Writing this book was similar. It demanded far more time, energy, and persistence than I initially thought it would require. There were countless drafts and painstaking iterations before we arrived at a version that felt worthy of sharing.

The intense writing-thinking process required a complete reordering of my life. I dedicated my mornings—sometimes entire days—to this book-writing project. Thankfully, my consulting practice had grown to the point where I had a team in place to handle most of the day-to-day client management duties. That afforded me the time and space required to focus on thinking, writing and research. And for that I am deeply grateful to everyone who supported me through it all.

Could I have written what turned into something resembling a 700 + page textbook with fewer pages? Probably. But I'm reminded of Blaise Pascal's quote, later echoed by Mark Twain: "I'm sorry I wrote you such a long letter; I didn't have time to write a short one." It actually takes even more time to distill something clearly and succinctly. Perhaps with another year, I could have shaved this down to 270 pages!

Still, despite its length, this book was never meant to be a quick read, it was meant to be a useful one. My goal was to write a practical, relatable, and relevant book for growth-minded organizations—one that delivers, hopefully, critical insights to help you operationalize your purpose and meaningfully grow your business. If even one idea from this book helps you unlock more of your potential, focus on what truly matters, or align your business more closely with your purpose, then this effort will have been well worth it.

I hope the ideas and frameworks in this book—the 7P Business Alignment Model (BAM) that combines alignment coaching and fractional support—will prove to be a transformational part of your own journey toward becoming who you're meant to be and achieving what matters most.

In fact, writing *Focus on What Matters* has been a deeply personal journey of alignment and the result of applying the very same principles contained within it. What you hold in your hands is both the framework and the product born out of it.

However, the frameworks and ideas only matter if people are being positively impacted and connected with one another in ways that encourage our collective learning and betterment. Through the Purpose Matters Community, we hope you will stay connected, invite others and continue building a force for good alongside like-minded and like-hearted leaders.

Interestingly, in his later work, Maslow introduced "self-transcendence" as an even higher level of the hierarchy that goes beyond self-actualization to alignment with: "higher goals and purposes... contributing to causes greater than personal interests, often through spiritual experiences or a sense of unity with a larger whole".[2]

Peter Drucker wisely reminds us that:

"The number of people who are really motivated by money is very small. Most people need to feel that they are here for a purpose. Unless an organization can connect to this need to leave something behind that makes this a better world, or at least a different one, it won't be successful over time."[3]

Thank you for allowing us to walk alongside you on your purpose-driven journey. It's been an honor and privilege —and I look forward to where your path will lead next.

Aligned with purpose,

Steven

ACKNOWLEDGMENTS

This book like so many among hundreds of thousands of business books published each year is the result of countless hours of effort. Sometimes that effort looked like staring at a blank computer screen, struggling to construct a sentence or two that resembled a cogent thought. Other times, it consisted of walking around my neighborhood or taking a drive somewhere while wondering what I got myself into.

And after more than a thousand hours or so spent writing, reflecting, re-writing, researching and collaborating with others to refine and synthesize the ideas and frameworks that make up what is more akin to a textbook rather than a book that can be read cover to cover, I hope that at the end of the day it proves to be useful. If even one fellow human navigating their own business-life journey finds greater clarity or renewed purpose, and creates a meaningful result because of it, then the effort will have been worth it.

I am deeply grateful to everyone that accompanied me on this journey, especially Alfredo Romero, who served as a valuable sounding board and contributing author for the Pipeline and Product sections.

Over a period of nearly two years, many morning hours were spent at the Y Center located nearby at the graduate school that I attended which also served as our "writing studio". During these sessions, interspersed with breaks consisting of dry cappuccinos and mochas, we were able to develop and refine many of the ideas presented in this book.

I want to express my gratitude to the incredible editors whose insight, creativity, and expertise have elevated this work to far greater heights than I could have achieved alone. Your thoughtful feedback, constructive critiques, and purposeful guidance were instrumental in shaping each chapter.

To our copy editor, Lesa Boutin, who meticulously reviewed every chapter. Thank you for your editing recommendations that improved the book's coherence and flow. We're also delighted that you found it inspiring for your own entrepreneurial pursuits!

To Julie Sykora, a freelance editor who we utilized during the early stages and gave us our first glimpse into the difference a skilled editorial eye can make to improve our writing.

To Melanie Sterling, our book publishing consultant and coach whose encouragement and check-ins over the entire book project gave us the much-needed milestones and accountability to stay the course. She helped us through the entire process from advising us on cover design to getting ISBN numbers and preparing a version that we could upload to IngramSpark and Amazon and finally get our first copies printed.

To Lindsay Voss, my fellow Drucker Alumn whose sharp editorial acumen, combined with Drucker's perspectives, helped refine several chapters especially related to People, Purpose and Culture in a way that made more practical sense. She also encouraged me to use more "yin" oriented metaphors that weren't so heavily weighted towards my penchant for sports and combat analogies.

To my colleague and Executive Coach Dr. Michael Millar, who put on his consulting and editorial hat from time to time to help me clarify ideas and, more importantly, remind me to reframe and highlight whenever possible the idea of maximizing opportunities vs. only overcoming frustrations or solving problems! Thank you, Dr Millar, for your insightful questions that enabled me to probe deeper while staying true to my purpose.

Also, to my younger brother Brian, who isn't shy about pointing out things he sees can be improved and reminding me of the importance of human connection, relationships and community, something that would be difficult if not impossible for AI to replicate. The Purpose Matters Community can only grow and thrive with more leaders like him.

To Maria Sosnowski, who created and professionalized the book's index, which is like a search engine for the reader. At first I tried to index the book myself and then slowly realized I was in over my head after

ACKNOWLEDGMENTS

two weeks of suffering from a cognitively demanding and emotionally disorienting process when an author tries to index his own book!

To Daria Lacy, my book formatting expert who guided me through the "amazon jungle" that is Indesign and whom I spent countless hours with putting the innumerable edits that I was making back in a format that could be printed and published. I wouldn't wish upon anyone who doesn't have the expertise the difficulty and frustrations of trying to navigate the complexity of this intractable program.

In addition to all the human expertise that guided this book, I also want to acknowledge the transformative role of AI-powered tools in this editing process. These rapidly evolving technologies provided indispensable support in enhancing the text's quality, readability, clarity, and coherence. From catching grammatical mistakes to suggesting phrasing improvements, these tools were vital collaborators that augmented the human-centered creative process.

Here's an AI-generated (ChatGPT) explanation of our prompt, "Improve FOWM" (Focus on what Matters) that we used for every part of our book to accomplish our objective of creating a book that matters for our readers:

The "Improve FOWM" prompt, I understand it based on your preferences and instructions, is a request to enhance the content of your book Focus on What Matters: Aligning Your Business with Your Purpose. It means:

1. Refining the Writing: Improve clarity, coherence, and readability while keeping your unique voice and conversational tone. Ensure the content is engaging, actionable, and easy for SMB owners to understand.

2. Alignment with Purpose: Keep every section tied to the central theme—helping business owners focus on what matters by aligning their business with purpose.

3. Eliminating Redundancy: Removing repetitive or unnecessary information to ensure the writing is concise and impactful.

4. Ensuring Practicality: Incorporating actionable, relatable advice that resonates with SMB owners, reflecting their real-world challenges and needs.

5. Polishing for Flow: Use smooth transitions and clear structure so ideas connect naturally from one to the next.

6. Tailoring to SMB Owners: Prioritize simple, practical solutions and avoid abstract theory or overly formal language. Maintain a peer-to-peer, partnership tone.

7. Respecting Preferences: Follow your stylistic choices—avoiding corporate-speak, clichés, and jargon—so the writing stays grounded and authentic.

"In essence, the 'Improve FOWM' prompt is about taking your draft and elevating it to its best version, ensuring it effectively communicates your message, engages your audience, and reinforces your credibility as a thought leader for SMB owners. If there are specific nuances or instructions I need to keep in mind, feel free to let me know!"

While AI tools provided suggestions for improvement, all final decisions, ideas, and creative direction remain our own. We extend our gratitude to everyone—both human and digital—who contributed to shaping this work.

I also want to thank Ramona, for her unwavering positivity and support through much of this journey and the many times she accompanied me at the Y Center, Honnold Library, and in cafes around K-town near downtown Los Angeles during the book writing process. Fortunately for me, her job as an educator required a seemingly inordinate amount of paperwork and administrative tasks that kept her busy during those sessions!

Together, I hope we've created something that will continue to inspire and stay true to our mission of helping others focus on what matters, live with purpose, and unlock more of their potential with greater fulfillment, all while serving the greater good.

And if this book has, in some small way, encouraged you to take a step closer to what matters most in your own journey, then it has done its job.

In purpose and gratitude,

Steven

NOTES

Introduction- Why Alignment Matters

1. "Alignment Definition." Google Search Results. Accessed December 30, 2024. https://www.google.com/search?q=alignment+definition.

2. McKinsey & Company. "Enduring Ideas: The 7-S Framework." McKinsey & Company. Accessed December 30, 2024. https://www.mckinsey.com/capabilities/strategy-and-corporate-finance/our-insights/enduring-ideas-the-7-s-framework.

3. Senge, Peter M. The Fifth Discipline: The Art and Practice of the Learning Organization. New Y3.   Senge, Peter M. The Fifth Discipline: The Art and Practice of the Learning Organization. New York: Doubleday, 1990, 1994. Page 9.

4. Wartzman, Rick. "What Will You Do Differently on Monday?" Harvard Business Review, February 18, 2010. https://hbr.org/2010/02/what-will-you-do-differently-o.

5. Packard, David. The HP Way: How Bill Hewlett and I Built Our Company. New York: HarperBusiness, 1995.

Chapter 1: What Matters

1. Frankl, Viktor E. Man's Search for Meaning. Boston: Beacon Press, 2006, 106.

2. Plato. Apology. In The Last Days of Socrates, translated by Hugh Tredennick and Harold Tarrant, 38a. London: Penguin Classics, 1993.

3. bab.la. "Unexamined." English Dictionary. Accessed August 8, 2025. https://en.bab.la/dictionary/english/unexamined.

4. Drucker, Peter F. The Effective Executive: The Definitive Guide to Getting the Right Things Done. New York: Harper & Row, 1967.

5. Drucker, Peter F. The Essential Drucker: Selections from the Management Works of Peter F. Drucker. New York: HarperCollins, 2001, p. 47.

6. Drucker, Peter F. The Effective Executive: The Definitive Guide to Getting the Right Things Done. New York: Harper & Row, 1967.

7. Drucker, Peter F. Management: Tasks, Responsibilities, Practices. New York: Harper & Row, 1973.

8. "One hour of effective planning can save ten hours of doing," commonly cited in productivity literature; origin unknown.

9. Gray, David. "What Makes Successful Frameworks Rise Above the Rest." MIT Sloan Management Review. Reprint #62424, 2021. Available at MIT Sloan Management Review.

10. This quote is widely attributed to Albert Einstein—"If I had an hour to solve a problem, I'd spend 55 minutes thinking about the problem and 5 minutes thinking about solutions"—though no direct source confirms he ever said or wrote it. A similar sentiment appears in Ideas and Opinions (New York: Crown Publishers, 1954), where Einstein states, "The formulation of a problem is often

11. "A complex problem is a bunch of simple problems combined," commonly attributed to problem-solving literature; origin unknown.

12. Abraham H. Maslow, Motivation and Personality, 2nd ed. (New York: Harper & Row, 1970), 35–37.

13. Simply Psychology. (2021). Maslow's Hierarchy of Needs. Retrieved from Simply Psychology.

14. Gallup. State of the American Workplace. Washington, D.C.: Gallup, Inc., 2017. https://www.gallup.com/workplace/238085/state-american-workplace-report-2017.aspx.

15. University of Minnesota College of Continuing and Professional Studies. "The Role of Professional Development in Employee Retention." Accessed December 30, 2024. https://ccaps.umn.edu/story/role-professional-development-employee-retention.

16. The Conference Board. "Without Professional Development, More Than Half of Employees Would Consider Leaving Their Job." The Conference Board, March 15, 2023. Accessed August 8, 2025. https://conference-board.org/press/professional-development-survey-retaining-talent.

17. Joseph Campbell and the Power of Myth. Directed by Catherine Tatge. Hosted by Bill Moyers. Public Broadcasting Service (PBS), 1988.

18. Héctor García and Francesc Miralles, Ikigai: The Japanese Secret to a Long and Happy Life (New York: Penguin Books, 2017).

Chapter 2: Customer Matters

1. Peter F. Drucker, Management: Tasks, Responsibilities, Practices (New York: Harper & Row, 1973), 61.

2. "The Psychological Motivation Behind the Purchase of Luxury Watches," CPP Luxury, accessed January 1, 2025, https://cpp-luxury.com/the-psychological-motivation-behind-the-purchase-of-luxury-watches.

3. "Peter Drucker's Strange Discovery," California Institute of Advanced Management, accessed January 2025, https://www.ciam.edu/peter-druckers-strange-discovery.

4. Levitt, Theodore. "Marketing Myopia." Harvard Business Review, July-August 1960. Available at https://hbr.org/2004/07/marketing-myopia.

5. Ibid

6. Walt Disney Company. 2025. "About The Walt Disney Company." The Walt Disney Company. Accessed March 22, 2025. https://thewalt-disneycompany.com/about/.

7. Harper, Douglas. 2025. "Education." Online Etymology Dictionary. Accessed March 22, 2025. https://www.etymonline.com/word/education.

8. "Peter Drucker's Strange Discovery," California Institute of Advanced Management, accessed January 2025, https://www.ciam.edu/peter-druckers-strange-discovery

9. "Peter F. Drucker, Management: Tasks, Responsibilities, Practices (New York: Harper & Row

10. "Who is your primary customer?" - Harvard Business Review. Available at: Harvard Business Review

11. Drucker, Peter F. The Five Most Important Questions You Will Ever Ask About Your Organization. San Francisco: Jossey-Bass, 2008.

Chapter 3: Culture Matters

1. Scaling Up DFW. "Actions to Live By: Creating Culture - Webinar Replay." Accessed January 2, 2025. https://scalingupdfw.com/actions-to-live-by-creating-culture-webinar-replay/.

2. Chartered Management Institute. Understanding Organisational Culture. Accessed January 2, 2025. https://www.managers.org.uk/~/media/Files/PDF/Checklists/CHK-232-Understanding-organisational-culture.pdf.

3. Edgar H. Schein, Organizational Culture and Leadership, 4th ed. San Francisco: Jossey-Bass, 2010.

4. Change Management Review. "Why Culture Eats Change Management for Breakfast." Accessed January 3, 2025. https://change-managementreview.com/why-culture-eats-change-management-for-breakfast/. While the saying "Culture eats strategy for breakfast" is widely attributed to Peter Drucker, there is no verified evidence that he coined or used this phrase.

5. GuruFocus. "Buffett, Munger, and Lynch on the Circle of Competence." Accessed January 3, 2025. https://www.gurufocus.com/news/2064642/buffett-munger-and-lynch-on-the-circle-of-competence.

6. Institute for Strategy & Competitiveness, Harvard Business School. "Unique Value Proposition: Creating a Successful Strategy." Accessed January 3, 2025. https://www.isc.hbs.edu/strategy/creating-a-successful-strategy/Pages/unique-value-proposition.aspx

7. Core Competencies Framework for Discovering Strengths developed with OpenAI assistance. ChatGPT [AI Model]. Accessed January 3, 2025. https://openai.com/chatgpt.

8. Shiftbase. "Organizational Values: Definition and Importance." Accessed January 3, 2025. https://www.shiftbase.com/glossary/organizational-values..

9. MIT Sloan Management Review. "Effective Leaders Articulate Values and Live by Them." Accessed January 19, 2025. https://sloanreview.mit.edu/article/effective-leaders-articulate-values-and-live-by-them/

10. Harvard Business Review. (2021). Why Company Culture is More Important Than Ever. Retrieved from Harvard Business Review

11. Forbes Communications Council. "How to Build a Strong Employer Brand That Attracts Top Talent." Forbes. Last modified May 10, 2022. Accessed January 3, 2025. https://www.forbes.com/councils/forbescommunicationscouncil/2022/05/10/how-to-build-a-strong-employer-brand-that-attracts-top-talent/

12. Harvard Business Review. "Company Culture Is Everyone's Responsibility." Harvard Business Review, February 2021. Accessed January 14, 2025. https://hbr.org/2021/02/company-culture-is-every-ones-responsibility.

13. e-Buddhism. 2025. What You Think, You Become. What You Feel, You Attract. What You Imagine, You Create - Buddha. Accessed March 16, 2025. https://e-buddhism.com/what-you-think-you-become-what-you-feel-you-attract-what-you-imagine-you-create-buddha/

14. Your Time to Grow. "How Journaling Can Help You Develop Leadership Skills." Your Time to Grow. Accessed March 21, 2025. https://yourtimetogrow.com/journaling-help-develop-leadership-skills/.

15. Living Your Future Now: The Transformative Power of 'Acting As If'." Katie Bellamy Blog, April 26, 2024. https://www.katie-bellamy.com/blog/living-your-future-now-the-transformative-power-of-acting-as-if

16. Ibid

17. Forbes Business Council. "Creating Your 2024 Leadership Vision Through the Art of Visualization." Forbes, January 16, 2024. Accessed March 21, 2025. https://www.forbes.com/councils/forbesbusiness-council/2024/01/16/creating-your-2024-leadership-vision-through-the-art-of-visualization/

Chapter 4: Purpose Matters

1. Oxford English Dictionary, online version, s.v. "purpose," accessed January 3, 2025, http://www.oed.com.

2. Peter F. Drucker, "The Practice of Management" (New York: Harper & Row, 1954), 37.

3. "Peter Drucker: The Man Who Invented Management," BusinessWeek, November 28, 2005, 74.

4. Drucker Institute. "About Peter Drucker." Drucker Institute. Accessed January 4, 2025. https://www.drucker.institute/about-peter-drucker/.

5. Peter F. Drucker, Management: Tasks, Responsibilities, Practices (New York: Harper & Row, 1973), 38-39.

6. Stoever, Henry. "Why Purpose Matters Now." The CEO Magazine, June 20, 2024. https://www.theceomagazine.com/business/management-leadership/the-benefits-of-purpose/.

7. George Labovitz and Victor Rosansky, The Power of Alignment: How Great Companies Stay Centered and Accomplish Extraordinary Things (New York: Wiley, 1997), 1.

8. Zeno Group. "Global Study Reveals Consumers Are Four To Six Times More Likely To Purchase, Protect And Champion Purpose-Driven Companies." Forbes, June 17, 2020. https://www.forbes.com/sites/afdhelaziz/2020/06/17/global-study-reveals-consumers-are-four-to-six-times-more-likely-to-purchase-protect-and-champion-purpose-driven-companies/.

9. Einstein, Albert. "We cannot solve our problems with the same thinking we used when we created them." As cited in various sources, though actual source uncertain.

10. Jaworski, Bernard, and Virginia Cheung. Creating the Organization of the Future: Building on Drucker and Confucius Foundations. Leeds: Emerald Publishing Limited, 2023, 102.

11. Saint-Exupéry, Antoine de. "When you want to build a ship, do not begin by gathering wood, cutting boards, and distributing work, but awaken within the heart of man the desire for the vast and endless sea." As cited in various sources, original source uncertain.

12. The mission statement beginning with "We endeavor to proactively empower value-added synergies…" was generated with AI assistance using ChatGPT, an AI language model by OpenAI. Accessed March 2025. Available at: https://openai.com/chatgpt.

13. Drucker, Peter F., The Five Most Important Questions You Will Ever Ask About Your Organization. San Francisco: Jossey-Bass, 2008, p. 3.

14. McDonald's Corporation. "Our Values." Accessed January 3, 2025. https://corporate.mcdonalds.com/corpmcd/our-company/who-we-are/our-values.html.

15. The Coca-Cola Company. "Our Purpose & Vision." The Coca-Cola Company. Accessed January 4, 2025. https://www.coca-colacompany.com/our-company/purpose-and-vision.

16. Tesla. "About Tesla." Tesla, Inc., accessed February 2025. Available at: https://www.tesla.com/about.

17. Amazon.com. "Customer Obsession and Commitment to Innovation Push Amazon.com to #1 in Customer Service, According to National Retail Survey Released Today." Amazon Press Center. November 2006. Accessed January 4, 2025. https://press.aboutamazon.com/2006/11/customer-obsession-and-commitment-to-innovation-push-amazon-com-to-1-in-customer-service-according-to-national-retail-survey-released-today.

18. Nike, Inc. Mission Statement. "Bring inspiration and innovation to every athlete in the world. (If you have a body, you are an athlete.)" Accessed July 19, 2025. https://about.nike.com/

19. IKEA. "The IKEA Vision and Business Idea." IKEA. Accessed January 4, 2025. https://www.ikea.com/us/en/this-is-ikea/about-us/the-ikea-vision-and-values-pub9aa779d0/.

20. Business Model Analyst. "Tesla Mission and Vision Statement." Business Model Analyst. Accessed January 4, 2025. https://businessmodelanalyst.com/tesla-mission-and-vision-statement/.

Chapter 5: Chart the Course: OKRs

1.   Stephen R. Covey, The 7 Habits of Highly Effective People: Powerful Lessons in Personal Change (New York: Free Press, 2004), 98.

2.   Future Startup. "An Introduction to OKR: How Tech Giants Like Google, Amazon Set and Achieve Goals." Future Startup. October 8, 2019. Accessed January 4, 2025. https://futurestartup.com/2019/10/08/an-introduction-to-okr-how-tech-giants-like-google-amazon-set-and-achieve-goals/.

3. Paul R. Niven and Ben Lamorte, Objectives and Key Results: Driving Focus, Alignment, and Engagement with OKRs (Hoboken, NJ: Wiley, 2016), 4.

4. Foundation for Critical Thinking. "Defining Critical Thinking." The Foundation for Critical Thinking. Accessed March 21, 2025. https://www.criticalthinking.org/pages/defining-critical-thinking/766.

5. Peter F. Drucker, The Practice of Management (New York: Harper & Row, 1954).

6. Andrew S. Grove, High Output Management (New York: Vintage Books, 1995), 76.

7. John Doerr, "Good Example OKRs," What Matters, accessed January 4, 2025, https://www.whatmatters.com/okrs-explained/good-example-okrs.

8. "Objectives and Key Results (OKRs): A Comprehensive Guide," The Process Hacker, accessed January 4, 2025, https://theprocesshacker.com/blog/objectives-and-key-results/#h-key-results.

9. Steven Levy, "When John Doerr Brought a Gift to Google's Founders," Wired, February 19, 2018, accessed January 4, 2025, https://www.wired.com/story/when-john-doerr-brought-a-gift-to-googles-founders/.

10. Ibid

11. John Doerr, interview by Kara Swisher, Recode Decode, Vox, May 19, 2018, https://www.vox.com/2018/5/19/17369636/transcript-kleiner-perkins-john-doerr-book-recode-decode.

12. "Firms with structured management practices fare better," Cornell Chronicle, October 2024, accessed January 4, 2025, https://news.cornell.edu/stories/2024/10/firms-structured-management-practices-fare-better.

13. "Measurement Myopia," Drucker Institute, accessed January 4, 2025, https://drucker.institute/thedx/measurement-myopia/.

14. William Bruce Cameron, Informal Sociology: A Casual Introduction to Sociological Thinking (New York: Random House, 1963), 13.

Chapter 6: Stay the Course: OKR Best Practices

1.   Anonymous, "The Apollo mission was off course 90% of the time, but they still reached the moon by continually making small adjustments," widely attributed online, origin unverified.

2.   Ben Lamorte, The OKRs Field Book: A Step-by-Step Guide for Objectives and Key Results Coaches (Hoboken, NJ: Wiley, 2022)

3.   Ibid

4.   Ben Lamorte, The OKRs Field Book: A Step-by-Step Guide for Objectives and Key Results Coaches (Hoboken, NJ: Wiley, 2022), 9.

5.   Ben Lamorte, The OKRs Field Book: A Step-by-Step Guide for Objectives and Key Results Coaches (Hoboken, NJ: Wiley, 2022),.

6.   Niven, Paul R., and Ben Lamorte. Objectives and Key Results: Driving Focus, Alignment, and Engagement with OKRs. Hoboken, NJ: Wiley, 2016, p. 4.

Chapter 7: Focusing on What Matters

1.   Covey, Stephen R. First Things First: To Live, to Love, to Learn, to Leave a Legacy. Simon & Schuster, 1994, p. 161.

2.   Merriam-Webster Dictionary. "Focus." Merriam-Webster.com Dictionary. Accessed January 3, 2025. https://www.merriam-webster.com/dictionary/focus.

3.   Merriam-Webster Dictionary. "Distraction." Merriam-Webster.com Dictionary. Accessed January 3, 2025. https://www.merriam-webster.com/dictionary/distraction.

4.   CNBC. "Bill Gates and Warren Buffett Say This 1 Trait Is the Key to Success." Accessed January 3, 2025. https://www.cnbc.com/2017/06/22/bill-gates-and-warren-buffett-agree-this-trait-is-key-to-success.html.

5.   Beahm, George, comp. I, Steve: Steve Jobs in His Own Words. New York: B2 Books, 2011.

6.   Lencioni, Patrick. The Four Obsessions of an Extraordinary Executive: A Leadership Fable. San Francisco: Jossey-Bass, 2000.

Chapter 8: Aligning Your Time with What Matters

1. Drucker, Peter F. The Effective Executive. New York: Harper & Row, 1967, p. 26.

2. Drucker, Peter F. The Effective Executive: The Definitive Guide to Getting the Right Things Done. New York: Harper Business, 2006, p. 51.

Chapter 9: Develop the Right Fit Employee Profile

1. Schutz, Peter. The Driving Force: Extraordinary Results with Ordinary People. Leadership Publishing, 2005.

Chapter 10: Hire Right-Fit Employees

1. Collins, Jim. Good to Great: Why Some Companies Make the Leap... and Others Don't. HarperBusiness, 2001, p. 13.

2. Smart, Geoff. Who: The A Method for Hiring. Ballantine Books, 2008, p. 22.

3. Willis Towers Watson. "Managing Employee Pay in High Inflation Markets." WTW Insights, November 2024. Accessed [insert access date]. https://www.wtwco.com/en-us/insights/2024/11/managing-employee-pay-in-high-inflation-markets?utm_source=chatgpt.com.

4. Flanagan, John C. "The Critical Incident Technique." Psychological Bulletin 51, no. 4 (1954): 327–58. Accessed December 30, 2024. https://psycnet.apa.org/doi/10.1037/h0061470.

5. Stillman, Jessica. "Why You Shouldn't Trust Your Gut When Hiring." Inc., March 27, 2017. Accessed December 30, 2024. https://www.inc.com/jessica-stillman/hiring-job-interviews-daniel-kahneman.html.

6. Adler, Lou. Hire With Your Head: Using Performance-Based Hiring to Build Great Teams. Hoboken: John Wiley & Sons, 2007, [page number].

Chapter 11: Build the Right Fit Team

1. Branson, Richard. The Virgin Way: Everything I Know About Leadership. New York: Portfolio, 2014.

2. Wikipedia contributors. "Information Silo." Wikipedia. Last modified [date of last modification], accessed January 5, 2025. https://en.wikipedia.org/wiki/Information_silo.

3. Coaching Leaders. "Peter Drucker on Strengths and Leadership." Accessed January 5, 2025. https://coachingleaders.co.uk/peter-drucker-on-strengths-and-leadership/.

4. Drucker, Peter F. "How to Make People Decisions." Harvard Business Review, July 1985. Accessed March 21, 2025. https://hbr.org/1985/07/how-to-make-people-decisions.

Chapter 12: Let Go of Misfit Employees

1. Drucker, Peter F., and Joseph A. Maciariello. Management: Revised Edition. New York: HarperCollins, 2008.

2. Henry Ford, "My Philosophy of Industry," interview by Fay Leone Faurote, The Forum 79, no. 4 (April 1928): 481.

3. Peter Drucker, Men, Ideas, and Politics (Boston: Harvard Business Press, 2010).

Chapter 13: Identify the Right-Fit Customer

1. Lee, Harper. To Kill a Mockingbird. New York: Harper Perennial Modern Classics, 2006. Originally published 1960.

2. Global, Abundance. 2024. "Emotional Branding in Building Long-Term Customer Loyalty." Abundance Global. October 23, 2024. https://www.abundance.global/emotional-branding-in-building-long-term/.

Chapter 14: Attract the Right-Fit Customers

1. Shah, Dharmesh. "The more advocates you have, the fewer ads you have to buy." HubSpot,https://blog.hubspot.com/service/building-relationships-with-customers

2. Levitt, Theodore. 1969. The Marketing Mode Pathways to Corporate Growth. http://ci.nii.ac.jp/ncid/BA03405953.

Chapter 15: Retain and Grow Loyal Customers

1. Steve Jobs. Quoted in Brent Schlender and Rick Tetzeli, Becoming Steve Jobs: The Evolution of a Reckless Upstart into a Visionary Leader (New York: Crown Business, 2015), 187

2. Robinson, Phil Alden. 1989. Field of Dreams. United States: Universal Pictures.

3. The original quote from Emerson's journal is "If a man can write a better book, preach a better sermon or make a better mouse trap than his neighbors, though he builds his house in the woods, the world will make a beaten path to his door." (Quoteresearch. 2015. "Quote Origin: If You Build a Better Mousetrap the World Will Beat a Path to Your Door – Quote Investigator®." March 24, 2015. https://quoteinvestigator.com/2015/03/24/mousetrap/.)

4. Wikipedia contributors. 2024. "Customer Lifetime Value." Wikipedia. April 11, 2024. https://en.wikipedia.org/wiki/Customer_lifetime_value.

5. (Exploding Topics, n.d.). Retrieved January 14, 2025, from https://explodingtopics.com/blog/customer-retention-rates

Chapter 16: Let Go of Misfit Customers

1. Peter F. Drucker, "The purpose of business is to create and keep a customer," quoted in Goodreads. Accessed January 2025. Available at: https://www.goodreads.com/quotes/70385-the-purpose-of-business-is-to-create-and-keep-a?utm_source=chatgpt.com."Peter F. Drucker, Management: Tasks, Responsibilities, Practices (New York: Harper & Row

2. Franklin, Sam. 2022. "The true cost of eCommerce returns: Stats and best practices for minimizing loss." Bloom (blog). October 7, 2022. https://www.letsbloom.com/blog/true-cost-of-ecommerce-returns/.

Chapter 17: Align Your Product/ Service

1. Drucker, Peter Ferdinand. The Effective Executive, 1986. https://dx.doi.org/10.4324/9780080549354.

Chapter 18: Optimize Your Product/Service

1. Haden, Jeff. "20 Years Ago, Jeff Bezos Said This 1 Thing Separates People Who Achieve Lasting Success From Those Who Don't." Inc., accessed January 9, 2025. inc.com/jeff-haden/jeff-bezos-success-quote.

2. Staff, Gameball. "A Good Product Just Isn't Enough Anymore With Ron Kaufman, CEO of Uplifting Service." Gameball (blog), July 9, 2023. https://www.gameball.co/blog/a-good-product-just-isnt-enough-anymore-with-ron-kaufman-ceo-of-uplifting-service.

3. Loyalty Experience Platform, Annex Cloud Loyalty Management Solution. "21 Customer Retention Statistics for 2023 That Will Surprise You," December 4, 2024. https://www.annexcloud.com/blog/21-surprising-customer-retention-statistics-2023/.

Chapter 19: Innovate Your Product/Service

1. Hesselbein, Frances. Hesselbein on Leadership. San Francisco: Jossey-Bass, 2002. Pg 20.

2. Drucker, Peter F. Innovation and Entrepreneurship: Practice and Principles. New York: Harper & Row, 1985, pg 35.

3. Galli-Debicella, A. (2021). How SMEs Compete Against Global Giants Through Sustainable Competitive Advantages. Journal of Small Business Strategy, 31(5), 13–21. https:// doi.org/ 10.53703/ 001c.29812

4. Adobe. "Design Thinking: A Beginner's Guide." Adobe Creative Cloud. Accessed March 21, 2025. https://www.adobe.com/creative-cloud/design/discover/design-thinking.html.

5. Ries, Eric. "The Lean Startup Methodology." The Lean Startup. Accessed March 21, 2025. https://theleanstartup.com/principles.

Chapter 20: Measure What Matters to Your Customer

1. Drucker, Peter F. Innovation and Entrepreneurship: Practice and Principles. New York: Harper & Row, 1985, 35.

2. Clayton M. Christensen, The Innovator's Solution: Creating and Sustaining Successful Growth (Boston: Harvard Business Review Press, 2003), 75.

3. Reichheld, Fred. "The One Number You Need to Grow." Harvard Business Review, December 2003. Available at: https://hbr.org/2003/12/the-one-number-you-need-to-grow.

4. Qualtrics. "Net Promoter Score (NPS): The Ultimate Guide." Qualtrics XM. Accessed March 21, 2025. https://www.qualtrics.com/experience-management/customer/net-promoter-score/.Ibid

5. Ibid

6. Ibid

7. SurveySensum. "What Is a Good Net Promoter Score (NPS)?" SurveySensum Blog. Accessed March 21, 2025. https://www.survey-sensum.com/blog/what-is-a-good-net-promoter-score

8. Reichheld, Fred. The Ultimate Question 2.0: How Net Promoter Companies Thrive in a Customer-Driven World. Boston: Harvard Business Review Press, 2011.

Chapter 21: Align Your Process with Purpose

1. Stephen R. Covey, The 7 Habits of Highly Effective People: Powerful Lessons in Personal Change (New York: Free Press, 2004).

2. Ibid

3. Peter F. Drucker, Management: Tasks, Responsibilities, Practices (New York: Harper & Row, 1974), 45.

4. Peter F. Drucker, The Effective Executive (New York: Harper & Row, 1967), 36.

5. Boutros, Tristan, and Jennifer Cardella. The Basics of Process Improvement. Productivity Press, 2016

6. Project Management Institute. "Lean Project Management: Applications and Advantages." PMI, accessed December 29, 2024. https://www.pmi.org/learning/library/lean-project-management-7364.

Chapter 22: Optimize and Map Your Process

1. JSB Network. "Process Improvement." JSB Network. Accessed March 22, 2025. https://www.jsbnetwork.com/process-improvement.

2. The W. Edwards Deming Institute. "If You Can't Describe What You Are Doing as a Process..." The Deming Institute. Accessed March 22, 2025. https://deming.org/2589-2/.

3. JSB Network. "Process Improvement." JSB Network. Accessed March 22, 2025. https://www.jsbnetwork.com/process-improvement.

4. Firmao. "Process Mapping Before ERP or CRM Implementation." Accessed January 2, 2025. https://firmao.net/blog_net/crm/process -mapping-before-erp-or-crm-implementation.

5. Asana. "What Is Process Mapping? Definition, Examples, and Benefits." Asana Resources. Accessed March 22, 2025. https://asana.com/resources/process-mapping.

6. Boutros, Tristan, and Jennifer Cardella. The Basics of Process Improvement. Productivity Press, 2016

Chapter 23: Systematize What Matters: Process Playbook

1. Deming, W. Edwards. The New Economics for Industry, Government, Education. MIT Press, 1993, p. 62.

2. Interfacing Technologies, "What Is RASCI/RACI?," Interfacing, accessed December 28, 2024, https://interfacing.com/what-is-rasci-raci.

3. Digital Leadership. "RASCI Definition, Examples and Roles Streamlining Framework." Digital Leadership, July 13, 2023. https://digitalleadership.com/rasci-definition-examples-and-roles -streamlining-framework/.

Chapter 24: Problem Solving Matters

1. African Proverb. "If you want to go fast, go alone; if you want to go far, go together." Widely attributed to African oral tradition.

2. Napoleon Hill, Think and Grow Rich (Meridian, 1983). Insights on mastermind groups and their value in fostering accountability and diverse perspectives.

3. Kim, Steven. "Problem Solving Using Integrative Consultation." Purpose Matters Consulting, March 27, 2025. https://www.purposematters7.com/post/problem-solving-using-integrative-consultation.

4. "Blind Men and an Elephant." Wikipedia. Accessed December 28, 2024. https://en.wikipedia.org/wiki/Blind_men_and_an_elephant.

5. "Lights of Guidance: A Bahá'í Reference File," Bahá'í Works, accessed December 28, 2024, https://bahai.works/Lights_of_Guidance/Consultation#583._Every_Member_to_Express_Freely_and_Openly_his_Views.

6. 'Abdu'l-Bahá. *Selections from the Writings of 'Abdu'l-Bahá*. Accessed January 3, 2025. Selections from the Writings of 'Abdu'l Bahá | Bahá'í Reference Library

7. Drucker, Peter F. The Effective Executive. New York: Harper & Row, 1967.

8. Schwarz, Roger. "How to Design an Agenda for an Effective Meeting." Harvard Business Review, March 19, 2015. Accessed December 28, 2024. https://hbr.org/2015/03/how-to-design-an-agenda-for-an-effective-meeting.

9. Parabol. "How Does Parabol Work?" Parabol. Accessed March 21, 2025. https://www.parabol.co/how-does-parabol-work/.

10. Lean Enterprise Institute. "5 Whys." Lean Enterprise Institute. Accessed March 21, 2025. https://www.lean.org/lexicon-terms/5-whys/.

11. Wikipedia contributors. "Brainstorming." Wikipedia. Last modified November 20, 2024. Accessed December 28, 2024. https://en.wikipedia.org/wiki/Brainstorming

12. Universal House of Justice. "28 November 2023 – To the Bahá'ís of the World." Bahá'í Reference Library. Accessed March 21, 2025. https://www.bahai.org/library/authoritative-texts/the-universal-house-of-justice/messages/20231128_001/1#973422615.

Chapter 25: Profit on Purpose

1.   Drucker, Peter F. "Profit for a company is like oxygen for a person. If you don't have enough of it, you're out of the game. But if you think your life is about breathing, you're really missing something." Quoted in Frances Hesselbein, Hesselbein on Leadership. Jossey-Bass, 2002.

2.   Deloitte. "Purpose-Driven Companies: The Key to Thriving in a World of Rapid Change." Deloitte Insights. Accessed January 9, 2025. https://www2.deloitte.com/us/en/insights/topics/marketing-and-sales-operations/global-marketing-trends/2020/purpose-driven-companies.html.

3.   Patagonia example

4.   Drucker, P. (1994). The Theory of the Business. Harvard Business Review. Retrieved from hbr.org

5.   Ibid

6.   Harvard Business School Online. "Hypothesis Testing: A Step-by-Step Guide." Harvard Business School Online, September 2, 2020. Accessed March 21, 2025. https://online.hbs.edu/blog/post/hypothesis-testing.

7.   Magretta, J. (2002). Why Business Models Matter. Harvard Business Review. Retrieved from hbr.org

8.   Drucker, Peter F. Management: Tasks, Responsibilities, Practices. New York: Harper & Row, 1973.

9.   Drucker, P. (1994). The Theory of the Business. Harvard Business Review. Retrieved from hbr.org

Chapter 26: Optimize Profit Decisions

1.   Marsden, Paul. "Business is all about solving people's problems—at a profit." Goodreads. Accessed January 9, 2025. https://www.goodreads.com/quotes/561272-business-is-all-about-solving-people-s-problems---at-a.

2.   Investopedia. "Opportunity Cost." Investopedia. Last modified September 19, 2023. Accessed January 9, 2025. https://www.investopedia.com/terms/o/opportunitycost.asp

3. Econlib. "Opportunity Cost." The Library of Economics and Liberty. Accessed January 14, 2025.

4. Investopedia. "What Is the Difference Between Economic Profit and Accounting Profit?" Investopedia. Last modified March 30, 2023. Accessed January 9, 2025. https://www.investopedia.com/ask/answers/033015/what-difference-between-economic-profit-and-accounting-profit.asp.

5. Munger, Charles T. "USC Business School Keynote Speech." Speech, University of Southern California, 1998. Retrieved from Farnam Street. https://fs.blog/charlie-munger-thinking/.

6. Ibid

7. Wechsler, David. The Measurement of Adult Intelligence. Baltimore: Williams & Wilkins, 1944.

8. Ibid

9. Oxford University Press. "Intelligence." Oxford Learner's Dictionaries. Accessed January 14, 2025. https://www.oxfordlearners-dictionaries.com/definition/english/intelligence.

10. Misattributed to Albert Einstein. "Everybody is a genius. But if you judge a fish by its ability to climb a tree, it will live its whole life believing that it is stupid." While

widely attributed to Einstein, there is no evidence supporting this claim. For discussion on its attribution, see Quote Investigator. Accessed January 14, 2025. https://quoteinvestigator.com/2013/04/06/fish-climb/.

Chapter 27: Maximize ROI of What Matters

1. Stephen R. Covey. The 7 Habits of Highly Effective People (New York: Free Press, 1089).

2. Damodaran, Aswath. "Return on Equity (ROE) by Sector (US)." Stern School of Business, New York University. Accessed January 14, 2025. https://pages.stern.nyu.edu/~adamodar/New_Home_Page/datafile/roe.html.

3. Investopedia. "Law of Diminishing Marginal Returns." Investopedia. Last modified August 16, 2023. Accessed January 9,

2025. https://www.investopedia.com/terms/l/lawofdiminishingmarginalreturn.asp.

4. Vena Solutions. "Average Profit Margin by Industry: How to Benchmark Your Business." Vena Solutions Blog. Accessed January 14, 2025. https://www.venasolutions.com/blog/average-profit-margin-by-industry#:~:text=The%20average%20gross%20profit%20margin,average%20gross%20profit%20at%2012.45%25.

5. Indeed. (2023). Profit Sharing: A Guide to Sharing Profits with Employees. Retrieved from indeed.com

6. Watson, Stu. "A plan that rewards employees with a share of the fruits of their labor draws a direct connection between work and reward." Edward Lowe Foundation. Accessed January 14, 2025. https://edwardlowe.org.

Chapter 28: Keep Improving What Matters

1. Franklin, Benjamin. "Without continual growth and progress, such words as improvement, achievement, and success have no meaning." Quoted in Goodreads. Accessed January 9, 2025. https://www.goodreads.com/quotes/314089.

2. Abdu'l-Bahá. "If you plant a seed in the ground, a tree will become manifest from that seed..." The Promulgation of Universal Peace, p. 450. Accessed January 9, 2025. https://reference.bahai.org/en/t/ab/PUP/pup-450.html.

3. Buscaglia, Leo. "Change is the end result of all true learning." Quoted in Goodreads. Accessed January 9, 2025. https://www.goodreads.com/quotes/217978.

4. "How do you eat an elephant? One bite at a time." Source unknown, widely attributed in motivational literature and speeches.

5. "Lao Tzu, Tao Te Ching, Chapter 64."

6. Allen, Woody. Quoted in Peter Guber, Tell to Win: Connect, Persuade, and Triumph with the Hidden Power of Story. New York: Crown Business, 2011.

7. Anonymous. Common motivational saying. Widely attributed in leadership and self-help literature.

8. Dweck, Carol S. "People with growth mindsets take charge of their learning and continuously seek opportunities to improve." USOC Mindsets. Accessed January 9, 2025. https://garyhorvath.com/wp-content/uploads/2016/11/USOC-MINDSETS-by-Carol-Dweck-2.09.pdf.

Chapter 29: Enjoying the View?

1. AZ Quotes. "Nelson Mandela Quote." https://www.azquotes.com/quote/592260.

2. Sacred Structures. "The Story of Three Bricklayers – A Parable About The Power of Purpose." https://sacredstructures.org/mission/the-story-of-three-bricklayers-a-parable-about-the-power-of-purpose/.

Chapter 30: Slow Down, Be Still and Listen

1. Lamott, Anne. Help, Thanks, Wow: The Three Essential Prayers. New York: Riverhead Books, 2012.

2. YouTube. "Sissel Kyrkjebø - Slow Down (Live Performance with the Tabernacle Choir)." YouTube video, 5:04, posted by The Tabernacle Choir, July 21, 2019. https://www.youtube.com/watch?v=EFe84U__kt8.

3. Equip for Life Coaching. "Letting Your Soul Catch Up." Equip for Life Coaching, 2016. https://equipforlifecoaching.com/2016/letting-your-soul-catch-up/.

4. Campbell, Joseph. The Power of Myth. Edited by Betty Sue Flowers. New York: Doubleday, 1988.

5. Victor Cheng, The Strategic Outlier Letter (newsletter, January 9, 2025).

6. Harvard Health Publishing. "Mindfulness meditation may ease anxiety, mental stress." Harvard Medical School Blog, January 8, 2014. https://www.health.harvard.edu/blog/mindfulness-meditation-may-ease-anxiety-mental-stress-201401086967.

7. Fogg, BJ. "Forget big change, start with a tiny habit." TEDxFremont, November 2012. https://www.youtube.com/watch?v=AdKUJxjn-R8.

8. Mayo Clinic Staff. "Dehydration: Symptoms and Causes." Mayo Clinic, https://www.mayoclinic.org/diseases-conditions/dehydration/symptoms-causes/syc-20354086.

Chapter 31: The Hero's Journey to What Ultimately Matters

1. Campbell, Joseph. The Hero's Journey: Joseph Campbell on His Life and Work. Edited by Phil Cousineau. Novato, CA: New World Library, 2003.

2. Phrases.org.uk. "The darkest hour is just before the dawn." https://www.phrases.org.uk/meanings/darkest-hour-is-just-before-the-dawn.html.

3. Quote Investigator. "Our Greatest Glory Is Not in Never Falling, But in Rising Every Time We Fall." https://quoteinvestigator.com/2014/05/27/rising/.

4. BrainyQuote. "Mary Pickford Quote." https://www.brainyquote.com/quotes/mary_pickford_105053.

5. Pew Research Center, "The Future of World Religions: Population Growth Projections, 2010-2050," accessed January 2, 2025, https://www.pewforum.org/2015/04/02/religious-projections-2010-2050.

6. New King James Version (NKJV). The Holy Bible, Matthew 22:37-39. Available at: https://www.biblegateway.com/passage/?search=Matthew+22%3A37-39&version=NKJV.

7. Sahih International. The Quran, Surah Adh-Dhariyat (51:56). Available at: https://quran.com/51/56?translations=20.

8. Bahá'u'lláh. Gleanings from the Writings of Bahá'u'lláh. Available at: https://www.bahai-library.com/writings/bahaullah/gwb/101.html.

9. English Standard Version (ESV). The Holy Bible, Micah 6:8. Available at: https://www.biblegateway.com/passage/?search=Micah+6%3A8&version=ESV.

10. Bhagavad Gita, Chapter 2, Verse 55. Available at: https://www.holy-bhagavad-gita.org/chapter/2/verse/55.

11. Dhammapada, Chapter 16, "Love." Available at: https://ancient-buddhist-texts.net/Texts-and-Translations/Dhammapada/16-Love.htm.

Chapter 32: Preparing for What Matters Next

1. Keller, Helen. (1903) 2006. The Story of My Life. New York: W. W. Norton & Company.

2. BPM. "What Is the Difference Between an Exit Plan and a Succession Plan?" BPM Insights. Accessed January 9, 2025. https://www.bpm.com/insights/what-is-the-difference-between -an-exit-plan-and-a-succession-plan.

3. Calder Capital. "Effects of Owner Dependence on Business Valuation." Accessed January 9, 2025. https://www.caldergr.com/ effects-of-owner-dependence-on-business-valuation.

4. ExitGuide. "Using Comparable Sales in Business Valuation." Accessed January 9, 2025. https://exitguide.com/comparables.

5. Internal Revenue Service (IRS). "Fair Market Value Definition." Accessed January 9, 2025. https://www.irs.gov/publications/p561.

6. Sageworks. "The Hidden Value or Value Killer in Your Business." Forbes, May 16, 2016. Accessed January 9, 2025. https://www. forbes.com/sites/sageworks/2016/05/16/the-hidden-value-or-value -killer-in-your-business/#30a9301d71b9

7. Ibid

8. Ibid

9. McGregor, Mary Ellen Biery. "These 8 Stats Show Why Many Business Owners Can't Sell When They Want To." Forbes. February 5, 2017. Accessed January 9, 2025. https://www.forbes.com/sites/sage-works/2017/02/05/these-8-stats-show-why-many-business-owners-cant-sell-when-they-want-to

10. Hamilton, Brian. "Many Business Owners Overestimate Their Business Value." Forbes, May 16, 2016. Accessed January 9, 2025. https://www.forbes.com/sites/sageworks/2016/05/16/the-hidden-val-ue-or-value-killer-in-your-business.

11. MidStreet. "Seller's Discretionary Earnings (SDE) Explained with Examples." MidStreet Blog. Accessed January 9, 2025. https://www.midstreet.com/blog/sellers-discretionary-earnings -explained-with-examples.

12. Peak Business Valuation. "Valuation Multiples for a Small Business." Peak Business Valuation. Accessed January 9, 2025. https://peakbusinessvaluation.com/valuation-multiples-for-a-small-business/?utm_source=chatgpt.com.

13. Peak Business Valuation. "Factors That Affect a Valuation Multiple." Peak Business Valuation. Accessed January 9, 2025. https://peakbusinessvaluation.com/factors-that-affect-a-valuation-multiple/?utm_source=chatgpt.com.

Chapter 33: Implementing What Matters: the 7P BAM

1. Peter Drucker, The Daily Drucker: 366 Days of Insight and Motivation for Getting the Right Things Done (New York: HarperBusiness, 2004), 236.

2. Carol S. Dweck, Mindset: The New Psychology of Success (New York: Random House, 2006), 246.

3. Fogg, BJ. Tiny Habits: The Small Changes that Change Everything. Boston: Houghton Mifflin Harcourt, 2019.

Chapter 34: Overcoming Implementation Challenges

1. Monticello. "If You Want Something You Have Never Had… (Spurious Quotation)." Thomas Jefferson Encyclopedia. Accessed March 19, 2025. https://www.monticello.org/research-education/thomas-jefferson-encyclopedia/if-you-want-something-you-have-never-had-spurious-quotation/.

2. Tribus, Myron. "Quality Management in Education." Journal for Quality and Participation, January–February 1993, 5. Available at http://www.qla.com.au/Papers/5.

3. Peter F. Drucker, The Effective Executive, HarperBusiness, 2006, p. 285.

4. "Success comes from good decisions, good decisions come from experience, and experience comes from a lot of bad decisions." Often attributed to Tony Robbins, though the original source remains uncertain.

5. Dweck, Carol S. Mindset: The New Psychology of Success. New York: Ballantine Books, 2006.

Chapter 35: Right-Sizing the Support You Need

1. Drucker, Peter F. The Effective Executive. New York: HarperBusiness, 1967, p. 127.

2. Project Management Institute. A Guide to the Project Management Body of Knowledge (PMBOK Guide). 6th ed. Newtown Square, PA: Project Management Institute, 2017, p. 131.

3. Bezos, Jeff. "2017 Letter to Shareholders." About Amazon, April 18, 2018. Accessed December 30, 2024. https://www.aboutamazon.com/news/company-news/2017-letter-to-shareholders.

4. Ibid

5. Ibid

6. Ibid

7. Ibid

8. Ibid

9. Drucker, Peter F. Management Challenges for the 21st Century. New York: HarperBusiness, 1999.

10. Centers for Disease Control and Prevention. "About the Program: Obesity." Last reviewed June 7, 2022. Accessed December 30, 2024. https://www.cdc.gov/obesity/php/about/index.html.

11. Drucker, Peter F. The Effective Executive. New York: Harper & Row, 1967, p. 256.

12. Reece, Ed. "Consulting leads from the front, coaching leads from behind, and advising walks side by side with the client." ReeceCorp. Accessed December 30, 2024. https://reececorp.com.

Chapter 36: Choosing the Right Support

1. "Project Management Triangle." Wikipedia: The Free Encyclopedia. Last modified November 2024. Accessed January 2, 2025. https://en.wikipedia.org/wiki/Project_management_triangle.

2. New York Post. "LeBron James' Alleged $1.5M-a-Year 'Biohacking' Routine: Does It Work?" New York Post, November 8, 2024. https://ny-post.com/2024/11/08/health/lebron-james-alleged-1-5m-a-year-bio-hacking-routine-does-it-work/

Appendix

1. QLA. "A New Good Idea." QLA Blog, accessed December 30, 2024. https://www.qla.com.au/blog/leading-improvement/a-new-good-idea/.

Afterword

1. Twain, Mark. Quoted in "If I Had More Time, I Would Have Written a Shorter Letter", Quote Investigator, April 28, 2012. "I didn't have time to write you a short letter, so I wrote you a long one

2. PositivePsychology.com. "Hierarchy of Needs: A 2024 Take on Maslow's Findings." PositivePsychology.com, April 2024. Accessed June 2025. https://positivepsychology.com/hierarchy-of-needs/.

3. Drucker, Peter F. The Essential Drucker: The Best of Sixty Years of Peter Drucker's Essential Writings on Management. New York: HarperCollins, 2001.

Index

Bhagavad Gita, 493
bias, 199–200, 229
Bible, 492, 493
blind men and elephant parable, 384
blind spots, 538–539
bliss, following, 46
Blockbuster, 55–56, 318–319, 321, 325
bottlenecks, identification and elimination of. *See* Process Mapping
B Players, 232–233
brainstorming and prioritization framework, 397–398
branding, 78, 93, 254, 406
Branson, Richard, 207
bricklayers parable, 467
Buddha, 80
Buddhism, 494
Buffett, Warren, 64, 136
burnout
    overview, 470
    acting to prevent, 484, 485
    focus and, 136
    purpose misalignment and, 92
    reflection questions for, 470, 475
Buscaglia, Leo, 446
Business Alignment and Growth Advisors, 523
Business Alignment Coaches (BACs). *See also* 7P Business Alignment Model (BAM); Purpose Matters
    as accountability partners, 516–517, 523
    consistency and, 518–519
    constructive group dialogue

and, 385
continuous improvement and, 446–447
course corrections and, 448
focus and, 137
inertia and, 526–527
knowing/doing gap and, 537–538
role of, 520–521, 531–532, 542, 545
routines and, 520
support structure for, 95
time management and, 158
business benefits, defining, 56–57
business models
    overview, 405–406, 414–415
    defined, 406
    key components of, 407–413
    reflection questions for, 415–416
busyness, habitual, 478
buyer's remorse, 270
buy-in, time-tracking and, 162, 166

C
Cameron, William Bruce, 120
Campbell, Joseph, 46, 479–480, 489
cause-and effect, 393–396
celebration
    of achievement, 468–470, 472–473
    company culture and, 78, 132, 178, 343
    of learning process, 457, 515
    of success, 78, 131, 518
celebration-motivation-achievement loop, 471

Center for Economic Studies, 120

change. *See also* continuous improvement; exit planning
  collaborative change management and, 520–521, 523
  growth needing, 445–446
  inertia and, 447, 458, 526–527, 533, 571
  resistance to, 303, 526, 571, 637
  starting small, 519
  support for, 531

channels, business models and, 409

character, hiring for, 171

Chartered Management Institute, 63

Cheng, Victor, 482

Christensen, Clayton, 331

Christianity, 492

churn rate, 263, 266

circles of competence, 64

Clark, Dick, 63

closing shop, 499

CLV (Customer Lifetime Value), 261–267

coaching role, 542–544

Coca-Cola Company mission statement, 100

collaborative change management, 520–521, 523

collective wisdom, using, 383–388

Collins, Jim, 191

communication, 338–339, 378, 389–390

company culture
  overview, 81–85
  alignment of core values and core competencies and, 73–74, 82
  celebration and, 78, 132, 178, 343
  of continuous improvement, 83, 311–312, 314, 457, 460
  core competencies and, 64–69, 82
  core values and, 69–76, 82, 83
  cultivation of, 77–81
  defined, 63, 82
  of experimentation, 327–328
  gap between actual and desired culture, 78–81
  hiring and, 44–45, 186
  importance of, 63–64, 78, 81, 84–85
  of improvement, 303, 311–312, 314
  learning culture, 132
  performance evaluation and, 235
  reflection questions for, 85–87
  sacred space and, 481
  self-actualization and, 44

Comparative Value Pricing Analysis, 272, 276–280, 281

competencies vs. traits, 173–174, 178–182, 186, 579–583

competitive advantage
  company culture and, 83
  distinct value and, 66–67
  innovation and, 321–322
  monitoring competitors for, 308, 313–314
  optimization and, 303
  purpose and, 93

545–546
challenges in, 525–526
coaching vs. consulting vs.
    advising and, 542–544
collaborative change
    management and, 520–521,
    523
consistency and, 516–519,
    522–523, 537, 546
goals, variation of, 513–514
growth mindset and, 514–516
importance of, 566
inertia and, 447, 458, 526–527,
    533, 571
learner mindset and, 389,
    530–531, 533
Pick Two Principle and, 551–
    554
as process, 516
range of effort for, 519–520
reflection questions for, 523–
    524, 534–535
right distinctions and, 528–
    530, 533
strategic reflection and, 27–31,
    482–483, 485, 527
subject matter expertise and,
    540–541, 543–544
incremental improvement
    innovation vs, 317–321, 322,
    325
    optimization and, 304, 311,
    313
indirect cost analysis, 272, 274–
    276, 281
inertia, overcoming, 447, 458,
    526–527, 533, 571
Informal Sociology (Cameron), 120
information, accuracy

assessment of, 386–387
informed decisions, 202–203

innovation
    overview, 325–328
    alignment with purpose,
    322–323
    benefits of, 321–323
    framework for, 323–324
    incremental improvement vs,
    317–321, 322, 325
    methodologies for, 324–325,
    327
    reflection questions for, 328–
    329
innovation meetings, 457
Integrative Consultation (IC),
    383–388
intelligence, 423–425
intelligent decision-making,
    423–424
intention, 30
internal analysis (SWOT), 292
interviews, 199–201, 205
Inuit people, 529
iPhone, 319, 325
Islam, 492–493

J
James, LeBron, 558
Jaworski, Bernie, 95
Jefferson, Thomas, 525
job descriptions, as not job
    posting, 201
job platforms, use of, 192
job postings, 197–198, 201–202,
    205
Jobs, Steve, 136, 261,
job satisfaction, 44

451
  right distinctions and, 529
  sales mix analysis and, 273
  values and, 294–295
"Marketing Myopia" (Levitt),
  54–55
market rates, defined, 195
Marsden, Paul, 417
Maslow, Abraham, 41
Maslow's hierarchy of needs,
  41–45, 46, 50, 642
mastermind groups, 383
McDonald's mission statement,
  100
measurement. *See also*
  assessment; Key
  Performance Indicators
  (KPIs); Net Promoter Score
  (NPS); return on investment
  (ROI)
  of Customer Lifetime Value,
  261–267
  Drucker on, 120
  Return on Equity, 429–430,
  439
  of time spent, 140–141, 164.
  See also time management
meditation, 483–484
meetings, 389–393, 457, 629–630
memo writing, 539–540
mentors, need for, 490, 495
Michalowicz, Mike, 631–639
Microsoft, 340
milestone goals, 226, 227
mindfulness, 479–481, 483–484,
  485, 570
mindset
  of curiosity and humility, 389,
  530–531, 533, 538–539

detached, 385–386
fixed mindset, 456
growth mindset, 456–458, 459,
  514–516, 522
learner mindset, 389, 530–531,
  533, 538–539
profit first, 638
progress-growth, 448–449, 456
on work, 467
*Mindset: The New Psychology of
  Success* (Dweck), 456, 514
minimally acceptable standards,
  221
minimally tolerable outcomes
  (MTO), 125
misalignment, impacts of, 18,
  19–20, 24
misfit customers
  overview, 280–282
  identification of, 272–280, 281
  problems with, 269
  reflection questions for, 282–
  283
misfit employees, 219–220.
  See also performance
  evaluations; weeding out
  employees
mission, 47, 323, 347
mission statements
  defined, 114
  development of, 95–101
  OKRs and, 114–120
  OKRs not aligning with, 130
  refinement of, 104
mistakes, avoidance of, 423
modeling. *See* leading by example
motivation, 92, 471
MTO (minimally tolerable
  outcomes), 125

analysis, 276–280
of employees, 212–214, 216,
 623–625
EPI survey on exit planning,
 501–502
strengths, identification of, 292
sustainable profitability, 271, 281
Swimlane Maps, 361
SWOT analysis, 292
systematic abandonment
 principle, 28–29, 140

T
tactical meetings, 392
tactical vs. strategic focus, 527
talent acquisition. *See* hiring
Task & Duty List (TDL)
 Framework, 585–594
task analysis, 585–586
tasks, defined, 585
tasks and duties, documentation
 of, 143–150, 585–594. *See
 also* People-Data-Things
 (PDT) Framework
tasks and duties, functional
 vs. personality-driven
 structures, 209–214, 215
task statements, 142–145, 586–
 587
task steps, 587–588
teams, 207–217, 356, 357. *See
 also* People
technical capabilities, culture vs.,
 65–66
technical competencies, 181–182
technology, leveraging of, 307,
 313, 357
termination. *See* weeding out
 employees

Tesla, 101, 103–104, 320, 340
theories, evidence and, 407
theory of the business, 406
things-related tasks, 183–184,
 599–600
thinking, changing of, 94
time, value of, 430–432, 439, 564
time management. *See also* Focus
 Alignment Framework
 (FAF)
 overview, 165–166
 alignment and, 545–546
 Drucker on, 155, 156–157,
  164, 165–166
 importance of, 155, 165
 intentionality about spending,
  136
 measurement of, 140–141
 reflection questions for, 166–167
 Toggl use for, 156, 158–165
 What Matters Time, 157–158,
  166
 Zero-Based Time Budgeting,
  140
*Tiny Habits: The Small Changes
 that Change Everything*
 (Fogg), 518
Title VII, 626
to-do lists, OKRs as not, 131
Toggl, 156, 158–165
Toggl champions, 163
trade-offs. *See* opportunity costs
traits vs. competencies, 173–174,
 178–182, 186, 579–583
transition planning. *See* exit
 planning
Tree Diagrams, 143, 587–588
Tribus, Myron, 355, 526, 571
trust, consistency and, 294

About the Authors

STEVEN KIM is the Founder and Principal of Purpose Matters, a consulting and coaching firm that helps small and mid-sized businesses grow through purpose-driven alignment and fractional executive-level support. He partners with business owners to attract and retain more right-fit employees and customers, align their teams, and lead with greater clarity and focus on what matters most.

His integrative and holistic approach combines strategic insight with hands-on guidance to help leaders build more aligned, resilient, and fulfilling organizations.

Steven holds a degree in Economics from UC Berkeley and earned both an Executive MBA and an MA in Management from the Drucker School of Management at Claremont Graduate University.

ALFREDO ROMERO is a subject matter expert in marketing, sales, operations, and product management. Through his work at Purpose Matters and ALROM Marketing, he helps small and medium-sized businesses grow their organizations using data-driven strategies, common-sense problem-solving, and best practices from other industries. His work around the globe has resulted in success from increased customer knowledge and segmentation to product development and launch to lead generation and sales training.

Alfredo holds a degree in Economics from Pomona College and an MBA from The UCLA Anderson School. In addition to leading ALROM Marketing Consulting, he also teaches at Pomona College in Claremont and the College of Business Administration at Loyola Marymount University.

www.ingramcontent.com/pod-product-compliance
Lightning Source LLC
Chambersburg PA
CBHW041731240326
41458CB00163B/6931/J